# "HERE"

*Jerry C. Cooper '23*

Number 128
Centennial Series of the
Association of Former Students,
Texas A&M University

"A person gets something at Texas A&M which is not to be found anywhere else in the world . . . I can't define it. I can't describe it. And neither can you. It's that something that others admire and only Aggies understand. But it's as real as life itself. Unable to describe it, we call it the Spirit of Aggieland. And if you don't feel something tingle inside you when you hear it set to music, as we just heard here this evening, then you are not an Aggie."

—James W. Aston '33, 1949 Campus Muster Address

# "HERE"

## The Muster Speeches
## at Texas A&M University

EDITED BY
Jerry Cullum Cooper '63

FOREWORD BY
Col. Michael Edward Fossum '80

TEXAS A&M UNIVERSITY PRESS
COLLEGE STATION

This paper meets the requirements of ANSI/NISO Z39.48–1992
(Permanence of Paper).
Binding materials have been chosen for durability.
Manufactured in the United States of America

Library of Congress Cataloging-in-Publication Data

Names: Cooper, Jerry C., 1941– compiler, editor, writer of supplementary
    textual content.
Title: "Here": the Muster speeches at Texas A&M University / Jerry Cullum
    Cooper '63.
Other titles: Centennial series of the Association of Former Students, Texas
    A&M University; no. 128.
Description: First edition. | College Station: Texas A&M University Press,
    [2018] | Series: Centennial series of the Association of Former Students,
    Texas A&M University; number 128 | Includes index.
Identifiers: LCCN 2017035142 | ISBN 9781623496005 (cloth: alk. paper)
Subjects: LCSH: Texas A & M University—Alumni and alumnae. | Agricultural
    and Mechanical College of Texas—Alumni and alumnae. | Texas A & M
    University—Alumni and alumnae—Biography. | Agricultural and Mechanical
    College of Texas—Alumni and alumnae—Biography. | College orations—Texas
    A & M University. | Speeches, addresses, etc., American—Texas—College
    Station. | LCGFT: Speeches.
Classification: LCC LD5309 .H47 2018 | DDC 378.764/242—dc23 LC record
available at https://lccn.loc.gov/2017035142

*For Richard "Buck" Weirus '42, whose infectious "can do"*
*attitude for always getting the job done helped*
*spread the "Spirit of Aggieland"*

Publication of this book is generously supported by

Kathy Havel, for her husband, Mike Havel '76, whose love of Aggieland has spread the legacy and traditions of Texas A&M University to friends and family (including his Mustang wife);

and

Nancy and Leroy "Shafe" Shafer '67, in memory of Neal C. "Clint" Ward and George Mack Antilley—two Aggies whose lives ended too soon.

Neal C. Ward '67, a US Air Force captain (posthumously promoted to the rank of major), was piloting an A-1H Skyraider when he was shot down over Laos on June 13, 1969. He was the roommate of Shafe Shafer when they both served on Corps of Cadets staff. An animal science major from Pasadena, Texas, Clint was a distinguished student, a distinguished military student, and a Ross Volunteer. He was named Who's Who Among Students in American Universities and Colleges, and he was one of the early recipients of a Houston Livestock Show and Rodeo Scholarship.

George Mack Antilley '69, the brother of Nancy Shafer, died in a car accident during his freshman year. A graduate of Abilene High School, Mack was majoring in agricultural economics. He was a member of the Corps of Cadets, Company D-1 "Spider D."

The Muster table, which holds the primary candle that begins the Roll Call for the Absent, is the work of Texas A&M University architecture professor Rodney C. Hill. His previous contributions include the seven walnut panels in the Memorial Student Center depicting the history of A&M and its programs. Rodney's wife, Sue, assisted in the completion of his wood carving projects. Used by permission of the artist.

# Contents

*A gallery of illustrations follows page 183.*

# Foreword

As proud former students of Texas A&M University, we Aggies love our traditions and our school.

I did not grow up steeped in Aggie heritage and was the first in my family to attend this university. I joined the Cadet Corps for the sole purpose of getting a cheap dorm room because the non-reg (non-Corps) dorms were full and apartments were too expensive. As a freshman in 1976–77, I was overwhelmed by the bewildering array of traditions and expectations as one of the "Keepers of the Spirit of Aggieland." After finally getting used to the buzz haircut and the fundamentals of cadet life, I settled into my college courses and tried to take each new surprise as it came my way. And my life was changed forever for the better.

After getting through most of my freshman year, I thought I had all of this Aggie stuff figured out, and I was proud to be a member of the Corps of Cadets. We had marched into Kyle Field before football games, built our first bonfire, could recite the inscriptions on most of the buildings and monuments on campus, done countless pushups, and never missed a Midnight Yell Practice. While walking around campus on a spring night, I could almost feel the presence of great Aggies who had come before me and had walked these same paths—perhaps also enchanted by a row of blooming dogwoods glowing in the moonlight along the old Military Walk.

With just a few weeks to go before the end of the school year, it was time for something I had not experienced before, Aggie Muster. My Corps outfit marched over to G. Rollie White Coliseum and my fish buddies and I climbed to the top row of seats right up next to the rafters.

We got there early, and I remember being bored and worrying about the lost study time with final exams just around the corner. As the building became more crowded, I noticed people gathering on the floor in front of the stage. These were not students—most were adults of various ages. As they clustered into groups, some were hugging and laughing, while others were embracing in tears. I still had not figured out who these people were when it was time to start and they all settled into seats in front of the stage.

As the program proceeded, my freshman thoughts drifted between physics and chemistry and the beautiful music and poetry. When they announced it was time for the Roll Call, I remember standing and looking down on the scene far below with no clear understanding of what would come next. A name was read from the roster. Voices from the floor and the stands answered, "HERE!" and a lit candle appeared. Followed by another. And another.

With a shock, I finally understood what it really means to be a Texas Aggie. You're not just an Aggie while you are a student; you are an Aggie for life. And when your time is done, your family and friends will gather one last time in your memory to answer the Roll Call in your name. I also realized that someday—hopefully many years in the future—my name would be on that Roll Call, too.

Respect, Excellence, Leadership, Loyalty, Integrity, and Selfless Service (the words over the entrances to Texas A&M's Memorial Student Center); duty, honor, country; and an intense love for each other and our university. That's what it means to be a Texas Aggie.

In the years since my first Aggie Muster, I have been honored to attend Musters wherever I've been stationed, including West Berlin during the Cold War. It has also been my honor to speak at Muster ceremonies in many cities across the country.

I cherish Aggie Muster as our most hallowed tradition, and I am proud of the work my friend and editor, Jerry C. Cooper '63, has done to compile this extensive collection of Muster speeches. In these pages you will discover a treasure of insights into the Spirit of Aggieland.

—Col. Michael Edward Fossum '80
US Air Force Reserve (retired)
NASA Astronaut (STS-121, STS-124, ISS-28/29) (retired)
Vice President, Texas A&M University
Chief Operating Officer, Texas A&M University at Galveston

# Preface

In the mid-1980s, a young Texas A&M English professor named John C. Adams (not to be confused with John A. Adams Jr. '73, Texas A&M historian and author of countless Aggie books) stopped by *The Texas Aggie* magazine office in the Clayton W. Williams Jr. Alumni Center. He was working on a study of Aggie Muster speeches delivered on campus since World War II. I shared with him a number of speeches that I had collected and helped him find a few more. He published *The Voices of a Proud Tradition* privately in 1985, which included twenty-seven of the forty speeches delivered since 1946. Unfortunately, the local printer he used had legal problems with another publication, suddenly ceased operation, and left Brazos County. Except for a small number of the books purchased by the Association of Former Students, the supply of *Voices* dried up immediately.

As Professor Adams explained in his preface to *Voices* in 1985: "The annual Aggie Muster speech is the keynote address given at Texas A&M University each San Jacinto Day, April 21 . . . Muster is a proud tradition and the Muster speeches have for years been the voice of that tradition . . . As I have sifted through and collected the available Muster speeches delivered at A&M, I have discovered an enduring set of values that echoes across generations of speakers. Many Muster speakers are distinguished by their deep sense of indebtedness, similar to patriotism, to Texas A&M. They recognize that Texas A&M is what it is today because of the quality of the choices that people have made there for over 100 years. They also recognize that choices are continually being made about the future of A&M. Their speeches attempt to amplify and celebrate the values that have traditionally guided these choices."

Adams went on to discuss the "art of speechmaking or rhetoric," outlining Aristotle's three kinds of persuasive speech: Forensic—to prosecute or defend issues about human actions (often used in the courtroom); Deliberative—counsel or advice concerning future actions; and Epideictic or Ceremonial—dealing with the present and seeking to praise or lay blame for historical events. Adams concludes, "Although on occasion it may include elements of the other kinds of speeches (surely at times it has been wholly deliberative), the historical emphasis of the Muster speech is distinctively epideictic." This is partly because it is traditionally given on San Jacinto Day in honor of the battle that won Texas' independence.

"The Muster speeches evidence a deep concern," he continued, "for national and international issues and an ambitious, optimistic desire to take a stance, and attempt to solve the most pressing problems of the time. In sum, the Muster speeches are expressive of hope, an enduring set of values, and a community of ideas, not necessarily learned in the classroom, but nevertheless shared by former students."

Adams concluded that although "the overall meaning of the Muster speech is difficult to comprehend . . . the Muster speeches are repositories of ideas—significant ideas—spoken by people who were called upon to 'say a few words.' At their very best, these speeches reflect a set of values that are central to Aggieland and go to the heart of the experience of being an Aggie."

While the speeches vary greatly in theme and content, each speaker showcased a unique viewpoint on the history, traditions, and heritage of the Aggie Spirit.

Professor Adams's analysis holds true for the speeches added since the 1985 publication.

Other than continuing to collect speeches as they were delivered at Aggie Musters from the late 1980s and into the new century, I didn't think much more about it. The next several years were spent contacting the speakers or their families and editing the speeches into a single manuscript. In doing so, I came across nine campus Muster speeches that were unavailable when *Voices* was first published and discovered six newspaper articles that provided some detail on the speeches that were still missing.

The 1949 speech given by James W. Aston '33 was obtained when his widow sent a recording of the entire Muster program taken from a phonograph record found in his belongings.

The 1950 address of Marion S. Church '05 was discovered on a tape recording in the A&M archives. It was first assumed that it was strictly a political speech until a few comments near the end regarding San Jacinto and Corregidor made it clear that he was addressing the cadets at Texas A&M on Muster Day.

When I wrote to the University of Houston Chancellor's Office to get a biography of Gen. A. D. Bruce '16, the return mail included a copy of his 1960 Muster speech with his handwritten notations in the margin. A similar inquiry to Olympic Silver Medal shot-putter C. Darrow Hooper '53 likewise brought a copy of his 1965 address.

While checking for the campus locations of each Muster, I discovered that the entire speech of Texas A&M agronomy professor and World War II Medal of Honor recipient Eli L. Whiteley '41 had been printed in *The Battalion,* the A&M student newspaper. On Easter Sunday in 1962, with the campus nearly vacant, Muster was conducted inside the MSC Ballroom, where Whiteley urged support for change. The fact that it was the only Muster speech to be printed in *The Battalion* appears significant. It is highly likely that A&M's president, Gen. James Earl Rudder '32, and other administrators read Whiteley's speech and were encouraged by such a statement coming from a war hero. The following year (1963) the name of A&M changed from the Agricultural & Mechanical College of Texas to Texas A&M University and women were admitted to A&M on a limited basis.

The 1973 speech of longtime Vietnam prisoner of war James E. Ray '63 was lost until I realized that virtually his entire address was in my story about his return from captivity in the July 1973 *Texas Aggie* magazine. This, along with quotes from a write-up in *The Battalion,* was incorporated into this book.

Stepping down after thirty-one years as editor of *The Texas Aggie* in 2002, I continued to collect speeches and began to look through my files. I realized that I had the material to do an updated edition of *The Voices of a Proud Tradition* and wanted to get this collection into the hands of Aggies and friends of Texas A&M. While exploring this possibility, the project languished for more than a decade.

In the meantime, I continued to collect addresses at each year's Muster ceremony until I now have information on seventy-three Muster speeches since 1944—sixty-eight actual manuscripts along with five newspaper write-ups.

Oftentimes, speakers depart from their written notes and add comments that occur to them while making their presentation. In order to reflect these remarks accurately, I have listened to audio and video recordings of Muster ceremonies to ensure that the speeches herein convey the sentiments actually delivered by the speakers. In addition, I made corrections of obvious typographic errors and sentence construction while inserting clarifications to provide context for readers. In addition to the speeches, two appendixes are included—the first provides the years, speakers' names, campus locations of ceremonies, and source of the speeches, and the second features traditional poems about Muster and Aggie traditions.

# Introduction

*The Magic of Muster*

"HERE!"

With this single word, Texas Aggies throughout the world annually pledge their loyalty, love, and allegiance to the Aggie Family. Each April 21, San Jacinto Day, the anniversary of the battle that won Texas its independence from Mexico in 1836, brings renewal and dedication to an ideal that sets the Aggie Family apart from all others—the Aggie Spirit.

"HERE!" is the response from classmates, family, and friends as the names of Aggies who have died during the past year are called in a "Roll Call for the Absent" during the concluding moments of each ceremony. On the main campus of Texas A&M University in College Station, Texas, and at several hundred locations around the world, Aggies gather to pay homage to their friends and fellow Aggies who have made what an A&M poem by Philo H. Duval Jr. '51 calls "The Last Corps Trip."

Muster is this and more. It is the twenty-one-gun salute by the Ross Volunteer firing squad. It is the fading notes of Silver Taps carried on a quiet breeze.

"Being composed of the Alumni of the College," the 1883 program of the Ex-Cadets Association stated, "many of whom annually pass from its halls into the bivouac of life, it is but meet that we should form and ever preserve an organization for uniting us fraternally, and always at necessity's call, extend a helping hand to an old comrade. In reunion we meet and live over again our College days, the victories and defeats won and lost upon drill ground and classroom. Let all Alumni answer at roll call."

The 1942 Corregidor news report, containing the Aggie roll call that Maj. Tom Dooley '35 compiled for Maj. Gen. George F. Moore '08, gave added emphasis to the A&M tradition and fostered the ceremony we know today as Aggie Muster.

The definitive story of Aggie Muster is told in great detail by John A. Adams Jr. '73 in *Softly Call the Muster: The Evolution of a Texas Aggie Tradition* (Texas A&M University Press, 1994).

English professor John C. Adams's 1985 edition of *The Voices of A Proud Tradition* asked, "What is the Muster Speech?" While the origins of the Muster speech are uncertain, for many years it has played a significant part in the annual Texas A&M Muster ceremony on San Jacinto Day, April 21. The Aggie Muster celebrates the 1836 battle that won Texas independence, and former and current students from Texas A&M University gather together wherever they are around the world to reaffirm bonds of love for each other and to reunite themselves with those Aggies who have passed from this life.

Adams wrote that the Muster addresses "reflect a deep concern for the importance of friendship, self-reliance, personal sacrifice, duty, and leadership." The speakers urge their views in both celebration and defense of these principles. At times they speak emotionally, at others with much attention to reason, to statistics and facts, but always with conviction.

In 1952, then-state senator Searcy Bracewell '38 dramatically recalled Gen. Sam Houston's 1836 order for scout Deaf Smith to destroy the bridge over Vince's Bayou. This denied both the enemy and his own soldiers an avenue of retreat from the Battle at San Jacinto. Bracewell then urged Muster attendees to "take the reins of responsibility."

Two years later, Texas Governor Allan Shivers, a University of Texas graduate, praised A&M for teaching "the arts of peace as well as the arts of war" and lauded its contributions to science, agriculture, and engineering. "Its true strength," he concluded, "seems to lie in that spirit which enables this school to produce fine American citizens. I'm talking about honest, God-fearing, conscientious American citizens who are proud of their freedom and who are willing to give their lives, if necessary, to protect it." In 1950 Shivers ordered that the full-size Liberty Bell replica given to the State of Texas be placed at Texas A&M in recognition of the sacrifices made by Aggies in the defense of the nation. It hangs in the rotunda of the Academic Building to this day.

Texas land commissioner Maj. Gen. James Earl Rudder '32 (president of Texas A&M from 1959 to 1970) expressed the importance of voting and public service in his 1956 address. "I have never known any Aggie to show any apathy or lethargy in any matter connected with Texas A&M College," he said. "We need that same enthusiastic spirit in the halls of government—from the local school board all the way to the White House."

Houston attorney Mayo J. Thompson '41 urged Aggies in 1969 to "become involved" and pointed out that non-Aggies, in spite of their criticism and fault-finding, "desire to be more like us, for they see in us . . . the spirit of camaraderie, the spirit of fidelity . . . the true spirit of the Muster."

In 1977 former Vietnam War POW James E. Ray '63 delivered his second campus Muster address, emphasizing the importance of discipline and awareness of human relations in achieving goals. "The most effective units in my experience," he said, "have been those in which there was a high level of mutual leader/follower respect. High standards, firm discipline and a strong sense of identity with the unit. . . . I know this sense of cooperative teamwork at every level in an organization is possible because I've seen it work."

Former A&M faculty dean Dr. Haskell M. Monroe spoke in 1983 when he was president of the University of Texas at El Paso. After pointing out numerous reasons why he considered himself an Aggie, he characterized Aggies as "part of an endless maroon line, which for 107 years has marched nobly toward high achievement, thoughtful concern for others and the defense of freedom."

Longtime National Football League referee M. L. "Red" Cashion '53 defined the Aggie Spirit this way in 1990: "You must Live it—to Understand it; You have to Share it—to Feel it; and most of all, You have to Give it—in order to Receive it!"

Then, in 1994, Texas A&M University–Kingsville history professor Andrés Tijerina '67 described how he followed his brother, Albert Tijerina '65, to A&M, only to come face to face with a "tall, blond Anglo roommate." On their first day Tijerina told him "if he ever tried anything with me, by golly, he was going to have to fight one mean Mexican . . . and this guy just looked at me in amazement and said, 'I just came here to be an Aggie like you.' It was the first time I had ever been perceived as something other than a Mexican."

When Reed Arena opened in 1998, former A&M football coach Eugene Stallings '57 delivered the longest address in Aggie Muster history and recited two lengthy poems without having a single note or cue card. Woven through his speech were the names of many prominent Aggies and remembrances of their contributions to help illustrate the Aggie Spirit.

Brooke Leslie Rollins '94 attended her first Aggie Muster in 1990, as a freshman. After serving as student body president, she returned to campus as Muster speaker in 2007 to relate the stories of nine members of her husband's Aggie family and that of a close friend of her husband's who died in the Iraq war to illustrate the strong ties Aggies have for their school.

Former A&M president and US Secretary of Defense Dr. Robert M. Gates told the 2009 Aggie Muster about the "22 Aggies who have made the supreme sacrifice for their country in Iraq and Afghanistan. Ten of them were students while I was president. I signed the diplomas of four of them, shook their hands and handed those diplomas to them, and witnessed their commissioning. For eight of them, I probably signed the paper that sent them into combat, and for nine I wrote the condolence letters to their families."

Many of the speeches seek to do what has been thought impossible—explain the Aggie Spirit to students, former students, and even those outside the Aggie Family. A number of them succeed admirably. Some of the speakers attempt to define the meaning of Aggie Muster and talk about A&M traditions, such as the Twelfth Man, Silver Taps, Gig 'Em, Bonfire, the Aggie Ring, and Reveille. Others recount A&M's leadership in wartime and accomplishments on peacetime fronts. Several define the elements of a great university, the importance of personal discipline, and the characteristics of a Texas Aggie.

In two very special speeches, A&M's original 12th Man, Dr. E. King Gill '24 (1964 address) and Col. Tom Dooley '35 (1978 address) share the very personal stories of their involvement in the birth of revered traditions. Gill relates the events at the Dixie Classic in 1922 that gave rise to A&M's 12th Man, and Dooley tells how he gathered Aggies' names during the incessant bombing and shelling of Corregidor to send back the story of the "1942 Muster" on the "Rock."

Only two individuals have delivered more than one campus Muster address—James W. Aston '33 in 1949 and 1961 and James E. Ray '63 in 1973 and 1977.

Although the majority of Muster speakers have been Texas Aggies, nine of them are not Texas A&M former students. Those include Gen. Dwight Eisenhower, World War II Supreme Allied Commander, and two of the three governors to address Muster—Colorado Governor Dan Thornton (1953) and Texas Governor Allan Shivers (1954). A&M presidents Dr. Jack K. Williams (1971) and Dr. Robert M. Gates (2007) are among this group, along with book publishing executive Col. Willard Chevalier (1947), Rev. Sam Hill (1948), former A&M faculty dean Haskell M. Monroe (1983), and former Texas A&M head football coach R. C. Slocum (2016).

# "HERE"

# First Muster Packets
# Mailed Worldwide (1943)

From *Softly Call the Muster: The Evolution of a Texas Aggie Tradition*, by John A. Adams Jr. '73 (Texas A&M University Press, 1994):

> In 1943, E. E. McQuillen '20, executive secretary of the Association of Former Students, decided to use the word *Muster* for the April 21st observance. To spread the word, he assembled the first written Muster packets for distribution to the various Texas A&M clubs, mothers' clubs, and military installations around the world. The packets contained a detailed program outline, greetings from A&M President Dr. T. O. Walton, and a Muster poem about Corregidor, "The Heroes' Roll Call," by Dr. John Ashton '06, a member of the college English faculty.

From *The Battalion*, April 22, 1943:

> As a part of the National Capital A. & M. Club's program, a [radio] broadcast was put on at 5:15 yesterday afternoon with Secretary of Commerce Jesse H. Jones and US Senator Tom Connally as speakers. The Texas Quality Network honored A. & M. with a broadcast, "Cavalcade of the Fighting Texas Aggies," from 8:30–9:00 p.m.
>
> Dr. T. O. Walton, President of A. & M., in a radio message to the 1943 Muster of the Fraternity of A. & M. men, stated: "Tonight more than ten thousand former students of the A. and M. College of Texas are serving in the armed forces, 8000 of them as officers. More than a hundred of our boys have lost their lives in this war; 40 are listed as prisoners of the Japs; and scores of men are missing in action. The military heritage that is A. and M.'s is exemplified by the deeds of her sons on the fighting fronts of the world. The Spirit of Aggieland that binds men closer than brothers, marches on!"

# E. E. McQuillen '20
*1944—Guion Hall*

E. E. McQuillen '20.
Photo from editor's
collection.

Everett Eugene McQuillen was born June 9, 1898, in Palestine, Texas. His college education was interrupted by World War I, but he returned to complete his animal husbandry degree and graduate as valedictorian. He was a lieutenant colonel in the Corps of Cadets, associate editor of the *Longhorn* (yes, that's what the A&M yearbook was called from 1903 until 1949), president of his senior class, and captain of A&M's Southwest Conference champion 1920 basketball team. He earned a master's degree at the University of Wisconsin before returning to A&M to teach animal husbandry and to work in insurance for several years.

Becoming active with the Association of Former Students, he was instrumental in obtaining a $25,000 gift for A&M's Student Loan Fund in 1925 from the Sears, Roebuck Agricultural Foundation. In the fund's first year, 500 A&M students benefited. In 1926 he was named executive secretary of the association upon the resignation of Col. Ike Ashburn. For two decades, he provided exemplary leadership for the Texas A&M alumni organization. Between 1929 and 1937, McQuillen and his assistant, Lonnie B. Locke '22, took salary cuts to keep the association going during the Depression.

In the 1930s, he helped establish the Opportunity Award Scholarship Program, which initially provided needy students $125 per semester and a campus job. In the early 1940s, McQuillen initiated the banquets that welcomed graduating seniors into the association for over half a century. In 1942 he introduced the concept of "annual giving," which encouraged continuing support from former students. "Mr. Mac" was president of the American Alumni Council and served as its national director of funds.

McQuillen resigned from the association in 1947 to become executive director of the Texas A&M Development Fund. He raised funds to build the Memorial Student Center (MSC) and developed the Gold Star Fund to help children of A&M servicemen. (For twenty-one years he lived in a house where the MSC now stands.) His success led to creation of the Texas A&M Foundation in 1953, which he also directed until retiring in 1963. In 1975 he was inducted into the Texas A&M Athletic Hall of Fame. E. E. McQuillen died January 6, 1979.

## First Memorial Roll Call

E. E. McQuillen's 1944 Muster address has been lost to history. The following newspaper write-up of the event appeared in the April 22, 1944, issue of *The Battalion*.

### First Ceremony Held by Corps in Muster History

Adding their voices to the thousands of others around the world, last night the A. and M. Corps for the first time in Muster history met in Guion at eight p.m. to hold a Muster ceremony of their own.

Probably the largest group of Aggies to attend any single Muster, the traditional program was followed by 1200 students. The affair was opened with the "National Anthem," which was followed by a roll call by classes, each class answering in unison when their name was called. Next the "Aggie War Hymn" was sung by the Corps and an explanation and history of the San Jacinto Day celebration was made.

The remainder of the program consisted of the reading of a message sent by Jake Hamblen '27 [president of the Association of Former Students]; an address made by E. E. McQuillen, Secretary of the Ex-Students Association; the singing of the "Twelfth Man"; and the Memorial Roll Call by Dr. John Ashton '06. The names called were Herbert Smith '39, Lt. Joseph P. Lindsley '41, Robert Derace Moser '42, Edwin Pat Patterson '43, Harold Louis Delfraisse '43, Dick Downing '43, Claude A. Riggs '44, Pvt. Richard Andrew

Stromberg '44, Aviation Cadet James C. Black '45, Rex Watson Bynum '46, Eugene Depew '47, and John Richard Carlson '47.

The ceremony was closed with the sounding of Silver Taps, played by six buglers of the Aggie Band and the playing of the "Spirit of Aggieland," with Pat Owens at the console of the organ.

# Lt. Clifton H. Chamberlain '40

## *1945—Guion Hall*

Lt. Clifton H. Chamberlain '40. Photo from editor's collection.

Clifton Henry Chamberlain Jr. was born March 26, 1918, in Yadkinville, North Carolina. His family moved to Texas in 1926. Commissioned following graduation with a degree in petroleum production engineering, he was called to active duty with the 54th Coast Artillery Regiment in February 1941. In June he was assigned to the 59th Coast Artillery Regiment and was stationed on one of the small islands near Corregidor. He was a Japanese prisoner of war for 999 days from the surrender of Corregidor in May 1942 until he was liberated by US forces in February 1945.

Returning to the United States, he was stationed at Fort Crockett as artillery engineer, adjutant, and commander of harbor defenses of Galveston, Texas; attended artillery school at Fort Bliss; and instructed at the Seacoast Branch of the Artillery School at Fort Scott, California. In 1947 he was transferred to the Corps of Engineers and was given a regular army commission.

He graduated from the Engineer Officer Advance Course at Fort Belvoir, Virginia, in 1950 and was assistant professor of military science and tactics at Georgia Institute of Technology for three years. He graduated from the Command and General Staff College at Fort Leavenworth, Kansas, in 1954. For the next three years, he served in Italy as action officer in the plans and operations division, Allied Forces Southern Europe. Returning to the United States, he was division engineer for the 9th Infantry Division and commander of the 15th Engineer Battalion before working his way up to chief of the engineering division of the Corps of Engineers Ballistic Missile Construction Office.

He served a year in Korea as commander of the 11th Engineer Battalion, attended the Industrial College of the Armed Forces, and retired in 1966 as chief of the Military Engineering Division, Directorate of Topography and Military Engineering in the Chief of Engineering's Office, Washington, DC.

His decorations include two Legion of Merit awards, Army and Air Force Commendation Medals, the Bronze Star, and the Purple Heart. He died February 17, 1988.

## Campus Muster Speech

Clifton Chamberlain's 1945 Muster address has been lost to history. The following information is adapted from the newspaper write-up of the event in *The Battalion*.

Saturday night at 8 p.m. the joint Cadet Corps–Brazos County Muster ceremony filled Guion Hall. In conjunction with the Muster, an all-girl orchestra from Sam Houston State Teachers College performed at a show to raise funds for a proposed monument honoring longtime A&M mascot Reveille. They also played for a Corps dance in Sbisa Hall.

Silver Taps was held that night.

*The Battalion*, the A&M student newspaper, listed the names of some 450 A&M former students then known to have died in World War II.

The campus Muster committee learned of Lt. Chamberlain's release from a letter his parents forwarded to the Association of Former Students office: "Dear Mother, Reborn January 30, 1945, at 7:30 A.M. Am well and so happy I can't describe how I feel. After three years of uncertainty, to be back with your own people is heaven."

In addition to speaking at the 1945 Muster, Clifton Chamberlain came back to campus for the 1969 Muster with Aggie survivors of Bataan/Corregidor Urban C. Hopmann '39, Tull Ray Louder '41, Harry O. Fischer '29, and Jerome McDavitt '33. They brought with them an American flag that American POWs made from red, white, and blue strips of parachute cloth from a supply drop when they were liberated from the POW camp at Cabanatuan, Luzon.

As this book was being prepared, Clifton Chamberlain's son, William "Clif" Chamberlain '71, presented the Texas A&M University Archives with a scrapbook that his mother had created containing news clippings, personal correspondence, and other memorabilia of his father's military service, POW status, and release from captivity.

# Gen. Dwight D. Eisenhower

*1946—Kyle Field*

Gen. Dwight D. Eisenhower. Photo from editor's collection.

Born October 14, 1890, in Denison, Texas, Dwight David Eisenhower grew up in Abilene, Kansas, and graduated 61st out of 164 cadets at the US Military Academy at West Point in 1915.

After beginning his military service at Fort Sam Houston, Texas, where he met his wife, Mamie, he was stationed at various posts in the United States. Following a tour in the Panama Canal Zone, he graduated first in a class of 275 at Command and General Staff School. He served under Gen. John J. Pershing in Washington, DC and with Lt. Douglas MacArthur in the Philippines. He took command of US forces in the European theater in 1942 after serving in the War Plans Division under Army Chief of Staff Gen. George E. Marshall. Later that year, he was named commander in chief of the Allied Expeditionary Force. He directed the invasion of North Africa and commanded the Allied invasions of Sicily and Italy in 1943. He briefly was Allied commander in chief, Mediterranean theater, before becoming supreme commander, Allied Expeditionary Force, in January 1944. In June of that year, he directed the D-Day landings at Normandy. Germany unconditionally surrendered eleven months later.

Following World War II, he was Army chief of staff until 1948 when he assumed the presidency of Columbia University. While serving in that capacity, he visited the Texas A&M campus on November 9, 1950, for the inauguration of A&M president M. T. Harrington '22. The next year he became the first commander of the newly formed Supreme Headquarters Allied Powers Europe (SHAPE). In 1952 he was elected president of the United States and served two terms until 1961.

Eisenhower addressed 10,000 at Texas A&M's Homecoming Muster at Kyle Field in 1946, expressing his gratitude to current and former students who served as military officers in World War II. He also expressed his "lasting admiration" for the accomplishments of Texas A&M's ROTC program and its graduates.

Eisenhower died March 28, 1969.

## "Speech for Texas Agricultural and Mechanical College"

This visit to Texas A&M allows me to pay a first installment on two debts, both of them long overdue. One is to acknowledge, in this Easter morning ceremony, the magnificent contribution made by your college in the gaining of the Allied victory of 1945. The other is to pay tribute, through this largest of all ROTC units, to the vital role played by the entire ROTC system in that bitter contest.

Through the lean years following 1918, at a time when possibility of another war seemed, to the public mind, so remote as to challenge the sanity of any individual of contrary view, the nationwide ROTC system steadily turned out reserve officers. Between 1919 and our entry into World War II, it produced 112,000, of whom 58,000 were still on the rolls in 1941. In the early days of mobilization, when officer procurement was one of our most critical problems, we had this substantial body to employ. General Marshall called it at the time, "our principal available asset."

The ROTC of this one institution furnished the Army 7,000 officers—far more than any other college. Figures—and I have already submitted you several—are sometimes more eloquent than words. No more convincing testimony could be given to the manner in which the men of Texas A&M lived up to the ideals and principles inculcated in them during their days on this campus than the simple statement that the Congressional Medal of Honor has been awarded to six former students [the total would eventually be seven], that forty-six took part in the heroic defense of Bataan and Corregidor [this total is closer to ninety], and that nearly 700 are on the list of our battle dead [more than 900 gave their all]. As one of the field commanders with whom served many of the veterans in this homecoming gathering, I can feel only a lasting admiration for the ROTC of Texas A&M. This admiration extends to the individual as well as to the institution that produced you.

You met the sternest of all tests. No matter how deep and instinctive our hatred of war, we still are quick to recognize that the weakling cannot measure up to the standard it sets.

Even people who have been so fortunate as to remain strangers to the terror of the diving plane and the nerve-shattering thump of bursting shells, who have not known the sickening smells, the dust, the mud, the stifling heat, the freezing cold of the battlefield or the bone-deep weariness of marching and firing and digging and crawling, who have not felt the sadness of blank files in the ranks—even these can sense that respect is won in combat only by manifestation of virtues we most admire in men—courage, devotion, endurance, discipline, optimism, mutual help, loyalty.

To these qualities there must be added, for success, still another, and vital, ingredient.

It is leadership.

You veterans here know, better than others, that the highest commander cannot, by himself, provide the leadership necessary to tactical victory. He must be supported by a great organization of devoted assistants, the base of which must be the captains, the lieutenants, the sergeants and corporals—every man that has a position of responsibility over another in the battle. Through days and months of experience, you veterans learned to distinguish between the true and the false, between the man who leads and the one who seeks under the cloak of undeserved authority to escape his own proper share of the costs that must be paid to achieve any positive and worthwhile purpose.

You well know that the officer who pretends to a position of human rather than of mere official superiority, who deliberately thrusts upon his men added danger, suffering or exhausting work in order that he may himself escape their full impact, is not, in the eyes of his men, an officer and a leader, regardless of the weight of the insignia he carries upon his shoulder.

During the war, a broad survey was made to determine what qualities enlisted men considered most important in a good officer.

Our soldiers thought the two prime requisites were: first, his ability or competence; secondly, they named his interest in the welfare of his men. As to his personal attitude, Major General John M. Scaffold described it well to the cadets at West Point back in 1887. He said, "The discipline which makes the soldiers of a free country reliable in battle is not to be gained by harsh or tyrannical treatment. On the contrary, such treatment is far more likely to destroy than to make an army. He who feels the respect which is due to others cannot fail to inspire in them regard for himself; while he who feels disrespect towards others . . . cannot fail to inspire hatred against himself."

It is the commander who shares, naturally and unpretentiously in every problem of the group, who gains the confidence of his men and gives them his own, who shares with them every turn of fortune, who takes no thought of himself until every need of all his men has been accommodated, who learns from them as much as he can teach them, and who expresses in every word and deed his pride of belonging to the whole, that invariably gains for himself the greatest reward that can come to any man.

This reward is the respect, esteem and love of his associates. Moreover, his is an elite unit. Such a man is a stranger to resentment from his men. They accord—they demand for him—a position before the world that comes only to those who have rendered honest service to their fellows.

It is this type of officer that the ROTC must develop. It cannot be done in days or weeks; it requires months of training, of study, of reflection. That nation's war needs in officers—if war should again come to us—cannot possibly be met without the ROTC. No regular establishment can meet the requirements in numbers, while shorter, emergency periods of training, although effective in the rapid selection and specialized combat training of promising material, cannot provide the opportunity for full development of the promise into rounded, understanding leadership.

For it is not true that leaders are born—never made. That notion is a tattered remnant of a system that went out with the bow and arrow. It's true that a real leader must be inherently endowed with certain essentials, among which are personal integrity, intelligence, common sense, and stability under pressure. But this is the raw material that reaches its ultimate effectiveness only under wise and persistent development. Given the rich stock of American manhood to draw upon, selection and training will continue to produce an even more magnificent body of unit leaders than those who in the last war led 8 million other Americans to the most decisive and the greatest victory, with the lowest losses, that the world has ever known.

The ROTC accomplishes, to a remarkable degree, both the selection and this training. A college course is by its nature a selective and screening process. By and large, those who graduate are tested risks for carrying through to a successful conclusion the diverse enterprises of modern military science. The ROTC man receives much more than military training. He is subjected to an increasingly difficult series of mental challenges. He gains information and, more important, he gains tolerance, appreciation, and understanding of the problems of mankind. He grows, matures, broadens in interests. His training is calculated to give him a feeling of confidence and sureness, but not an attitude of superiority and snobbishness toward his fellow men.

In our country, we hold that every man should have the opportunity to rise to any station in his chosen profession commensurate with his ability. This is not merely a pretty theory in the Army. It is our guiding principle. We provided the Military Academy, to which entrance lies in the hands of our elected representatives of the people: we established the CMTC [Citizen's Military Training Camps] before the war and the officer candidate schools during the war: we commissioned specialists direct from civil life; and finally, gave battlefield commissions to men who displayed the ultimate requirements of an officer in being able to lead troops successfully in the face of the enemy. The wartime Officer Corps of the American Army was the best the American nation could provide. It had no artificial limitations due to race, color, or creed. Its record is one to thrill every true American. Its splendid leadership enabled our Army to defeat two of the most powerful military machines the world has ever seen. To say that some officers might have done more or done better should not be allowed to obscure the main issue.

The soldier of our citizen army recognizes his commander as one of his fellow men. He has no fear and must not be allowed to have any fear of that officer as a man, no feeling of inferiority toward him as a citizen of this republic. The American way of life has taught each to think for himself, to be an individual, to be self-reliant. It has engendered within him the desire for success and achievement.

At the same time he has learned, from his daily contacts, to recognize intelligence and integrity and the qualities of leadership in others. He is not a follower by nature but will extend himself to the utmost for those in whom he feels he can place his trust. He knows the value of organization and of discipline.

It is out of such stuff that American armies have always been made. To the American military commander, this truth offers an opportunity and a challenge. An opportunity in that these men can, by proper leadership, be welded into an unbeatable army. A challenge in that it calls for the exercise of the highest degree of justice, imagination, and initiative to explore and develop the potentialities of the young Americans in his charge.

The education of the officer never ends. The global nature of the recent war, with its close relationships to the political, industrial, and economic life of the nation, has made plain the need for more than purely military skills and knowledge, particularly in those who are to bear responsibilities in the higher staffs, or with other government agencies. Here again, the educational practices absorbed in the ROTC are certain to assist in the continuous broadening and growth of the individual.

I cannot close without suggesting to you more human and more profitable employment of the qualities developed in the ROTC than mere success in battle.

We have briefly surveyed the soldierly virtues that are essential to victory in war.

But not yet has been solved the problem of employing these virtues, which sustain the truth that man was created in the image of God, to serve as effectively the cause of peace as the demands of war. Must we admit that only the compulsion of a common, deadly fear can produce the teamwork that is as necessary to the peaceful concert of peoples as it is to batter and crush a stubborn foe? Why is it that the demonstrated abilities of a great nation and her allies to produce an equal progress toward the heart's desire of every individual on that earth—can't provide assurance that he may pursue his peaceful desires in tranquility and absence of fear?

The answer again is leadership, and again the answer must comprehend leadership in all walks of life, in all spheres of influence. Knowledge of the world—of other countries and peoples as well as our own, understanding of the need of strength to support good intent, and of the need for organization for the constructive work of peace. These, supported by energetic, tireless leadership, are the greatest need of a near-chaotic world.

The graduate of ROTC must acquire in his makeup the elements of mental and moral fitness, the desire to help and inspire his fellows, that will mark him for leadership in any community in this land. If he is truly trained, he will be the man to rely on—the one to respect—in danger or in calm.

He is one of the great hopes of this nation—of civilization itself.

# Col. Willard T. Chevalier

*1947—System Administration Building Lawn*

Col. Willard T. Chevalier.
Cushing Memorial
Library and Archives.

Willard Townshend Chevalier, vice president of McGraw-Hill Publishing Company and one of America's most outstanding civil engineers, was visiting the Texas A&M campus at the time he was invited to speak at Aggie Muster. He addressed 1,500 students, former students, and friends of Texas A&M at the annual San Jacinto Day event, held on the lawn of the Administration Building. Chevalier had been president of the American Road Builders Association after graduating with a civil engineering degree at Brooklyn Polytechnic Institute in 1910. He participated in the design and construction of the New York subways and the New York State Barge Canal. He served as a captain, major, and lieutenant colonel in France with the 11th Engineers and was a colonel in the reserves from 1937 to 1948.

## Build Character and Culture*

Colonel Chevalier's 1947 Muster address has been lost to history. The following information is from newspaper write-ups of the event. During the ceremony, it was announced that a large granite "T" monument to longtime A&M mascot Reveille had been completed at the entrance to Kyle Field.

From the *Bryan Eagle*, April 22, 1947: "Col. Willard Chevalier, noted educator and publications executive (Vice-President of McGraw-Hill Publishing Co.), paid homage to the Texans of 111 years ago who won

*Speech title assigned by editor

freedom and fame on the field of San Jacinto. He praised the A&M College of Texas for the advantages it was taking from the sacrifices of these early Texans."

From *The Battalion*, April 22, 1947: "The way of honoring those that have passed on is to build character and culture at this great institution."

# Sam Hill

## *1948—System Administration Building Lawn*

Sam Hill. Photo from editor's collection.

Samuel Bernard Hill was born September 17, 1906, in Amelia, Virginia. After graduating from San Antonio Military Academy, he earned an AB degree from Austin College in Sherman in 1929 and a BD from Austin Presbyterian Theological Seminary in Austin in 1932. He served as pastor at churches in Bartlett, Cuero, and Beeville and started a parochial school in Victoria. Noted author George Sessions Perry devoted a dozen pages in his 1942 book, *Texas, A World in Itself*, to Victoria and to Hill.

Hill began his Victoria pastorate in 1941 and the next year left to become a training officer with the US Army Air Corps. Hill commanded the Air Corps unit being trained at Texas A&M in 1943–44. He achieved the rank of lieutenant colonel before being discharged in 1946.

His younger brother, David Lee "Tex" Hill '38, a member of Troop A Cavalry at A&M, flew torpedo bombers for the US Navy and became the second leading ace with Gen. Claire Chennault's "Flying Tigers" against the Japanese in China before the attacks on Pearl Harbor and the Philippines. Joining the Army Air Corps after war was declared, Tex was belatedly awarded the Distinguished Service Cross in 2002.

On February 1, 1948, Sam Hill was named chaplain of the A&M College of Texas and was serving in this capacity when he delivered the Muster address that April 21. He was the first A&M chaplain in some thirty-five years and was a nonsectarian religious advisor to the more than 4,000 A&M students. He resigned his post at Texas A&M on October 1 after eight months of service.

Sam Hill died December 19, 1994, in Hunt, Texas.

# Campus Muster Speech

Reverend Hill's Muster address has been lost to history. The following is from the *Bryan Eagle*, April 22, 1948:

With a gathering of nine thousand students, former students, wives and guests seated on the lawn in front of the administration building joining in, representatives of the Student Senate of Texas A&M College at 6 p.m. Wednesday staged the home campus ceremony of the world-wide Aggie Muster. Some three hundred similar ceremonies were conducted throughout Texas and others throughout the world.

Texas Aggies, wherever they might be, gathered for the traditional April 21 ceremony honoring San Jacinto Day and pledging anew their allegiance to their school.

John Stiles, senior student from Cisco, served as Muster chairman here, with Clifford Harris, student chaplain from Gail, giving the invocation and Charles Harrison, senior from Groesbeck, reading the "Roll Call for the Absent." Called were the names of five A&M students who died since the last annual muster, with friends and classmates answering "Here."

Music by the 160-piece A&M Band, the 60-voice Singing Cadets male choir and playing of Silver Taps by the bugle corps set the atmosphere for an impressive ceremony. A volley by an honor guard from the Ross Volunteers climaxed the roll call.

Principal speaker was Rev. Sam Hill, now chaplain of the college, with a brief speech by A. E. Hinman, Corpus Christi, president of the Association of Former Students.

# James W. Aston '33
## *1949—Guion Hall*

James W. Aston '33.
Photo from editor's
collection.

James William Aston was born October 6, 1911, and raised in Farmersville, Texas. At Texas A&M he was a Distinguished Student, captain and fullback of the football team in his senior year, a member of the Ross Volunteers, president of Senior Court, and cadet colonel of the Corps of Cadets. He received his BS in civil engineering.

Aston worked for the City of Dallas, where he was named city manager in 1939. In 1941 he took leave to enter active duty in the military as a lieutenant. He quickly rose to the rank of colonel and was named chief of staff of Air Transport Command in November 1945. His decorations include the Distinguished Service Medal and the Legion of Merit.

Following World War II, he accepted a position as vice president of Republic National Bank in Dallas in December of 1945 and would become president and CEO in 1965. He was named chairman of the board and CEO of the Republic of Texas Corporation in 1974.

He was president of the Texas Bankers Association, the Cotton Bowl Athletic Association, and the Dallas Citizens Council. He was on the National Council of the Boy Scouts of America and was appointed to the Governor's Energy Advisory Council in 1973.

Aston was named to the Sports Illustrated Silver Anniversary All-American Football Team in 1957. In 1961 he served as president of Texas A&M's Association of Former Students and delivered the campus Muster address for a second time. (Only two individuals have delivered two campus Muster speeches.) Aston was chosen a Texas A&M Distinguished Alumnus in 1967, and a dormitory at A&M was named in his honor in

1975. He was inducted into Texas A&M's Athletic Hall of Fame in 1968 and into the Corps of Cadets Hall of Honor in 1997.

For fifty years he was married to Sarah Orth, whose face appears on the columns of the Jack Williams Administration Building at Texas A&M.

James Aston died October 2, 1995.

## Only Aggies Can Understand*

*This campus Muster address by James Aston was unavailable until his widow, Pat Harris Aston, reported that she had a phonograph record of the 1949 Muster ceremony. A transcription of his remarks follows.*

Mr. Chairman, fellow Aggies, and friends, it is fitting indeed that the world's largest military school, the school which has provided more officers for the defense and security of this country than any other institution, should hold an annual muster to pay our respects to those who have preceded us and for those of us who remain to rededicate ourselves to duty, to God, and to country.

Thus, the Aggie Muster has a twofold significance. First, we are reminded of our debt to those men of Texas A&M, your classmates and mine, who gave their lives in war or who lie disabled in the veterans hospital, or whose future has otherwise been darkened so that you and I might enjoy the privileges of a free and democratic country. We're also reminded of our debt to the other Aggies who have passed on to their reward from earthly stewardship. And while they did not sacrifice their lives on the battlefield, they gave the best they had through art, sciences, and the professions and thus made their full contribution toward a better world. No occasion can be more sacred than one where we honor those who have honored us. No debt can be greater than ours.

The other significance of the Aggie Muster is to remind us of our duty as Aggies to the past, present, and future. We're the beneficiaries of

---

*Speech title derived by editor from speech contents

the tireless and unselfish sacrifices of those we honor today. But we're also the recipients of responsibility, which to faithfully discharge will require the best you and I possess.

I am certain that, if those we honor today could speak to us, they would echo in unity the statement made by Dr. George W. Truett to an assemblage in Dallas a number of years ago. Dr. Truett said, "Hats off to the past. Coats off to the future." The true degree of our love and appreciation will be measured by what we do from now on.

It's a great privilege to be an Aggie. A person gets something at Texas A&M which is not to be found anywhere else in the world. There are thousands of colleges and universities where a person can get a degree in his chosen field, but there is but one Aggieland. Maybe it's because it's a democratic school where there is no distinction between financial means, where clothes and privileges are the same. Maybe it's because it's a man's school with dormitory life. Maybe it's because it's a school where there's no prejudices to religion or station in life. I can't define it. I can't describe it. And neither can you. It's that something that others admire and only Aggies understand. But it's as real as life itself. Unable to describe it, we call it the Spirit of Aggieland. And if you don't feel something tingle inside you when you hear it set to music, as we just heard here this evening, then you are not an Aggie.

It was the Aggie Spirit which motivated and guided the lives of those whom we honor tonight and it's in their honor and in recognition of our duty that we pledge the best that's in us to faithfully and aggressively discharge the responsibilities which are ours.

Responsibilities of an Aggie start from the day of enrollment as a freshman and they are permanent from that day on. Responsibilities of a student are no different from the responsibilities of an ex-student. The traditions of Aggieland are many and, while I will not attempt to enumerate them all, I will mention a few, which as we are reminded today have become our duty to uphold.

An Aggie has respect for law and a respect for authority regardless of whether it be state, institutional, or social. We're asked sometimes to question the wisdom or application of a law, rule, or order, but an Aggie is trained to follow the order to the nth degree. Aggies are noted for their leadership. They are good leaders because they are good followers and are obedient to authority. An Aggie is tolerant of his fellow man.

Another tradition of Aggies is the will to win. Not to be first necessarily, but to do our best, whether it be in the classroom, on the campus, on the athletic field, or in the business world. Fair play is a tradition for which sons of Aggieland are noted. No one is victorious where victory is achieved other than according to the rules of the game.

And no tradition, no duty of an Aggie is more important than the duty of being a gentleman at all times and under all circumstances. Thus, as we meet here tonight and in hundreds of places around the world, in honor of those who have honored us, let us resolve again to ourselves, to A&M College, to friends and classmates who have passed from this world, to God and to country, to do our part as Aggies. To uphold the great traditions of this college, so that when your name and my name are called at some future Aggie Muster, someone will rise and proudly hail, "Here."

# Marion S. Church '05

*1950—Guion Hall*

Marion S. Church '05.
Photo from editor's
collection.

Marion Somerville Church was born in 1884. He was the first designated commander of Texas A&M's Corps of Cadets. Following graduation, he attended law school and became a noted attorney in Dallas. With three members of the Dallas A&M Club, Church formed a regiment of cavalry to serve in World War I. In October 1918, the unit was at full strength, but the war ended the following month.

In the 1920s, Church, with the able help of Carl C. "Polly" Krueger '12, reorganized the Association of Former Students. They traveled the state to build support for the fledgling alumni organization. Church was association president in 1923–24, and Krueger was president the following year.

In January 1951, Church was featured as one of the "Texans in Action" in *Texas Parade* magazine, then published by Ike Ashburn, formerly the A&M commandant and executive secretary of the Association of Former Students.

Church managed four family-owned farms, gleaning the latest scientific procedures from Texas Agricultural Experiment Station bulletins. He served as general counsel to the State Democratic Executive Committee. When he died July 18, 1959, he gave his collection of 750 cookbooks to the Texas State College for Women (now Texas Woman's University).

## Live to Honor San Jacinto*

*Church's speech has been transcribed from audio tape in the Texas A&M University Archives. The recording appears to be missing the opening lines of the speech.*

[*audience laughter*] Well, what are you going to do about it? What are you going to do about the present government emasculating your Constitution? What are you going to do about 'em changing your form of government? What are you going to do about them taking the rights of Texas away from you?

What are you going to do about moving all of the regulations of your people, your society at Washington? I'd rather have to go to Mexico City, because we could control those rats down there. But they're smart; they're smart in Washington. They love such people as is up there. They don't like to see 'em convicted. And when he is convicted, your Secretary of State says, "I'm still for it." I'd rather go to Mexico City and I'll go up there and risk my life as well as my liberty.

Why? Why did the United States fight England? It was a centralized government, taking away from the colonies the right of home rule. What did Patrick Henry say? Oh hell, even a schoolboy knows that Patrick Henry said, "Give me liberty or death." He didn't say, "Give me free false teeth, free bustles, free coffee." [*loud audience laughter*] Yes, my friends, they cut us apart from that great country and I'm sorry for the English people and the mistakes they made because my father was an Irish man of north Ireland and he loved that native land, but he became a United States citizen.

Yes, they've gone so far that when a baby's born they donate $13 to its birth and when it dies, when it's 70 years old, it donates an $80 coffin free to bury it. I had rather be a pauper and free and be buried where the crows could pick my bones than to be a slave and be buried free by a tyrant in an $80 coffin. And you'd better feel the same way. You'd better let this spirit of San Jacinto soak in on you. You'd better realize . . . Well, what was the motto way back yonder of the Spanish-American

*Speech title derived by editor from speech contents

War? I was just a little boy. I heard 'em sing it. "Christ was born across the sea to make men holy; let us die to make men free." Free. Freedom is what I'm trying to say. Not economic freedom, but personal freedom. The freedom of private enterprise to run your peanut raws through as long as you want to and pack 'em any way you want to. That's what they were talking about. That's the kind of freedom. Christ was born across the sea to make men holy; let us march and die to make men free.

What did we think in World War I? We wasn't talking about pensions then. We wasn't talking about all of this planned economy then. I was a part of that transaction as a soldier. I was thrilled. Woodrow Wilson says, "Let us make the world safe for democracy." Remember? What did he mean? What did we mean? Why did we supply the greatest number of officers to that army than any school in the United States? To go over there and win pensions for the world? To go over there and get false teeth for the world? To go over there and get free medicine from doctors that can't get to you?

No!

Fighting to make the world safe for democracy. Democracy! What kind of democracy? Democracy where the citizen owned the government and where the government didn't own the citizens. We go on another administration or two like we're going, you're going to be owned and your government will own you. You've got the choice that says as a citizen you own your government. And let your cry, let your motto be "Liberty, not Gifts." Don't make a wet nurse out of your government, ol' Aggies. Make a choice there to provide you a place to wax and to protect you. Personally I don't know but one way—to work—to make a living. There's three ways to make a living outside of working, and that is by inheritance, charity, or robbing. Now if you can figure out any other way, you're smart. I guess I've talked long enough. [*laughter*]

But what I'm trying to say—this is a serious case. This is your life; this means your prosperity; this means your liberty and the liberty of your children. Upon you, such as you, depends the future of this nation. Whether it shall be free or whether it shall be slave. That's why I'm yelling so up here this first chance I've had at a group of fine young men to say what's been in my soul a long time.

You say to me, how in the world can I, just one individual, change all this, if we want to change it. Well, you can get two little brass cannons like we had at San Jacinto and go to shooting. You can get muzzle-loading guns and sharp toads and stick it in Mexicans or New Dealers. [*laughter and cheers*] And I tell you what you can do. You can take that brass collar off your throat. It's choking you ever' time you vote, whether you're a Democrat, socialist, or Republican. And vote for tax cuts. Vote for the United States and quit voting for parties and men. When you do that, you won't be slaves. You'll be free men. Free men. And then our celebration each year will not be a mockery. But we will live to honor San Jacinto and our departed dead that died at Corregidor and splashed ashore in death at Normandy.

And may the world be saved by the United States to make the world free. And may the United States be made free by us—decent, patriotic citizens that want to be free and not chattels of a government. We want to own our own government and not have anybody own us. When we shall have done that, then we have paid homage and tribute to our institution and Texas and to our departed dead.

I thank you.

# James H. Pipkin '29

*1951—Memorial Student Center Lawn*

James H. Pipkin '29.
Photo from editor's
collection.

James Harold Pipkin was born March 29, 1907, in Huntsville, Texas. His father was a Baptist preacher, and he was a member of a large family —one of nine children. The family moved to Bryan in 1909, where he attended grammar and high school.

After studying at Texas A&M, Pipkin entered the University of Texas Law School, where he received his Bachelor of Laws degree in 1931. On December 1, 1934, he entered the service of the Texas Company (Texaco, Inc.) in the legal department at Houston. In 1938 Pipkin was admitted to practice before the Supreme Court of the United States.

In February 1942 he was transferred to New York as assistant to the executive vice president, and on September 15, 1949, he was appointed assistant to the chairman of the board. On September 1, 1950, Pipkin was named general manager of industrial and public relations. He became an executive vice president in 1962 and joined the board of Texaco in 1971.

In 1950 Pipkin received the honor medal of the Freedoms Foundation, Inc., Valley Forge, Pennsylvania, for "outstanding achievement in bringing about a better understanding of the American way of life." Pipkin was selected by the 1949 official awards jury of the Freedoms Foundation to receive the medal for a speech that he delivered in Abilene, Texas, in March 1949 entitled, "Is Our Freedom in Danger?"

James Pipkin died February 9, 1979.

# "Son, Remember . . ."

Now, in this place, we have come to a solemn and sacred hour. This being the forty-seventh annual Muster, wherein we pay our tribute of gratitude and affection to those men who once studied in these halls and have now passed from this earthly scene. I trust you will forgive me if I, a layman, center what I have to say around a text of Holy Scripture. It is found in the Gospel according to St. Luke, Chapter Sixteen, and consists of only two words:

"Son, remember . . ."

A new-born baby has no memory, nor is it expected to have one. The mother who holds it in her arms loves it none the less. But the case of a man is different. One of the most pitiful sights in the world is that of a grown man who has lost all recollection of his past. He can remember nothing of his childhood and youth, nor can he recall the lessons of experience or the standards by which he learned to live. He can only look out upon a world he does not understand, with empty, bewildered eyes.

And what is true of an individual is, if anything, even more tragic when set upon a greater stage. A school, a state, a nation or a society that has forgotten its own past, that knows no more the great sources of its own vigor, stands in desperate peril.

It is well, of course, that we live in the realities of the present with our eyes upon the future. But it is also well to remember that the roots of both present and future lie deep in the soil of what has been. Without accumulated experience we should be no more fit to solve the problems of today and tomorrow than are the apes in the jungle or the beasts in the fields.

The ability to remember is, perhaps, mankind's most primary possession. Certainly it is the pre-condition of all intelligent life, the accumulator and relator of experience, the guardian of those standards of right and honor cherished by our fathers before us, and given to us in turn as a sacred trust. Without it, devotion to "life, liberty and the pursuit of happiness" would be meaningless and absurd.

Today, here, we have come to an hour of remembrance.

I can speak this personally only for myself. But when I came from my mother's home this morning, just a few hills away, and saw again this loved and remembered scene, a thousand memories flooded into my mind: not of places, merely, but of faces and names, words spoken, hand clasped in hand, incidents of the classroom and campus, the music of the band rising in the clear autumn air, the team running on the field, the fierce ebb and flow on the turf below, the sustained thunder from the stands of the united voice of the "twelfth man" projecting its will-to-win to the eleven visible men.

Doubtless each of you experienced feelings like mine, though other faces and other years may have risen up before you. We do this because we share in a great tradition, greater than the single memories of any one of us. And though years pass, faces change, visible appearances alter, the spiritual core of that tradition remains unaltered and undiminished.

Possibly there are men here today who were graduated from A&M before I was born. Some of you students were babes in arms when I studied here. In all these years the faculties have changed. Buildings have been torn down and buildings have arisen. Familiar names have become almost forgotten and new names have become honored. What, then, is it that we share in common? What is it that binds us together as one, that will always bind us together? What but the invisible, undefinable, yet intensely palpable spirit of A&M? An outsider might not have any idea of what I am talking about. But you know. You have felt it. It has entered into you so that your whole life, no matter how long you live or where you live it, is richer and better for it. And, if you are a true son of A&M, the life you live and the deeds you do will reflect credit and honor upon the school we are not ashamed to say we love.

Today we look back over seventy-five years in the life of this college. They have been, perhaps, the most eventful seventy-five years the world has ever known. The apparently stable and settled world order of 1876 has been broken and melted in the furnaces of two great global wars, and that is not the end of it. The physical conditions of human life, particularly in America and Europe, have been vastly and fundamentally improved. Yet social conflict has rent the world, and today, an ancient reaction to bondage parading under a new name challenges all that our fathers held dear and indispensable to liberty.

If somehow President [Thomas] Gathright and his five fellow-professors could be transported in time from their two brick buildings and five small cottages to be with us now, to sit where we sit, they would not recognize the buildings and physical equipment which we sometimes call "the college." Yet, if they could know the changes that have come upon the world, if they could see how, over three-quarters of a century, A&M has adapted itself in instruction and in service, they would feel no cause for shame. They would recognize where they are, would know that the dream they dreamed has not been abandoned but fulfilled—to an extent which in all probability they did not foresee.

They would see how the original curricula have been carried on and expanded, new curricula added, serious scholarship genuinely valued, until today A&M stands academically as the peer of any institution of higher learning in the land. They would learn what, in a practical way, A&M has meant to the people of Texas and this country. With amazement they would witness how its great stream of men has gone forth to enrich not only the life of the Mother State of Texas, but the life of the nation and of the world. On the farm, the range, in business and industry, the sciences, the professions, and in the calling of the soldier, the sons of A&M have left an indelible and often glorious impress.

Could they be here today, it would move those men of 1876 [the year A&M opened its doors] to know how in every armed conflict the sons of A&M have served and borne themselves with honor. It would amaze them, remembering the small beginning, to be told that in World War II A&M gave more of its sons to be commissioned officers than any other college or university in the land, not even excepting the United States Military Academy at West Point. They would be saddened, indeed, as we are saddened today, to know how many of these men will never return. Yet they would not be cast down, for they were of a generation that had to learn, as we have learned, that the price of liberty comes high; that in times when it stands in peril those who love it must maintain it, if necessary, with their lives.

Here, and in many other parts of our land today, the sons of A&M are mustering. Those still living who cannot be with us in the body are most surely here in spirit. And as they and we call the roll of the absent, our hearts rise up together in gratitude to Almighty God for those we were privileged to call a friend and who today, we may believe, gather in a higher place than this to answer to a greater muster.

Yet as I counsel each of you "Son, remember!," it is not in any sense in our minds that today marks a final culmination in the work and spirit of A&M. The marching years go on. This is a bivouac upon the way. Seventy-five years lie behind us, and our spirits are filled with their glory. But this is not an ending. Better years than we have known lie before us. Many of us here today, please God, will muster in this place twenty-five years hence, when A&M celebrates completion of its first hundred years. What a year 1976 will be! Perhaps those who muster here then will say, "Why, the men of 1951 could not have dreamed the growth and greatness that lay in the years just before them!" Men of 1976, I hope that you may be able to say all that, and more. Yet even your triumphs, like ours, will be only a beginning. A hundred years from now surely the men of another generation will stand muster here, to thank God for progress and service we shall not be here to see, though we can predict it with confidence.

For no matter how many years may pass, no matter what physical changes come, no matter how the generations rise and fall away, A&M, that is to say, the essential spirit of A&M, will never pass away so long as its sons remember and cherish their heritage, so long as it remains within them as a living thing.

And what is the underlying basis of that heritage?

Is it wealth, power, possessions? It is none of these things. While the rewards of honest and intelligent effort should be despised by no man, the foundation upon which our fathers built goes far deeper. It is a foundation based upon human character: the life of integrity lived out in reverence and fear of God.

From the beginning of Texas it was one of her glories that here any man stands upon the basis of his individual worth and accomplishment. The men of 1836 did not ask "Who was your grandfather?" They asked, instead, "What kind of fellow are you? Can you stand on your own feet? Can you pull your own weight—and a little more?" Texas was no place for the weakling and the parasite. Such of these as came soon left for home.

And because those early "Texians" put character, self-reliance, and courage first, they bred here on that foundation a proud race of men who built a state and a way of life that is the envy and the admiration of the world. It didn't "come easy." The riches of nature did not fall like ripe fruit into the laps of an indolent people. It came hard. But because what we have here was earned by fighting, risk-taking, and plain hard work, its taste is sweeter in our mouth.

Today in America we are witnessing a widespread and tragic decline from the pioneer spirit. Millions of people today are thinking in terms of guaranteed security, rather than in terms of effort and accomplishment. They think the world owes them a living, and they imagine that if they only vote for it at the ballot box, an easy life will be theirs without effort, or with little effort, to earn it.

Such people could never have made Texas. Nor can such people keep Texas great. They do not understand that an economy of abundance comes only from constant initiative, daring, and work. Those who desire ease at little cost to themselves really want to live on the effort and toil of other people. They want to build a parasite state.

Now the people of Texas and our country generally have never been slow to fulfill their Christian duty of helpfulness toward the unfortunate and the distressed. They will always continue to do so. But those who want to build a parasite state of ease without effort for those people who are able to earn their own way, fail to see a grim reality behind the glittering promises of their leaders. The stark reality is that a parasite state could not endure for a generation, but would fall into economic ruin. Men who are willing to work and produce for themselves and their families will not long consent to support millions of parasites in virtual idleness.

The health and vigor of any state or nation depend upon maintenance of the character of its people. If the enervating philosophy of "security first" should prevail in Texas, Texas will be finished, its sons and daughters unworthy of the strong men and devoted women who struggled and conquered here to secure us our great inheritance.

But to suppose such a condition is to know that it will never happen here. Never will the sons and daughters of San Jacinto become a race of weaklings! And one reason why this may be predicted with confidence is the continuing influence of the school in which we are gathered.

You who are students here, you who have been students here, know well how A&M stands like a mighty fortress for those potent truths and principles upon which the greatness of Texas has been founded. In a day when older and once-proud educational institutions have abandoned the ancient and simple virtues and convictions to grope about in a fog of their own making, the light of Texas A&M shines as a bright and undiminished beacon. It provides not only sound scholarship; it impresses also those basic truths which must be cherished if men are to remain men: the supreme importance of personal integrity, the sturdy dignity of individual independence, the sterling value of men who can walk proudly among their fellows and humbly before their God.

So long as a continual stream of such men pours from the halls of A&M, we can have confidence in the future of Texas.

When young Sam Houston, aged twenty, went off to join the army in 1813, his mother gave him two gifts: a musket and a plain gold ring. Inside the ring was engraved a single word which Elizabeth Houston said must forever shine in the conduct of her son.

The musket he used until it wore out. The ring he wore until he died. He wore it in triumph and in trouble. He wore it in the House of Representatives, in the Senate, in the governor's chair in Nashville and in the successive capitols of Houston and Austin. It was on his finger when he cornered and crushed Santa Anna at San Jacinto, 115 years ago today. The word engraved within it was also engraved upon his heart. For whatever Sam Houston had of faults and failings, and they were doubtless many, he was a titan who lived according to his principles and always maintained his integrity.

During his lifetime the ring and the word engraved within it was a mystery to his friends—even to his great and good friend Andrew Jackson. Yet the one word there was the key to his character, to his unfailing reverence for womanhood, his unwillingness to meet slander in his darkest hour with aught but silence, his personal courage, his willingness to stand alone when he thought he was right.

After Sam Houston's death, his wife Margaret removed the plain gold band from his finger and held it up so that his children could read on its inner surface the word that had guided and summed up his life. The word was: HONOR. To all of you gathered here, including myself, but particularly to you younger men now students in these halls, I join together the two words with which I began, and the word given us by the Father of Texas: "Son, remember—HONOR."

So long as that purpose animates our lives, the spirit of Texas A&M will live.

# Searcy Bracewell '38

## 1952—System Administration Building Lawn

Searcy Bracewell '38.
Photo from editor's
collection.

Born January 19, 1918, in Houston, Joseph Searcy Bracewell graduated from Texas A&M in 1938 with a BA in history. As a student, he was drum major of the Fightin' Texas Aggie Band and a Ross Volunteer. He obtained his law degree in 1940 from South Texas College of Law in Houston.

Called to duty in the US Army in World War II, he handled logistics on the staff of Gen. George Patton's Third Army, earning the European Theater Medal with five battle stars. He was discharged as a major in 1945 and, with his father and brother, established the law firm that became Bracewell & Patterson. The firm came to be known as Bracewell LLP and employs 450 attorneys with offices in nine cities and three countries. He retired in 1988 as a senior partner.

From 1947 to 1959, Bracewell served two years in the Texas House of Representatives and ten years in the Texas Senate. He authored bills establishing the University of Texas M. D. Anderson Cancer Center and the UT Health Science Center Dental School. He chaired the Texas Water Development Board from 1969 to 1971 before becoming interim president of South Texas College of Law in 1974. He was chairman of the board of trustees of the Texas A&M Research Foundation, president of the Houston Grand Opera, on the boards of the Houston Foundation and the Houston Lyric Theatre Foundation, and a vice president of the Houston Chamber of Commerce.

He was a vice president of Texas A&M's Association of Former Students in 1977 and was named a Distinguished Alumnus of Texas A&M in 1978. In 2002 he was inducted into the Corps of Cadets Hall of Honor and named the Texas Aggie Bar Association Lawyer of the

Year. He chaired the Chancellor's Century Council and the Board of Visitors of Texas A&M University at Galveston and served as president of the Association of Former Students' Sul Ross Group, which consists of A&M graduates who have been out of school more than fifty-five years. He died May 13, 2003.

## Destroying the Bridge*

In the report which General Sam Houston made to President Burnet after the battle of San Jacinto he said:

> At half-past three o'clock in the evening, I ordered the officers of the army to parade their respective commands, having in the meantime ordered the bridge on the only road communicating with the Brazos, distant eight miles from our encampments, to be destroyed, thus cutting off all possibility of escape.

With the destiny of Texas hanging in the balance, Houston exhibited a keen insight into the frailties of man, and expressed a keen cognizance of a human weakness which existed on that day as much as in 1952.

He realized, I think, that by destroying one seemingly insignificant bridge, he had at the same time removed the great stumbling block of men in all ages—the inherent desire to escape. The one foremost hindrance to human greatness—the separating wall between valor and success on the one hand, and mediocrity, if not dishonor and failure, on the other.

That bridge meant more than a means of physical escape; it signified a refuge from the dishonor of failing to discharge responsibility—it signified a haven for that certain reprehensible substitute for sacrificial effort.

In all ages, men have unconsciously sought to escape from responsibilities—not only physical escape, but psychological as well. All men are plagued by the destructive power of escapism. Men everywhere have sought the bridge when faced with seemingly insurmountable

*Speech title derived by editor from speech contents

obstacles—when faced with great responsibilities. The complexities of this modern society have, in all probability, increased our natural reluctance to measure up, toe-to-toe, with the increasing responsibilities brought about by complexity. Difficult is the task and as challenging today as it always has been.

Through the years Texas A&M College has gained the respect of the world at large because the men of Aggieland, since its inception, have exemplified the strength which begets strength. The tradition of a willingness to pick up the reins of responsibility when others were hesitant to do so—a willingness to plunge into the water and swim, and even perish, if need be, in the attempt.

Were historians to write of men—men without great political or economic significance to flavor their careers; strong men who by their strength made others strong; men who, realizing that, unless they discharged the responsibilities, the responsibilities would go undischarged; men who had a keen realization that there is no such thing as a minor responsibility—then the pens of historians would continuously write of A&M men past and present who divorced themselves from the escapism of the political theorists and the fashionable intellectuals and the like—men who accepted community and civic responsibility without hesitation or fear of personal consequence—men who plowed the fields when the fields needed plowing—who performed scientific research when it needed to be done—who built the bridges when they needed to be built—men who died when someone had to die—men, who by their actions, made other men strong.

An unknown poet said it this way [the lines are from "To the Fighting Man" by Pfc. Charles W. Bodley]:

> I want to walk by the side of the man who has suffered and seen
>     and knows,
> Who has measured his pace on the battle line and given and taken
>     the blows.
> Who has never whined when the scheme went wrong—nor scoffed
>     at the failing plan—
> But taken his dose with a heart of trust and the faith of a gentle-
>     man;

Who has parried and struck and sought and given and scarred
with a thousand spears—
Can lift his head to the stars of heaven and isn't ashamed of his
tears.

I want to grasp the hand of the man who has been through it all
and seen;
Who has walked with the night of an unseen dread and stuck to
the world-machine;
Who has bared his breast to the winds of dawn and thirsted and
starved and felt
The sting and the bite of the bitter blasts that the mouths of the
foul have dealt;
Who was tempted and fell, and rose again, and has gone on trusty
and true;
With God supreme in his manly heart and his courage burning
anew.

I'd give my all—be it little or great—to walk by his side today;
To stand up there with the man who has known the bite of the
burning and the fray;
Who has gritted his teeth and clenched his fist, and gone on doing
his best,
Because of his love for his fellow man and the faith in his manly
breast.
I would love to walk with him, hand in hand, and together journey
long.
For the man who has fought and struggled and won is the man
who can make men strong.

As we reflect in pride today on the glory of a great heritage which was
guaranteed by the valor of the men of San Jacinto, and which has been
preserved in other subsequent military conflicts—and as we especially
pay tribute to the Aggies of yesteryears who gave the full measure of
devotion, that in so doing, you and I could have a glorious opportunity
to meet the responsibilities of our day—may we turn from our natural inclinations to escape in our own complacency and inertia—let us

feel the pounding of a heart eager to accept the numerous challenges thrown in our path.

The men of San Jacinto went on to gain the glorious victory which rocked the world and stimulated the cause of freedom everywhere. The knowledge that this bridge of escape had been destroyed was uppermost in their thoughts—that the destiny of Texas as well as their own destiny rested with the manner in which they acquitted themselves. The bridge across Vince's Bayou, the stumbling block behind them, was no more. With their faith resting in the Almighty, and that spirit which we hold traditional at A&M College burning in their manly breasts—there was no obstacle to victory.

Let us resolve anew that the Spirit of Aggieland, which idealizes that which has made America great, shall permeate the atmosphere where free men gather everywhere.

Let us be ever aware that the bridge affording escape has been destroyed. Let us rejoice in its destruction. And when we answer the roll call for those Aggies whose voices are not now audible, let's let our answers have the significance of a faith in the future, as was theirs, who knew no bridge behind them.

# Gov. Dan Thornton

*1953—Memorial Student Center Lawn*

Dan Thornton. Photo from editor's collection.

Born January 31, 1911, in Hall County, Texas, Isaac J. Thornton (he christened himself Daniel) moved with his family to Lubbock. He worked in the Texas cotton fields, entered junior livestock work, and later became state president of Texas 4-H Clubs.

After attending Texas Tech University and the University of California at Los Angeles, Thornton and his wife, Jessie, to whom he was married for thirty-eight years, established a Hereford cattle herd in Springerville, Arizona. In 1940 they moved to Gunnison, Colorado, and within five years their "Thornton Triumphant" Herefords were internationally known. At the National Western Stock Show in Denver in 1945, two of their TT bulls sold for $50,000 each, a world record at the time.

Dan Thornton entered public life in 1948 when he was elected to the Colorado State Senate. In a dramatic campaign in which he flew to almost every town in the state, he was elected governor for two successive terms, beginning in 1951. He spearheaded Dwight D. Eisenhower's campaign for president, was chairman of the National Governors Conference in 1953, and president of the Council of State Governors. Also in 1953 Eisenhower appointed Thornton to the President's Commission on Intergovernmental Relations.

While governor, Thornton focused on advertising what Colorado had to offer and promoted significant municipal and industrial growth. He also halted gambling in the state and signed the State Fair Employment Practices Act. The US Air Force Academy was established in Colorado Springs during his tenure. Thornton retired from politics after an unsuccessful US Senate race in 1956. He died in Carmel, California, January 19, 1976.

# "America's Immeasurable Strength"

President Harrington, Distinguished Guests, and Aggies everywhere:

Ever since I was a small boy on our family farm near Slaton, Texas, I can remember each year Aggies gathering for Muster Day. Of course at first it couldn't mean much to me, as a kid, but as the years went by, it was easy to learn that here annually was one of the grandest, most traditional events that any college in the country ever held. I have often wondered if those first students who met in 1903 to honor the Battle of San Jacinto had even the slightest thought that they were beginning a celebration and observance which has come to be—not a local tradition, if you please—but an international tribute by Aggies everywhere—in battle or in peace—to Aggies everywhere who proved that their love of a free country was greater even than their love for life itself. To you ex-students here today, it is a great opportunity to renew your Aggie days and to become more conscious of your Texas and college heritage. To you Aggies, it gives you an opportunity to resolve that you will follow in the proud loyalty and unswerving paths of predecessors. To me, it is an inspiration and a tremendous personal honor.

It seems rather unusual to me, as a native of Texas, to now be the governor of another state which, of course, in many ways excels the state of Texas. For example, if we were to level out the state of Colorado to the average altitude of Texas, Colorado would be three and one-half times the size of Texas. There are many other facts which I shall not bore you with at this time as I know you did not come here to hear me talk about the state of Colorado.

I might say at this time that I am also a little apprehensive about the contents of this speech as my administrative assistant in my office in Denver added some finishing touches and he, incidentally, graduated from your friendly neighboring university at Austin. Be that as it may, I know that school loyalty ends where Texas loyalty begins. I am reminded of a Texas youth who, a few years ago, was passing through a small town in one of the New England states. He had just a few hours to spare before making his train connection, and in going for a stroll he happened to pass by the local cemetery where a funeral was being held for one of the not-so-well-known natives, a local ne'er-do-well. During the ceremony, the preacher asked the few people participating in the funeral if anyone had a few words to say about the deceased. There was a long silence, and all of a sudden the young man from Texas spoke up and said, "Well, if no one has anything to say about the deceased, I'd like to say a few words about Texas!"

Last July, I had the great pleasure of attending the National Governors' Conference in Houston with the other governors, as guests of my fine friend, Governor Allan Shivers. At that time, we went out on that tremendous ship channel and visited the San Jacinto Monument, and we had an opportunity to get two very definite, vivid impressions. First, an actual living of the historical past and significance of that Texas event as we walked up those great marble steps, and through the rotundas with their memorable displays, and, secondly, an impression of the tremendous industrial growth and progress of that area. Of course, this area is not alone in this tremendous growth; it is duplicated in the great northern cities of this state, the forests of East Texas, the oil derricks and skyscraper office buildings in West Texas, the agricultural development in the Rio Grande Valley, and almost any place else you want to mention in the Lone Star State.

From these two impressions, I want to develop the theme for this Muster Day talk—how and why the greatest traditions and heritages of our nation are actually our immeasurable strength.

There is no need, I know, for me to repeat any of the details of the Battle of San Jacinto. They are all well known to you. What I would like to bring to your attention is the underlying, driving, motivating force which made the achievement of Gen. Sam Houston at San Jacinto possible and the liberation of Texas a fact instead of a dream. What I want to talk about is America's intangible, and her immeasurable, strength which does not have its origin in armaments, battleships, guns, tanks, or even in the atom bomb, nor in our inexhaustible resources as we normally think of them. This immeasurable strength has its roots deep in every individual American—it is our greatest natural, God-given resource: the consecration of the American to his right and to his privilege and duty as custodian of our American heritage of freedom.

On the morning of April 19, Gen. Houston said in a dispatch, "This morning we are in preparation to meet Santa Anna. It is the only chance of saving Texas. We have only 700 men to march with, besides the camp guard. We go to conquer. It is the wisdom of necessity to meet and fight the enemy now." That is what he did.

I am going to risk drawing a conclusion from this dispatch of Gen. Houston and his resulting victory at San Jacinto. How was this result possible? What made the difference between victory and defeat? He was outnumbered; he had waited in vain for promised reinforcements; he had every justification for discouragement, gloom and pessimism— yet he said, "We go to conquer."

Back of that statement was the consecration of a man to his belief, to his conviction that Texas must be free. It is of this quality, of this greatest American resource, that I would speak. There has been no advance in any direction without the consecration of an individual to his objective, regardless of the amount of endeavor expended. Consecration compels an undeviating devotion which cannot be turned aside because of apparently inadequate resources; it compels self-forgetfulness; it begets the will to risk and expend all, even to making the supreme sacrifice that an ideal may be attained, that an objective may be reached. Consecration is the driving force which will not be denied.

There is in every man a "something beyond himself," a hunger, a yearning, a reaching beyond the material. Call that quality what you wish, but it differentiates man from animal. It is his claim to immortality: his approach to a life of integrity lived out in reverence of God and service to his fellow man. To me it is man's ability, with the help of God, to dedicate himself to the attainment of an ideal. It is diametrically opposed to a Godless ideology, which today, is our greatest enemy. It is our responsibility to face the reality of today's danger; to meet the threat of destruction with the assurance born of consecration to our democratic way of life. Herein lies our own preservation and the hope of the world.

Our founding fathers were dedicated to the cause of freedom: These United States exist today because of such men as Washington, Sam Adams, Benjamin Franklin, and Sam Houston who were ready to suffer personal sacrifice that freedom might be born.

History is replete with untold numbers of instances and examples where ridicule and even persecution were heaped upon some individual because of his perseverance in pursuit of an envisioned possibility—an ideal. Advances made in science were often made at the risk of personal danger that a great truth might be discovered. After its discovery, experiments with unknown potentialities were undertaken. Did fear enter into the discovery of electricity, roentgen rays, the process of nuclear fission? I doubt it—the realization of possible danger was there, but it was not a deterrent to the research expert. Why? Because of his consecration to his objective.

The story is the same in every field of endeavor, whether it is medical research, mechanical experimentation, social reform, or making a better mouse trap. Consecration gives the impetus, generates the energy, recognizes no barriers, overcomes all obstacles.

We, in America, have a wonderful heritage, unique in many respects and precious beyond calculation. We are the custodians of our heritage of freedom and must be dedicated to its preservation. It is our responsibility—each one sharing his just portion. There is no such thing as a minor responsibility in this republic; this responsibility rests upon each individual. It is a shared freedom which we enjoy—it therefore must be a shared responsibility. Sharing responsibility presupposes its acceptance by the individual. In the acceptance of that responsibility, convictions and beliefs must be translated into action. Many a person has been guilty of giving "lip service" to a cause, and while "hot air" may fill a place in our Western life, I never knew it to heat a room or cook a meal.

In the last two decades we have traveled far; sometimes up, sometimes down. The road has been devious. At times we seemed to be lost in a maze of chaotic conditions.

It would not be fair if we do not recognize the good which we have accomplished. For the worth of any endeavor must be judged from an overall perspective and not by one isolated instance of failure.

We have been alarmed by the threat of "creeping socialism." And well we might be. It is our duty to educate ourselves in the effects of such marked trends in our national economy, through the study of other nations who have succumbed to the destructive influences of socialism, fascism, and communism. I will not digress into the slave labor of millions of Russians. We all know too well that glaring example of the suppression of individual freedom. What I would like to stress is the subtle encroachment of such influences which led to the nationalization of certain industries in England. Coal, steel, and transportation were nationalized, and what was presented as a panacea for their ills now has proved to be a fraud and a deception with devastating effects upon their economy. The irony of the situation is that these steps were taken largely because of the Labor Party's active endorsement of them, but from whom their far-reaching effects were subtly concealed. The greatest vigilance on the part of every American is necessary if we are to make a report to our children of our successful stewardship of their heritage.

We have "contained" communism in Europe. We must not overlook what might happen in our own backyard. In 1948, it was necessary to recall our ambassador to Guatemala because of threats to his life. Why? Because he spoke up for American business and thus incurred the active animosity of communist-infiltrated trade unions in that country. United Fruit and Pan American Airways experienced grave troubles from the courts dominated by the communist agents in their labor parties. These facts are known to our state department, of course, but I want every American to be cognizant of the fact that an ocean does not necessarily separate us from danger. There is no greater fallacy than the oft-accepted axiom, "Tis folly to be wise, when ignorance is bliss." The inevitable result of such ignorance is devastation from which recovery is long and difficult, if not impossible. Our consecration to our American way of life can leave no stone unturned, no possibility of danger unexplored, lest we allow ourselves to be destroyed.

Let us look at another phase in our economy. We have been told that small business has suffered, that mortality in that field has been high; but small business is still an important instrument in our free competitive enterprise system. We are justly proud of our mass production firms, but they are not equipped to handle small orders and special jobs. That is for a small outfit who fills the assembly line of the mass producer. One auto company buys from nearly 1,100 different smaller firms. Sears-Roebuck buys from more than 8,000 firms, more than double the amount of ten years ago. Macy's sells articles from more than 15,000 manufacturers. Statistics show that small business takes in 35 cents out of every dollar. Small business is the freest segment of the American economy and the strongest bulwark against a managed economy. It is the source of new blood for our free enterprise system. Let's have more of it. Here the dignity of man gains stature. Here is a source of America's greatness. Our natural resources are the materials, our productive genius is our tool; but where are the blueprints? I'll tell you where—they are in the soul of the man who can envision the objective while it is yet far off; the man who has a burning, all-consuming desire to reach that objective. It has been said that freedom is indivisible, and if we want to enjoy it and fight for it, we must be willing to extend it to everyone. It is our devotion to our "shared concepts and kindred objectives" that binds us and makes us invincible.

And so, as long as Aggies and Americans everywhere pause a few minutes each year in their busy and diverse lives, to recollect our own proud heritage—which cannot be obliterated by a bomb blast—our strength will grow stronger every year. Your Muster Day ceremony today is 50 times prouder and more traditional than the first one 50 years ago. Every year you meet will more than impress upon you the grandeur of our land and the greatness of our type of government.

Keep it up—make it greater—you may think it is a local tradition, but it is actually much more; it is a national asset—for peace, growth, and progress.

# Gov. Allan Shivers

*1954—Memorial Student Center Lawn*

Allan Shivers. Courtesy Texas State Library and Archives Commission.

Robert Allan Shivers was born October 5, 1907, in Lufkin, Texas, and was raised on a farm in the Tyler area. By age thirteen, he was working at a sawmill after school and during the summer. His family relocated to Port Arthur, where his father became a district judge and Allan completed high school.

In 1925, Shivers dropped out of the University of Texas at the end of his freshman year to work at an oil refinery. He returned to school in 1928, received his BA degree, and passed the state bar exam in 1931, two years before completing his LLB degree. After practicing law in Port Arthur for a year, Shivers (at age twenty-seven) was elected the youngest member of the Texas Senate.

Entering the US Army in 1943, he served with the Allied Military Government for Occupied Territories in North Africa, Italy, France, and Germany until 1945, when he was discharged as a major with five battle stars and the Bronze Star. Returning from World War II, he briefly managed his father-in-law's business enterprises in the Rio Grande Valley before being elected Texas lieutenant governor in 1946. He assumed the governorship in 1949 upon the death of Beauford Jester and served as governor for seven and a half years.

Shivers broke ranks with the Democratic Party over Texas' rights to the oil-rich Tidelands, a ten-and-one-half-mile-wide strip of submerged lands beyond the low-tide mark of the Gulf of Mexico. The issue became a turning point of the presidential election of 1952 in which Shivers delivered the state's electoral votes to Dwight D. Eisenhower, who pledged to sign a bill confirming Texas' right to the property.

As governor, Shivers appointed future Texas A&M president J. Earl Rudder '32 commissioner of the Texas General Land Office in 1955 following the Veterans Land Board scandals. When a full-size replica of the Liberty Bell was presented to each of the states, Shivers sent Texas' replica to Texas A&M, where it is displayed in the Academic Building rotunda.

Retiring from politics in 1957, Shivers returned to managing his father-in-law's holdings. He served as president of the United States Chamber of Commerce, chairman of the advisory board of the Export-Import Bank of the United States, and chairman of the University of Texas Board of Regents. Shivers died January 14, 1985.

# Understanding the Aggie Spirit*

It is a high honor and a distinct privilege to join you today in paying solemn tribute to A&M men who have given their lives for freedom and in this rededication to the principles which they championed.

It is altogether fitting that, half a century ago, the Aggies who started this tradition selected San Jacinto Day as the time for it. All Texans, whether or not they have ever had any connection with Texas A&M College, must feel a great sense of pride, just as I do, in its accomplishments and in the spirit which has made those accomplishments possible.

You call it the Twelfth Man spirit and the Spirit of Aggieland. It is that. But it is also much more. Basically, it is the same spirit which was displayed by the 700 men in General Sam Houston's command 118 years ago today at San Jacinto, where they conquered Santa Anna's 1,600-man army. It is, in reality, the same spirit which has made it possible for our nation to emerge successfully from every war in its glorious history. You know as well as I, of the many significant and heroic contributions made by A&M men in the greatest of those wars.

For as long as I can remember, and certainly for as long as most of you can remember, we have either been fighting a war or fearing that we would become involved in one.

---

*Speech title derived by editor from speech contents

This is a glorious era in which we live, and yet it is no exception. Today, as it has so many times in the past, the shadow of war hangs over us. The threat of a godless ideology, of power-crazed international gangsters and hoodlums, poses again the problem this world has never been able to solve. But it is a problem that all Americans should have high hopes of solving. Most of the world has put its faith in American leadership and in our country's attempts to establish a permanent peace. Our country must continue to put its faith in God as we renew our efforts to bring about lasting peace on earth.

I feel certain that most of you men, training here in the methods of war, hate war as most military men do. Most of our country's great generals—among them many graduates of Texas A&M—probably hate war even more than the average American citizen because they know its true horrors.

Sam Houston hated war. Like the generations of Texans who have enjoyed the freedom he made possible, he hoped that Texas and the nation would be able to put aside the instruments of war and enjoy the fruits of peace forever.

On the day after the battle of San Jacinto, General Houston sat under a tree, munching an ear of corn while his men debated the fate of General Santa Anna, their prize captive. Houston interrupted their discussion and began scattering corn by the handful among them.

"My brave fellows," he said, "take this along with you to your own fields, where I hope you may long cultivate the arts of peace as you have shown yourselves masters of the art of war."

Texas A&M is a college that teaches the arts of peace as well as the art of war. For many years, its graduates have been proving that it does an exceptionally good job in both fields.

There may be even more significance than Houston himself realized in the fact that he scattered kernels of corn to his men as he talked to them of the arts of peace and the art of war. Today, we must realize that war and peace are inseparably connected with corn, grain, cotton, and the many other vital commodities which the Good Lord has enabled the American people to produce in such enormous quantities.

A&M has made many significant contributions—through research and the improved methods developed here—to efficient farming methods which have helped America become the richest nation on earth. Perhaps it will make even more significant contributions to the solutions of many of the domestic problems we now face. Many of our country's domestic problems, of course, have international implications. We should keep in mind that while we are worried about the effects our huge farm surpluses will have on our economy, there are people in this world who are starving. We cannot blame this paradox— people starving on one side of the world while people on the other are worried about having too much—on the mere geographical differences. The major transportation problems were solved long ago, leaving only the problems of diplomatic negotiation, methods of payment, and distribution.

In my humble opinion, this situation offers the people of America one of the best opportunities in their history to help themselves by helping others. Over-production of food in this country offers a serious threat to the stability of our economy; at the same time, it has the potential of keeping many thousands of people in other countries from starving. I think we can all agree that well-fed people are less likely to start wars than are people on the brink of starvation.

Just as I think agriculture poses our foremost domestic problem nationally, I am firmly convinced that water presents the number one problem now facing the great state of Texas. This, too, is a field in which A&M has helped Texas make great progress in the past. The research now being done here on the problems of water scarcities and soil erosion, plus the engineers being trained by A&M to cope with these problems, could result in solutions for which Texas would be eternally grateful.

Texas usually has plenty of water; but all too often, it has too much water in the wrong place at the wrong time and not enough in the right place at the right time. Last week, for instance, a delegation of twenty-eight West Texas counties came to my office one morning seeking drought relief. That afternoon, a group in South Texas appealed to my office for flood relief.

We need better storage and distribution facilities for the water we have and for the vast amounts of water that now flow unused to the Gulf of Mexico.

A water resources committee established by the Fifty-third Legislature is studying the problem now. It already has found that there are many places in our state streams where huge amounts of flood waters could be impounded. It has found, too, that improving our water supply through the use of such reservoirs could produce great industrial growth for Texas. Undoubtedly, A&M-trained engineers will have a part in solving this problem.

I have been talking about agricultural and engineering problems—problems which I believe Texas A&M has helped, and is helping now, to solve. In my opinion, however, the sphere of Texas A&M's influence extends over a much broader area than these I have mentioned. For more than three-quarters of a century, A&M has been producing fine soldiers, leaders in agricultural development, excellent scientists and engineers. Its true strength, however, seems to lie in that spirit which enables this school to produce fine American citizens. I am talking about honest, God-fearing, conscientious American citizens who are proud of their freedom and who are willing to give their lives, if necessary, to protect it.

It is strange but true that America has long been famous for having citizens who give their lives—but otherwise not fifteen minutes of their time—for the preservation of freedom and democracy. Many people who would willingly die for the right to vote will not expend the slightest amount of time and effort necessary to take advantage of that right.

Basically, all of America's wars have been waged simply for the right of the free ballot—for the right to the type of government and the type of leaders we want. The departed Aggies we honor here today made the supreme sacrifice fighting for that right.

At some future date, we, too, may be called upon to make identical sacrifices. But we are prone to overlook the fact that almost every day we should protect such rights by making the trivial sacrifices necessary to exercise them.

In America, we have managed since 1776 to preserve the God-given right to be governed by ourselves—to elect our government leaders and to call them to account whenever necessary.

Too often, however, we are inclined to let others worry about these things. Too many of our citizens shrug their shoulders and dismiss all government activities as "just politics." There are many capable men who could make valuable contributions to their fellow citizens by serving in public office, but who refuse to become interested on the grounds that politics is a dirty business. If politics is a dirty business, isn't the real dirt on the hands of those who refuse to spend the time and effort necessary to clean it up?

The problem of getting more of our citizens to take a more active interest in government, in my opinion, is one of the most important ones we face. It is a problem we must solve if we are to make sure that those we honor here today shall not have died in vain.

No one, I suppose, can truly understand your Spirit of Aggieland until and unless he has actually been a part of it. As one who has observed it for many years, however, I think I know a little about it. That is why, as I said earlier, I am convinced that it is more than just the spirit of a great college. If it were not more than just that, I doubt seriously that Muster ceremonies similar to this one would ever have been held at Guadalcanal, at Corregidor, at Anzio.

Throughout the world, people have witnessed the Aggie Spirit; and I feel certain that many of them have become convinced, just as I have, that down through the years it has received a helping hand from the Greatest Teacher of them all.

Most of the great military men I have known have been deeply religious men. In fact, I do not believe that any man can be truly great, in any field, without being deeply religious. I think it is altogether fitting and proper that prayer has become an integral part of your Muster ceremony, which today is being observed by more than 400 different groups of former A&M students throughout the world.

I think it is in keeping with the best traditions of A&M that, once each year on San Jacinto Day, Aggies are called upon to rededicate themselves not only to freedom, to their college, and to their country, but to high Christian principles and ideals as well.

One of the most famous quotations to come out of World War II, I believe, was this: "There are no atheists in foxholes."

It is true that almost everyone, no matter how calloused and indifferent he may seem toward religion, calls on the Lord for help in times of great stress, danger and trouble. It is a pity that so many of us wait until such occasions to call on Him, when we should be seeking His guidance constantly in our daily living.

It will take His help, as well as all of the resources and abilities at our command, to solve the many great problems confronting our state and our nation.

On October 4, 1876, in the ceremonies officially opening Texas A&M College, Governor Richard Coke said: "Texas is preparing to embrace and be worthy of the great destiny which the big years of the future have in store for her."

It seems to me that this statement is just as true today as it was then. I am confident that Texas A&M College will continue to play a major role in preparing our state for its great destiny.

# Gen. Otto P. Weyland '23

*1955—Memorial Student Center Lawn*

Gen. Otto P. Weyland '23.
Photo from editor's
collection.

Otto Paul Weyland was born January 27, 1903, in Riverside, California. His family moved to the Taft Ranch, near Corpus Christi, Texas, when he was eight. At Texas A&M, he received the nickname "Opie" and was commander of the Aggie Band. He earned his college expenses operating a candy concession.

He worked briefly with Western Electric, then entered the US Army Air Service, where his classmates were Charles Lindbergh and future aircraft manufacturer James S. McDonnell. From 1927 until 1942, Weyland proceeded through a variety of assignments from instructor at Kelly Field to chief of staff of the Sixth Air Force. He earned his first star in 1943 and went overseas to command a World War II fighter wing. In February 1944, Weyland accepted command of the XIX Tactical Air Command, the combat unit that gained acclaim for its air support of Gen. George Patton's Third Army in its dash across France in the spring of 1945. Weyland pinned on his second star and became commander of the Ninth Air Force and participated in six major campaigns.

Gen. H. H. "Hap" Arnold, commander of the US Air Force, later said, "When the German commander, Gen. Erich Elsner, surrendered the riddled remnants of what had been a 200,000-man force, he made no bones about the fact that he was surrendering to 'Weyland's air force.'" It marked the first time in history that ground troops surrendered to air action.

Following the war, after earning his third star, he alternately headed the Tactical Air Command and the Far Eastern Air Forces, where he directed operations in the Korean War. In July 1952, Weyland became

Texas A&M's first four-star general and reorganized Japan's air defense forces and aircraft industry. He was commanding general of the Tactical Air Command from 1954 until his retirement in 1959.

His decorations include two Distinguished Service Medals, the Silver Star, the Distinguished Flying Cross, and the Legion of Merit.

Texas A&M presented him an honorary doctorate in 1946. He was named a Distinguished Alumnus in 1976 and inducted into the Corps of Cadets Hall of Honor in 1995. He died September 2, 1979.

## Guarding Our Heritage with Honor*

Mr. President, distinguished guests, and fellow Texas Aggies.

I am happy and grateful that I can be back home for this annual Muster. Over the years I have attended many Musters in many parts of the world—Washington, Panama, England, France, and Germany, and more recently, Korea and Japan.

Several of those meetings were held in combat zones while our country was at war and, these, even more than the meetings held during times of peace, brought home to me the full impact and significance of the Muster tradition. Even while calling the roll of our comrades who paid with their lives to maintain their freedoms and traditions, our thoughts would turn back here, to the cradle of the Texas Aggie Spirit. And when I looked around at the men at those meetings, I was proud at what I saw—proud of the men who loved their independence but who were ready and willing to leave their homes to fight the tyranny that threatened the peace of their families. Then, too, would my thoughts go back to those rugged individualists who settled in Texas and who dropped their peacetime tools to fight the despotic intruders at the Alamo, at Goliad, and at San Jacinto. I am grateful to General Sam Houston and those early Texans, not only for making this a free country 119 years ago today, but for passing on to us the heritage of honor in all things, duty to country, and bravery born of conviction of purpose.

---

*Speech title derived by editor from speech contents

To these principles we rededicate ourselves today, and well we should, for even though we are now in an era of prosperity, we enjoy but an uneasy peace. We are living in what may well prove to be the most critical period in the history of the United States, one in which the threats to our security and freedoms have never been greater. Communist forces have made clear their ultimate objective of dominating the entire world, forcing the Communist system on all free nations, and of destroying our very way of life. The Reds operate to achieve their time-tables of expansion by political, economic and psychological pressures wherever possible. Failing in these measures, they resort to military force. We have seen that they prefer the divide-and-conquer technique to achieve control of expanding fringe areas, with a view to avoiding the awful retribution of American air power inherent in major military aggression.

It would be foolhardy, indeed, for us to ignore the fact that they possess land armies numerically superior to ours, or that their air and naval forces are second only to our own. We know that their military strength is supported by vast natural resources, an expanding industry with a controlled totalitarian economy, and that they possess nuclear weapons.

Knowing these things, we must accept that we face an enemy capable of launching an all-out global assault against the free world or, if he chooses, he can pursue his goal of world domination by means of a series of limited aggressions in widely scattered, remote areas, using the puppet forces of satellite countries.

To meet this double-barreled threat, we have had to maintain a vast atomic retaliatory capability and to develop adequate mobile combat forces in readiness so that the Communists would be convinced there can be no profit in either global war or in further limited aggressions or "brush fire" wars, such as Korea.

In developing these forces, we have recognized that the United States cannot match the masses of raw military manpower available to the Communists, and that we accordingly must take fullest advantage of our superior technology and industry. The highest form of expression of military technology lies in air power, and air power has emerged as the key and decisive element of modern war. This is not to say that air power alone is enough. Adequate provision of modern, well-trained and equipped land and naval forces, in proper balance to meet the threats of today and tomorrow, is also essential if we are to retain our way of life.

We in America are not alone in our determination to resist further aggression. The other freedom-loving peoples and free nations of the world face the same dangers, and look to us for leadership in consolidating the strength of all free nations to meet the common peril. Separately, these smaller countries would have little chance of survival. Collectively, their strength is enormous and greatly reduces the load on our own country. Their contributions to the common cause will vary according to their individual capabilities. Some countries are rich in essential raw materials; others are small but highly industrialized nations which can process the raw materials of their neighbors; some are rich in manpower and can provide excellent land fighting forces even though they cannot afford air forces. Still others contribute to the over-all cause simply by virtue of their geographical location and suitability for air or naval bases. But they are all drawn together, regardless of race, color or creed, by their common love of freedom and self-determination.

Because of our tremendous and unexcelled industrial capacity, superior technology, and leadership in the air, the burden of providing the air forces for the security of the free world falls largely upon the United States. This was true in World War II, it was true in Korea, and will be true in the future.

Our air power has been developed and is consistently being refined and improved to fulfill this responsibility. The United States Air Force is a tremendously complex organization. The combat power of the USAF is vested in our strategic air forces, tactical air forces, and air defense forces. These are backed up by an air training command to develop the air and ground crew members and other highly trained specialists; by an air materiel command to procure, maintain and overhaul our aircraft, technical equipment and other supplies; by a Research and Development organization which assures that our aircraft and equipment are the finest that American ingenuity can provide; by a global air transport service and air base system to support our widely flung operations; and finally, by our educational system which assures the most advanced professional competence of our officers and airmen.

With the advent of Soviet long-range bombers, capable of reaching anywhere in the United States, coupled with their development of atomic and thermonuclear weapons, the problem of air defense of this country has become very real indeed, and our air defense system is being built up accordingly.

Our long-range strategic air forces are maintained in instant readiness to strike at the enemy's war-sustaining resources, should all-out war occur. They have been and continue to be the greatest single deterrent to major Communist aggression or all-out war.

Referring again to the pattern of Communist conspiracy, it is evident they wish to avoid for the time being, and wisely so, an all-out war. It has become increasingly clear that any armed conflict of their choosing in the near future will be of a limited nature, such as Korea.

This fact has called for increased emphasis upon our tactical air forces, ready to move quickly to any threatened area of the world. These mobile and highly flexible tactical air forces are comprised of fighters, high performance reconnaissance, fighter bombers, tactical bombers, and combat transports. These are the forces which fight the air battle for control of the skies, to strike enemy military forces and materiel in rear areas before they can be brought to bear on friendly forces, and which create the conditions most favorable for the employment of friendly land forces. We form a closely knit team with army forces, and provide close combat air support to influence the land battle and to assist our comrades on the ground in achieving their objectives with the fewest possible casualties. These tactical air forces are ready to go into action either in conjunction with our own army forces, or with the ground forces of those friendly nations who may be rich in manpower but cannot afford adequate air forces.

Well, regardless of whether we are at peace or at war, the Texas Aggies are always on hand to make this a better world. The training you get here is the finest in the world to produce well-balanced citizens, capable either of contributing to the civilian economy or of taking up arms in defense of our country. Most of you will probably find your way into your chosen civilian profession, but it is comforting to know that you can be depended upon in time of emergency to join your comrades in the military services. Many of you will come into the Air Force or the Army, either temporarily or permanently. Throughout the military services, the spirit and professional competence of A&M men are well known and respected—Air Force and Army leaders are always eager to have them. It is a source of pride that during the emergencies of World War II and the Korean War, there were more officers in the Army and the Air Force from Texas A&M than from any other single institution! I personally hope that many of you will choose the Air Force as a career. It is a good life—rich in the satisfactions which come of honorable service to the nation.

If those early pioneers and patriots of April 21st, 1836, are looking down today, I am sure they feel that their sacrifices were not in vain; that those who followed them carried on the good work they started: and that you men here, and Texas Aggies elsewhere gathered for today's Muster ceremony, may be fully trusted to guard our national heritage of liberty and freedom, of human rights and the dignity of man, and our traditions—with HONOR.

# Maj. Gen. J. Earl Rudder '32

*1956—Memorial Student Center Lawn*

Maj. Gen. J. Earl Rudder '32. Photo from editor's collection.

Born May 6, 1910, in Eden, Texas, James Earl Rudder attended John Tarleton Agricultural College (now Tarleton State University) and transferred to Texas A&M in 1930. Rudder majored in industrial education, lettered in football, and graduated in 1932.

Commissioned a second lieutenant in the US Army Reserve at graduation, Rudder was a football coach and teacher at Brady High School and Tarleton College until called into active duty for World War II in 1941. In 1943, as a lieutenant colonel, he organized and trained the 2nd Ranger Battalion, which scaled the steep cliffs of Pointe du Hoc on June 6, 1944, to silence enemy guns endangering Omaha and Utah beaches during the D-Day invasion. Gen. Omar Bradley stated, "No soldier in my command has ever been wished a more difficult task than that which befell the thirty-four-year-old commander of this Provisional Ranger Force."

In December 1944 he took command of the 109th Infantry, which helped repulse the last-ditch German attack in the Battle of the Bulge. Rudder was a colonel when released from active duty in 1946. He retired from the Army Reserve as a major general in 1967. His decorations include the Distinguished Service Cross, Legion of Merit, and Silver Star.

Rudder was mayor of Brady, Texas; commissioner of the Texas General Land Office; and vice president of Texas A&M. He was named the sixteenth president of Texas A&M in 1959 and was instrumental in the renaming of Texas A&M University and admitting women on a limited basis in 1963. In 1965, he was also named president of the Texas A&M University System. He initiated the Texas A&M Century Study and the Long Range Planning Committee, which outlined A&M's future growth. Rudder served as president until his death March 23, 1970.

Rudder was posthumously named a Distinguished Alumnus of Texas A&M in 1970. He was an inaugural inductee into the A&M Corps of Cadets Hall of Honor in 1993. The Rudder Tower and Auditorium complex at Texas A&M bears his name, and a larger-than-life statue of him stands at the south end of Military Walk.

## Honesty, Integrity, and Common Sense*

One hundred and twenty years ago today, a ragged, ill-equipped band of 700 Texans—who had been retreating for weeks—suddenly turned around and defeated a vastly superior force to win freedom for Texas.

There could be no more appropriate date for Aggies everywhere to pause and pay homage to those who have given their lives for freedom from that date until this. The realization of what their supreme sacrifices have meant, and the importance of this heritage, brings a deep and sincere feeling of humility to me. I can think of no greater honor which could come to any Aggie than to be called upon to speak at this annual Muster Ceremony.

It is unfortunate but true that we cannot merely celebrate our freedom and pay tribute to those who created and protected it without some fear of what is going to happen to that freedom. Even as we celebrate, we face grave dangers which are just as real, if not as apparent, as those which General Sam Houston faced in 1836.

We are living in the Atomic Age. It is altogether possible today by military might for a mere handful of people to conquer an entire country and to hold all of those people captive in an iron grip. This is an awesome threat; however, we need only to reflect on the fighting spirit of Sam Houston and his ragged band to realize that military power alone is not the complete answer. The spirit of those dedicated to a cause can be a most powerful influence in any endeavor.

*Speech title derived by editor from speech contents

For years, outsiders have been trying to analyze the world-famous Spirit of Aggieland. It has been honored throughout the world, and almost every passing day adds to its fame. Although it is universally admired, it can be fully understood only by those of us who have studied together, worked together, and lived together here at our beloved College. It is that intangible thing that enables us to perform the difficult task right away and to take only a little while longer to do the impossible.

It is, furthermore, a natural starting point for the battles which must be waged against enemies of democracy.

The most dangerous of those enemies, in my opinion, is the widespread tendency on the part of our people to ignore political and governmental activities. Loyal, patriotic Americans too often seem to forget that our country did not become great by letting the "other fellow" do the things which had to be done. When you leave a duty up to the other fellow, he is going to do it his way. In dealing with the life or death of our freedom—as we do at almost every election—we cannot afford to let someone else exercise the privileges for which so many gallant Americans have given their lives.

The well-known Biblical parable in the fourteenth chapter of St. Luke tells us that when the INVITED guests refused to attend a banquet, the Master filled their places with anyone he could find on the highways and byways. In our seats of government, none of the places go begging. If there is no unselfish, conscientious, honest American who is willing to serve, there is always someone with purely selfish motives to fill the vacancy. Political hacks, special interest groups, power-mad bosses and others who would use our government for selfish motives are constantly looking for opportunities to move in and take over.

Their chances of success are directly proportionate to the number of Americans who take no interest in the affairs of government.

If you owned stock in a business enterprise, you certainly would take a keen interest in its affairs. You would be happy to exercise any power at your command to see that it was operated honestly and efficiently. Our government is one of the biggest businesses in the world. We are its stockholders because everything we have and everything we ever hope to have depends upon it. Our vast opportunities and our wonderful freedom are our investment in it. They could be wiped out overnight if we became careless enough to let America be taken over by the termites which are gnawing at the foundation of the American way of life.

In government, there is no middle ground; either we govern ourselves, or someone else will move in to govern us. It has often been said that in a democracy, people can have government as good as they demand but that they usually get government as bad as they will tolerate.

One of the things which makes Texas A&M College so great is the keen interest taken in it by its students and ex-students. Aggies, in school and out, love A&M enough to defend it in every way possible. I have never known any Aggie to show any apathy or lethargy in any matter connected with Texas A&M College.

We need that same enthusiastic spirit in the halls of government—from the local school board all the way to the White House. We need men who will defend freedom just as vigorously in the County Courthouse as they will on a foreign battlefield. It is just as important to fight with ballots in peacetime as it is to fight with bullets in time of war.

We need men who will give willingly of their time to promote honesty and integrity in government—men who will do the right as God gives them the ability to see the right.

America is a land of tremendous assets. Our natural resources, our production methods, our free enterprise system, our scientific achievements, our special talent for management and organization—all of these things have contributed to the highest standard of living the world has ever known. But the one thing that probably has contributed the most is the free, enthusiastic, driving spirit with which Americans are so bountifully endowed. Take away that spirit and America probably would do little more with its national assets than have many other nations which are just as rich in natural resources.

This is the same spirit which made Sam Houston withstand the storms of his era to emerge a national hero. It is the same type of spirit that I saw in the Hüertgen Forest Battle in World War II.

I asked for volunteers to run a tape through a mine field, in order to give the rest of our men a guided path through the field that would keep them from stepping on a mine. While the three were placing the tape, one of them—a towheaded youngster about twenty years old—stepped on a mine and lost his foot. He was brought back to the aid station, and when I went in to talk to him, he began to cry. I tried to comfort him, and told him that he would soon be going home to see his family and his friends for the first time in more than a year. I tried to comfort him and assure him that his injury was not as tragic as he might consider it at first. When I finished, he looked at me and said, "Colonel, it's not my foot I'm worrying about. You gave me a job to do and I didn't finish it."

Like this lad, the men we honor today for creating and protecting our freedom were unable to finish the job because the job of fighting for freedom is never finished.

Each of us is obligated to do a part of that job, simply because we are fortunate enough to be citizens of a free country. Whether it be serving in some position of public trust or merely taking an active interest in and participating in governmental affairs, we should be as deeply concerned about a job unfinished as that brave lad in the Hüertgen Forest.

Aggies understand leadership. They know that a good military leader must have more than chevrons on his sleeve or brass on his collar to get men to follow him. If he has the spark of leadership for which Aggies are famous, men will follow him anywhere.

The Lord has told us that every man should utilize the talents which God has given him. The talent of leadership, which so many of you are demonstrating here, is badly needed throughout our country.

Nothing can do a greater job today in fighting the enemies of democracy than can the spirit, the leadership and the devotion to duty which is so much a part of Texas A&M. These are things we must use in the future to improve our government and the general welfare of our beloved State.

It is not enough merely to go to the polls every year or so. That is just one of the duties with which every American citizen is charged. To perform that duty properly, he must take an active, continuing interest in public affairs every day of the year. Another important duty, more often ignored than intelligent voting, is participation in conventions and other political affairs which give one the opportunity to voice his own opinions.

Each of us should consider seriously our opportunities to serve in public office. Capable men should not complain about unfair government when they, themselves, fail or refuse to offer themselves for public service. Actual participation drives home better than anything else the real importance of ability in governmental posts. One of the things which makes the Aggie Spirit so dear to us is the fact that we participate in it. We are a part of it.

We cannot be true to the real Spirit of Aggieland, and to those Aggies who have made the supreme sacrifice, merely by being prepared to do our duty in time of war. Service to our country must be a part of our everyday lives. We must be mindful of our many civic responsibilities and obligations. We must be willing to serve in church work, in welfare movements and in the countless other activities which help make up the moral fiber of America.

We must seek to improve our state and our nation. Many problems lie before us—important problems such as the water shortage, the need for bringing more industry to Texas, the need for keeping our government the servant of the people, the need for solving as many problems as possible on the lowest practical level of government. Standing out above all these is the need for men of honesty, integrity and common sense in the halls of government.

This is rightfully a day for rededication to the principles which we cherish and which Aggies before us have cherished. Aggies of today have an enviable opportunity—and a challenge—to carry the Spirit of Aggieland to our fellow citizens. I am strongly convinced that this spirit can be used to help supply the leadership necessary to bring about more widespread participation in the affairs of government.

There is a line in that great Aggie song, "The Spirit of Aggieland," which says, "True to each other as Aggies can be." In order to be true to each other, we must be true to our principles, to our heritage, and to our country; we must discharge cheerfully and to the best of our ability the duties born of citizenship in the land of the free.

As we leave this Muster here, let us join together, as Aggies, in the firm resolve to discharge our day-by-day duties in a manner that will be in keeping with the heritage handed down to us by those we honor here today.

# Gen. Bernard A. Schriever '31

*1958—Memorial Student Center Lawn*

Gen. Bernard A. Schriever '31. Photo from editor's collection.

Bernard Adolph Schriever was born September 14, 1910, in Bremen, Germany, and became a naturalized citizen in 1923 after coming to the United States in 1917. He received his early education in San Antonio and graduated from Texas A&M in 1931 with a BS degree in engineering.

His military career began with the acceptance of a field artillery reserve commission upon graduation. Following flight training at Randolph Field, Schriever earned his wings and a commission as a second lieutenant in the Air Corps Reserve in 1933. While at Wright Field, Ohio, he graduated from the Air Corps Engineering School and in 1942 received an MA in aeronautical engineering from Stanford University.

In 1942 Schriever joined the 19th Bomb Group in the Southwest Pacific, where he flew sixty-three World War II combat missions in the Southwest Pacific. Beginning in August 1943, he was chief of staff, Fifth Air Force Service Command, until September 1944, when he assumed command of Advanced Headquarters, Far East Air Service Command.

Following graduation from the National War College, he returned to US Air Force headquarters in 1950. In May 1954, he became assistant to the commander, Air Research and Development Command (ARDC). In August he also assumed command of the Western Development Division, Headquarters, ARDC (redesignated the Air Force Ballistic Missile Division). In this position he directed intercontinental ballistic missile development and the initial Air Force space program.

His awards and decorations include the Distinguished Service Medal, Legion of Merit, Air Medal, Purple Heart, and two unit citations. He was rated a command pilot. In 1962 Schriever was named a Distinguished

Alumnus of Texas A&M and in 1993 was inducted into the Corps of Cadets Hall of Honor.

Schriever retired in 1966 but continued in an advisory capacity on numerous government boards and councils. In June 1998, Falcon Air Force Base in Colorado Springs, Colorado, was renamed in his honor. He died June 20, 2005.

In 2009 his life story was published in Neil Sheehan's *A Fiery Peace in a Cold War: Bernard Schriever and the Ultimate Weapon.*

## The Human Factor*

General Schriever's 1958 Muster address has been lost to history. The following article by Ronald Easley appeared in the April 22, 1958, issue of *The Battalion.*

> Fierce lightning and rumbling thunder failed to thwart Maj. Gen. Bernard A. Schriever's address at the 55th annual Aggie Muster on the Memorial Student Center lawn yesterday evening.
>
> Just as the final notes of taps sounded, large drops of rain fell on the scrambling crowd of some 5,000 people.
>
> Gen. Schriever, Class of '31, spoke on the human factor—the most important factor in preparing our nation's defense. He said the two elements that make up defense are technology and military. . . .
>
> For technology, the first factor, the period since the end of World War II has been the most dynamic, the speaker said. He pointed out that there has been more development in this period than in all the years preceding.
>
> "This development has revolutionized warfare and changed the whole military posture of our country.
>
> "Merely outproducing the enemy as we did in World War II is today as outmoded as the bow and arrow," Schriever went on. He called "qualitative superiority," or a superiority in the number of men technically trained in scientific warfare, the most important thing.

*Speech title assigned by editor

In 1946 the United States was superior to Russia in the number of atomic weapons. Since then the Reds have advanced rapidly and are probably ahead of us now, he added.

"This means we should work all the harder to maintain our present qualitative superiority," he commented.

"In the past Texas A&M has done a great deal in putting technically trained men into industry and must continue to do its part in the future.

"The second factor presents an even greater challenge to our nation. A&M's prominence rests upon her military program and she must continue to play her part in the military preparedness of the country," remarked Schriever.

Schriever deplored what he called "the rebellious attitude of the average high school graduate toward the imposed discipline of the military." This, he said, has in turn resulted in a lack of self discipline. These were the findings of a survey made by the Air Force of more than 10,000 high school graduates.

An Air Force psychiatrist found that one-third of the American prisoners in Red Chinese prison camps during the Korean War yielded to the Communist proddings, Schriever pointed out.

"This indicates the lack of an adequate moral code, poor general education and military unpreparedness in our men," he added.

# Olin E. Teague '32

*1959—Memorial Student Center Lawn*

Olin E. Teague '32.
Photo from the editor's
collection.

Olin Earl "Tiger" Teague was born April 6, 1910, in Woodward, Oklahoma. At 120 pounds, he played football and baseball at Texas A&M, earning the nickname "Tiger" for his tough and tenacious character.

In his sophomore year, his father had a heart attack, and Teague had to pay his own educational expenses. He fed show calves and shoveled manure for twenty-five cents per hour, worked on the construction of the original Kyle Field, and cleaned up and sorted mail from 4:00 to 8:00 a.m. and from 7:00 to 11:00 p.m. at the campus post office. It is said that he lived in the livestock arena, where J. E. Loupot and other buddies would bring him hot and oftentimes cold leftovers from the mess hall. He somehow found time to serve as Company G Infantry commanding officer in A&M's Corps of Cadets and was a member of the elite Ross Volunteers.

He left his job as South Station superintendent for the US Post Office in College Station to volunteer for Army service during World War II. He led the 1st Battalion, 314th Infantry Regiment of the 79th Division, in its attack on Utah Beach during D-Day. He was severely wounded on a recon patrol near the Siegfried Line and endured twenty operations and almost two years in the hospital. Discharged as a colonel, his combat decorations included the Silver Star and Bronze Star, the French Croix de Guerre, two Purple Hearts, and the Combat Infantry Badge.

In 1946 he won a special election to represent Texas' Sixth District in Congress. He was an outspoken advocate for American veterans, authoring the GI bill that extended education benefits to Korean War veterans. He served on the West Point Board of Visitors and was named a Texas A&M Distinguished Alumnus in 1966. He retired from Congress in 1979 after serving as chairman of the Committee on Veterans Affairs and as second ranking majority member of the Committee on Science and Astronautics. He chaired the Subcommittee on Manned Space Flight and the Legislative Oversight Committee. Teague was inducted into the Corps of Cadets Hall of Honor in 1993. He died January 23, 1981, and is buried in Arlington National Cemetery.

## Bold Leadership*

This is a moment of particular importance to each and every one of us.

It is a moment of reflection, of prayer, of Thanksgiving for the past, of hope in the future.

It is a moment in which each one of us realizes even more than usual that we are something more than just individuals—we are a part of a great and continuing tradition, part of an ever-widening pattern.

In the course of arriving at this moment—the fifty-fifth annual Muster of Texas A&M—we have each of us benefitted in innumerable ways from the splendid tradition of the past.

Today—on the hundred and twenty-third anniversary of the winning of Texas independence—we participate with Texas A&M men all over the world in a living tradition of loyalty and comradeship.

And also today we dedicate ourselves to the challenging and essential task of making our own constructive contribution to the existing tradition which our forebears have built.

I was a senior at this great institution of ours in 1932.

At first glance, twenty-seven years does not seem a particularly long time—yet, since 1932 the world has changed more rapidly and completely than during any similar span of years since the beginning of recorded history.

In 1932 the United States and the rest of the world were in the throes of deep economic depression, but there was no thought or danger of war, we imagined.

*Speech title derived by editor from speech contents

True, a small cloud the size of a man's hand had just appeared on the horizon to the west of us. Three months before our 1932 muster, Japanese marines had landed in China and a war had started between those two countries. And, with increasing regularity, dispatches from Germany included mention of a raucous and peculiar-looking politician named Adolf Hitler.

But there was not a one of us who dreamed that those two unconnected events would, in six short years, breed other events which would eventually disrupt and distort the lives of the more fortunate among us, and take the lives of those less fortunate.

The story which dominated the newspapers of the day was the Lindbergh kidnapping, and we of that year's senior class were thinking more about how we were going to earn a living in an economically depressed United States than about anything that was going on in Asia or Europe.

But it was the war that saw Texas A&M contribute the full measure of its gallantry by giving up more of its sons to be commissioned officers than any other college or university in the land. It was a war, too, that added a long list of names to that sad roster of courageous young men who helped purchase victory and freedom with the down-payment of their lives.

But, above all, it was a war that changed the entire course of civilization. Because of that war the world will never again be the same.

For in the midst of the fighting—on August 6, 1945—suddenly we discovered that mankind had caught lightning in his hands.

He had mastered the atom.

The city of Hiroshima had 318,000 inhabitants. It was a city of parks and playgrounds, factories and churches. In a matter of seconds it was a seething, blackened mass. One bomb had obliterated sixty percent of the city. In an area of 4½ square miles scarcely a living thing survived.

That one bomb, for all practical purposes, ended the war. For that we were grateful. Our first reaction was relief and joy. After almost five years we had peace at last.

But eventually there came a second reaction—concern.

This fearful weapon was in our hands—to use as we saw fit. We could use it to build a brave new world of tomorrow, or we could use it to create a holocaust unprecedented in its savagery and total effect.

On August 6, 1945, mankind had struck a new hour.

Hitherto man had never quite been able to keep pace with his own inventive genius. He always seemed to lack the mental and spiritual maturity to prevent the perversion of his inventions, so that they inevitably did almost as much harm as they did good.

Now mankind could no longer afford such immaturity.

And the questions arose—were we really the masters of the atom—or had we merely released a power that would master us?

Of course, the final answer to that question is still in doubt.

At first we made the tragic mistake of thinking we could monopolize the secrets of nuclear fission by building a wall around them. We underestimated the Russian capacity. The Soviets jumped over the wall. In one generation, they literally leaped from the oxcart to the cyclotron. The wall, which we had foolishly hoped would be our safeguard, almost became our prison.

And, of course, the research and development which led to Hiroshima led also to the creation of a fantastic new world—a world of guided missiles, the Sputnik and the race for control of outer space.

Make no mistake about this: The orbits which circle above our heads constitute the most compelling fact of our times.

The nation that controls outer space controls the world.

If outer space becomes a province of the world's most ruthless imperialists, then freedom will fall into eternal jeopardy.

But, if the conquest of outer space is achieved by men of good will—then we shall have the opportunity of adding a new dimension to freedom and with it, the achievement of permanent and total peace.

There are those who would minimize the military and defense potentials of outer space. They claim the race between Soviet Russia and the United States is purely a propaganda battle.

These critics would have us ignore the problem of special satellites and concentrate our money and our scientific genius on the development of earthbound weapons which would make us impregnable to attack.

I wholeheartedly disagree with this view.

I think it both inaccurate and dangerous.

Naturally, we must continue to accelerate our production and development of new weapons. But we need more than a mere military posture to succeed. We need more than a sterile weapon psychology.

If that were enough to keep the world's peace there would have been no fighting in the Near East. There would be no Berlin crisis.

Even if we were able to make ourselves impregnable (and Soviet advances in science make that a very doubtful assumption), how could we prove it? How could we convince the rest of the world? The rest of the world would see in the satellites the tangible proof of Soviet progress. They would balance those manifestations against our mere assertions of invulnerability, and they would naturally look to Russia as the leading power of the earth. The battle would be lost before it was begun.

There is no doubt about this: Once the United States appears to have fallen so far behind Russia in scientific development that recovery is impossible—then we shall be in mortal peril as a nation and as a civilization.

This means greater production of our missiles. It means greater submarine production. It means development of the power of total and instant retaliation.

It means all of these things.

But it also means much more.

It means the redevelopment of the pioneering spirit—the daring and brilliance that have always characterized this nation—in the pursuit of peace. It means the development and exploitation of trained imagination. It means bold leadership.

It means the creation of an intellectual climate in which our greatest brains and our greatest talents can make their full contribution.

It means that we as Americans must prove to all the world that we have the capability of lifting the age in which we live, so that all men everywhere will be able to walk on higher ground because of our imagination and our idealism.

In the light of this, I would like to speak now directly to you seniors who will soon be leaving A&M to make your way in this troubled and challenging new world.

It was my privilege to be selected for service in the House Committee on Science and Astronautics. This is by far the most important assignment I have had in my twelve years in Congress.

In this capacity, I have had the opportunity of listening to the leading scientists of the western world discuss the future in terms which, if they had been used just a handful of years ago, would have branded their user a lunatic.

I am convinced that we stand on the threshold of an unlimited future—a future without horizons—a future of infinite potentialities. The scientific advances of the past will read almost like a footnote to the advances yet to come.

When I sat where you are now sitting as an undergraduate, I thought I was facing a challenging future.

Compared to what you face, the challenge of 1932 was mere child's play.

In the world you face, there will be no room for mere passengers— no room for intellectual or spiritual deadheads.

There will be room only for men of character and with the education to make a positive contribution in one way or another to the preservation of our free society.

Gone forever is the time when men can relax and tolerate the status quo. There has been too much of that in the past, and we have paid dearly for it.

You will have to recover and improve upon the tradition of revolutionary exploration which created this nation and made it great. It will no longer be sufficient for an educated man to conform. From now on he must perform.

You will have to preserve and champion our traditional values in the face of bitter opposition.

The pace of scientific development will be vastly accelerated—not slowed.

Just two years ago, the problem of putting an earth satellite into orbit seemed almost impossible of solution.

We have passed that point of development so swiftly that earth satellites are almost obsolete. For the first time in the history of the universe, the inhabitants of one planet have been able to penetrate their own gravitational field and reach these other planets.

And even though the problems seem almost insurmountable now, I am convinced that, sooner than we anticipate, human beings will be flying through space and interplanetary travel will be an accomplished fact. In your lifetime you will see men upon other planets.

The implications of this are enormous.

Outer space is man's last and greatest frontier.

Frontiers require intelligence, courage, daring, hard work. They break and destroy those who do not possess these virtues, or who fail to use them well.

The space frontier contains limitless potentials, limitless challenges.

For instance, in outer space lies the power to control the world's weather, to change the tides, alter climates, create new seasons. In outer space lies the power to revolutionize the entire technology of communications.

In outer space lies the hope of total, permanent peace.

It will be the task of your generation to win this last, essential frontier and to hold it.

It will be an enormous task—but it must be undertaken—and successfully undertaken.

Success will require responsible men—loyal men—men who cherish freedom above all earthly things—men of training and imagination endowed with leadership and toughness of mind.

And to you I say this: In the future which you will inherit, you will find constant cause to thank God you have been trained at Texas A&M.

You have been well prepared academically. But you have also been inoculated with the important intangibles—intangibles which are taught better here than anywhere else on earth. I refer to those intangibles I have mentioned: self-reliance, imagination, loyalty, courage, daring, industry, honor.

These have been the proud characteristics of A&M men in the past. I remember General Randolph Pate, Commandant of the Marine Corps, telling me recently that in all his experience he had never had an officer from A&M who was not a top officer.

Texas A&M produces natural leaders. It has a tradition of producing men who have best moved their country along by leading.

That is your strength.

Opposite you is a society with a tradition of producing men who can serve their country only by being led.

Hold fast to your tradition.

Hold fast to what you have been taught.

Hold fast to what you believe.

If the world is to be moved from dissolution—and I am convinced it will—it will be saved by you and by others like you in every corner of the entire free world.

But this is not something that will be done for you. It is something you must do yourself. Peace is not something that is handed to you on a silver platter. Freedom is never won or lost in a day.

Peace must be struggled for, worked for, and won. Freedom, to be preserved, has always needed a constant mutuality of sacrifice, effort and care.

We do not operate under any divine exemption from the lessons of history. The conquest of space—the preservation of freedom—the achievement of total peace, will require the total endeavor of all men of good will, all men of ability, of education and training, all men of courage and daring.

The weapons necessary for victory are in your hands. They have been forged here at A&M and they have been forged well. Don't slacken your grip on them. Don't let them fall from your grasp. Don't let them become blunt or rusty.

On our roll of honor there are hundreds of names of gallant young men who gave up their most precious possession—their life—so that honor and decency and freedom would prevail upon this earth.

They were believers in the American dream—a dream that some day men shall bear no burdens save of their own choosing—that they shall walk upright in pride and self-respect, masterless, and worship their God as they see fit.

At the moment, they wait expectantly to learn whether their sacrifice was in vain, whether humankind was worth the saving, whether the dream was a foolish fantasy.

You—and your generation—must supply that answer.

I am confident that you will prove worthy of the challenge.

Thank you and God bless you.

# Lt. Gen. A. D. Bruce '16

*1960—Memorial Student Center Lawn*

Lt. Gen. A. D. Bruce '16.
Photo from editor's
collection.

Andrew David Bruce was born September 14, 1894, in St. Louis, Missouri. He graduated from Texas A&M in 1916 with a BS degree in dairy husbandry. He entered the US Army as a second lieutenant at Leon Springs, Texas, during World War I. As one of the 2nd Infantry Division's youngest battalion commanders, he received the Distinguished Service Cross for actions near Verdun, at Chateau Thierry, in the Marne (where he was wounded), at St. Mihiel, and in the Meuse-Argonne offensive at Blanc Mont.

At the outbreak of World War II, Bruce headed the Army's Tank Destroyer School. He established Fort Hood, Texas, and developed a force that would knock out some 2,600 German armored vehicles, including 300 in the Battle of the Bulge. In 1943, he assumed command of the 77th Division (the Statue of Liberty Division), which marched steadily from Guam to Okinawa in some of the fiercest fighting in the South Pacific. His forces made the famous end run behind Japanese lines to recapture Leyte in the Philippines. In a key battle of that war, the 77th Division conquered the fortress island of Ie Shima, which became known as the place where popular war correspondent Ernie Pyle was killed by a sniper.

Following the war, Bruce served as a military governor in Japan and as commandant of the Armed Forces Staff College before retiring in 1954. In September 1954, he became the third president of the (then private) University of Houston. He was named the university's first chancellor in December 1956. Before retiring in August 1961, he led the university to full accreditation, strengthened its faculty, raised its academic standards, and won state support.

Bruce was named a Distinguished Alumnus of Texas A&M in 1968 and inducted into the Corps of Cadets Hall of Honor in 1993. He died July 28, 1969, and is buried in Arlington National Cemetery. A State of Texas historical marker was erected in his memory at Fort Hood in 1972.

## A Pledge and Responsibility*

I've just read the *Batt* [*The Battalion*, Texas A&M's student newspaper] and have heard the talks here. I realize I shall repeat some things already said. But, my English prof, the beloved professor David Brooks Cofer, said repetition is good for emphasis. Hence, I shall not change my speech.

Often I have heard this statement: "It must have been a handicap in the army to not be a graduate of West Point." My answer has always been, "No, I never found this to be true."

I noticed once a year West Pointers had a get-together. Once a year, no matter where we were, we Texas A&M graduates got together for our annual Muster. . . .

Nothing can compare to it.

I qualify in one respect for this appearance here today. I am an Aggie and very proud of that fact. But as I look at you here today and think of the past, I cannot help but feel that there are those who are far better qualified to speak to you on this Muster Day.

Better, indeed, for all of us this afternoon if old Sam Houston could speak. It would be priceless if an Aggie who gave his life in World War I, or World War II, or in the Korean engagement could speak to us and inspire us with great words. However, there is consolation in knowing that we the living are a testimonial to all of them.

We are here today because of the sacrifice made by the men at San Jacinto on that 21st day of April in 1836, when a valiant Texas Army under Sam Houston won one of history's most decisive battles.

We are here today because of our Aggie comrades who have passed on in body, but remain with us in spirit.

*Speech title derived by editor from speech contents

Our Muster tradition dates back 57 years to April 21, 1903, when the Texas A&M Cadet Corps, some 300 strong, met together to observe the independence of Texas and to pay homage to those gallant sons of Goliad, the Alamo, and of San Jacinto. That band of Aggies pledged that April 21 would be a day of mustering for A&M men wherever they might be "forever afterwards." These Aggies also stated that this observance would be a time to pay homage to all A&M men who have passed on. And to unite us more completely with these Aggie friends, it was decided that a living comrade would answer "Here" when the roll call for the absent was read.

And so it has been.

Since its start by that small group of Aggies, the occasion has come to be one of the greatest A&M traditions. It has become a symbol of the great loyalty and respect which binds the men of A&M to their college and to each other.

Our Muster is more than just a ceremony. It represents a pledge and responsibility which has been handed down by A&M men from generation to generation and from year to year.

Our Muster tradition has been an opportunity for A&M men to renew each year their loyalty and unity. The basic foundation of our friendship for each other and our love and devotion for Texas A&M and our country has been this loyalty and unity.

This tradition has survived for 57 years and during three wars.

Musters have been held under all kinds of conditions and in all parts of the world. Little bands of Aggies have gathered on April 21 in the Philippines, in Japan and on many remote islands in the Pacific. They met together in North Africa, the Middle East and Europe. Sometimes they came together in an atmosphere of quiet and seclusion. Often they congregated near the battlefront within sight of the enemy and within range of gunfire. Whether it was in the cold and wilderness of Alaska or on some desolate, lonely island, our Aggies always managed to get together for a Muster.

For example, you know one Texas A&M Muster was held on April 21, 1942, on Corregidor in the Philippines not long before it was captured. Many present at the Muster did not survive; others suffered for years as prisoners.

In connection with this Muster, let us review another Muster. On the morning of April 16, 1945, the 77th Infantry Division made a landing on an island called Ie Shima. This island should not be confused with Iwo Jima, which the marines had such a tough fight to capture in February and March, and the scene of the world famous picture of "Raising The Flag."

At the eastern end of the island of Ie Shima there is a village of concrete houses, in back of which is a pinnacle 607 feet high. This last-stand position of the enemy had hundreds of pillboxes, caves in limestone sometimes three stories high, and emplacements in the concrete houses. They had lots of mortars, artillery and antitank guns. Tunnels connected some of the positions. It was a veritable fortress. The approach of this fortress was slow. The fighting was severe.

You will recall that Ernie Pyle was killed.

I prepared an inscription for a wooden sign to mark his grave as follows: "At this spot the 77th Infantry Division lost a buddy, Ernie Pyle, 18th of April, 1945."

Today it is on his permanent monument.

We inched forward on April 20. Our men reached within 50 feet of the top of the mount and had to pause on account of the pinnacle. The enemy launched a vicious counter-attack, but the line finally held.

Instructions were issued to all A&M men that we would have to hold our Muster in our own companies or battalions or headquarters. We couldn't assemble everyone together. We earnestly hoped to capture this island on April 21. On that day the attack was made by successive blows. First the west side advanced, then the south. Finally, at 10:30 a.m., six men struggled to the top.

I sent the following message to the Governor of Texas: "The 77th Infantry Division, after a bitter pillbox-to-pillbox, house-to-house, cave-to-cave fight, planted our American Flag on the highest point of the strongly defended mountain pinnacle on Ie Shima. Men from Texas planted a Texas Flag on Bloody Ridge of the pinnacle fortress [the scene of the heaviest fighting] in honor of those gallant Texans who gathered together at Corregidor to remember San Jacinto on 21 April 1942."

Our famous Aggie Muster was held by small groups as planned. I was present with a few in the area of Division headquarters. Several "Heres" had to be answered, but we felt mighty proud to capture a veritable fortress that allowed us to vindicate, in a measure, that heartrending Aggie Muster held three years before on Corregidor.

It is irony, indeed, that those Aggies of 1903 had little idea that the custom they founded would be observed under such a variety of places and conditions. But it was their inspiration, their loyalty, and their unity that made it possible.

The spirit that emanates from our Muster tradition has been one of comfort and common purpose. It is our one great tie with Texas patriots and Texas Aggies, living and dead.

These Musters have been held in times of peace, in times of "cold" wars, and in times of "hot" wars. And in every instance, Aggies have not been found wanting or lacking the determination to aid a cause, help a friend, or perform a service.

A splendid record has been written by the Aggies who are with us today in spirit. Too often this record has been written in blood. Aggies have always been among the first to serve their country . . . in peace and in war. Their fitness and ability as fighters have made them the envy of many. Their accomplishments in more peaceful pursuits have, likewise, endeared them to many men. But, it has been in war that many Aggies ended their careers.

And, as we meet here today, we find our nation still involved in a "cold" war against the enemies of freedom, decency, and all we hold sacred and dear.

The facts of today may prompt us to ask these questions: Have we, the living, kept faith with our Texas patriots and with our Aggie buddies who have died? Have their fighting and sacrifices been without results?

I think not.

The battle for peace is a never-ending struggle. It will not be concluded so long as there are evil forces abroad in this world trying to enlarge their territories and spreading their Godless ideologies. Aggies have not shed their blood for a lost cause. For there is no greater cause than freedom.

The Aggies who have died on ridges, fields and streams in all parts of the world can sleep as peacefully as their ancestors who fell at the

Alamo, Goliad, and San Jacinto. It is for we the living to continue where they left off. We must continue the seemingly unending search and fight for freedom. We will have failed our departed Aggie buddies and Texas patriots only when we have refused to take up the struggle.

Many of us here today have been intimately acquainted with many of the events connected with the battle for freedom. We need no reminder of what happened. We know the debt of gratitude that society owes our patriots of yesteryears and yesterdays. It is our hope, I know, that it will not be necessary again for Aggies, or anyone else, to fight.

However, we will not fear the day if it comes. As Aggies we accept the challenge when it arrives and are content that it will not be without purpose. We will strive to keep faith with our Texas patriots and Aggie buddies. On San Jacinto Day of each year, we can re-dedicate ourselves to the task of preserving that most perfect and cherished state of freedom and peace.

In conclusion, let us today take advantage of this opportunity again and resolve that we . . . as individual Aggies . . . will never lose sight of the goal of freedom and never forget those who have "carried the ball" thus far. When the call to duty or service is made, let us hope we have the courage to say loud and clear . . . Here!

Let it be an echo of the "Here" uttered by those asleep in their graves in our country, Europe, the Middle East, North Africa, the Philippines, and Korea.

Let us never forget our heritage at San Jacinto.

# James W. Aston '33

*1961—Memorial Student Center Lawn*

James W. Aston '33.
Photo from editor's
collection.

James Aston, vice president of Republic National Bank in Dallas, delivered the campus Muster address in 1949 and 1961. Only two individuals have delivered two campus Muster speeches. (See the earlier chapter for a biographical sketch of Aston.)

## Do We Know the Truth?*

Mr. Chairman, Fellow Aggies and Friends:

Twelve years ago I was privileged to address the student body at the annual Aggie Muster here on campus, and it is a great honor to be here again.

I am sure that the Aggies who are today conducting a worldwide Muster observance in more than 250 designated spots, not only throughout Texas but also around the globe, wish they could be here for this assembly, for we meet here on historic ground. It was on this campus that nearly 40,000 former students of Texas A&M, those who commemorate this occasion, received in substantial measure the basic training for leadership which has distinguished this great school in the arts, sciences, and professions. Since the custom of holding annual Aggie Muster began in 1903, these meetings have come to hold deep, traditional significance to all Aggies everywhere. Each of us, in his own way perhaps, pauses briefly to re-examine the high ideals and purposes which were such an important part of his college years. To most of us, these Musters also mean times of looking ahead, as best we can, to try

*Speech title derived by editor from speech contents

to evaluate what tomorrow will bring, and what it means to us both as individuals and as a people.

In its essential spirit, the Aggie Muster is a memorial to Aggies who have gone before us; the many who have laid down their lives for our country in time of war and in peace. It is a time, too, for grateful acknowledgment of others who are dedicated to serving mankind in many fields throughout the world, often without regard for monetary reward or acclaim. We should honor them here and wish them Godspeed.

The question before us now is how we can best memorialize our great heritage, the inspiring traditions of selfless service, and insure the continued opportunities that only a free society can provide.

Of course, it is with reverence, ever abiding respect, and appreciation that we answer "Here" for our departed brothers, but this service is also for the living to rededicate self and effort to the guarantee of continued freedom. In this connection we perhaps face the greatest challenge in history.

Looking about us on every hand today, we sense an unrest, an uncertainty, and even an element of doubt about where this country is going, about what is going to happen to us. This is only natural, for we are living in a time of tremendous change. We must remember that times of great progress have always been times of equally great uncertainty. Just try to imagine that consternation which arose among the citizenry when Galileo first trained his telescope skyward, then started telling people what he had seen! Think of the uncertainties which troubled Europe in the wake of Columbus' discoveries. And, just to bring things up to date, the other day a young Russian placed us in something of a similar state by making an hour-long rocket ride around the earth.

Leading educators today have begun to pay more and more attention to the rate of change in our society, rather than to the changes themselves. Never before in history has the rate at which change occurred had the importance and the impact on our everyday lives that it has today.

Some companies find themselves reaping major portions of their profits from products which not only were nonexistent six years ago, but which probably had not even been imagined!

Almost daily, we hear of breakthroughs in the various sciences which open the doors upon even greater changes than those experienced thus far.

Look for a moment at the discoveries which have occurred in the span of the last year, and which are being undertaken even now. We all are familiar with the probes into outer space. Most of us are aware of exploratory work being conducted in the oceans of the world, and with project "MOHO" [Mohole] in the Pacific, an effort to probe record depths in the earth's crust [to obtain samples of the earth's mantle]; this endeavor has already proved richly rewarding to our scientists.

Everywhere we see new fruits of scientific discovery—the petrochemical industry, with such by-products as synthetic fibers, wonder drugs, new industrial materials and many other advantages; in electronics and communications, with computers and allied devices rapidly revolutionizing the methodology of modern business; in transportation, with atom-powered transport in various forms promising to move the world's commerce more efficiently.

These are only a few examples which highlight the rapidly changing world about us, and we must not doubt for a moment that even greater change lies ahead. For instance—education (development of the knowledge and skills with which to manipulate the physical resources at our disposal) has been the bedrock base for growth and progress as we know it. But, what is the truth? Do we know? We know now more than we did before—but do we know the truth? I need not emphasize to you who are gathered here how important a factor Texas A&M College has been and continues to be in the search, the growth and the development of the truth!

As we move further into this era of change, this great institution and all other educational institutions everywhere are entrusted with a tremendous responsibility. Theirs shall be the role of channeling and directing those changes which occur, so that mankind will be the beneficiary, not the victim of change.

For all of us the future holds great promise. But to realize the bounties of that promise, we must have the courage to meet the challenges which lie ahead. We cannot achieve positive goals if we give in to the fears which are voiced on every side almost daily. Today is the unparalleled age of opportunity and I challenge each of you—the sons of Texas A&M—to carry the torch of excellence; for only through excellence can we retain the freedom which we treasure so much, and only in this manner can we fully discharge our responsibilities to the present and the future, and to those in whose honor we answer, "Here!"

# Eli L. Whiteley '41

## 1962—Memorial Student Center Ballroom

Eli L. Whiteley '41. Photo from editor's collection.

Eli Lamar Whiteley was born December 10, 1913, in Florence, Texas, and grew up on a farm on the North San Gabriel River between Liberty Hill and Georgetown. He won the Medal of Honor during the Battle of the Bulge in December 1944.

As a first lieutenant, he took charge of a company of 96 men that had been ordered to take a small but key town defended by some 300 Germans. During fighting that reduced company strength to seven men in fighting condition, Whiteley was injured seriously on two different occasions. When the fierce battle was over and the city had been taken, he refused to leave his platoon until ordered to do so. Whiteley's Medal of Honor citation reads as follows:

> While leading his platoon on 27 December 1944, in savage house-to-house fighting through the fortress town of Sigolsheim, France, he attacked a building through a street swept by withering mortar and automatic weapons fire. He was hit and severely wounded in the arm and shoulder; but he charged into the house alone and killed its 2 defenders. Hurling smoke and fragmentation grenades before him, he reached the next house and stormed inside, killing 2 and capturing 11 of the enemy. He continued leading his platoon in the extremely dangerous task of clearing hostile troops from strong points along the street until he reached a building held by fanatical Nazi troops. Although suffering from wounds which had rendered his left arm useless, he advanced on this strongly defended house, and after blasting out a wall with bazooka fire, charged through a hail of bullets. Wedging his submachine gun under his uninjured arm, he rushed into the house through the hole torn by his rockets, killed 5 of the enemy and forced the remaining 12 to surrender.

As he emerged to continue his fearless attack, he was again hit and critically wounded. In agony and with one eye pierced by a shell fragment, he shouted for his men to follow him to the next house. He was determined to stay in the fighting, and remained at the head of his platoon until forcibly evacuated. By his disregard for personal safety, his aggressiveness while suffering from severe wounds, his determined leadership and superb courage, 1st Lt. Whiteley killed 9 Germans, captured 23 more and spearheaded an attack which cracked the core of enemy resistance in a vital area.

Returning to Texas A&M in 1946, he became an associate professor in the Department of Agronomy. He died December 2, 1986, and lay in state in Texas A&M's System Administration Building (now the Jack K. Williams Building) before a military ceremony carried him to the cemetery. He was posthumously named a Distinguished Alumnus in 2012 and inducted into the Corps of Cadets Hall of Honor the same year.

## A&M Can Change*

*Eli Whiteley's Easter holiday address was delivered in the Memorial Student Center ballroom to a small audience. His entire speech was printed in the April 26, 1962, issue of The Battalion, the only campus Muster address that has, to date, been published in its entirety in the student newspaper.*

Today we have gathered here to carry on one of the greatest traditions of A&M. The event that we are commemorating began many years ago with a small group of men who gathered at Washington-on-the-Brazos to draft Texas' Declaration of Independence.

This group of men had dreams of freedom from oppression, dreams of self government and a desire for independence. They were men with strong wills, who declared their freedom from Mexico on March 2, 1836. This act led to the Texas war for independence. It also led to the Alamo, Goliad and finally to San Jacinto. On April 21, 1836, Texas won her independence from Mexico.

*Speech title derived by editor from speech contents

This was not the final battle for the independence of Texas. After Texas was admitted to the Union in 1845, another war was fought. The Mexican War finally established Texas' freedom from Mexico. The years following the Mexican War were years of great expansion and progress; they led, however, to some of the darkest years in the history of our state and nation—the Civil War.

These dark years were not fruitless, however, because out of them came the greatest experiment in education that the world has ever known. The Morrill Act of 1862 establishing the land grant colleges and universities was, I think, exclusive of the Constitution, the greatest single act that the Congress of the United States has ever passed.

More people have received greater benefits from this law than any other single law. What courage it must have taken to embark on such a program in those dark days of the Civil War. It was a program that would develop into the greatest educational program ever established in this or any other nation. Our own college is a part of this program.

The Texas Legislature passed the act making A&M a land grant college in 1871. A&M opened its doors to six students on October 4, 1876, and since that time has grown to be one of the great educational institutions of the state and nation. This year we are joining with the other land grant colleges and universities to celebrate the act that led to their establishment.

A&M is 85 years old, so we have not reached the century mark, but we are approaching it with anticipation. What changes will the next 15 years bring to our institution? What changes should we make so that we can better serve the people of our state?

This college belongs to the people of Texas and its primary function is to serve the people of Texas. With this in mind, the administration of A&M embarked on a study to determine our place in the future educational system of Texas. One hundred outstanding citizens of Texas were asked to serve on a committee to chart the course of A&M through the next few years, so that when we reach the century mark we will be in the best possible position to serve the people of Texas.

At the same time the Century Council is making its study, our own faculty, staff and students are conducting an internal study. It is hoped that these studies will offer a blueprint for the future of A&M during the next 15 years. We cannot predict the future, but we can look at the past and make some estimate.

How has the college changed to meet the needs of the people of Texas? We need to go back only to the post–World War II period to find excellent examples of the flexibility of our school; in that period with the influx of a large number of ex-servicemen, A&M changed to meet the needs of the people of Texas.

Bryan Air Force Base was utilized to house freshmen students. Classes were taught in barracks and office buildings. Housing for married students was developed. Classes were taught at early and late hours. During this time A&M launched a multi-million-dollar building program. Hundreds of thousands of dollars were spent for new equipment for our classrooms and laboratories; new faculty and staff members were added; new courses were added to the curriculum; old courses were updated or dropped.

The need for more highly trained graduates was recognized—new graduate courses were offered; the enrollment in our Graduate School in 1946 was 313, in 1955 it was 512, and in 1961 it was 725. The number of students in the Graduate School more than doubled in 15 years. The Data Processing Center was established to meet the pressing needs in this area. The Nuclear Science Center was established to fill the need in this vital field of study. And only recently the Maritime Academy was established to train marine transportation and engineering officers.

And as we enter the space age, A&M is offering courses in space technology to train engineers in this important field. These are only a few of the changes that have occurred in the past 15 or 16 years. But they show that A&M can change and has changed to meet the needs of the people of Texas. I feel confident that A&M will make even greater changes in the next 15 years.

But these changes have occurred in the past. What about the future? The material offered in the courses that are taught will change! It will become more advanced. Due to the amount of knowledge that has accumulated in the past, it will be necessary for the college to receive better-trained students from our high schools.

These students, in order to finish college in four or five years, will have to know more when they enter college than some of us knew when we were sophomores or juniors in college. The college will need to have our support in order to bring this about. We must demand for our children the best possible training in grade school and high school. Our support in this area will help the college to do a much better job in teaching our children.

There will be changes in the ratio of graduate students to under-graduates. The ratios between agricultural, engineering and liberal arts students will change. These changes will be influenced by the law of supply and demand and by the calibre of student that A&M graduates.

If A&M is to grow and take its proper place in the educational system of Texas, it must make changes in policy so that it can fulfill its obligations to the people of Texas. The administrative officers, the staff and the faculty are fulfilling their roles in the development of our school. What is the role of the former students in this development?

This is difficult to define. We who have graduated from A&M feel that it belongs to us and that we belong to it. Those of us who have sons want them to come to A&M to find the same types of friendship and fellowships and to experience the great traditions that have become a part of the student life. All of these things are fine, but we also want our sons to get the finest possible education.

This will be possible only if the administrative officers, the faculty and the staff cooperate. We as ex-students can play a vital role in help-ing them do their jobs by giving them the support they need. How can we accomplish this? First, we can give to the Development Fund. You are all familiar with this fund and the many fine uses it has had in the past.

Second, we can give our time to work for the good of A&M. This means that we give our best when asked to perform a service. Third, we must sell A&M by promoting the college at every opportunity. We must tell other people about the fine job that the school is doing even though we may not like some of the policies of the college.

A&M cannot fulfill its role in the educational system of Texas with-out the support and goodwill of the people of Texas. We need to tell again and again the dynamic story of its accomplishments. Through the decades, Texans' goodwill toward and assistance to A&M has been tremendous. The net balance in the bank of public goodwill is still high. But time may run out on us one of these years.

We need to mobilize all of our resources promptly behind an effective public relations program. I don't mean that we should open a public relations office. We simply need to tell the story of A&M to friends and acquaintances in a sincere, simple and straightforward manner.

Fourth, and this, I think, is the most important part of our role as ex-students, we need to support the decision of the administrative officers. Changes that are made by the Board of Directors, the chancellor, the president and the deans of the colleges are to be accepted. Changes have always been made in the policies under which A&M has operated.

Without these changes under the able administrations of such men as [Lawrence Sullivan] Ross, [Thomas] Walton, [Gibb] Gilchrist, [Frank] Bolton, [Earl] Rudder, and [Thomas] Harrington, A&M could not have achieved its place of greatness in the educational system of Texas. These men and the Boards of Directors under which they served were faced and will be faced with many decisions, some of them that will chart new courses for A&M.

These will be bold steps to prepare the college for its place in the future. We as ex-students must take our place and give the college the support it needs. In these next few years of crises let us be able to say as the Apostle Paul said to Timothy, "I have fought a good fight, I have finished my course, I have kept the faith."

# L. F. Peterson '36

## 1963—Memorial Student Center Lawn

L. F. Peterson '36. Photo from editor's collection.

Leland Fred Peterson was born January 28, 1914, in Temple, Texas. He went to Temple Junior College before receiving his BS from Texas A&M. He worked his way up from an oil field roustabout to chief petroleum engineer for Stanolind Oil and Gas Company. After dissolving his international consulting partnership of Keller and Peterson (1953–70), Peterson continued as an independent oil operator and petroleum engineering consultant.

In 1963, while serving as president of the Association of Former Students and on Texas A&M's Century Council, Peterson was appointed to the Texas A&M Board of Directors by Governor John Connally and served until 1975. He was president of the board from 1967 to 1969. As a member of the board, Peterson helped to make decisions concerning two important issues that would significantly change Texas A&M. In 1963, Texas A&M expanded its admission rules to become a coed campus in spite of the voiced opposition of many students, past and present. Also in 1963, the Texas Legislature passed a bill changing the name of the Agricultural & Mechanical College of Texas to Texas A&M University. The initials "A&M" became a symbol of A&M's heritage.

Peterson served as a member of the Texas College and University System Coordinating Board from 1975 to 1981. He was named a Distinguished Alumnus of Texas A&M in 1976. Peterson died July 1, 1985.

# Program of Excellence*

General Rudder, Mr. Chairman, Aggies, and Friends of Texas A&M:

It is a privilege and a great honor to be asked to speak at this annual Muster here on the campus of our great college. This is my first Muster on the campus since I was a student here 27 years ago. This great Aggie tradition of Muster is today being conducted and observed in more than 280 designated sites, not only in Texas, but throughout the world. Thousands of former students of this college are in Muster ceremonies at this time, renewing their friendships and honoring the dead. Every living Aggie would like to take part in this ceremony on the site of the original Muster. This Muster program ties a great day in Texas history to a great traditional practice by Texas' great student body, the Texas Aggies. I wish now to direct my remarks to Excellence in Higher Education in Texas and the role of Texas A&M in this effort.

The Texas system of higher education is relatively young, since it has only been 127 years since the victory of San Jacinto, and only 87 years since Governor Richard C. Coke, the father of public education in Texas, signed into law the Constitution of 1876. Our public schools, high schools, junior colleges, colleges and universities have come a long way, but we still have to do a lot of catching up in order to reach the levels of excellence so necessary to the economy of this State.

There have been many statements made by learned men on the importance of excellence in our colleges and universities, but a recent statement by Governor John Connally said, "As the space age dawns, Texas stands at the educational crossroad. We have had a good system of higher education always, and we have a good one now, but being good is not enough if we are to fill the major role destiny has assigned to us in this new and wonderful age. These are two areas of vast importance to all Texans: namely, education and industrial development, and they go together. Business in this complex space age needs laboratories as well as labor."

It has been proven time and time again that industry follows brain power. For example, in the State of California, there are 23 state-

*Speech title derived by editor from speech contents

supported colleges and universities. California has the model public school, junior college, college and university system of this country. Much has been written and spoken about their program of education and its success. As a result of this modern, up-to-date, excellent system, California now receives more than 40% of all United States defense contracts, which alone bring $200 million in annual contract expenditures to that state. By comparison, Texas receives less than 2% of these government defense contracts. California, although a younger state than Texas, is, as of 1962, first in population in the United States, and first in per capita income. In addition to California, other states with superior systems of higher education are leading the way. We hear the familiar phrase "closing the missile gap," and it will be closed, but Texas, in order to get on the team, must close the "higher education gap" if this state is to prosper with the leaders.

Now, just what is the problem for state-supported schools? First, the State of Texas must develop a plan for our colleges and universities perhaps along the lines of the plan of education in the State of California or other leading states. This plan should determine the needs for trade schools, junior colleges, undergraduate colleges, and the universities. It should be designed to meet the future needs of the state and to provide excellence in every public school: trade through the highest degree-granting university, but under a system of satellite or feeder controls. In other words, each school would have excellence in its own program, but each school would fit into the overall program in a proper place. The responsibility of every school would be defined and exact, and each school in its proper place would strive for excellence at its level of instruction and service.

Now, excellence means to me that every student, instructor and administrator in every school in this education system is aspiring to accomplish the very best of his or her capabilities. To make our schools competitive in excellence with schools in other states, we need to provide the administration with the more talented personnel and with physical equipment which enables the talented personnel to accomplish their very best. As to the students in this public school program for excellence, there is a sorting-out process involved, and it is definitely a part of the program for excellence. In this country and in this state, we are proud of our democracy where all are given equal rights of justice, protection, representation and taxation, and these rights are carried over somewhat into education. Certainly through the high school level our children are taking about the same work, but after this level is attained, the assertion of competitive ability rightfully takes over to a greater degree.

Every young girl or boy has a different level of capability as a student. Many parents now tell their children the only way to prosper today is to have a college education, and certainly there is wisdom to this statement, but the truth is, every high school graduate does not have the capabilities, the motivation or the aspiration to become a college student and graduate. Our counseling and testing systems are a means of sorting out these students. The United States is a land of multiple chances, and a great number of students are given a trial in college. It is impossible to bring all the prospective college students to the university; therefore, the junior colleges and other four-year colleges, according to the adopted plan, give these young men and women their chance to perform as college students. Not all of these people will make it in college; many will drop out and learn a semi-skilled profession not requiring a college degree. Others will do well in four-year colleges, and those with unusual capabilities will go on to graduate study. Under such an educational program we can keep Texas' young people in Texas. With new industry we need the technicians, the college graduates, and post-graduates from our universities if this state is to become a leader with other technological and industrial states. The State of Texas must take on the burden of taxation, increased tuition and private giving necessary to bring about this plan of excellence in all levels of education.

In my opinion, the A&M College's role in this drive for excellence is as follows:

First—This University must strive and aspire for its place as the number one university in its major areas of undergraduate instruction; namely, Agriculture, Engineering, Veterinary Medicine, Architecture and the Physical and Natural Sciences.

Second—This University should be the only school in the higher education system offering graduate degrees of excellence in Agriculture, Engineering, Veterinary Medicine, Architecture and in some areas of Arts and Sciences.

Third—This University should be the only school, or certainly the number one school, with Agriculture and Engineering Experimentation and Extension Services.

Fourth—Other schools in the A&M College system should strive for excellence in their respective areas of undergraduate instruction, with the A&M College as the nucleus of the system. The member colleges of the System would send their undergraduate students and their more gifted graduates to A&M College for their further education.

Where do we stand in this drive at A&M College toward a program of Excellence?

The overall state program is certainly on its way. Here at A&M, we are already ahead of many of the state schools and universities due to the following facts and accomplishments. The Faculty-Staff-Student Study on Aspirations was completed and supplied to President Rudder in the spring of 1962. The Century Council has completed their studies and made their report. The Board of Directors on November 16, 1962, in response to the Century Study Report, presented their Blueprint for Progress at our great College Convocation. The Board of the College is already making decisions along the lines of the recommendations of these studies. We have already on our campus an inspired administration, faculty and student body. General Rudder and his staff are actively formulating plans which will elevate this school from a good university to a university of real excellence.

It has been a great honor and pleasure to participate in this great tradition and to discuss these problems of education in Texas and at A&M College with you. In closing, I would like to quote from a Chinese philosopher, who made this statement three centuries before Christ. He said, "When planning for a year—sow corn; when planning for a decade—plant trees; when planning for a life—train and educate men."

Thank you.

# E. King Gill '24

*1964—System Administration Building Lawn*

E. King Gill '24. Photo from editor's collection.

Earl King Gill was born January 1, 1902, in Dallas. He became Texas A&M's original 12th Man, whose willingness to serve in the Aggies' 22-14 win over Centre College on January 2, 1922, inspired the continuing A&M tradition of students standing throughout football games. The following season he caught an eleven-yard pass to score the first touchdown in a 14-7 win over the University of Texas in Austin.

Gill graduated from A&M in 1924 with a BS degree in engineering. He coached high school sports for a year at Greenville and then entered Baylor School of Medicine. He graduated from Baylor in 1929 and went directly into the US Army Medical Corps. He set up an eye, ear, nose, and throat practice in San Antonio and moved to Corpus Christi in 1935. During World War II, he returned to the Army Medical Corps for five years, serving at Goodfellow Field in San Angelo and the School of Aviation Medicine at Randolph Field near San Antonio. He commanded the base hospital at Majors Army Airfield in Greenville and completed his duty with the Far Eastern Air Force at Fort McKinley in the Philippine Islands. Gill and his wife returned to Corpus Christi, where he practiced ophthalmology until Hurricane Celia damaged their home and they moved to Rockport in 1970, the same year he lost part of a finger in a hunting accident. He retired at the age of seventy in 1972, five years after having been slowed by a heart attack.

While at A&M, Gill earned eight letters in football, basketball, and baseball. He was inducted into A&M's Athletic Hall of Fame in 1969. In 1980, the Class of '80 dedicated a Twelfth Man statue, sculpted by G. Pat Foley, that stood at the entrance to Kyle Field until major renovations caused the statue to be move to the Rudder Foundation plaza. The life-size depiction of E. King Gill will always remind Aggies of the part he played in establishing one of the many traditions that make Texas A&M a unique institution. Another, larger statue was placed outside Kyle Field.

Gill died December 7, 1976.

## A&M's 12th Man—The True Story*

Mr. President, distinguished guests, ladies and gentlemen, and fellow Aggies:

No human being could but be very humble, very grateful and appreciative of this honor you have given to me, coming from a student body that I love.

I recall the last war when I was in the Philippines. The group of officers that I was with were required to check the bulletin boards at headquarters at least three to four times a day. On one occasion in the center of one was a notice which read: "There will be a meeting of A&M men in tent 402 at 7 p.m. tonight." An officer standing beside me remarked: "You Aggies beat anything I have ever seen. We can establish a beachhead on one of the islands out here and in a short time, there will be a sign stuck in the sand reading 'There will be an A&M meeting here tonight.'" I think this demonstrates what other people think of Aggies. They may not particularly like us, but they respect us. I also took advantage of a trip to Corregidor where one of our most famous and hallowed Musters was held during the siege of the "Rock" by the Japanese. This loyalty and dedication equals anything in our history. It is well that we should pause here and pay homage to these and other A&M men who have moved along the way.

I have asked a number of A&M students what should I say today. I received an answer from one of them, Pat Nance, who said, "Tell us how the 12th Man tradition originated and how has being a Texas Aggie affected your life." The first is easy to tell, the last more difficult.

*Speech title derived by editor from speech contents

The story of the 12th Man was originated by E. E. McQuillen '20 about 1939–40 when A&M was enjoying its greatest football teams, one a National Champion. The school was asked to dramatize a football incident that would be suitable for radio. McQuillen thought of the incident when I was called out of the stands to take my place on the bench. It occurred in a post-season game on New Year's Day, 1922, 42 years ago.

The place was Dallas, and the old wooden stadium, seating about 10–12,000, was near where the present Cotton Bowl is located. The teams were Texas A&M, champion of the Southwest Conference, and Centre College, which had won nine games and was considered the National Champions. They boasted of three All-Americans on their team, a rather unheard of thing during this time. The game had several unusual aspects: It was the first post-season game in the southwest; it was to produce the publicity making the conference recognized over the United States; and it was the beginning of the 12th Man tradition at A&M.

Personally, I had been a substitute on the team during the year but had left the team after Thanksgiving to give my time to basketball. Anyway, I didn't think I had a chance to play. In those days the teams dressed in a downtown hotel and rode to the stadium in cabs. I lived in Dallas and was home for Christmas. It was quite easy for me to ride with the team to the stadium and easier to get into the game. Anyway, I didn't have the $3.00 admission. After we were in the stadium and on the bench, I was asked to spot players from the stands, and that is how I was up with the student body. During the first half, A&M received so many injuries that it appeared we would not have enough men to finish the game. So I was called from the stands. I went under the wooden stands, no dressing room mind you, and took off my civilian clothes and put on an injured player's [Heine Weir's] uniform. From there I took my place on the bench to remain there to be used if it was necessary. This is the true story of the incident of the 12th Man.

How it has affected my life and emotions: For one thing, it has made me feel humble and proud to think that I might represent the finest body of young men in the US. Any one of them could be the 12th Man, but he must be ready to stand and fight for the things that are right and the traditions of this country and this school. It has made me a better man and a better doctor, and last but not least, a more responsible citizen. It has, on a lighter side, made me the prime target for the many A&M jokes that come along.

It is my sincere hope that there will always be the Muster, and there will always be a Cadet Corps at A&M. For without it, there will be no A&M; for in it are found many of our most precious and hallowed traditions. As we reach into the future, it is well that we remember the past. May we be dedicated to turning out A&M men of high calibre— dedicated and responsible leaders. May this be our aim—we must not fail.

# Clarence Darrow Hooper '53
*1965—System Administration Building Lawn*

Clarence Darrow Hooper '53. Photo from editor's collection.

Clarence Darrow Hooper was born January 30, 1932, in Fort Worth. He set a national discus record at North Side High School. At Texas A&M, the 6-foot, 3-inch Hooper won the NCAA shot put in 1951 and captured the Silver Medal with a throw of 57 feet and ¾ inch at the Helsinki Olympics in 1952, missing the gold by 2 centimeters. He also earned three letters as an end and place-kicker for the A&M football team. In 1965 he was inducted into the Texas A&M Athletic Hall of Fame and became a member of the Texas Sports Hall of Fame in 1979.

After earning a master of engineering degree in civil engineering in 1954, he served two years as a US Air Force lieutenant, training the Army Corps of Engineers in the design and construction of forward theater airfields.

In 1956 he started working for Gifford-Hill and Co., Inc., as a design and construction engineer. After fourteen years in staff engineering, production management, and as general manager of ready-mix concrete operations in Atlanta, Georgia, he became part owner of Texas Testing Laboratories, Inc., in Dallas. In 1977 he founded Hooper & Associates, Inc., providing geotechnical engineering and construction materials testing services. In 1991, Hooper sold the geotechnical engineering operation to one of his sons. In 1999 he sold the remainder of the firm to another son and his two partners.

Hooper received Texas A&M's Outstanding Engineering Alumnus Award in 1987 and was named a Distinguished Graduate of A&M's Department of Civil Engineering in 2000. He served on advisory councils for A&M's College of Engineering and Department of Civil Engineering and was a trustee of the Dallas Independent School District.

## Dynamics of Change and Innovation*

Thank you, General Rudder, for establishing my right to talk to this Muster as one who appreciates the significance of this date in Texas history and Aggie tradition, too.

This commemorative service honoring the memory of those brave Texans at San Jacinto and those Texas Aggies that have died during this year reminds each of us of our indebtedness to these men and to the ideas they fought for. What they gained for us through their sacrifice, we have today. But the vision to change and innovate, to challenge, to improve and to achieve for our contemporaries and for our children is the greatness of these men which we must emulate. The "Dynamics of Change and Innovation" is our heritage.

Change takes place daily about each one of us. I live in Dallas, a city which we like to call a dynamic city. Things are on the move and the pace is invigorating. Where a city block of 2-story brick buildings stood across from our office yesterday or last year, now stands an imposing 50-story bank building. Marble and glass from the street to the clouds. This is an investment in your future; you are the men that will introduce the changes, innovations, and inventions that will fill this building with new jobs, new companies, and even new industries.

Our Love Field in Dallas, that has been controversial for most of its recent useful life, is a facility that undergoes constant change. The newly constructed 8,000-foot runway sends planes to all destinations now, but you are aware that plans are being laid for future supersonic air traffic to be served by a regional airport jointly owned by Dallas, Fort Worth, and the surrounding communities. While plans progress on this regional facility, new construction for additional parking at Love Field continues so that today's demands are met.

*Speech title derived by editor from speech contents

The economic feasibility of the Trinity River Canal from the Gulf Coast to Dallas and Fort Worth is a program that will change the economic use of many raw materials and transportation facilities. Problems that have slowed the progress of this program have revolved around questions of federal participation in financing the construction and operation of this transportation and flood control project. The magnitude of construction costs of close to one billion dollars causes us to immediately turn to Uncle Sam to come up with the money. However, the importance of maintaining our free enterprise economic approach is an essential ingredient in our continued growth as a state and nation. To achieve a partnership of federal, state, and local government with private business is important to the successful realization of this project. Our growth measured by the $600 billion/year gross national product is a milestone that many admire in passing, but it must force us to consider how we got there and how do we continue to move upward.

The decision of Arlington State to divest themselves of the Texas A&M University System is a change that I'm sure has caused you some mixed emotions. It certainly has given me some. Here is a school that is geographically located perfectly for the Dallas–Fort Worth community. A location of terrific potential—for students as well as the surrounding community and local industry. That this school must grow to meet today's and tomorrow's needs is, I think, obvious to everyone. For them to think that their growth would be faster and/or better by affiliating with TU rather than A&M is their own decision to make, but it always hurts to feel that someone else can do more for them than we can. But it would hurt even more for us to continue in a relationship that is not mutually attractive. We must re-evaluate our system at each change and continue to move ahead with our own plans for the future—for excellence.

In carrying out our plan for excellence, we have passed some "change" milestones that bothered us perhaps unnecessarily. We have changed our name to coincide with the stature that we have enjoyed for years. We are now, in name as well as in deed, a University. We all pondered the proposal to change the name with prejudices of tradition and the desire to preserve memories rather than to plan for the years ahead. If our former name conflicts with our goals of excellence, then which do we compromise? After the problem has been thoughtfully considered, and a solution proposed by those charged with the responsibility for excellence, then we should endorse these plans and even make them our own. Realizing at each change that perhaps we will be wrong in our appraisal of the situation, but to know that to refuse all change will certainly stifle all improvement.

Another controversial issue constantly alive on our campus is compulsory military training. This issue cannot be studied without considerable personal feelings on the part of a student or former student. We have too many memories of what the conditions were when we personally were confronted with the student life situation. But external factors such as draft quotas, brush fire wars and changing ROTC programs keep demanding the continual consideration of our campus military establishment. We can't isolate ourselves from the effects of these changes. We must adjust our campus military policies to meet our objective of excellence.

I know one change that we're all in favor of. When Randy Matson ['67] is poised in the shot put ring anyplace, anytime, the world's shot put record he set on April the 9th is liable to be broken. And the world record book had better be changed to reflect it. The improvements in technique, training and ability of competitors in the shot put is undeniable; the record book traces the changes. Good changes in technique and training improve the distance, and bad changes are lost in the search for improvement. The increase in track records continue to advance, sometimes slowly and sometimes with quite dramatic improvement. To look ahead and anticipate what records will be 10 years from now in 1975 stretches the imagination. Ten years ago, one of my contemporaries, Parry O'Brien, had just broken the 60-foot shot put barrier and changed the technique and training regimen. Now our fine sophomore is making everyone think in terms of when do we go through the 70-foot mark. Randy's results in shot putting represent all of us in symbolizing our desire to improve on past performance.

The realignment of our football coaching staff this spring is a change intended to bring about an improved football season record. We have constantly sought to react to the importance of this vehicle of public image building. This school deserves to field a winning team. Gene Stallings and Hank Foldberg are in harness to do just that.

One item of importance to each of us Aggies and to our school in pursuit of excellence is the Aggie image in the eyes of other Texans and people we contact in student, business, and personal life. Our intense school loyalty and devotion to one another as Aggies has made other people envious to the point of continuously circulating what must be called "Aggie Jokes." Perhaps we should be proud of this interest by others, but it has been a source of agitation to me since the day I entered here as a freshman. Just as the Texan image has been ridiculed all over the world as oil rich, uncultured, and blustering, we as Aggies have had more than our share of being the target of those people who lack the feeling of deep attachment to school that is the heart and spirit of this university. The Spirit of Aggieland is an affirmative stature as opposed to the negative drive of others that seek to rise by ridicule or belittling our allegiance. However, we need to be aware that our reactions to this prompting is a test of our right to stand firm in loyalty but with an open mind to listen to improvements or help from unexpected directions. The Aggie image that we promote must back up, in action, those goals of excellence we have set for ourselves. People of Texas must be able to feel uniformly proud of our students, our graduates and our continuing program of teaching and research. The continued success of our school is dependent on the support of not only former students, but on our being able to continually convince the taxpayers of Texas that the school we have here deserves their continued and increased financial and moral support.

As we honor today the deeds and ideals of those early Texans that sacrificed for us at San Jacinto, and to memorialize those Aggies who have died during this past year, let each of us prepare ourselves to meet changes required to meet today's changing world and to be ourselves the initiators of change to improve our image, our school and our State of Texas.

# Penrose B. Metcalfe '16

*1966—System Administration Building Lawn*

Penrose B. Metcalfe '16.
Photo from editor's
collection.

Penrose Blakely Metcalfe was born November 24, 1893, on the XQZ Ranch, operated by his father, Charles B. Metcalfe, a rancher and state legislator. He graduated with honors from San Angelo schools and entered A&M in 1912. He majored in animal husbandry, graduating in 1916 with a BS degree in agriculture. He saw service in World War I, enlisting in the aviation section of the US Army Signal Corps in 1917. He became a pilot in 1918 and was discharged from the service as a captain in the Army Air Corps.

A dedicated public servant, Metcalfe served five years as a member of the Tom Green County school board, eight years as a member of the Texas House of Representatives, and eight years as a member of the Texas Senate. He spoke frequently before youth farm organizations throughout the state. He was interested in young people and their problems and advancement and helped a great many of them obtain their education.

Metcalfe died in March 1970.

## Never, Never, Never Die*

I had definitely intended to keep my remarks completely free from any personal references, for many reasons, but the wonderful introduction just given me by President Rudder has sort of shaken me up a little and certainly stirred my heart. I have a lot of Irish in me, which sometimes causes me to become a little emotional.

*Speech title derived by editor from speech contents

It is true that I have for a very long time taken especial interest in young people. Next week my 1916 Class at A&M will celebrate, on this campus, its 50th anniversary—that's a lot of years!

Through all this half-century, I have kept closely in touch with A&M and pretty well informed as what the overall picture here really was. I have done this largely through the students, for I consider their attitudes and reactions the ultimate test of the success of this—or any other—educational institution.

Right now there are young men, whom I have known ever since they were boys, in every class here; in the graduate school, on the faculty and on the administrative staff right on up to and including the one who has just introduced me, your splendid president, Earl Rudder.

I have shared their problems and ambitions, their joys and sorrows, and sometimes may have even helped some of them a little. Although most of them are mature men now, they are still the same youngsters to me—in fact they will always remain my very own boys in whom I am well pleased.

When members of your Student Senate called and wrote me that the Student Body wanted me to make a talk here this evening, I was greatly pleased and felt so highly honored at the invitation that I accepted without the slightest delay—before they had time to back out! Since then, I have given a lot of thought and study to A&M Musters, their history, what they signify and what their origin was, in order that I might have something to say that would be appropriate to this important and revered occasion.

Association of Former Students President Royce Wisenbaker '39 has made a highly interesting and informative discussion of the written and factual history of the Muster, and there is no need for me to comment on this phase further.

In my studies and research, it quickly became apparent that only a definite and strong cause could have brought into being a tradition which has endured so strikingly and which has increased each year in scope and widespread participation.

I realized it was bound to rest on a fundamentally sound basis to have developed the importance it rightly occupies, wherever Aggies are together on this day each year.

It then occurred to me that it might be a fruitful and sensible idea to look into what lay far behind the history of its founding.

As I moved along in this quest, I more and more had the feeling that those loyal cadets in 1903, aided and encouraged by a wise faculty and administration, must have had an impulsion further than a gathering just to honor the heroes of the Battle of San Jacinto and our own departed Aggies, worthy as such an immediate objective undoubtedly was.

That whatever inspired those young men in 1903 must have been some force or belief—perhaps intangible—which had been principally acquired when they became students at A&M—but which became great and strong and inherent in their characters and hearts. That once one could determine just what this motivation was, the genesis of the Muster was bound to be clear and cogent.

As the first Muster started out to honor primarily the heroes of San Jacinto, I was impressed with an idea that perhaps a brief review of how conditions were in Texas at that time [1836] and immediately precedent thereto, might be helpful in finding a solution of my search.

In those days Texas was a strange land. It was crushed by war and its people had very little money, no reservoir of clothing or food, poverty, and very few of the necessary munitions of war.

It was a land of turmoil and travail when the new Republic was born. But it still was a land which had its dreams.

Certainly many of the founders were originally actuated by selfish purposes, by a desire for new lands they might acquire and own; some were looking for financial gain and others sought political power.

Their principal assets were a courageous people and a deep-seated hope for liberty and safety, and a land to live in which had a government responsive to the people.

But when it became evident their common welfare was in danger, they laid aside their personal and selfish motives promptly and without restraint.

They rose up all over Texas, willing and ready, if need be, to give up their lands, their livestock, their crops and all their worldly goods in order to secure that liberty which they valued more than all they had built or owned, and even their precious lives.

We Texans all recall, with much satisfaction and pride, that the War for Texas Independence was not a war fought by the people of Texas against the people of Mexico. Quite the contrary. It was a war fought by a civilian army of the sovereign, independent people of Texas, against the professional, hired forces of a harsh military dictator. And, in those gallant non-professional forces of Texas, there were numerous fearless men who were citizens of Mexico, or of Mexican descent, who bravely fought—and many of whom gave their lives—side by side with the rest of the Texans.

The Texas revolutionaries had another asset—and this, to my way of thinking, was the most important and enduring of them all. This was the belief that their individual lives were of lesser overall importance than the securing and establishing, beyond any revocation, of the right of liberty and freedom for their fellow men.

In their modest and simple way, they honestly and sincerely subscribed to that great truth which had been set out more than two thousand years ago, that: "Greater love hath no man than this, that a man lay down his life for his friends."

This was one of the guiding precepts of the heroes who made the sacrifices which brought the Republic of Texas into being. Our Texas way of life—in fact that of all America—is founded on the principle of a love for our fellows, and the hope and desire that they will always be free to enjoy their lives, liberty and the pursuit of happiness.

Only through the guidance of such a belief, coupled with the courage and determination to carry it through without stint or termination, could the noble aims of those great and farsighted people have ever been achieved.

Of course it is self-evident that conditions today are vastly different from what they were in 1836. Then it was only Texas that was in a state of uncertainty and insecurity.

Today it is the entire world that is in turmoil and confusion.

A short time ago I read, with much pride and approval, accounts of the recent telegram signed by thousands of you students here and sent to the President of the United States, supporting America's unselfish and difficult efforts in Viet Nam to secure a decent and free way of life for those long-suffering people.

This was a typical Aggie reaction and ran true to form. It also indicated that you realistically and correctly evaluate the global situation of today. And that you—awesome as the facts may be—recognize that America alone in the world, has the power, and the will, and the faith to cope with all that confronts us, and maintain some balance and hope in world affairs. Any pull-back, however slight, can only precipitate more trouble, more wars, and eventually cost more lives of young Americans.

Of course we neither sought, nor like, nor desire this fearful responsibility. Now that it is here we cannot but face up to it and try to grin and bear it, until such time as peace can be won and all the peoples of this earth can live without fear of destruction.

When this institution was established and first opened its doors nearly a century ago, it was inevitable that the sound and lofty principles upon which Texas was founded would be carried into this school, and thence into the lives and sentiments of all the students here.

Pursuant to its destiny, throughout close to one hundred years of existence, years of growth and service, Texas A&M has been the development ground for a number of worthy and desirable traditions. Unquestionably one of the very finest and most sacred of these is that of the Muster.

The observances of the Muster each year, all over the world, have served as a renewal and reaffirmation of one more tradition which I consider is the greatest tradition of all. This is the existence here, ever since A&M was born, of an inherent, and intense, and all-pervading loyalty of students for their country, for their school, and a never-failing love for their fellows.

> Here the free spirit of mankind at length
> Throws its last fetters off; and who shall place
> A limit to the giant's unchained strength,
> Or curb his swiftness in the forward race?
> [from William Cullen Bryant's "The Ages"]

This well-nigh sacred tradition is a priceless legacy, left to us by those of our fellows who have gone on before and whose memory we honor here today. It will always remain vibrant and strong because it is enshrined in the minds and hearts of all Aggies everywhere. And, thanks be to our Maker—it can never, never, never die.

# Maj. Gen. Raymond L. Murray '35
## *1967—System Administration Building Lawn*

Maj. Gen. Raymond L. Murray '35. Photo from editor's collection.

Raymond Leroy Murray was born on January 30, 1913, in Los Angeles, California. At Texas A&M he lettered in basketball, was an All Southwest Conference end in football, and was a regimental commander in the Corps of Cadets.

After being commissioned following graduation, he served several years in China during the Sino-Japanese War and a year in Iceland. As a major, Murray won the Silver Star and a promotion to lieutenant colonel commanding the 2nd Battalion, 6th Marines, at Guadalcanal. His second Silver Star came less than a year later leading the 2nd Battalion at Tarawa. Six months after that, he received the Navy Cross for directing the initial assault on Saipan despite serious wounds. Communications specialist Leon Uris later used his commander to model the character "Highpockets" Huxley in his acclaimed novel *Battle Cry*, which was made into a movie.

Following World War II, Murray served in numerous Marine Corps training commands and as commanding officer of the 3rd Marines and executive officer of the 5th Marines. As commander of the 5th Marine Regiment in Korea, he earned his third and fourth Silver Stars and the Legion of Merit during action in August and September 1950. He was awarded the Distinguished Service Cross for extraordinary heroism during the 1st Division's historic breakout at the Chosin Reservoir, and two days later won his second Navy Cross and a promotion to colonel for leading his depleted and exhausted men in defending key resources before launching a counterattack that decimated enemy forces.

After directing Marine Corps training, he was promoted to brigadier general and served in Okinawa and as commanding general of the Marine Corps base at Camp Pendleton, California, and the Marine Corps Recruiting Depot at Parris Island, South Carolina. After promotion to major general he was inspector general of the Marine Corps and assistant chief of staff, G-3, at Headquarters Marine Corps before his final tour as deputy commander of III Marine Amphibious Force in the Far East. He retired August 1, 1968, and was inducted into the Corps of Cadets Hall of Honor in 1999. Murray died on Veteran's Day, November 11, 2004, shortly before a sixty-foot flagpole was dedicated in his honor at a bridge in Oceanside, California, that had been named for him the previous year.

## Knowledgeable, Dedicated Leadership*

This is a proud moment for me. Thirty-two years ago, I left this campus and became a second lieutenant in the United States Marine Corps. Because our installations are located principally on the Atlantic and Pacific coasts, it has not been convenient for me to return to the campus except at occasional times when I was en route from one coast to the other. In spite of the long periods between my visits, however, I have felt close to the school because of the many A&M men I have met and been associated with through the years. In fact, of the eight Aggies who entered the Marine Corps in 1935 and 1936, four are Major Generals and still on active duty. Two others have retired within the past three years.

A&M, as you are aware, has provided leadership in our armed forces for all the years of its existence, and the point I wish to make to you today is that now and into the future, the need will continue to exist for the leadership that our school so ably provides.

When I was five years old, American doughboys, among whom were many Aggies, helped bring to an end the terrible war that had devastated parts of Europe. The armistice of 1918 ended the war that had been fought "to make the world safe for democracy." It was hailed as the

---

*Speech title derived by editor from speech contents

"war to end all wars." For insurance, good men established the League of Nations.

I grew up during the peaceful years of America in the 1920s and 1930s. Of course there were a few minor disturbances in the world during those years of "peace." The Greco-Turkish War of the '20s left us the present bitter legacy of Cyprus.

While I was an Aggie like you, fighting the battle of the books here at College Station, US Marines fought skirmishes and rebuilt a couple of nations in the Caribbean. The year I graduated and was commissioned, Mussolini's legions invaded Ethiopia. With guns, tanks, and planes, Japan was persuading China to become a member of "the greater East-Asia co-prosperity sphere," while Russia and Finland fought in the ice and snow of the Arctic Circle.

Nazi storm troopers occupied the Ruhr Valley, annexed Czechoslovakia's Sudetenland, and then swept into Poland. Twenty years after the Armistice, a second world war to end all wars and make the world safe for democracy had begun. It proved to be more widespread and more devastating than had the first world war, or any other war in the history of mankind.

The equivalent of a division of Aggies sacrificed personal comfort and desire, for duty and country, and led the American G.I.s—soldiers, sailors, and Marines to victory. And many of those whom we honor today made the supreme sacrifice in that war.

In the aftermath of Hiroshima and Nagasaki, the awesome weapons created by the technology of our modern civilization caused reasonable men to be certain that war had become too horrible for any civilized nation to contemplate waging again.

These reasonable men established the war-crimes tribunals and a United Nations peace-keeping organization to prevent that dread horseman of the apocalypse from ever again riding forth to scourge our civilization. But the echoes still reverberated from the bells that heralded the dawn of peace, and the formal treaties ending World War II had not yet been signed by civilized men, when armed conflict raged in Greece, the cradle of western civilization: and in Jerusalem, where the Prince of Peace walked.

Shortly thereafter, Aggies once again led and bled when violence shattered the morning calm of Korea. And more names were added to our memorial Muster. Even today Korea knows not peace, only an uneasy peace.

Since that truce was enacted in Indo-China, Egypt, Indonesia, Hungary, Pakistan, Malaysia, Tibet, Iraq, West Iran, the Congo, and South Vietnam, the hounds of war have been unleashed. From east to west, back and forth across the earth, they have ravaged the land, and people have died defending their homes, their freedoms, and their families. Even today, as we honor our fallen heroes, who gave their lives so that we might live in freedom, war boils in Vietnam, and simmers in a dozen other places.

I hope I have made it clear that, in my lifetime, although reasonable men and powerful nations have earnestly sought peace and the means for preserving it, even the most Christian nations, with the most advanced technology of our modern civilization, have become embroiled in war. And it seems fairly certain, given the strains and pressures that now exist in the world, that in our lifetime, and for the foreseeable future, although we dream of and hope for peace, war will be the sober reality.

You, and your sons after you, will be called upon to lead your fellow Americans as warriors. More than two thousand years ago, Aristotle observed that all that was necessary for evil to triumph was for good men to do nothing. One may also logically assume that until the millennium when all strong warriors are good men, it behooves all good men to be strong warriors.

The holding of this Muster is overwhelming evidence of the unmeasurable contribution which Texas Aggies have made as good men and as strong warriors, so that you and I could continue to enjoy the freedom and the way of life that they had known. And their mantle of responsibility and leadership has now descended upon your shoulders. I therefore urge you to accept the challenge eagerly and to prepare for it to the utmost of your ability. For the task of the leader is becoming increasingly harder and more complex. When I took the oath of a second lieutenant of Marines in 1935, our recruiters could be highly selective in the few recruits they accepted—most were high school graduates and many had attended college. The private first class was an experienced, tested and proven veteran, relatively mature in age and skilled in the profession of arms. Usually he was the product of a stable home where God and country were synonymous with virtue. The weapons and tactics we employed were relatively simple. Our rifles were single shot, bolt-action Springfield 03's. We could direct air strikes and naval gunfire by semaphore flags when our radios failed. Our enemies in World War II and Korea were readily identifiable: they wore uniforms and deployed on the battlefield in the conventional manner.

But those of you who will become lieutenants in these times must cope with leadership problems which my generation of lieutenants never imagined. It has been predicted that the Vietnam War may last for several more years, and many of you will see duty there. Many of your troopers may be high school dropouts, from broken homes, who have grown up in an atmosphere where patriotism is embarrassing, authority resented and ridiculed, and the draft is something to dodge.

It will be incumbent upon you to lead these men so that they can operate computer-directed missiles, maintain the radars which drop bombs from supersonic jets on unseen targets, or simply shoot automatic M-16's with fire discipline so that your ammunition resupply does not become an insurmountable logistics burden at a critical moment.

You will have to engage and destroy an enemy who fires from ambush and then disappears in the jungle, while you avoid accidentally destroying the lives and property of innocent people whom this enemy hides among and uses for a shield.

You must not only fight in this environment but you must also help to rescue a primitive, illiterate people from economic, social, and political chaos, literally building them into a nation. The French were there a hundred years and they failed. Indeed the task sometimes seems impossible.

But we must try. There is no alternative if you wish your children and grandchildren to enjoy the free air and precious rights which we have taken for granted. If we fail, how long can our nation endure, where can we find liberty and justice, surrounded by totalitarian enslavement?

Already it is only a rowboat ride away from Key West, and there are mighty efforts to spread it. Nearly a billion communists are being indoctrinated and committed to bring about our downfall. Perhaps among our own people, too, some of the manifestos and Mao Tse Tung should be required reading, for he has written down the plan and the strategy. His lieutenants, or minions, must slavishly obey his divine precepts.

No one has dictated to you, and no one will, what your courses of action must be. Your privilege, your responsibility, your sacred trust as free men is to devise, judge, invent, accept or reject, build upon the wisdom, the contributions, of all those good men who have gone before you. It is now your task to perpetuate and make work the noble experiment of mankind begun in our land in 1775. And it will be your obligation to extend the fruits of your experience to those who need and seek them.

As far as the mind's eye can peer into the future, your country, and the world, will need the courage, the skill, and the dedicated leadership of good men who are strong warriors. The need has never before been more critical nor the challenge more demanding.

I have spoken of the continuing need for military leadership. Since the military is my profession, I am vitally interested in the military leadership of the future.

The requirement for civilian leadership is no less compelling. I am seriously disturbed about certain manifestations that I see in our country. The apparent growing disregard of respect for the law, the apparent growing dependence of people in all walks of life on government and its agencies to take care of them. The apparent diminution of desire on the part of individuals to make their own mark in the world.

I can understand the confusion and concern of people who feel overcome by the increasing complexity of life, but if we are to remain a free and independent nation; if we are to continue to advance and grow, we must develop leaders who have their feet on the ground and who can by their words and actions inspire others to return to the virtues which have made our nation great, leaders who can explain and make sense out of the complexities that face us.

Those of you who are not in the military program have an equally important responsibility to prepare yourself for leadership of the civilian community. No matter how competent and dedicated our military leaders are, the battle is lost if there is not an equal capability and determination in the civilian community.

You face problems greater than any in our history. The increasing mechanization of our society; the headlong increase in scientific knowledge; the social problems that refuse any longer to remain under the rug, out of sight.

Yes, knowledgeable, dedicated leadership is needed more than any other time in the history of our nation.

I am confident that history and this memorial Muster will bear me out, that you and the Texas Aggies who follow you will prove equal to the compelling task. And the spirits of those we honor today will be with you to sustain you in your darkest hours, and to applaud your successes.

They had their day of gallantry and victory, but now, truly, the eyes of Texas and the nation are upon you.

# Maj. Gen. Wood B. Kyle '36
## 1968—System Administration Building Lawn

Maj. Gen. Wood B. Kyle '36. Photo from editor's collection.

Wood Barbee Kyle was born March 3, 1915, in Pecos, Texas. After graduating from Texas A&M with honors, he resigned a commission in the US Army Infantry to accept appointment as a Marine second lieutenant. His first overseas assignment was in Shanghai, China, with the 6th Marines. After an assignment aboard the USS *Lexington*, he joined the 2nd Marines as a captain and was promoted to major a month after heading across the Pacific in July 1942.

Assuming command of the 1st Battalion when his commander was wounded at Guadalcanal, Kyle refused evacuation for his own wounds. He was awarded the Silver Star in that battle, and he earned a second one for personally leading an attack on the heavily defended central sector of Tarawa in November 1943. A month later, he was promoted to lieutenant colonel and participated in the invasions of Saipan and Tinian.

After teaching at the Command and General Staff School, Kyle served with Fleet Marine Force Pacific and at Headquarters Marine Corps where he was promoted to colonel. He commanded the 4th Marines in Kaneohe Bay, Hawaii; headed the Tactics Branch for the Marine Corps Landing Force Development Center; and was chief of Joint Plans Branch in Europe from 1954 to 1961.

Promoted to brigadier general, Kyle commanded Fleet Marine Force, Atlantic, before returning to Marine headquarters in 1963 to become deputy chief of staff (research and development). In 1966 he became a major general and was given command of the 3rd Marine Division in Vietnam, where he earned the Navy Distinguished Service Medal. A year later, as commanding general of the 5th Marine Division, Fleet

Marine Force at Camp Pendleton, California, he received the Legion of Merit. Kyle retired in May 1968 after thirty-two years of active duty and worked for FJM Corporation for several years. He died October 25, 2000.

## Aggie Marine Corps Generals*

President Rudder, Ladies and Gentlemen:

It has certainly been several years since I was last privileged to visit Texas A&M. Certainly, this is not by choice, since this great university has been a part of my life and my family's life since before the turn of the century. My father graduated from Texas A&M in 1898. My uncle E. J. Kyle graduated in 1900 and, a few years later, after completing post-graduate work, returned as a professor. Later he was to serve this university (then college) as Dean of Agriculture for many years. As Chairman of the Athletic Council, he was principal fund-raiser for the construction of Kyle Field, which was later named in his honor. My brother graduated here in 1934; also, numerous cousins have attended this university over the years.

This is my 32nd Muster since graduation in 1936. Looking back over those years I count that ten of these Musters have been outside the United States—various countries in the Pacific, Southeast Asia, and Europe. I mention this not because it is important that I as an individual have spent these years overseas, but because it is typical of the life of A&M men who have made the military service their career. And, in a broader sense, it is indicative of the national policy of our country over these years.

Since the end of World War II over twenty years ago, our country and our countrymen have worked, fought, bled and died to stem the spread of communism from its bases in Russia and China to other areas of the world. It has involved us in two major wars, numerous minor actions such as Lebanon and Santo Domingo, and "show of force" and other operations that are too numerous to even mention.

---

*Speech title derived by editor from speech contents

This has been the greatest campaign ever waged by any nation. Its scope has been so vast that only our country, the greatest country ever to exist on this earth, could have supported it over these many years. Only those who have lived through this period and have been intimately associated with this effort are fully aware of its impact on almost all the nations of our world. It will be many years before a complete history is possible—much of the information is still classified and will remain so for several years hence. On the whole, this has been a successful campaign. There have been many reverses, but they do not compare in importance to our successes.

We are now engaged in the second great war of this protracted conflict that commenced almost a quarter century ago. So much time has passed that many of our senior citizens have lost sight of the basic purpose of this campaign, the same purpose that led to our military presence in South Vietnam today. Many of you were not even born when we started this crusade.

Secretary of State Dean Rusk, when he accompanied the president on his trip to Vietnam last year, told the assembled general officers that our reason for being in Vietnam was simply to stop the spread of communist control to all of Southeast Asia. It is just as simple as that and needs no embellishment.

This is the same basic objective that our nation has pursued for over twenty years. We have done the same in Europe, the Middle East, Central and South America, the Caribbean, and in Korea. The only difference is the place—now it is Southeast Asia and we have become involved in war with a determined enemy who will not give up.

As the Vietnam War has dragged on, we find an increasing bitterness and opposition to our role, both within our country and by some life-long friends abroad. Many of these dissenters are obviously irresponsible people, but on the other hand there are intelligent, responsible citizens in positions of great trust and importance who bitterly oppose the US involvement in Vietnam. There are major segments of the national news media who have abandoned their legitimate mission of reporting the news and now devote their major effort to discrediting our government, our military services, and our chief executive for our actions in Vietnam. The dissension and bitterness in our country has grown to the point where it is the single greatest issue confronting our government. I am sure that many of you, the same as I, are wondering just what is happening to our country. The answers are not readily apparent.

But, if you accept the thesis that today we are fighting to stop the spread of communism, then you must remember that this global conflict started over twenty years ago. That is a long, long fight. It has cost us untold millions of dollars and the lives of thousands of our men. In its earliest days, the threat was more apparent since it involved Western Europe, an area close to us in many ways. At other times it was in our own hemisphere and this was too close to home for comfort. As the conflict spread to the remote areas of Asia, the reasons for our involvement became less clear and consequently received less support by our people. You probably recall that the war in Korea was most unpopular in this country.

It appears that many of our people have grown weary of this long conflict and are no longer willing to fight to contain communism. True, many of them honestly believe that it is no longer a threat to our security. Of course, everyone has a right to his own opinions, but the cry we hear most often is that this war is illegal and immoral. If that is true, then everything we have done since World War II to save the free world is also illegal and immoral. I would hate to be the one who told all the widows who have lost their husbands, all the mothers and fathers who lost their sons, all the children who lost their fathers, that they died in vain while engaged in illegal and immoral acts. I would hate to think that the years I have spent away from my family on foreign shores, the days on the battlefield, have all been in vain.

But, we will not settle this issue today and, in fact, not in the near future. People will believe what they believe and many will preach their beliefs. We will not stop them because that is the way of our great country. That is why the Pilgrims came to this land. I just hope that those who preach dissent will remember that the right to preach dissent does not exist under a communist regime. I cannot believe that it is illegal and immoral to fight for the rights that we all enjoy.

Texas A&M men have played a great role in this long campaign. It is difficult to gather accurate statistics; but, we do know that over the years A&M has provided more leaders for our armed forces than any other school, exclusive of the military academies. At certain times it has provided even more.

For instance: In World War II there were more graduates of Texas A&M serving as officers in the US Army than there were graduates from West Point. Remember that at this time the air force was a part of the Army.

Since 1960, Texas A&M has produced more than 3,000 officers for active duty in the armed forces: 2,000 Army, 1,000 Air Force, 40 Navy and 80 Marines. We do not know for sure how many of these are currently serving in Vietnam, but it is probably around 700.

We can account for 80 graduates of Texas A&M who have reached the general officer or flag officer rank. I suspect there are more than that.

Let me mention just a few of these. In 1935, there were four graduates of Texas A&M commissioned in the Marine Corps. Despite the fact that there is less than a 5% chance that a second lieutenant will reach general officer rank, three of these officers did it. Odell Conoley, known as "Dog Eye" Conoley here, reached the rank of brigadier general and retired a few years ago. Ray Murray, member of the infantry here, is now a major general. Until recently he served as the Deputy Commander of III Marine Amphibious Force, the Marine Corps command in Vietnam. He was evacuated because of illness about a month ago and is now well on the way to recovery. Bruno Hochmuth, member of the cavalry, reached the rank of major general. In March 1967, he relieved me as Commanding General of the 3rd Marine Division in Vietnam. Until recently this division's area of responsibility was the two northern provinces of South Vietnam, including the DMZ. Bruno performed in his usual outstanding manner until November 14, 1967, when his helicopter was shot down just north of the city of Hue. He died in the crash.

In 1936, again there were four graduates who entered the Marine Corps. This was my class, and we were not quite as fortunate as '35. Hollis Mustain, member of the cavalry, was killed in action as a lieutenant colonel while commanding an infantry battalion in Iwo Jima. Ed Hamilton, member of the engineers, was seriously wounded in action on the island of Bouga[i]nville in World War II. He was subsequently retired for physical disability in the rank of lieutenant colonel. Ormond Simpson, member of the band (infantry), is now a major general commanding the Marine Corps Recruit Depot, Parris Island, S.C. I am the fourth member of that class.

I do not know the officers of the other services so well, but let me mention a few: those who reached the top rank (four stars) in the Army: General George H. Beverly, Class of '19; General Jerome J. Waters, Class of '13.

In the US Air Force: General O. P. Weyland, Class of '23, retired after commanding the Tactical Air Command, US Air Force; General Bernard A. Schriever, Class of '31, following a distinguished career in the development of missile systems of the nation's space program, retired after commanding the Air Force Systems Command.

Needless to say, there are thousands of others who have left this great university to assume positions of leadership and responsibility in our armed forces and other agencies of our government.

It would be impossible to even attempt an assessment of the value of this great institution to our nation's way of life.

I do know that in my area (the military) the reputation of Texas A&M is known far and wide. Simply stated, it is the best—and you can be sure of that.

It has been an honor and a privilege for me to attend this university and to be invited back here today.

# Mayo J. Thompson '41
*1969—System Administration Building Lawn*

Mayo J. Thompson '41.
Photo from editor's
collection.

Mayo Joseph Thompson was born May 12, 1919, in Houston. He received his BS degree in economics from Texas A&M in 1941. While at A&M, Thompson debated throughout the Southwest Conference, directed Aggie Tau News, and was awarded "best drilled" in his battery. After graduation, he entered the US Army and served with the 7th Infantry in World War II in the Pacific theater of operations. He retired from the Texas National Guard as a colonel in 1958.

In 1949 he received his LLB degree from South Texas College of Law and served as adjunct professor there. He entered private practice and became a noted specialist in admiralty law. In 1973 he was confirmed by the US Senate as a commissioner of the Federal Trade Commission. In 1975 he joined the firm of Akin, Gump, Strauss, Hauer, and Feld as a senior partner and retired in 1980.

Thompson participated in the founding of A&M's Center for Education and Research in Free Enterprise and was recognized nationally as "Free Enterprise Man of the Year" in 1976. He also served on the board of Gifford-Hill and Co.

Thompson spoke at Texas A&M commencement exercises in 1973, was Centennial Year president of the Association of Former Students in 1976, and served on the board of the Aggie Club (now known as the 12th Man Foundation). In 1979 the Texas Aggie Bar Association named him Aggie Attorney of the Year. For three years he was on Board of Visitors of Texas A&M University at Galveston.

He was a founding member of Texas A&M's President's Endowed Scholars program and provided valuable support for A&M's Corps of

Cadets and A&M's renowned Student Conference on National Affairs (SCONA). He was named a Texas A&M University Distinguished Alumnus in 1980. Thompson died July 15, 2007.

## "Texas A&M—An Island of Light"

The Spirit of Liberty began the pulse beat of this great nation 180 years ago when a few men perceived that Government could not survive by human judgment alone.

This same Spirit of Liberty began the pulse beat of this State of Texas, then a nation, when some 130 years ago, again, a few men perceived that government could not survive by human judgment alone.

Each of these great adventures marked its genesis with a constitution and laws. These constitutions were a product of human experience, not of abstract reason. Long before 1787 and 1836, men craved some means of assurance that their resort to Life, Liberty and the Pursuit of Happiness would not turn upon man's subjective concepts.

These great writings provide us with documentary evidence of man's emergence toward government by the consent of the governed, and by the rule of law.

It is then fair to say that within the background of the two Constitutional Conventions that framed these great writings is actually the entire history of man's search for an adequate safeguard against abusive government, either for or in behalf of a majority or a minority. We are truly a society who have contracted with the rule of law.

Violation of law may occur for various reasons. Some people may feel that the law is unjust, such as our modern students of civil disobedience sometimes reason, or others disobey it because they have not learned to live within it. In either case, disobedience, civil or criminal, is brought about simply because people have not been taught to respect and cherish the rule of law.

Broadly speaking, the chief reliance of law in a democracy is the habit of popular respect for law.

Any government is only worth having as long as it can openly tolerate dissent and free channels of expression. Once we fear the extremes of associations or speech, then we acknowledge the weakness of our bond.

However, disobedience is a long step from dissent. Civil disobedience involves a deliberate and punishable breach of legal duty. No matter what it is called or how it is justified or rationalized, civil disobedience demeans democracy's processes of social change and eventually destroys democracy itself. Civil disobedience is a counsel of despair and defeat, and is altogether undemocratic.

Of course, only the most bigoted chauvinist would claim that America is without some glaring faults, but there has never been a Utopian society on earth and there never will be unless human nature is remade.

Since inequities will mar even the best-framed democracies, the injustice rationale would allow a free right of civil resistance to be available always as a short cut alternative to the democratic way of petition, debate and assembly. The lesson of history is that civil insurgency spawns far more injustices than it removes.

Our laws guarantee wide opportunities to use mass meetings, public parades and organized demonstrations to stimulate sentiment, to dramatize issues, and to cause change. However, the rights of free expression cannot be mere force cloaked in the garb of free speech.

Experience demonstrates that it is not a far step from what to many seems to be the earnest, honest, patriotic, kind-spirited multitude of today, to the fanatical, threatening, lawless mob of tomorrow. And the crowds that press in the streets for noble goals today can be supplanted tomorrow by street mobs pressuring for precisely opposite ends, and herein lies the danger.

Civil disobedience is an assault on our democratic society, an affront to our legal order and an attack on our Constitutional Government. To indulge civil disobedience is to invite anarchy.

The greatest danger in condoning civil disobedience as a permissible strategy for hastening change is that it undermines our democratic processes. To adopt the techniques of civil disobedience is to assume that representative government does not work.

There is no man who is above the law, and there is no man who has a right to break the law. Civil disobedience is not above the law, but against the law. When the civil disobedient disobeys one law, he invariably subverts all law. When the civil disobedient says that he is above the law, he is saying that democracy is beneath him. His disobedience shows a distrust for the democratic system.

Now or never law must assert its supremacy. At this high tide in human events, it must for today, and for posterity, be established that at all costs domestic disorder and violence will not be further tolerated; that the shameful abuse of the Constitutional rights of the peaceful majority by the shameless, dissonant, and vicious will no longer be countenanced; and that this nation, under God, shall be governed by law.

It is, of course, within the knowledge of all here today that civil disobedience is rampant in this great land of ours. There is virtually a flood tide of riot, commotion, indulgence, an air of permissiveness, and most surely we will reap the whirlwind—unless a new day dawns. Today it seems that anything self-pleasing is acceptable, and old ways or traditions of a moralistic or legalistic nature are no longer the main guidelines. We would do well to remember that the moral order of good and evil always transcends man's made-for-the-moment plans.

A government or a society is only as strong as the moral fiber of its people. I submit that it is time to pause and take inventory of where we are and where we are heading. It can safely be said that we have been cast adrift from our traditional moorings and no one is immune from this storm and bewilderment that engulfs us today.

This government and these people cannot long retain their vigor without resolve to build anew on a framework of meaningful principles to serve as guidelines for the future. If we do not, we will continue in interminable confusion, aimlessly drifting in a sea of uncertainty. It is against this somewhat awesome and ominous backdrop that we meet here today to commemorate a great event in history and celebrate this great University's grand Muster.

Nothing that we say or do here today will or can in any way alter one fact or circumstance that preceded our assembling here on such an auspicious occasion, but let me quickly add that the resolve that we take with us today as we depart can very much affect the facts and circumstances of the future.

As we stand here and reflect upon this school's outstanding administration and faculty, and as we look out on this sea of bright, young

American manhood, we veritably swell with pride over the conduct and example that have been demonstrated by all those connected with Texas A&M. It makes me proud to say, "I am a Texas Aggie."

Truly, it can be said that this school, on account of her administration, faculty, and student body, is an island of light.

This school, steeped in custom and tradition as it is, is the envy of all who witness its role in the scheme of things today, Aggie jokes notwithstanding. Since we are all beneficiaries of such a great legacy from this school, it is incumbent upon us to bear faithful witness and fidelity to her in all our days and years. It is mandatory that we do nothing to bring her shame. If we are to merit the splendid title, "Texas Aggie," we must constantly keep uppermost in our minds that we all are ambassadors, representing not only ourselves in that which we say or do, but representing another, Texas A&M.

In order that we might be best prepared to meet this obligation, there must be a plan and purpose that will fit us all. In this connection, I see a clear way.

First of all, and I wish to emphasize—first of all—we must set and keep our spiritual nature in order. Being first in order of importance, it can be and often is somewhat difficult to do. Especially is this true where the how to do it is obscure. The how has been so complicated by so many that often a simple solution offered by one is rejected out of hand as unworkable because it is so easy and simple. We must begin with being rightly related to God. In my considered judgment, the best way to establish a right relationship with God is more than adequately explained in the Book of Books, the Bible. It should be read in its entirety. It is the only Book that I know that tells us where we came from, what we are to do while we are here, and where we are going when we depart this world. On page after page, we find promise after promise to the faithful. One of the greatest such promises is found in the Book of First Samuel. In that book can be found a dialogue between God and the Prophet Samuel. In the midst of this dialogue, the clear voice of God sounds down from the ramparts of Heaven, and He promises all men:

"He that honoreth me, him will I honor."

How simple this is, but how mighty and majestic. Be rightly related, always keeping in mind:

"He that honoreth me, him will I honor."

Another thing that we can do is work hard. Hard work purifies the soul. In doing this, we do not leave the impression with others, and most especially we do not delude ourselves, that we hold to the view that the world owes us a living. Honest work is its own reward, and this school has made it possible for thousands who have worked hard to attain high and important positions in every field of endeavor. The accomplishments of A&M men, when considered as a whole, is second to none. We need not be defensive about being a "Texas Aggie," but to the contrary, being one should serve to drive us on toward attaining honest and legitimate goals.

Next, I exhort you to always do right. There is much too much permissiveness today. This leads to error, miscalculation and singular failures. Be honest, forthright and candid in all your actions. I remind you that there is a right way and a wrong way. There is the truth and there is the lie. Always do right; it will please most, and confound the rest.

So frequently today we hear the expression that qualified persons should "become involved" and help solve the existing issues. There is ample opportunity for us to do this very thing. It goes without saying almost that we, assembled here today, constitute a significant number of this government's and this society's caretakers.

Such people of ability among us have an obligation to "become involved" and to want to improve the society in which we live. We should be willing to speak and to write and to educate. We should be willing to press for prompt corrective governmental action. We should try on every occasion to be actively engaged in the practice of daily life.

We should advance solutions, and those solutions must be intelligent, responsible and fair to all. We must not tinker with society, but do all that we can, using legitimate, democratic methods, to help restore a sense of balance and reason, which is so sadly lacking today. I exhort you all to become involved.

Your speaker did not bring with him much in the way of credentials, but I did bring with me a host of deep-seated convictions—not opinions, but convictions. I hasten to explain the difference. An opinion is something that we have. A conviction is something that has us. One of those convictions that has me is that there is no other group in this great state that can observe, without guile and without hypocrisy, an occasion such as this, one that commemorates and pays homage to our heroic forebears and our departed fellow Aggies. For this school teaches, and her sons learn, that it is not being "square" to be characterized as an institution of tradition. Indeed, one of the most cancerous conditions ailing modern society is the neglect of customs and traditions.

Therefore, all of us can be justifiably proud of the honor that we pay today to those great heroes of the past and our own departed brothers. It is a right and privilege as we do this that few other groups can claim.

A word of caution. Regrettably, outside the maroon and white circle, many of our fellow citizens, as they observe this school and her sons, are quick to criticize, quick to find fault, quick to revile, and quick to make light of us. Secretly, I believe that deep down in the innermost recesses of their minds and hearts they desire to be more like us, for they see in us something not seen in every man. This which they see is the spirit of camaraderie, the spirit of fidelity, and verily, this is the true spirit of the Muster.

Because we are constantly viewed from all sides, as we resolve this day to become rightly related, to work hard, to always do right, to become involved, seeing that we are compassed about with so great a cloud of witnesses, let us lay aside every weight which does so easily beset us, and let us run with patience the life that is set before us, looking unto God, the Author and Finisher of all things good.

Even as we do this, as ambassadors for Texas A&M, we shall also become living letters of the true Muster Spirit.

Thank you.

# Yale B. Griffis '30

## 1970—System Administration Building Lawn

Yale B. Griffis '30. Photo from editor's collection.

Yale Berger Griffis was born December 29, 1909, in Aguascalientes, Mexico. His accomplishments were numerous while a student at Texas A&M. He was named a Distinguished Student in both his junior and senior years; was a member of the Fightin' Texas Aggie Band for four years, the Ross Volunteers his junior and senior years, and the cross country team for four years; and served as associate editor of the 1930 *Battalion* and the 1930 *Longhorn* yearbook (now known as *The Aggieland*). He was selected one of eleven outstanding students in the Class of 1930.

Upon graduation from A&M, Griffis studied law at night at the Dallas Law School and graduated in 1936 as president of his law class. In 1942 he was called into active duty in the US Air Force as a second lieutenant serving at numerous air bases in the United States and overseas. After being released from active duty in March 1946, he continued as a reserve officer, retiring in 1969 with the rank of colonel. His many professional activities include membership in the American Bar Association, the Dallas Bar Association, the Texas Bar Association, and the Texas Trial Lawyers Association. Griffis died July 11, 1985.

## A Sacred Trust*

President Luedecke, Mrs. Rudder, members of the faculty, our distinguished guests today, members of the student body and ladies and gentlemen.

*Speech title derived by editor from speech contents

Perhaps one of the attributes of an Aggie is the ability to put things always in the proper perspective. When Buck Weirus [executive director of the Association of Former Students] called me and told me that I had been selected to be the speaker today, he said, "Now there's something I'm going to tell you." I said, "What is it?"

"Well, you were definitely not our first choice for the speaker."

And I said, "Ohhh?" And he said, "Yeah, we tried to get a man by the name of Richard Nixon and when he couldn't come, then we decided on you." And then I got a letter from Collier Watson, and Collier said, "Your part of the program is to make the talk and you can talk as long as you want to, just so you don't go over 20 minutes."

Some years ago I was attempting to make the Muster speech at Dallas, and Jimmy Flowers came to me and said beforehand, "Now, Yale, for heaven sakes, make it short and try to say something appropriate, will you?"

Forty years ago, a very happy young man was walking across the campus of Texas A&M. He was a very eager young man. And he was walking across the campus close to old Gathright Hall and President Walton's home. This young man had just graduated from Texas A&M and he thought as all of his classmates thought, and as all young college graduates have a right to think, that the world was his oyster and that life was like a ripe peach, waiting to fall into his outstretched hand. This was the day-of-days. This was the thrill-of-thrills. Life was beautiful and in the words of a song popular in that day, he was looking at the world through "rose-colored glasses." In this state of elation, the young man meets one of his cavalry instructors, Captain George Walker, and in telling Captain Walker goodbye the young man hears these words: "Griffis, just remember, there are many things much more important in life than the almighty dollar."

These words by that beloved instructor have come back again and again in the years that have gone in between. Our class, the Class of 1930, graduated in a world that was steeped in a deep Depression. If any of us were fortunate enough to secure a job that paid us $125 a month, we knew that we were fortunate beyond our fondest expectations. A great many of our best engineers, our best minds, our best students were sent home from such great industrial complexes as Westinghouse and General Electric simply because of the economy of the day. Somehow, someway we struggled through the fog of the Great Depression only to find that it lifted upon the scene of the Holocaust of World War II. In that great conflict—as in World War I, as in Korea, as in South Vietnam, and now as in Laos—A&M men were in the fore, giving freely of their everything. And it is in honor of those brave lads, who gave their all from the battlefields of France to steaming jungles of South Vietnam, that A&M men and women around the world are mustered this evening.

What is it?

What is it?

What is the basis for this deep love and this deep loyalty that A&M men have for this school and for each other? What are the well-springs of these human emotions that lie hidden and buried deep within our hearts, but which literally engulf us anew each time we see the campus and recall to one another the sublime days spent in school? What is it that makes us know beyond a shadow of a doubt that the very finest thing that can happen to any teenage boy or young lady is to become a freshman at Texas A&M? What is it that makes us spiritually proud of the fact that we're Texas Aggies simply because of the fact that we are Texas Aggies?

Well, maybe it was that first yell practice that was held on the steps of the YMCA. Col. E. V. Adams, when you and I heard the band play "Wildcat" and we heard J. D. Langford, our head yell leader that year, tell us, "You freshmen, if you are not satisfied with your lot at Texas A&M, you make it better." Or perhaps it was that course in fish chemistry we almost failed, and would have failed, if it had not been for that certain sophomore that we thought hazed us unmercifully, but yet would go to any lengths to see that we passed our courses. Or perhaps it was that first baseball game when they passed around that plug of chewing tobacco and for the next four or five hours our entire body was a brilliant shade of chartreuse. Or maybe it was the 1967 football team that lost the first four only to storm back and win the Southwest Conference crown undisputed. Or perhaps it was those nights when April rolled around and we were unceremoniously awakened out of a sound sleep about two o'clock in the morning with a five-gallon can—I see you remember—with a five-gallon GI can of cold water thrown all over us and two more above us and we fell all over ourselves and the cans running down the hall trying to get the guy we knew who did it. Or maybe it was Final Review when we told the boys goodbye and we wept together unashamedly.

Yes, perhaps it was these experiences and a hundred others like them that you could name that give us that love and that loyalty that we have for this school and for each other and which go to make up what others refer to as that fightin' Texas Aggie Spirit.

But these experiences, these emotions do not complete the picture. For while we were sharing them we were also sharing another emotion—less colorful, perhaps, but equally as impressive. For during our days, we were attending classes, taking the courses, going to labs and learning those subjects by which and through which we would one day earn our living. A&M is a sincere school. It is a sincere school dedicated to its purposes. It was founded to teach the agricultural and the mechanical arts and it has never deviated from that purpose. But, along with these, it has excelled in the humanities and in the arts and sciences, and has made a contribution unequaled by any other college or university in the love and service that its sons have given for their country. A&M men are proud, wonderfully proud, of the service and love of country that they have given, are now giving and continue to give. We do not think it's smart to burn a draft card. We do not think it's smug to go up to Canada. We do not think it's cool to participate in any protest marches. And we consider the welfare of this nation and no other nation and only this nation to be of paramount interest to us in its conduct of its world affairs.

While we were thus learning to use these economic tools, we were also learning a valid set of values. We learned to live with one another and to trust each other's word. We learned to separate the truth from the theory, the facts from the fallacies, and the essentials from the non-essentials. We learned to keep our minds open for whatever the future might bring. And we learned that the attributes of character are much more valuable than intellectual prowess or the ability to accumulate this world's goods. From those who have gone on before us we have learned that a great faith in God and sacrifice will always be held in the highest esteem.

These then are the legacies that have been bequeathed to us by those who have gone on before us. And we hold them now as a sacred trust for those who will someday take our places. It is our responsibility to justify the sacrifices of our friends, our comrades, our classmates and our schoolmates in whose honor we muster this day.

A fairly obscure poet by the name of Will Allen Dromgoole once wrote a poem called "The Bridge Builder," and it contains a thought that I would like to leave with you this afternoon.

## The Bridge Builder

An old man traveling a lone highway,
Came at the evening cold and gray,
To a chasm vast and deep and wide,
Through which was flowing a sullen tide.

The old man crossed in the twilight dim,
The sullen stream held no fears for him;
But he turned when safe on the other side,
And builded a bridge to span the tide.

"Old man," cried a fellow pilgrim near,
"You're wasting your time in building here.
Your journey will end with the closing day;
You never again will pass this way.

You have crossed the chasm deep and wide,
Why build you this bridge at even-tide?"
The builder lifted his old gray head:
"Good friend, in the path I have come," he said,
"There followeth after me today
A youth whose feet must pass this way.
This stream which has been as naught to me,
To that fair-haired youth may a pitfall be;

He, too, must cross in the twilight dim—
Good friend, I am building this bridge for him."

# Jack K. Williams

*1971—G. Rollie White Coliseum*

Jack K. Williams. Photo from editor's collection.

Jack Kenny Williams was born April 5, 1920, in Galax, Virginia. He earned a BA degree from Emory and Henry College and received MA and PhD degrees from Emory University. After being a high school teacher and principal for a couple of years, he served as a heavy weapons officer with the 4th Marine Division in the South Pacific, where he was wounded during World War II. Leaving the Marines as a major, he achieved full professor rank at Clemson University, where he served as graduate school dean, dean of the faculties, dean of the college, and vice president. In 1966 he was named Texas' first commissioner of higher education and directed the Coordinating Board for Texas Colleges and Universities. When the legislature slashed the board's budget, he joined the University of Tennessee System as vice president for academic affairs and chancellor pro tem of that system's medical schools.

Named the seventeenth president of Texas A&M University and the Texas A&M University System following the death of J. Earl Rudder '32 in 1970, he capitalized on the changes Rudder had initiated. Working to improve the faculty and staff, recruit outstanding students, and build new facilities, he directed the university through its greatest period of growth. During his tenure, the Texas A&M University Press was established, Rudder Center and the Krueger-Dunn dormitory complex were completed, A&M was named a Sea Grant University, and the College of Medicine was born. In 1977 he relinquished the presidency to become chancellor of the A&M system. Two years later he resigned and became executive vice president and director of the Texas Medical Center, Inc., in Houston. Well-known Houston attorney Leon Jaworski said he was prepared to recommend that Williams replace him as president of the giant medical complex when Williams died of an apparent heart attack September 28, 1981. The System Administration Building at the east entrance to the Texas A&M campus was named in his honor in 1997.

## In the Footsteps of Giants*

This is one of the traditions for which Texas A&M University is known across the entire world—one of the traditions I knew about as a boy in southwest Virginia; one of the first traditions I saw practiced by A&M people, although I didn't know they were A&M people 'til they began talking about "It's Muster Day, let's say something about A&M." It's one of the honored and one of the revered and one of the highlights, one of the great things we do and it's one of the great things that you students years from now, wherever you are, will still be doing.

I have been part of a Muster once. I worked for the Coordinating Board and Gen. Earl Rudder asked me one day if I really were not sort of partial to Texas A&M University and I said I would plead guilty to that tender impeachment. And he said, "Since you have pled guilty, if you don't do the Austin Muster for me, I'll tell the University of Texas people you're on my side." So I did the Austin Muster in 1967 on 19th Street in Austin, Texas, and I was a hooked Aggie before, but I was thoroughly hooked thereafter.

I'm going to—after listening to these talks—I'm going to say this much about the people at Aggieland and elsewhere. You know, you and I are products of giants. We walk in the footsteps of giants and we do well to remember them because in each of us—in you and in me—there's a little bit of Michelangelo; there's a little bit of Benjamin Franklin; there's a little bit of Moses, the lawgiver; there's a little bit of every great scientist and writer and theologian and soldier who walked the face of the earth. Because what these people left, we have built on. And, whether we know it or not is really of no consequence to what I'm saying because that makes it nonetheless true. If you are a student at Texas A&M University, you are sitting in the seats occupied, figuratively

*Speech title derived by editor from speech contents

at least, by giants. And whatever you leave here knowing or thinking or being, this will be due in no small measure to the giants who preceded you. One of those was General Earl Rudder, a giant who preceded me as your president and who took this institution, which he had loved for so many years, and made it into a university of the first class. He had help before him. He had people like [President] Tom Harrington, he had Chancellor Gibb Gilchrist; he had many, many people, but he came at a propitious time in the history of this university when we had to meet the very serious challenge of change. And he brought us, you—all of you, whether you knew him or not—through the valleys of change. And so we walk largely in the shadows of giants like this.

That's why I guess the Muster means as much to me as I guess it does because they say if you want to see a fellow who really loves the South, transplant a Yankee down there and leave him for a while. If you want to see a fellow who really loves the Aggies, transplant somebody into your midst and leave him a while. I took root pretty quick. So, if I sound a little exuberant for A&M, there's a very good reason why. It's because I'm exuberant for A&M.

What will you see when you come back for your Muster ten years from now, twenty years from now? I'm not sure. Suppose you come back to this campus for a class reunion or for a Muster, not just to hear the roll call, not just to honor those who have gone away, but to see what the campus is and what the programs are and what people are doing. You may still meet some classmates who are still trying to get their degree. I know one thing. You'll talk and as you let years pile by you'll talk in very interesting riddles and circles for the young, because I listened to the old timers, the Distinguished Alumni of Texas A&M University. I went to a party with them and I listened to them talk and they are products of this great university and they are proud of it and they reflect on it.

They tell the stories of what they did, and of course they are elaborated a little by that time. We listened to the three men who were talking about their World War I experiences to each other—and this was a long time ago. They had already talked about their comrades who had been left in France. And one of them was talking about the little battle that his company had had and how many Germans they had run into and what a slaughter it was and how victorious the Americans were. And his friend said, "When you told it two years ago, the Germans were winning. And last year when the second man told it, it was a draw. And this year the Americans are completely victorious." And he said, with a twinkle in his eye, "As I get older, my memory gets better."

Your memories will get better. When you come back in ten years you'll find a campus with about 22,000 students, I think. You'll find about one-third of them girls and they'll be safely ensconced in dormitories with tolerant housemothers. You'll see football games from Kyle Field and I expect we'll be seating around 70[,000] or 75,000 people and we'll have the nation's number one football team for you. You know, I read the *Batt* [*Battalion*, the student newspaper] and I listen to all the news and I see what people write the letters to the editor about and I'm convinced when you come back here ten, twenty years from now the stands will still be singing "to *blank*, *blank* with Texas University" at whatever point in the song it comes. We will have some non-Texans in our student body, about as many as we have now, proportionately, just because of reciprocal agreements. I think the agreement is now that we let one Texan leave for Oklahoma if three Oklahomans come in, right?

We will have new branches of our institution. They will be located in various places in our state. And there will be free transfer between them and among them, not only on a one-shot basis, but I hope both to and from. I hope education within ten years, certainly A&M education, will be much more flexible and much more student-oriented as to the type of program and to its content and its nature. And I hope we can move from place to place in our system with a great deal more ease than sometimes is possible. You will see a new campus. You know that, of course; you've already watched in your college days a new campus take shape. You will see no fewer than three magnificent buildings of eight, eleven and fifteen stories, and maybe by then we'll like them so well, we'll build some more.

You can come to the System Building if you like and see the new elevator we're going to put in. We have a programmed elevator. As soon as it stops working fifty percent of the time we're going to take it out and replace it. We only have two weeks to go.

You're going to be finding your colleagues in the student body at that time living in refurbished, air conditioned, well-equipped dormitories. Their phone bills will be delivered to them by beautiful girls. Food will be so good that lines will, of course, form for hours before the doors open. We will be leading the nation in many things. We'll be leading the nation in marine science. I would expect within ten years that you will have your own professional programs by and large, your own law school. I would hope also that we will be in a position to have highly coordinated medical education, dental, pharmaceutical education, pro-fessional education which we can move into quickly and easily and with the use of A&M courses here applying toward the total degree. I would think we will have team teaching when you come back in those years to see your friends and to attend a Muster Day.

I would hope we will have our one million volumes in our library that we are striving for, but I would hope also that we will have worked all kinds of electronic operations in library arrangement so that we are on a knowledge network and can call to our own uses the great knowledge centers of the world. I would expect that our liberal arts and our teacher training would get progressively stronger each year and in ten years we will be sitting with the top institutions in those fields clearly. I would think our veterinary medical college would be doubled in its size. Perhaps and most certainly, I guess, through the building of facilities elsewhere in our state, but attached to or at least aligned with A&M. We should have space-age curricula in our engineering, our agriculture, our science, our business, our architecture and fields which we will offer.

Some things will not be changed when you come back, whether it's ten or twenty years or thirty or forty. There will still be the great traditions which bind us together and which give us a uniqueness and which give us memories that keep us—hearts and soul—with each other. There will still be a commitment on this campus, openly expressed and openly voiced and proudly voiced, to decency and dig-nity as essential qualities of civilized man. There will still be on this campus a commitment to a free republic—proudly and openly stated. There will still be a belief that the only recourse to success in our form of government is full participation in it by a knowledgeable citizenry. There will still be a commitment here—a strong commitment—to leadership exercised for the betterment of mankind. And there will be, as you most certainly know, a commitment to the love of your alma mater and to its love for you, the friendships you have formed here, to those that remain with you and those that have passed beyond. There will be a commitment to the memory of great experiences at your university and there will be a commitment to the debt you owe it and the promise it has for you.

And so today and tomorrow and ten or twenty years away we will gather as we do today and we will answer the roll call for our departed friends and we will remember them with love and in our prayers. And we will work tomorrow for them and in their memory because they were the giants who preceded us. And we will say for them at our Musters that our institution, Texas A&M University, will remain always in the forefront in everything it does.

Thank you.

# Larry B. Kirk '66

*1972—G. Rollie White Coliseum*

Larry B. Kirk '66. Photo from editor's collection.

Larry Byron Kirk was born August 8, 1939, in Dallas. He attended college for three years before enlisting in the US Army. He finished first in his advanced infantry training, went on to airborne school, and was assigned to the 82nd Airborne Division. Then he turned down a promotion and a chance to attend Officer Candidate School in order to complete his formal education at Texas A&M University. A Distinguished Military Graduate with a BA degree in business administration, he accepted a regular Army commission before completing Ranger and Master Jump School training. Reassigned to the 82nd Airborne, he was promoted to first lieutenant and sent to Vietnam.

After only three months in Vietnam, he won the Air Medal and two Bronze Stars for bravery as a combat platoon leader. Then on July 5, 1968, he was gravely injured by a land mine. The explosion tore off his leg and his right arm. Near death and with his military identification tags blown away, he was administered the last rites by chaplains of every faith.

In the three years following the battlefield incident, Kirk spent six months in a hospital bed in an army hospital and another nine months in a wheelchair. He endured ten operations and learned to walk with crutches and prostheses. While at Fitzsimons Army Hospital in Aurora, Colorado, he helped raise $42,000 to bring relatives of disabled veterans to the hospital for a Christmas visit with their loved ones.

His military career ended, he went on to become an active leader in business and civic affairs. Settling in Aurora, he became a dynamic force, serving at one time on seven different boards of directors. Kirk was selected in 1971 as one of the Ten Outstanding Young Men in America and served as executive vice president of the Colorado Jaycees. He was a Red Cross director and a charter director of the Citizens Committee against Airplane Noise and Pollution, helping mobilize Aurora and East Denver citizens to combat problems of low-flying aircraft at Stapleton International Airport. He established operating systems for a Colorado company, increasing its assets from $40,000 to $300,000 in less than two years. Kirk died March 17, 1997.

## Heritage*

Thank you.

I wish y'all wouldn't stand up like that. If y'all saw me on television the 19th of March, you'll know that when people stand up like that it has a tendency to make me cry. Don't do that, please.

First of all, I would like to say that it's an honor and a privilege to come back to Texas A&M to speak to you today. And I'd like to thank all those people who are responsible for my being here today. It's great to be back. This campus holds a lot of nostalgia for me. I left this campus and had a cartilage ripped out of my knee playing football and became disinterested in school, went in the Army as an enlisted man. But I couldn't stay away. I had to come back, and now I'm back again.

The campus looks great. They're changing things everywhere—buildings and streets and everything. I found out that I no longer know all of the buildings on Military Walk and when they were built. The students have somewhat changed. We have girls now. The curriculums have changed and they are changing all the time. I would like to impart one little food for thought for you and that is that change and progress are not synonymous terms. Those things which weather the years unchanged are called traditions and the Aggie Muster is one tradition I would like to see never change and never done away with.

Of course, if it wasn't for the Aggie Muster I wouldn't be here today. In fact, I almost wasn't here anyway. I was called to the door of death. I went and I looked and I didn't want to go, so they sent me back. If you

*Speech title derived by editor from speech contents

could have seen me four years ago laying in a tent in a battalion aid station, I was begging for morphine because I hadn't had any and the chaplain was giving me last rites and holding my hand and the doctor was sopping up the blood and trying to find a place to put three IVs. You'd have never thought that I'd be here today. And I wasn't real sure. But, it may be fitting that you've asked a person that has been close to death to come here and talk to you about our fellow Aggies who have reached the end of the road of life.

Aggies are special people. They all have certain characteristics about 'em, whether they be man or woman, which are unique and all similar. One of them is the undying spirit that these people have. Another is love—love for their school, love for their state, love for their country and love for their fellow Aggies. Another characteristic which pervades A&M is the positive mental attitude. Aggies are "can doers."

The hard times that you will share here together at Texas A&M will give you a quality which you will not find out in life, and that is unselfishness. Aggies learn to give and give to each other in many ways. The strong give stamina to the weak. And the weak give confidence to the strong. The learned give understanding to the befuddled. The successful give encouragement to the struggling. And our athletes have always given all the competition that the rest of the Southwest Conference could ask for. Texas A&M University gives excellence that other schools try to top. And our sophomores have always given our freshmen hell. But the dead have given us, the living, a thing called heritage.

Heritage is a gift given by those who have passed away. There is no way to measure a man until he has completed his whole life. Heritage is an intangible ingredient which instills pride in those lucky people who inherit it. We are gathered here today in tribute to those Aggies who have given us this gift and I would like to pay special tribute to the men that we've lost in combat. And I would like to quote to you from Dr. Martin Luther King, who once said, "You show me a man who has nothing to die for and I'll show you a man who has nothing to live for."

Pride. Boy, we've got a lot of it here at Texas A&M. We can be proud of this nation and the heritage bestowed upon us by the people from the beginning. Texas. We can be proud of the heritage bestowed upon us by those tenacious people who settled this country and would not give it up. And Texas A&M. We have a lot of heritage that has accumulated at this school since its inception in 1876. Pride is a motivator and pride is an achiever. Some of us have reached pinnacles and become famous and known worldwide. And others of us are low achievers. In other words, we go out and strive to climb a low mountain. But, whether your goals be high or whether they be low, it's how you accomplish them and did you do it better than anyone else. And these men that have passed away, regardless of their accolades or their little-known achievements; I would like to thank God for giving us these Aggies, who in this past year have given us a few more blocks of heritage to build on.

Thank you.

# Capt. James E. Ray '63

*1973—G. Rollie White Coliseum*

Capt. James E. Ray '63.
Photo from editor's
collection.

James Edwin Ray was born August 25, 1941, in Longview, Texas. He graduated from Texas A&M in 1963 with a BA degree in English and in 1976 received an MS degree in political science from Auburn University. While at A&M, he was a Cadet Corps lieutenant colonel, executive officer of the Second Wing, president of the Memorial Student Center Council and Directorate, a member of the Ross Volunteers, a member of the Student Senate, and was listed in Who's Who in American Colleges and Universities. He entered pilot training at Vance Air Force Base after his graduation and remained in the Air Force as a career officer.

He holds the Silver Star, the Legion of Merit, the Bronze Star with V (valor) with oak leaf cluster, the Air Medal, the Purple Heart with oak leaf cluster, and the Vietnam Service Medal. He was a first lieutenant when shot down during the Vietnam War and was promoted to captain while a prisoner of war from May 1966 until February 12, 1973. He earned the rank of major in 1975, lieutenant colonel in 1979, and pinned on colonel's wings in 1984. Ray attended the Air War College at Maxwell Air Force Base. He retired from the US Air Force in December 1990.

## Enduring Hardships*

*The following information is reconstructed from the July 1973 Texas Aggie magazine and the April 23, 1973, issue of The Battalion, A&M's student newspaper.*

*Speech title derived by editor from synopsis

[Captain Jim Ray was first acknowledged to be a prisoner of the North Vietnamese when Radio Hanoi broadcast his alleged "confession" two months after he was shot down on Mother's Day, May 8, 1966. In his address to this year's Campus Muster audience, he commented on that statement, which was his family's first indication that he was still alive.]

We [the POWs] are asked, "What did you think about while you were being tortured, while you were enduring the 'rope trick.'" Well, personally, I tried to concentrate on poems, scripture verses, some of the memory works that we as freshmen here had been required to learn and I tried to run these through my mind. The 23rd Psalm and the Lord's Prayer—notably.

The pain of that "rope trick" is an insidious thing—the tourniquet effect on the arms, the separation pain of the shoulders, the front of the chest where the clavicle attaches to the rib cage. It's just excruciating and yet it gets worse as time goes on. I found that I could not concentrate, I could not force my mind to concentrate on something as simple and yet as meaningful as the Lord's Prayer or the 23rd Psalm. And so as time wore on, I reverted to more simple verses and finally to just trying to count to 50, to 20, to 10. And I really got panicky when I found that I couldn't count to 10 because I could not keep a thought process going that long because of the interruption of pain.

It wasn't very much longer till I had made up my mind that when that guard came in I was going to beg for mercy and do whatever they wanted me to do. I thought often of the scripture "The spirit is willing, but the flesh is indeed weak". The guard came around about every five minutes or so making checks to see if we were ready to cooperate. So the next time he came in I had made up my mind that I was going to cooperate one way or another.

He came in and he had such a smug, arrogant look on his face that something just welled up inside me. When he sneered and said, "Now you will cooperate with the camp authorities!" I said, "Not on your life buddy!" and he left.

Boy, I hated myself. I wished I hadn't done that. So the next time he came around I used a bit more discretion, if I was able to even think of anything such as discretion at that time, and did what they demanded. That particular time, it was for a war crimes confession which they dictated.

[Later, when Ray had an opportunity to talk to other prisoners, they assured him that everyone had received the same reception and that no one had been able to endure. Ray went on to point out that his sense of humor, his Christian training, and the discipline he learned in high school and as a freshman at A&M helped him to survive. He recalled looking at the Vietnamese guards and telling himself that Tommy Dabney and Jack Mahand (sophomores who lived across the hall from him at A&M) "could do better than that."]

So undoubtedly, the mental and physical conditioning—hazing if you will, controlled hazing, has its benefits. Although at the time, 14 years ago, I would never have guessed it, it did help.

[Ray shared an event, not previously reported in the press, with the Muster crowd of more than 6,000. He told how the communists moved him and 13 other prisoners into the Hanoi Power Plant in August of 1967 in an attempt to prevent the US from bombing the installation.]

The mental duress of the 16 days that we spent at that power plant was considerable and yet each time we heard the alarm, each time we heard the bombs fall, we felt encouraged and our spirits actually were lifted, although at other times we feared for our welfare. It seems contradictory that we would rejoice to hear the planes coming in, to hear the bombs whistling in.

We could feel the simultaneous flash of light and the concussion . . . see the doors and windows of the building disintegrate . . . feel the concussion in our ears . . . and know that, in spite of what the enemy was trying to do, our nation was not going to be blackmailed. . . .

We also felt our spirits soar when the bombs came. We knew our blood would not be on the hands of American pilots, but on the hands of this Communist government that was so unscrupulous and defiant of international conventions and human decency as to stake prisoners at known strategic points.

[Ray noted that he and other former POWs discovered on their return that ultra-liberals and radical factions in America had been given "disproportionate coverage in the press. This hurt us a lot because our captors felt the radicals were spokesmen for the population. They saw that our treatment was being condoned, and they intensified it."]

We developed contempt for some of the "peace" representatives that visited us in Hanoi. Most of them were just naive in not recognizing that what they were being shown was a showcase of special prisoners.

[New York Times reporter Harrison Salisbury should have known better, Ray said, but he didn't do his job and search out facts. He just accepted what he was shown by the communists.]

Ramsey Clark was also a little naive but I cannot be as kind and generous with Jane Fonda. A person with her degree of talent and knowledge of theatrics cannot possibly have been misled or naive. Her husband's [political activist Tom Hayden, who was a principal organizer of Students for a Democratic Society] writings were given to us completely uncensored, her actions were praised by the communists, and we all feel her activities were a willful, deliberate participation in the communist cause.

[In his first press conference after release in February, Ray voiced support of amnesty for those who fled the United States to avoid the draft on the condition that they publicly acknowledge wrongdoing and complete a period of government service at least equal to the longest period of confinement experienced by the returning POWs.

At the gigantic homecoming celebration held for Ray in Conroe on March 4, he was presented a new Aggie Ring by Willard Clark '42 of Houston and a duplicate of his MSC Directorate Watch by Robert Haltom '44 of Fort Worth to replace the ones taken from him by his captors. He said he "shouldn't have been wearing them into combat, but at the time I thought I was invincible and wouldn't be shot down."

He stated that his driving concern was for confirmation of the status of America's Missing In Action servicemen and a return home for those still alive. He also called for support for "the men who have been disabled in the service of their country and to the families of those men who died that our nation, its ideals, and its goals might live forever."

Ray said that below the superficial changes he found upon his return, he saw the same basic ideals that had made American great.]

We must not let these ideals die. We must continue to instill in our young people the discipline that made our country strong.

# Sheldon J. Best '63

*1974—Kyle Field*

Sheldon J. Best '63. Photo from editor's collection.

Born December 29, 1940, in New York City, Sheldon Joseph Best was a member of Texas A&M's Corps of Cadets and student body president. After graduating from A&M, he entered the US Marine Corps. Assigned as S-4 (logistics) for the 5th Marine Regiment, 1st Marine Division, he completed jump school and was reassigned to 1st Force Reconnaissance Company. In August 1965, he was named the unit's executive officer and platoon commander as it was deployed to Vietnam. After a year in Vietnam, he was promoted to captain, served as aide to the chief of staff, Marine Corps Systems Command, and directed the Management Information Center in the Materiel Division.

In 1967, Best left active duty and entered the management training program at United Airlines. Over the next seven years, he served in positions of increasing responsibility before becoming vice president for in-flight services and then regional vice president for the Pacific Northwest. In 1982 he was named executive vice president and chief operating officer at AIRCAL, which was merged into American Airlines. Two years later he became a consultant to Texas Air Corporation and in 1985 assumed the presidency of Continental West Airlines for a year before being named CEO of Aerospatiale Aircraft Corporation and ATR Marketing, Inc. In 1989 he became executive vice president for marketing at Boullioun Aviation Services, Inc., and in 1996 established Best Consulting Company.

# Quality of Life*

When I met with Student Senate Vice President John Sharp this morning, I was told that there will be another vice president on this campus in a couple of weeks. If you weren't aware of that fact, it is Vice President Gerald Ford. So, you're going to have your share of vice presidents around here in the next few weeks.

For me, fellow Aggies, it is a unique privilege for someone my age, from the Class of 1963, to be invited back to A&M as the '74 Muster speaker. We were here several months ago and were privileged to address the induction banquet of the Ross Volunteers. Our ten-year class reunion was held last year in Houston where we were very warmly received by the "MOB" [Rice's Marching Owl Band]. I had to congratulate President Williams and the student leaders for the outstanding restraint that they demonstrated in keeping the student body in the stands. It reminded me of other days in Gregory Gymnasium in Austin, fifty-yard lines in Waco, Corps trips in Dallas, and an RV [Ross Volunteer] march in New Orleans in 1963, when our restraint was not as visibly demonstrated. What it caused me to reflect on was the sense of maturity and progress of Texas A&M in minds and spirits, and I guess that was the kind of spirit that felled the victory tree [a Rice University athletic shrine].

You know, as student body president in my senior year, we participated in a significant turning point in the progress of A&M toward academic excellence—a catch phrase of the '60s that is a reality in the '70s. A&M in 1974 is a university on the move, constantly changing to meet the needs of its students, state, and nation, through teaching, research, and extension work with a strong commitment to its proud heritage and traditions.

In my senior year we participated—often reluctantly—in decision-making that would change the name of this college to "University" and would alter the compulsory nature of the Cadet Corps, and bring women to A&M for the first time—at least for the first time legally.

*Speech title derived by editor from speech contents

Many of us will never forget the long weekend on campus when the coed decision was reached by the board of directors. General Earl Rudder, Cadet Colonel Bill Nix, and I put restraint to its ultimate test.

Several weeks later, several of us would travel to Austin to testify before a joint session of the legislature in opposition to coeducation. I, for one, vowed that no daughter of mine would ever go to A&M. Well, I'm ten years older, three daughters later, and I'm an officer with United Airlines with the direct responsibility for its 7,800 employees—7,200 of which are women. To borrow an advertising slogan, "We've come a long way, baby." After this weekend, I'm proud to say that I'd send any of my daughters to Aggieland to join the 3,990 women on our campus these days.

You know, on reflecting on these last ten years and what A&M has meant to me and others like me, I recall that during my first year out of A&M our nation buried a president at Arlington Cemetery. Six months later my wife and I buried a son at Arlington Cemetery. In the years that followed, many more would follow that long walk or be drawn up that beautiful Virginia hillside to take a place of rest among fallen comrades, family, and friends. Herein lies the deepest meaning of our Muster: the tribute to the comrades fallen in battle or taken from loved ones in a time of peace. Today we honor their memory and we reflect upon a quote from the Book of John that said, "Greater love hath no man than this, that he lay down his life for his friends."

We have lived since 1963 in what could be categorized as adverse times marked by assassinations, by riots, by Viet Nam (where I served as an officer in First Force Reconnaissance Company), difficulties with our economy, Mideast conflicts, fuel shortages which placed an unusual and heavy burden of artificial restraint on my industry, and, of course, Watergate.

With all the turmoil, there's a tendency to choose up sides and it becomes "they"—it is the politicians, it is the unions, the G.D. company, the faculty, the students, the administration. You know, ladies and gentlemen, we recognize that there will be differences. There always have been and there always will be. I submit that we Americans, we Aggies, we citizens of this world can stick together and can do things for one another—for our families, for our university, and our nation that won't cost the taxpayers one cent. We can do things for one another that will make our job, our homes, and our way of life more interesting and pleasant—but the initiative has to come from us. We have to care about one another. We have to find answers and not accept excuses. Ladies and gentlemen, in the tradition of Teddy Roosevelt, we have to become "activists." For, in this country of ours there are the doers and the doubters. I prefer to walk with the doers.

Henry David Thoreau once wrote, "If a man does not keep pace with his companions, perhaps it is because he hears a different drummer. Let him step to the music he hears, however measured or far away." Well, I submit in the cause of unity that the music to step out to is "The Spirit of Aggieland," which is a true reflection of the spirit of this great state, this great university and this great and this wonderful country we live in.

I would be remiss today if I didn't comment on the progress that I have witnessed this weekend at Texas A&M, and that has developed over the last ten years.

Would you believe, opera at Texas A&M? Well, I can recall that 12 of us took a trip to Houston my senior year—at university expense— thanks to Dr. Williams—a "cultural trip," it was called—so that we could see the museums, and the opera and fine arts, and go to dinner with Barron Hilton.

Now, however, you can eat with elegance atop a high-rise where Guion Hall once stood. Also, you can realize that girls in the ROTC will be there soon, and, with a push from the cadets, they're actually going to take an active part in cadet activities.

You know, these are only a few of the happenings that are going on at A&M today. They're fairly drastic departures from the mental picture most of you still have of Texas A&M, but for the most part they are additions and not replacements of old standards or cherished traditions.

The Corps is still strong and still producing more officers than any of the other institutions in the nation except the service academies. A&M's Cadets still stand head and shoulders above those from other schools in competition at summer camp. Some of these guys don't get their fill at summer camp so they follow this up with a jaunt to Ft. Benning for Ranger or Airborne training (they even accept Marines in Ranger and Airborne training, by the way).

The campus still ranks as the friendliest, and "Howdy" continues to be the byword. Midnight yell practices are as popular and wild as ever. The 12th Man still stands at football games and there are high hopes that kissing at the games will be more frequent next season (we'll leave that to Coach [Emory] Bellard and his staff). Silver Taps still produces the same effect on us as it will on you today.

So, while things are changing, they are also staying the same. In a way it's like the old saying, "It's not getting older, it's getting better." That's a nice saying about A&M's age as well as about its continuing improvement.

It's becoming a topic of conversation because massive plans are being laid for a celebration of its centennial in 1976. You'll be hearing a lot more about the centennial in coming months and will have an ample opportunity to participate in the observance in one form or another. While it is being given considerable thought by a lot of folks on campus right now, the centennial is still a couple of years away as far as most of you are concerned. So, you would probably be more interested about what has happened on campus recently—since last year's Muster.

It was a banner year with record enrollment, expanded programs, and the opening of new facilities at an unprecedented rate. Enrollment jumped to 18,520 students, a 10,000 increase from my senior year. The increase in the last year was 2,364 over a comparable period in 1972. The increase was one of the largest in the nation for a major institution and was achieved while maintaining a Scholastic Aptitude Test average of more than 1,050 for entering freshmen—well above the national average. The fall figures, as I said earlier, included 3,990 women and 3,733 graduate students. Incidentally, A&M now has more women enrolled than TCU or Baylor and more women than Rice has total students (and I guess there's some question about some of those students).

You know, this may be a good time to elaborate on my earlier remark regarding women taking ROTC and perhaps being in the Corps itself. The decision to admit women in the ROTC programs beginning next fall came after the university had received well over 100 inquiries from coeds. It should also be noted that the ROTC programs at every other college and university in Texas had previously gone coed. At the time, colleges and universities in Texas were watching A&M.

The Commandant emphasized that only ROTC was being opened to women, not admittance to the Corps of Cadets. Well, the cadets themselves, particularly the Corps staff juniors, soon initiated a study and came out with the statement that, "The Corps should be open to women to extend the outstanding training which the Corps provides and which makes the difference between an Aggie officer and any other ROTC graduate." One of the Corps leaders explained, "Considerable amount of thought, worry, and man hours have been dedicated to women in the Corps. The staff works for the love of the Corps and to provide for its continuing progress."

A&M has recently received authorization from the Texas College and University System Coordinating Board to initiate several new academic programs. These include a mental health education program to be conducted in cooperation with Baylor College of Medicine and a new professional-type doctor of engineering degree program.

If you think that A&M has changed too much too soon, let me assure you—opera is not one of the new course offerings. Opera is, however, a reality at A&M; thanks to a bold program undertaken jointly by the university, students, faculty/staff and the community. Operating under the banner of Opera and Performing Arts Society (OPAS), they brought a leading opera company to the campus for a very well-received performance of "The Marriage of Figaro" in February.

Getting back to academically related programs—the university has plans to start a new scholarly press this Fall. It will be known as "Texas A&M University Press." It'll be in the same building where decisions about changing the name of this university, coeducation, and the change in the Corps were decided by the board of directors, General Rudder, myself, and several other student leaders.

You might be interested in knowing that the Press will be headed by Frank Wardlaw, currently of t.u. (I still say "t.u." though I notice people are saying "UT" now), who has a very well-deserved national and international reputation in the scholarly publishing field.

You know, the value to the state and this nation of the importance of studies being conducted and the very great benefits that the public will derive from research at A&M will soon be recognized worldwide. Several A&M research projects today are aimed at helping solve the nation's energy problems. When we meet with Bill Simon, deputy secretary of the US Treasury, and formally with John Love in Washington, Texas A&M is a name that has some meaning to them. It is not just a school somewhere out in the middle of Texas. From the area of highway safety to the control of air and water pollution, there's a recognition that A&M has something to contribute.

One of the things that John Sharp didn't mention is the fact that I've worked in two presidential campaigns, one gubernatorial campaign, and one United States Senate campaign—most of which were on my own time, and you hear considerable comment about the "quality of life." It is important to us all—"quality of life" is not just a comment that relates to our environment, but it is life with our fellow man.

We have a moral obligation to improve this quality of life. You might wonder how we can do this. Well, first we do it by recognizing that every man and every woman is an individual like ourselves with hopes, ambitions, heartaches, financial obligations, and family. And second, by doing those little things that are the right and honest thing to do.

You know, those of us that are fortunate enough to call ourselves former students of Texas A&M can be well proud of our fine heritage. The men and women that walk this campus today are constantly seeking to improve and change, and that is the way it should be.

This morning I went to church services in St. Mary's. It was the church that I was married in on one of the most exciting days of my life—the day I graduated, the day I was commissioned in the Marine Corps, and the day I attended Final Review.

Being in that church, I remembered and reflected on the songs of the leader of the Singing Cadets, Bob Boone, and on the second platoon of the Ross Volunteers, who held our saber arch. I remembered that May 25th for me will always be a day with abiding memories to myself and my family.

Today, we return to A&M to pay honor to one another and especially to those who are no longer with us. For me, it is a very distinct honor to be able to share once again in a Muster ceremony on my beloved campus of Texas A&M—a thousand thanks for this opportunity.

# Reagan V. Brown '43

*1975—G. Rollie White Coliseum*

Reagan V. Brown '43.
Photo from editor's
collection.

Reagan Veasey Brown was born September 21, 1921, in Henderson, Texas. He completed his undergraduate degree at Texas A&M in marketing and finance in 1943. From 1943 to 1946 he served as a US Army captain in the 69th Infantry Division, with combat and occupation duties in the European theatre, where he was wounded.

After World War II, Brown owned a food, feed, and fertilizer business in Henderson for two years before joining the Texas Agricultural Extension Service in 1948. In 1956 he received his master's degree in rural sociology from A&M and became an extension sociologist, where until 1974 he worked with rural towns to upgrade their development. During this time, he also received a second master's degree from A&M in education and was named "Man of the Year" by *Progressive Farmer* magazine in 1968.

Brown was appointed special assistant to Texas governor Dolph Briscoe in 1974. He was a popular public speaker and represented Briscoe on over 4,000 occasions, delighting audiences with his East Texas wit and humor. Over the course of Brown's lifetime, he gave more than 7,000 speeches. He was an articulate advocate of the free-enterprise system and self-reliance. In 1977 he was elected commissioner of agriculture for the State of Texas and established Texas First, a job creation program.

A patriotic Aggie, Brown wrote an article about the US flag for the February 1972 *Texas Aggie* magazine after hearing a little boy ask his daddy why everyone stood up when the flag went by.

Brown died November 16, 1999.

# Rendezvous with Life*

It is great to be here today. I want to thank Tom for that very gracious introduction, and I want to also thank Larry for the great preparations he has made for this Muster. He did a masterful job.

Allan Seeger, shortly before becoming a casualty in World War II, penned the immortal poem about his "rendezvous with death." We are met today to pay tribute to Aggies that have crossed over, and for whom the muffled drums' sad roll has beat their last tattoo.

But today I want to talk to you about the rendezvous with life and the great responsibilities that you and I have. I look out at the live oak trees around the drill field and I remember that they were planted in memory of the Aggies that gave their lives in World War I. The more than 900 names on the plaque at the entrance to the Memorial Student Center are those who gave their all [in World Wars I and II]. Many of them were my classmates. I feel a sense of reverence as I look over the campus and feel the presence of those who once walked this hallowed ground. How great the sacrifices. How glorious the deeds. How magnificent the dreams.

You and I are now the custodians of the challenge. Next year will mark 140 years since the Battle of San Jacinto. Next year Texas A&M will be 100 years old. Next year, our country will be 200 years old. Our years are only a speck on the chronicles of history. During these years, the achievements of Americans and Texans have been tremendous.

On the Statue of Liberty in New York harbor there are inscribed these words: "Give me your tired, your poor, your huddled masses yearning to breathe free." And so they came from England and France, and Germany and Spain. They came from Africa and Italy and many other countries. Every color and every creed, longing to be free. These freedom-seeking men and women were your ancestors and mine. They plowed and they planted and they fought and they died. They pushed back the frontiers. They built the churches. They built the schools and the cities, and left you and me an opportunity to live free and to be judged by the tracks that we can leave.

*Speech title derived by editor from speech contents

Early America was a child left alone to stand or fall. The struggle was hard, but the pioneers did not give up. Their ideals sustained them. Strong men and strong women gave their lives so this country could grow and prosper and achieve greatness. They gave of themselves because they believed in the American dream of freedom. Freedom from want, and freedom from fear, and freedom from tyranny.

"Liberty," said Woodrow Wilson, "does not consist in mere declarations of the rights of man. It consists in the translation of those declarations into definite action." America stands today two centuries old as proof that our forefathers did indeed speak with actions as well as words.

Statesmen and poets and philosophers and a host of just plain Americans—average citizens—have in common one united bond—their love for the United States and what it stands for. General Douglas MacArthur voiced the patriots' creed: "Duty, honor, country." Those three hallowed words dictate what you ought to be, what you can be, what you will be!

John F. Kennedy spoke of personal integrity that makes Americans "Ask not what your country can do for you, but what you can do for your country."

The great anthems of America and her historical documents show the drive, the energy, and the faith in America that have been our strength throughout history.

Is there any heart in the audience today that is not stirred when we read Patrick Henry's oration as he shouted, "Is life so dear or peace so sweet as to be purchased at the price of chains and slavery? Forbid it, almighty God! I know not what others may choose, but for me—give me liberty or give me death!" Does it stir your spirit this afternoon as we envision the young Nathan Hale when he stood erect and said, "I regret that I have but one life to give for my country." Patrick Henry and Nathan Hale were ready to die for America.

The pages of our history record the names of hundreds of thousands of fellow Americans who did give their lives for America. The Concord Bridge. At Shiloh, the Alamo, Goliad, San Jacinto, San Juan Hill, Flanders Field, Bastogne, St. Lô, Guadalcanal, North Korea and Viet Nam and scores of other places are marked by the blood of American men and women. The muffled drums' sad roll has beaten their last tattoo. They paid the price. They made the supreme sacrifice that we all may be free.

To die for your country is noble. No greater sacrifice can be made than to lay down your life for your country and for your friends. But isn't it equally noble to live for your country? And that's the challenge that I want to make to you today. Live for America, Live for Texas and Live for Texas A&M as courageously as you would die for them. Live to make the American dream come true.

And what is that dream? What do Americans believe? We believe in democracy. Abraham Lincoln put it this way: "No man is good enough to govern another without the other's consent." Our democratic tradition stems from the founding fathers and is explicit in our great documents—The Declaration of Independence, The Constitution, and The Bill of Rights. We believe in liberty and justice. Kansas' *Emporia Gazette* editor William Allen White put it this way: "Liberty is the only thing you cannot have unless you are willing to give it to others." We believed in freedom of worship. Every man and woman worshiping God as he or she chooses. We believe in the rights of man. Ben Franklin said, "God grant that not only the love of liberty, but a thorough knowledge of the rights of man pervade all the nations of the earth so that a philosopher may set his foot anywhere on its surface and say, 'This is my country.'"

We have fought two great wars in the 20th century because we realize that those who trample on the rights of man were endangering not only our survival as a nation, but the survival of the rest of the free world. We believe in self government—that all men are created equal and this equality means equal in opportunity and equal in human rights. We believe in toleration of all of our diverse origins. We have learned not only to tolerate each other, but to welcome each other— our melting pot has produced a society that has learned to live together.

We believe in universal schooling. If you visit the Hall of Fame you will find an inscription under the name of the great educator, Abraham Flexner. It reads, "A common school is the greatest discovery ever made by man." This is an extremely American statement. Our free public schools are the greatest in the world and we are working to improve them.

We are outward-looking and forward-looking. The feeling that we are the custodians of freedom—a precious gift eventually to become available to all mankind—is perfectly compatible with American patriotism. The founders of our country found it possible to love their country and at the same time to feel that America had a certain responsibility to the rest of the world. They looked outward, and most of us in these anxious times follow their example.

We believe in dreams. Man is ever a dreamer. He searches for things afar, and he reaches way out yonder where all of his tomorrows are!

Behind the hand on the cradle and behind the hissing steam—behind the hand on the throttle there always has to be a dream. Martin Luther King said, "I have a dream that one day the valley shall be exalted, that every hill and mountain shall be made low, that the rough places shall be made plain, and the crooked places shall be made straight and . . . all flesh shall see it together."

Well, the list could go on. We must include in it that we believe in the future. We believe in the young people of our nation. You represent our greatest resource. What is to come already lies stirring in your eyes. I believe our boys and girls will lift their eyes to points beyond the horizon and their futures will glow with colors of infinite destiny. Poet Walt Whitman called this future "the years of the unperformed." The performance is up to you. You are the bridge between our past and our future. I believe you are the greatest generation of young people that our country or our world has ever known. I believe your bridges will be good ones.

1976 is our bicentennial year. Our land is young. Our strength is great. Our course is far from run. I ask each of you here in this great gathering today to look around you at our great state and our nation and find a place of expanded service.

Now I want to deviate just a moment from this text to say how proud I am of you who occupy the campus of Texas A&M. Since I've been on Governor Briscoe's staff, I've made over 230 meetings speaking to more than 100,000 people. They come down the aisles—your mothers and your dads—and they get me by the hands and they say, "My son (or daughter) is at Texas A&M." And sometimes those old hands are rough from hard labor and the sacrifices that they're making so you can be here. Many times their cheeks are moist as they speak of you and this school. I urge you to be a part of Texas A&M's strength—part of its greatness—part of its future and magnificence. Guard against those who might in any way tarnish its image by conduct or deed. Hold high its ideals.

We honor those who are gone, but accelerate in our hearts today our rendezvous with life. I challenge you to be a greater Texan, a greater American, a greater Aggie.

Faith has been our strength throughout history. "Always," as Helen Keller said, "we have it in our powers to rise and shoulder great burdens which destiny has placed upon us." Let us accept that challenge today as courageously as those who preceded us, and then let it be said when our job is finished: "These Americans, these Texans, these Aggies, used to the limit the talent God gave them. They were worthy of love and respect and of the sacrifices many people have made that they might achieve what they deem to be their task. They added what they could to the strength of America and to Texas and to Texas A&M. Their lives were lived well and there are no regrets."

Yes, you and I have a rendezvous with life.

We owe so much to oh so few—we pray dear God for strength and courage, too. To those that lit the torch that is tossed our way, we pledge that we will not fail our rendezvous.

Thank you.

# Charles G. Scruggs '45

*1976—G. Rollie White Coliseum*

Charles G. Scruggs '45.
Photo from editor's
collection.

Charles G. "Charlie" Scruggs was born November 4, 1923, in McGregor, Texas. He was president of the Texas Future Farmers of America before enrolling at Texas A&M in 1941. When Pearl Harbor was attacked, he joined the Army, completing Infantry Officer Candidate School. He spent the rest of World War II as a platoon leader in Europe.

After the war, he returned to A&M, where he wrote for the campus newspaper *The Battalion* and *The Agriculturist* magazine and received his bachelor's degree in agricultural administration in 1947. In his senior year he met *Progressive Farmer* editor-in-chief Eugene Butler and joined the magazine staff following graduation. During his career, he produced more than 500 magazine articles and two books. Scruggs was promoted to executive editor in 1972. Four years later, he was named editor and later editor-in-chief.

Scruggs was a key person in eradicating the screwworm, a costly livestock pest in the late 1950s. As founder and first president of the Southwest Animal Health Research Foundation, he organized a coalition of twenty Southwest livestock organizations to support and enlist federal aid for the multistate program. He established Texas Food and Fiber Abundance Month and was instrumental in creating the Texas Veterinary Medical Diagnostic Laboratories and establishing the Food Protein Center at Texas A&M University. He served on the Texas Tech University board of regents and was a member of the Texas College and University Coordinating Board. He was named "Man of the Year in Texas Agriculture."

Scruggs's affiliations with Texas A&M are numerous: vice chairman of the Agriculture Task Force, A&M Target 2000 study; councilor, Texas A&M Research Foundation; and member of A&M's College of Agriculture Development Council. Texas A&M University and the Association of Former Students named him a Distinguished Alumnus in 1982.

Scruggs died July 24, 2001.

## "How Will You Answer the Muster Calls of the Future?"

The pages of history are filled with stories of the many dramatic ways man has been called on to answer muster calls in the past.

There was a painful and fateful muster call at the Alamo 140 years ago. We know how those men answered, the price they paid, and the mental victory they won thereby.

Two hundred-plus years ago, other men had to answer a muster call. At that time the issues were less clear than those at the Alamo. But the consequences were just as dramatic.

The Colonies, as our country was generally known then, were torn apart by conflicting emotions. Most of our forebears of that day were descended from convicts, thieves, tragically poor peasants, and a few royal-blooded idealists—literally every kind and manner of person. Many came to America as a beneficiary of the "King's Mercy"—that is, they chose to settle in America rather than rot in a prison or sweatshop. Indeed, many of our forebears preferred pioneering to hanging.

In spite of this, nearly all had close and favorable ties to Great Britain —culture, family relations, trade, knowledge, tradition.

But they had to make a fateful decision: Should they cling to the past and the safety and security of a mighty—but oppressive—Britannia, or should they choose the unknown and cast their lot with an "unprincipled rabble without government, plans, money, or identified leaders"?

Their choice was heartrending—not at all as clear-cut as we imagine it was. At risk was family, fortune, friends—even life itself!

While we today pay homage to the glory of the American Revolution, it's important to understand that the events of that day could just as well be labeled the First American Civil War.

Brother broke with brother; father turned against son; family turned against family; even wives turned against husbands!

One colonist, as he was escaping from the Minutemen, wrote his sons: "If those wicked sinners, the rebels, entice you, believe them not, but die by the sword rather than be hanged as rebels, which will certainly be your fate if you join them!"

How would you have answered the symbolic muster call of that day?

While we cloak the Founding Fathers with a wreath of glory today, they had their difficulties, even among themselves. John Adams wrote his wife Abigail from "Phyladephia" in 1774.

> I am wearied to Death with the Life I lead. The business of the Congress is tedious beyond expression. The Assembly is like no other that ever existed. Every man in it is a great man—an orator, a critick, a statesman, and therefore every man upon every question must shew his oratory, his criticism, his political abilities.
>
> The consequence of this is that business is drawn and spun out to immeasurable length. I believe if it were moved and seconded that we should come to a resolution that three and two make five, we should be entertained with logic, rhetoric, law, history, politics, and mathematics concerning the subject for two whole days.

While we see everything clearly now through the hindsight of history, our Founding Fathers labored for more than two years. Abigail Adams in frustration wrote her husband: "I long to hear that you have declared an Independancy."

Finally, painfully, these men did answer that fateful muster on July 2, 1774, by inscribing their names forever to history.

Other muster calls have come. Almost all the members of my class at Texas A&M answered one. As we enrolled in 1941, we were to have been the graduating class of 1945. But about 800 of us lined up one day at old Ross Hall and heard our names called. A worn, folded little card that I treasure now tells the story of that day. It says:

> This is to certify that Scruggs, C. G., Private, was enlisted in the Army of the United States on the 5th day of December, one thousand nine hundred forty two for the duration and six months. When enlisted

he was 19 years of age, and by occupation a student. He has blue eyes, blond hair, ruddy complexion and is 6 feet zero inches tall.

Later entries read: *Infantry: campaigns: Northern France, Rhineland, Central Europe.* And the one Decoration and Citation I cherish most is the Victory Medal.

What a great word—Victory!

What would the world be like today if millions of Americans and thousands of Aggies had not answered the Muster Calls of the past when this great republic of ours faced crisis and challenge?

Let me point out, however, that the Muster Calls answered by those of us in World War II were easy to answer compared with the calls that you young people who are now at Texas A&M will be called upon to answer during the rest of this century. We hope none will be for war. But if you are called, I am confident you will answer, loud and clear, Here!

Instead, your Muster Calls will be more personal but equally serious. And the way you and millions of other young Americans answer these personal Muster Calls will do more to determine whether there will be an Aggie Muster here in 2076 than all the military campaigns of the past.

You and your generation will be called on to provide the means for Victory in such great struggles as the War Against Hunger, the Water Crisis, the Energy Crisis, and the Environmental Clash.

The food, water, energy, and population explosion crises will call for the most painful decisions ever made by man. How will you react to the problems of a world awash in a sea of hunger?

The horrible specter of famine lurks ominously in the future. Famine . . . hunger . . . these are strong and unbelievable words to us.

Let's look more closely at the horrible specter of hunger:

> Almost a thousand young children cluster at the compound each morning with tin cups to receive the stuff that sustains them. Young women dished out the pasty yellow substance. Others ladled out a vile green sauce of stockfish, palm oil and vegetables—all of which smelled like bad hog slop. But at least it was high in protein.

As the children began to finish their servings, first a few, then several jumped up and ran toward the big pots—now empty. Adults passed up and down trying to keep the kids seated; others drove back bunches of kids with sticks. As more finished eating, the mob of children became harder to control until—with a shriek—they boiled up and over each other, running, clawing toward pots and the hope of more food. They swarmed forward, indifferent to the whack-whack of the stick-wielding men screaming, groping, waving their tin cups in dust-flying chaos.

Outside, we moved past flocks of fragile skeleton-children with skins stretched drum-tight over tiny bones, past ragged refugees and ghostly beggar women with babies tugging at dry breasts.

Overhead a few buzzards husked their wings in dry air and soared in patient circles—for this place, like almost everywhere, reeked with the acrid sweetness of hunger and death.

From "Bangladesh—The Edge of Extinction,"
*Look Magazine*, April 1, 1969.

Is this sort of scene of concern to you? Will it affect your life? More than 350 years ago, the famous poet John Donne wrote [in *Devotions upon Emergent Occasions*]:

No man is an island,
entire of itself;
Every man is a piece of the continent,
a part of the main;
If a clod be washed away by the sea,
Europe is the less,
as well as if a promontory were,
as well as any manner of thy
friends or of thine own were;
Any man's death diminishes me,
because I am involved in mankind.
and therefore never send to
know for whom the bell tolls;
it tolls for thee.

My friends, as the world becomes more complex, as we crowd billions upon this planet and then shrink it further by transportation and communication miracles, the bell tolls more loudly for each of us.

Increasingly, we shall become, as Donne says, "involved in mankind." The words "population explosion" and "hunger" will form a litany that will ring continually through every discussion of substance in the last quarter of this century.

By the start of the 21st Century, the problems of population and hunger will likely totally eclipse all the things we think important today.

Who is going to feed and clothe and educate and bring up as responsible world citizens these billions of humans? Should America try to use its abundance to help feed the world? I think our answer must be yes. Any compassionate approach to today's living peoples would lead us to say that. But we must face up to the real test: Where is it going to lead us? Are we going to feed more people to produce more babies to demand more food to produce more babies, until finally it ends in world disaster?

The future decisions to be made are illustrated by a report of a missionary who served in China many years ago. He said that one year he and his associate had to decide whether to try to save the lives of 40,000 people with the food they had stored or whether they would let 10,000 die in order to be certain to save the other 30,000. They chose to let 10,000 die. You may have to face the problem—not of saving the lives of 10,000 people but of saving millions or perhaps tens of millions.

As one leader has put it, "We are in a race between the breeders and the feeders, and at the moment the breeders are winning." A great many say we can't do anything about this population problem. The fact is, we cannot afford not to do something about it.

And on whose shoulders will that responsibility fall? How will you answer the types of muster calls the missionary to China had to answer? These crises will threaten your home, your family, your way of life, your nation!

It is hoped that you will answer these calls correctly and well. And we hope there are some among you at this great University today who will provide the scientific and/or political breakthroughs or decisions—as have Aggies of the past—that will help the world live longer and better.

Then there are the Muster Calls that are more immediate, more personal: Integrity, Honesty, and Pride in this University.

I hope you will answer these personal Muster Calls in the affirmative and understand that we owe this great University and our Country a tremendous debt.

How can we pay these debts?

We can do this by declaring that we:

> Understand that the US has more right and goodness, more hope, and opportunity than we have failures; that we have more right than wrong.
>
> Refuse to abandon our moral principles of right and wrong.
>
> Will help others understand that we are a nation of laws.
>
> Understand that the right to criticize carries with it the responsibility to suggest and work for solutions.
>
> Cherish personal liberty and truth.
>
> Love America and worship God!

Most of all we should sing:
"America, America
God shed His grace on thee!"

# Maj. James E. Ray '63

*1977—G. Rollie White Coliseum*

Maj. James E. Ray '63.
Photo from editor's
collection.

Maj. James Ray delivered his first campus Muster address in 1973 when he was a recently released prisoner of war. He returned as the featured speaker for Muster Day in 1977. Only two individuals have delivered two campus Muster speeches. (See the earlier chapter for a biographical sketch of Ray.)

## Discipline and Human Relations*

When Dan asked me if there were any things I preferred to talk about or any things that I did not like to talk about, especially in view of the traumatic experiences that the prisoners of war face, I said, "Me mind?" I said, "After almost seven years up there, man I love it when it is my turn to speak to a captive audience." Yes, I really love it, with the butterflies and shaking knees and all. It's really a thrill to me to have been invited back for a second address to a group of students who embody the highest tradition of excellence that our nation has ever known. My hope for our great nation is that the spirit, the esprit de corps, the contributions, the dedication to excellence that have made Texas A&M the best university —the fastest growing in the country—that this spirit will be infused throughout our country to help us solve the problems that we face.

I am confident that the talent, the native ingenuity and the capabilities developed here at this great institution coupled with that famous Aggie Spirit can do just that and ensure that this nation, in spite of the problems that we face, in spite of the continuing growing pains,

*Speech title derived by editor from speech contents

adjustments to new evolving situations—I am confident in the future of our country with this kind of leadership to help guide it.

At my last Muster here in 1973, I emphasized how the training I had received here at Texas A&M had enabled me to endure and survive, and perhaps even in a few small ways, to succeed in some of the difficult battles that we faced in the captivity of a prisoner of war camp. I told of some of the experiences of torture, harassment, exploitation for propaganda—humiliations of every type that our captors could conceive—and I told you of how our training coupled with our ingenuity and our dedication to duty, honor, and country helped us to succeed in maintaining our morale and esprit de corps in that difficult circumstance that was based on the same type of spirit that we develop in men here at Aggieland. I even gave you some examples of the humor that men in difficult circumstances can develop to provide a little comic relief or to provide some of the insights into human nature that enable men to conquer difficult objectives.

One of my favorite stories grew out of the massive public relations campaign that was generated here in the mid-1969 time period. It included bumper stickers, athletic contests dedicated to those missing in action, killed in action, prisoners of war, and the tremendous letter-writing campaign that flooded the embassies of Communist countries throughout the world—especially the delegation of North Vietnam to Paris—with mail. We did not learn about many of these things until December of 1972, just a few months before the war was over, when some of the recent captives and members of the Linebacker II Operation—the B-52 drivers who had been so instrumental in bringing that war to a conclusion—were captured and came in and reported some of these activities to us.

In particular, one event that they brought to mind got us to thinking. They said that the Air Force's aerial demonstration team and the Navy's aerial demonstration team, the Thunderbirds and the Blue Angels, at the end of each of their air shows were doing a special pass for the missing men. Unfortunately, our captors in typical fashion cut off our communications, and so that night several of us were speculating on what this special fly-by would look like at the end of this air show, and some of the men mentioned the traditional missing man formation.

One of the other guys said, "No, I don't believe that would be quite adequate. It's got to be something more distinctive. I think I have the idea. I'll bet what they do is that they fly by and just as they approach the crowd, the man in the number three airplane—which traditionally represents the missing man—the number three pilot bails out, and comes floating down in a parachute. The airplane goes over and crashes in a big fireball and then everybody in the crowd runs out and beats the hell out of him." That would give you a little bit of an insight into how a prisoner thinks after several years.

However, in deciding on a topic for today, I would prefer not to dwell excessively on my experience as a prisoner of war. I would not like to become classified as a professional ex-POW I would rather look ahead and look more to current problems—problems that face us today— however—with respect to aspects of my readjustment to life back here in the United States, some of the ladies here would probably be more interested in how I got captured the second time.

When Becky and I were first dating, I introduced her to a number of the traditions here at Texas A&M and, in fact, I knew I was winning when I took her to the Wichita State game in 1973—I think that we won that one 55-7, so she became an instant fan of Texas A&M and all of its worthy traditions. For the first few weeks of our courtship we had a running battle over whether a particular distinctive color should be classified as maroon or burgundy. But again, I knew I was winning when we were in Galveston during the spring of 1973. They had a pretty severe flood down there, and in fact many of the roads were closed for several hours, and I knew I had won her over when she turned to me and she said, "Well, I can't think of anyone else I'd rather be burgundied with." So, as a result of all that, we now have a member of the Class of '97 with a sitter over in the MSC [Memorial Student Center] and a member of the Class of '99 is due to be delivered in about four weeks.

On such a significant occasion as this, I would like to call your attention to a couple of the problems which I noticed on my return after being out of the country for over seven years. Perhaps it was a little easier for me to perceive some of these problems, if I have perceived them correctly, because some of the trends, some of the problems that I am going to mention, have developed over that time period, and people have told me that being here and seeing how these problems evolved, seeing how these attitudes evolved, and evolving with those attitudes, made it more difficult for people really to see the same kind of Rip Van Winkle effect, or the same kind of shock effect that I had in being aware that two major trends have developed during my absence.

One of these was a general decline of discipline. Within our nation, it manifested itself in a number of different ways. A tremendously high and rising rate of crime. Tremendous problems with our welfare network—our welfare system in the United States. Problems within our schools where Johnny can't read—where people have become too involved and too caught up in the idea of "doing your own thing" or "if it feels good, do it," that they had neglected the kind of disciplines that are essential to long-range success.

The other movement that I saw, which I think is a beneficial movement, is a tremendous respect and concern for the rights of individuals, for the development of human relations, for an increase in the respect for the individual human being and human dignity regardless of race, regardless of national origin, regardless of sex, regardless of the old assumptions and the old prejudices which have hampered the development of our human resources. With that in mind, I would like to review with you some of the problems that we face in these two areas of discipline and human relations.

An era of unprecedented concern for human values and human goals has altered the face of nearly every organization in American society, and the institutions within the armed forces are no exception to this— but there is a major barrier impeding the tide of social evolution. We still find people of all ages and in all stations of life who view sound human relations as somehow incompatible, even inconsistent, with good discipline, high standards, and productivity. Believers in this incompatibility seem to cluster around two poles—one extreme says that concern for the individual constitutes or leads to permissiveness. At the other extreme, there is the feeling that complying with, and enforcing, high standards of discipline violates human individuality. The dichotomy between discipline and human relations seems to widen whenever there is an increased emphasis on one or on the other because this attention is misread by those of the opposite view as perhaps a shift in the wind, perhaps a matter of convenience, perhaps an emphasis on one is perceived as a de-emphasis or a repudiation of the other. But both of these extremes miss the point.

I would like to help clarify any misunderstanding and dispel it. I believe it would be beneficial to set out an unmistakable relationship between discipline and human relations. Briefly and simply stated, the relationship between the two in today's society is not one of incompatibility but one of inseparability. The requirements or high standards of professional performance, conduct, appearance, courtesy and productivity are more important to maintaining a cohesive and a productive organization than ever before. The leadership required to set and maintain the standards of today must be a leadership of firm but sensitive awareness—one that recognizes the individual's essential personal identity within a necessarily impersonal hierarchy. Since, in the final analysis, the success of any mission, the success of any organization, depends upon people, how they are treated is as important as how they perform or how they look or how they act.

Throughout my career in the military I've noticed that the best outfits—and this is especially true here of the military units at Texas A&M—the best outfits I've seen were not the ones that were loose, that were relaxed or casual, who were concerned so much with "doing their own thing." In fact, they tended to have the rock-bottom morale because in the long-run those organizations became schizophrenic, no one was really sure what was expected of him, no one was sure how far he could or should go, what was acceptable, when or with whom. These units quite expectedly did very poorly when called upon for a team effort or were placed in a competitive role. The most effective units in my experience have been those in which there was a high level of mutual leader/follower respect, high standards, firm discipline and a strong sense of identity with the unit. The rules of the game were clearly defined and uniformly applied. Everyone knew what was expected—knew where he stood—and people generally would not think about pushing these limits.

First of all, because they were involved with more important things—more important goals and more important pursuits. And second, because to do so would have let the rest of the team down. I know this sense of cooperative teamwork at every level in an organization is possible because I've seen it work. The only qualification is that this spirit must develop from within the organization. It can't be imposed from without—at least not over the long run. When problems are noted, people from the various headquarters or management groups can send in inspection teams, assistance groups, management teams, advisors, and they can help identify and solve some of the immediate problems at a given organization at a given time. But, while these aids are important, they rarely do more than put band-aids or cosmetic corrections on the problems. Only when we can institutionalize corrective action, when we can combine discipline and effective human relations, can we expect to achieve long-term solutions to basic problems.

I am pleased that we have very few chronic problems of this type and that the problems that we do face here at Texas A&M are generally solved very quickly because of the spirit of this great institution. So in a sense, I sort of feel like I'm preaching to the choir, and yet it is important that each of us—even though we may preempt some of these problems because of our spirit, our unity, our dedication to excellence—needs to be aware that they can crop up even here; and we need to know that these are continuing problems across our nation—very serious problems—so that as we go out to take up our roles in life, to take our stations, to take positions of leadership, we know the relationship between discipline on the one hand and sound human relations and respect for the individual on the other.

One of the best ways to avoid these extremes is to study the situation. Avoid pushing discipline to such a ridiculous extreme that it becomes Mickey Mouse or that it merely makes puppets of the subordinates in your organization. And while viewing the problems of human relations and individuality, you avoid pushing to the extreme an unguided, an uncontrolled attitude of "do your own thing" or "if it feels good, do it."

We need to strike a balance, and one of the best ways to do this is by training our young people, training our children. It begins in the home. It begins in the public schools—showing people how discipline is in their own long-range personal self interest. You know, self interest is one of the strongest motivators that psychologists have ever found. So, if we could convince people how discipline in short-range matters—

that foregoing one of the pleasures of life temporarily or cutting back on the relative emphasis placed on pleasures in favor of doing a little more hard work—perhaps a little more research, a little more practice in your professional specialty—can lead to long-range success. When we can convince people and can show them how short-range discipline contributes to long-range success, then we will have gone a long way to solving some of the attitude problems that our nation faces.

Today, many of you, especially those of you who have been freshmen this year, you have probably seen and felt predominantly only the restrictions of discipline, and yet tomorrow you will see and understand how discipline has been the key to success, the key to creativity and the key to victory. I can cite no more immediate example of that than the performance of the Singing Cadets as done today. There is a time when those men get together and they work, they practice, they learn a lot about the theory of music. They spend a lot of time putting that theory into practice when they could be out doing their own thing somewhere else—doing something that was easier. And yet because of their sacrifice, because of their practice and their dedication, they contribute a product that is just as representative of excellence as any that this great institution develops. But this is not limited to just the Singing Cadets, certainly. The Cadet Corps, the Aggie Band, our academic departments, our athletic teams, this whole spirit pervades this institution.

So, in that sense, I am really preaching to the choir. But as you take your place in life, as you go back to your individual communities, as you take your jobs, and as you take positions of leadership on parent/teacher organizations, on school boards, and civic organizations, if you can understand and apply this relationship between discipline on the one hand and good sound human relations and the appreciation for the dignity and the value of the human individual on the other, many of the problems that our nation faces now will disappear, but our nation needs that leadership.

In the sense that this Muster ceremony is a memorial to those Aggies who have departed this life, I am reminded of the words of President Lincoln as he stood on the battlefield at Gettysburg, Pennsylvania, when he said, "We cannot dedicate, we cannot consecrate, we cannot hallow this ground. The brave men, living and dead who struggled here have consecrated it, far above our poor power to add or to detract." I feel this is very significant to this occasion because those Aggies who have given their lives in the previous battles for our nation, those Aggies who performed, who made their mark in life, have set a standard that will be difficult for us to follow. It is a great challenge to us. And so, in that sense, to continue President Lincoln's words, "It is for us, the living, rather, to be here dedicated to . . . that great task remaining before us"—that we identify and solve and attack our nation's problems—that we may bind up our nation's wounds, the divisiveness caused by wars, and prejudices and racial conflicts—that we dedicate ourselves to preserving "government of the people, by the people, for the people."

I'm proud to be an Aggie, and I'm proud of the contribution that Texas A&M has made toward that goal. May it ever be so.

# Col. Tom Dooley '35

*1978—G. Rollie White Coliseum*

Col. Tom Dooley '35.
Photo from editor's
collection.

Thomas "Tom" Dooley was born December 18, 1913, and attended schools in McKinney, Texas. He graduated from Texas A&M in 1935 with a degree in agricultural engineering. While a student, he was voted one of the five most popular cadets. He served as captain of Corps staff, member of the cadet colonel's staff, and head yell leader.

As aide-de-camp to Lt. Gen. Jonathan M. Wainwright in the US Army during World War II, Dooley was taken prisoner by the Japanese on May 6, 1942. At the time of his liberation in August 1945, he had been promoted to the rank of lieutenant colonel. The next month, Dooley was selected by the US War Department to witness the surrender ceremonies of the Japanese aboard the USS *Missouri* in Tokyo Bay.

Dooley kept meticulous journals of his experiences on Corregidor and Bataan as well as throughout his captivity. These journals have been placed in the Texas A&M University archives by his wife and children. They provide a unique perspective and give an unflinching portrait of life as a US soldier in the Philippine Islands and as a prisoner of war of the Japanese.

Dooley prepared the famous 1942 Aggie Muster roll call for the Corregidor report at the request of Gen. George F. Moore '08. He tells the story of preparing that report in this Muster address.

Dooley died March 26, 2006, in Hopkinsville, Kentucky.

# The Corregidor Muster of 1942*

That's great. Forgive me, you start to get overcome when you come back to this school. I have. I want to thank you for asking me, including my wife, to this 78th Muster. Kind of chokes you up a little bit, but I'll simmer down in a minute.

I want to greet the Class of '33. I hope you have a nice reunion, and I hope you say sometime during this period, "I wish we'd been nicer to the class of '35."

When I look around on this visit and especially at this group tonight, it reminds me of that commercial—"You've come a long way, baby." I recall—I remember it well—that on December 3rd, 1931, a group of us walked up to the old administration building [Academic Building] to look at the bulletin board outside the Sergeant Major's office— Sergeant Major John King—because that's where they posted the first semester grades. You went up there to learn whether you'd be there next week. But what impressed me—what I'd remembered today—was at the top of the list it said, "Total enrollment: 1,975 students." I'm sure that's hard for all of you to realize. I'm sorry I didn't go far enough with my research to find out how many were there a week later. But it's a great change, and I'm happy to see the progress made by adding all these beautiful girls too.

People mention these Musters as beginning in 1883, or some say in 1903, and that they were held intermittently during those periods from 1883 through the 1920s. But as far as I can ascertain, and I spent four years here during the '30s, none were shown on the records. Perhaps we that attended in that period of the depression couldn't afford a muster. But they're great.

Of course, the reason Joe Marshall invited me here is because I happened to be in a certain occurrence in World War II, and I'm happy to come here and tell about that because I've wanted to do it ever since I came back during World War II.

A group of us were stationed in the Philippines. Although there were a number of Aggies there, quite a number of Aggies arrived on

*Speech title derived by editor from speech contents

the ships on November the 28th, 1941, just in time for the war to start on December the 8th for us because we were across the international dateline.

As a result of the Pearl Harbor attack, we were sort of out on a limb there because our resupply was completely cut off. We were immediately rationed—we had to ration ammunition and food because our mission then was to hold on as long as possible to prevent the Japanese from expanding further south, so that the troops back home could take that time to effect a build-up and recoup their losses and then start a successful campaign to end in Tokyo. I might add: To us who were there, it took them an awful long time.

But, early in December the Japanese landed on Luzon Island to the north and moved south. We effected a retrograde movement—US troops and Philippine troops, and did as well as we could—it did take time—and finally the pressure came to bear to the extent that Bataan, the peninsula down there, was forced to surrender on April the 6th, 1942. With that, the Japanese were able to move heavy artillery into positions where they could fire on the last US position, which was Corregidor Island. Having air superiority and heavy artillery to bear, the troops on Corregidor just had to dig in deeper. Naturally, movement was limited and communications were limited.

Along in mid-April, General George F. Moore—who was spoken of earlier—called me in. We were at adjacent headquarters in a tunnel protected by heavy rock. It was mentioned that General Moore was the class of 1908. I'd like to mention also that he was commandant of the Cadets and PMS&T [Professor of Military Science & Tactics] in the '30s. In 1942, he was commanding the harbor defenses of Manila and Subic Bay, and it was the last point that the Japanese had not occupied.

General Moore wanted to discuss the thought of the upcoming April 21st. Of course, he'd heard of past musters, but I didn't. But he knew that I was an Aggie. He said that he wanted to get a list of the Aggies still fighting there. Although the account nowadays says that they gathered on April 21st, it was impossible for that number of people to congregate because they could not be spared from their positions. So, we had a roll call, and a muster is a roll call. We got all of the Aggies listed, and I contacted one of the two correspondents still on the island. I don't remember whether he was UP or AP, but he was willing to use his carefully apportioned time—wire time—to get a story back to the States. We termed it the "Aggie Story."

At that time, it served several purposes. It gave a good plug for the state of Texas, which was a long ways away. It gave a good plug for Texas A&M, and it also served the purpose of notifying parents and wives at home of those that were still living and still fighting, because of the communication limitations there.

So, of that group which included those Aggies, we were unlike those at San Jacinto—we weren't successful in our fight. Corregidor was surrendered about two weeks later. It was May the 6th, 1942. Then came a long wait, and the survivors came back in the summer of '45, and that's when they learned that the Musters had sparked and continued during World War II. I'm sure some of you were here, but I was fortunate enough to attend the one on Kyle Field in 1946. Of course, that's when they really got going, and it is a great pleasure to be at this one today.

So, that's my story on the Muster at Corregidor. Let's hope that this tradition, rekindled in the time of war, will long endure in the time of peace.

Thank you.

Gen. Dwight D. Eisenhower delivered the Homecoming Muster address at Kyle Field on Easter Sunday, April 21, 1946. At the far left is Maj. Thomas Dooley '35, who served as an aide to Gen. Jonathan M. Wainwright at Bataan and Corregidor and was a POW for over three years. Next to him is Col. Olin E. "Tiger" Teague '32, who served in Europe during World War II and was congressman from the Sixth District of Texas from 1946 until 1978. Standing immediately behind General Eisenhower is Col. Bill Becker '41, who served as chairman of the Muster ceremony and who retired as a major general. Courtesy Texas A&M University Archives.

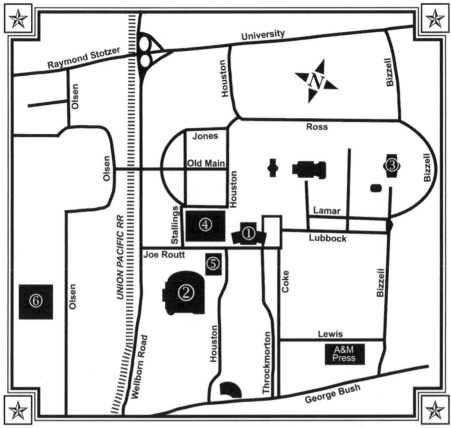

**AGGIE MUSTER LOCATIONS**

① GUION HALL
(Razed in 1971 for construction of University Center)

② KYLE FIELD

③ SYSTEM ADMINISTRATION BUILDING LAWN
(Jack K. Williams Building)

④ MEMORIAL STUDENT CENTER LAWN

⑤ G. ROLLIE WHITE COLISSEUM
(Razed in 2013 for expansion of Kyle Field)

⑥ REED ARENA

Texas A&M campus map showing the six locations of Aggie Muster ceremonies held on campus from 1944 to the present: (1) Guion Hall (1945–46, 1949–50); (2) Kyle Field (1946, 1974); (3) System Administration Building (1947–48, 1952, 1964–70); (4) Memorial Student Center (1951, 1953–63); (5) G. Rollie White Coliseum (1971–73, 1975–97); and (6) Reed Arena (1998–2016). Map by Anne Boykin.

Rare photograph of a concert in Guion Hall. Courtesy Texas A&M University Archives.

A seven-member rifle team fires a twenty-one-gun Muster salute outside of Guion Hall in 1949. Courtesy Texas A&M University Archives.

Stage party on the steps of the Memorial Student Center during the 1960 Aggie Muster ceremony. The speaker was Lt. Gen. A. D. Bruce '16 (in dark suit wearing sunglasses); also shown is Texas A&M's president, Maj. Gen. J. Earl Rudder '32 (standing to the left of the podium). Courtesy Texas A&M University Archives.

Students seated on the Memorial Student Center lawn for the 1961 Aggie Muster. Since the MSC lawn is considered part of the memorial to Aggies lost at war, Muster was the only time students were allowed on the MSC grass. Courtesy Texas A&M University Archives.

Students on the lawn of the System Administration Building in the mid-1960s. The Ross Volunteer firing squad, the Fightin' Texas Aggie Band, and the Singing Cadets are shown in the background. Courtesy Texas A&M University Archives.

The Aggie Muster reminder sign at the main entrance to the campus in 1985. Photo from editor's collection.

The Silver Taps buglers in the lobby of G. Rollie White Coliseum for the 1988 Aggie Muster ceremony. Photo from editor's collection.

The very first event in Reed Arena was the Aggie Muster of 1998. Photo by
J. Griffis Smith. Used by permission.

The candles lit during the Roll Call for the Absent surrounded the floor of Reed Arena in 2006. Photos courtesy of Texas A&M University.

# Lee H. Smith '57

*1979—G. Rollie White Coliseum*

Lee H. Smith '57. Photo from editor's collection.

Lee Herman Smith was born January 7, 1935, in Ector, Texas, and attended Sunset High School in Dallas. After graduating with a BS degree in math at Texas A&M, he earned an MS in engineering administration from Southern Methodist University, pursued doctoral studies at Iowa State University, and completed a PhD in statistics at Texas A&M.

He spent a decade in engineering with electronics and aircraft firms before entering academics at the University of Texas at Arlington in 1965. After achieving recognition in a series of administrative positions there and with the University of Houston and the University of Texas at Dallas, he was named president of Southwest Texas State University (now Texas State University) in 1974, the youngest president of a major university in the nation. During his seven-year tenure, Smith raised academic standards, created tenure management guidelines, implemented fund raising and development programs, and established an academic planning model. He also coauthored numerous research articles and a book, *Statistics for Business: A Conceptual Approach.*

After leaving academe in 1981, he held progressively more responsible positions with Travelhost, Inc., and was president of Standard Life Insurance Co., Intercontinental Life Insurance Co., and Voyager Expanded Learning, Inc. In 1999 he cofounded Umansys, Inc., to develop a patented, universally applicable automated enterprise management system.

## Not Just a Memorial Service*

It should go without saying, but for emphasis and the record I want to say that the privilege of being on this particular platform, in this particular position, for this particular event is one of the greatest honors of my life. Because we are an Aggie family, there are two other special people here who should share that honor with me. I want you to meet my wife, Eva, and my daughter Diette.

My remarks will naturally be directed to all Aggies everywhere, but I wish to direct my primary emphasis to the current students at Texas A&M University as we together contemplate the scope and significance of Aggie Muster.

As many of you know, and as Keith mentioned, I was also tremendously honored in the fall of 1976 when I was asked to bring greetings to Texas A&M University, on behalf of delegates from other universities and the learned societies, on the occasion of its centennial convocation. Those remarks comprised, without a doubt, one of the most heartfelt speeches of my entire life, so much so, in fact, that I toyed with the idea of repeating it here today. However, in deference to those of you who may have heard that speech at that convocation, I finally decided to take what I feel is the closest possible approach without an outright repeat. So, I've chosen to present a sequel to that delivery in both content and style. The formal subject of this speech is, of course, Aggie Muster, but you will recognize its essence as simply another futile attempt at the ever so desirable, but oh so virtually impossible, characterization of Texas A&M University.

Aggie Muster is truly a phenomenal memorial service. It is a special occasion when Aggies throughout the world pause to honor those who have passed from among the ranks of the physically living. It is that occasion when we rejoice as we commune officially with those spirits so strong and pervasive that they completely permeate our hearts and thoughts. It is that special occasion when we commemorate the glories of those Aggies who preceded us and pledge that we will exert every possible effort to see that those glories will be continually magnified

*Speech title derived by editor from speech contents

and multiplied by the Aggies to follow. Yes, Aggie Muster is indeed a marvelous memorial service; however, it is by no means *just* a memorial service. No, it is also a combined thanksgiving, reward, and rededication for those who participate in the Muster ceremony—a thanksgiving for the privilege of having been given the opportunity to earn the right to participate, a reward for the sacrifices made to earn that right, and a re-dedication to upholding the principles prerequisite to the constant and continued fulfillment of the responsibilities associated with that right.

No, Aggie Muster is by no means *just* a memorial service. It is a magnificent orchestration involving literally thousands of persons throughout the world. It is an exemplary implementation of an intri-cate and far-reaching extravaganza, the detailed plans for the next of which are initiated on an annual basis directly after the culmination of the Muster event of immediate concern. Through this orchestration (which epitomizes the proper management of the logistics of a difficult and complicated undertaking) is made available an almost countless number and variety of remarkable local approaches which combine to form a masterful global salute to the revered Aggies who have departed this earth.

No, Aggie Muster is by no means *just* a memorial service. It is an epic amalgamation of a multiplicity of equally desirable and spectrum-covering contrasts. What other event is simultaneously permeated by the formality of an inauguration and yet constantly softened by the informality of a family picnic? Where else will one encounter a col-lective which will in one instant reflect the macho of "old Army" and in the next instant exude the sensitivity of a Brahms lullaby? At what other event can an observer witness the protocol equivalent to any ambassador's reception and yet simultaneously be overwhelmed by the inherent equality of an ideal democracy? Where else can one, in three consecutive moments, encounter feelings which reflect the anxiety of a Broadway opening, the intensity of a religious conversion, and the relaxation evoked by a sauna bath? Where else can one simultaneously participate in a single ceremony which offers the excitement of a moon shot, the gaiety and frivolity of the state fair, the reverence of Easter sunrise services, and the solemn atmosphere of Silver Taps?

No, Aggie Muster is by no means *just* a memorial service. It is a roll call which manifests a way of life; a way of life that dictates that it is not nearly sufficient to meet one's own responsibilities as regularly, religiously, and loyally as possible—although that is definitely an implicit requirement of those who are granted the right to participate in the Muster. Indeed there is the concomitant expectation, nay demand, that one always, as is symbolized by the roll call, answer of one for the other, and both stand ready to meet the responsibilities of a fellow Aggie in need and simultaneously expect no less than the guaranteed, though not explicitly promised, reciprocation from any other Aggie.

No, Aggie Muster is by no means *just* a memorial service. It is an economic paradox like the Biblical pearl of great price. To that select few who have elected and have been selected to become Aggies, it comes as the greatest bargain in the world at absolutely no cost. On the other hand, this invaluable commodity is not for sale in the marketplace at any price whatsoever to those who have failed for any reason to qualify as members of our family—one of the most prestigious of all brotherhoods.

No, Aggie Muster is by no means *just* a memorial service. It is a potential personal significant emotional event for each Aggie in attendance, a rarity which takes on even more significance in view of the fact that most psychologists are in agreement that even the opportunities for truly emotional events do not come nearly so frequently in the lives of most persons. Even more rare is the propensity which Aggies have for converting these potentials into actual significant emotional events, thanks primarily to the lifelong conditioning and almost automatic emotional and spiritual preparation which immediately precedes each Aggie Muster.

No, Aggie Muster is by no means *just* a memorial service. It is the ultimate in multidimensional symbolism. It evokes the patriotism of the national anthem. It represents a discipline of right and wrong second only to the Ten Commandments. It brings to memory a code of fair play as sweeping as the Constitution. It is a reminder of a manifestation of adversity which challenges that encountered by Job, and a simultaneous promise of hope so well portrayed in Kipling's superb lines from the poem "If." It simultaneously conjures in our minds the competition of the Super Bowl, the pride of the Yankees, the fantastic togetherness of the survivors of Corregidor, the daring flight of the Spirit of St. Louis, all wrapped in the warmth of a Rembrandt, the nostalgia of a class reunion and the remarkable love of brother for sister.

No, Aggie Muster is by no means *just* a memorial service. It is a phenomenon which transcends the magic of make-believe. What futurist at the initial Aggie Muster could possibly have been so astute as to envision, much less so bold as to predict that fantastic scope and depth which it would ultimately achieve? What opium-filled mystic could ever have fantasized the emotion-packed high that only Aggies reach, and they only on Muster day? And would even Hemingway have dared create a fiction which would have as its theme a development so unbelievable as Aggie Muster, with one of its many sub-climaxes—an event so powerful as soldiers mustering together on Iwo Jima during World War II?

No, Aggie Muster is by no means *just* a memorial service. It is a promise for the future that exceeds the level of warranty of any will, insurance policy, savings account, or practically any other written or implied contract. It is a regularly occurring proof of the credibility of the promise that once a person makes those sacrifices required to earn the right to be called an Aggie, never a year shall pass from here to eternity when that person is not specifically and individually honored by those who some day will be the beneficiaries of that very same promise.

No, Aggie Muster is by no means *just* a memorial service. Nevertheless, as I've said, it is a memorial service, and so it is most appropriate that we explicitly and specifically pay tribute to those Aggies who have gone before us, that we may give thanks to God for the privilege of being today among the ranks of the physically living Aggies, and that we may pray to God for guidance of all Aggies who are to follow in our steps that they may preserve and enhance the heritage so generously bequeathed us by those whom we today pause to honor.

Most importantly, it is imperative that we and Aggies everywhere, on this special day of days, pay homage to that beloved institution which provided the initial impetus that gave birth to the unique bond so happily shared and treasured by Aggies everywhere. I personally do that best through the words of Earl Reum [in "A Wish for Leaders"], words which I've called upon before in similar situations. Mr. Reum has written these words as a challenge for all individuals. I wish today to quote that message for a very specific reason. For it is as though Texas A&M personified has said these words for every single individual who will ever find their way to this university as a student. In fact, Texas A&M not only provides the challenge of the message, it provides that unique way of life which maximizes the opportunity of each of its students throughout the ages to live up to the challenge. The message and the challenge and the ultimate way of life which I believe so well characterize Texas A&M are as follows:

> I wish you would know how it feels to run with all your heart and lose, and lose horribly. I wish that you could achieve some great good for mankind but have nobody know about it except for you. I wish you could find something so worthwhile that you deem it worthy of investing your life in it. I hope you become frustrated and challenged enough to begin to push back the very barriers of your own personal limitations. I hope you make a stupid mistake and get caught red-handed and are big enough to say those magic words, "I was wrong." I hope you give so much of yourself that some days you wonder if it is worth all the effort. I wish for you a magnificent obsession that will give you reason for living and purpose and direction in life. I wish for you the worst kind of criticism for everything you do, because that makes you fight to achieve beyond what you normally would. I wish for you the experience of leadership.

And so, Keith, Texas A&M University, as we honor your sons and daughters who are deceased, we realize full well that they serve only as surrogates through which we pass that highest honor which truly belongs to you. It is fitting then that I close once again in a very simple and straightforward fashion.

Texas A&M University, we admire you, we respect you, we salute you. Texas A&M University, we revere you. We shall be eternally grateful to you. We pray that you will continue your remarkable progress. Finally, as I have said, and as Keith has quoted, there is one phrase, one feeling, which is so powerful, that is so personal that one dare not use it but with great care. I shall take once again that personal privilege of saying it on this special day, for me and I know for thousands of others: Texas A&M University, we love you.

# Henry G. Cisneros '68

*1980—G. Rollie White Coliseum*

Henry G. Cisneros '68. Photo from editor's collection.

Henry Gabriel Cisneros was born June 11, 1947, in San Antonio. In addition to earning his bachelor's degree as a distinguished military graduate of Texas A&M, he received an MA in urban and regional planning from A&M in 1970. He was chosen as a White House Fellow in 1971 and then served as a captain in the US Army before earning an MA in public administration from the John F. Kennedy School of Government at Harvard University in 1973. In 1975 he received a PhD in public administration from George Washington University and was elected to the San Antonio City Council. After six years as a councilman, he was elected the first Hispanic mayor of a major US city in 1981 and served four two-year terms. Although supporters urged him to run for governor in 1990 and then US senator in 1992, Cisneros declined in order to remain close to his son, who had successful heart surgery in 1993.

Following the racial riots in Los Angeles in 1992, he flew to that city to try to calm its angry residents. That same year he worked on Bill Clinton's Democratic presidential campaign. When Clinton was elected, he appointed Cisneros as secretary of housing and urban development. Within eighteen months, his efforts to provide housing for homeless people and replace dangerous housing projects throughout the nation began showing results. He resigned from the cabinet in 1997 and was named president and CEO of Spanish-language broadcaster Univision Communications, the fifth most watched television network in the nation.

In 2000 Cisneros launched a community building joint venture to build workforce homes in central neighborhoods of major metropolitan areas. He served as chairman of CityView, which included component entities CityView West and CityView America. He and his wife, Mary Alice, founded American Sunrise, a nonprofit venture focusing on home ownership and after-school programs for central city children.

Cisneros has been president of the National League of Cities, deputy chair of the Federal Reserve Bank of Dallas, and a member of the boards of the Rockefeller Foundation, Enterprise Foundation, and American Film Institute.

## Soldier, Statesman, Knightly Gentleman*

We gather today to remember those who have passed from amongst this body. We remember them as friends and as classmates, as brothers and sisters, as Aggies, and as good men and women. That is a high and moving remembrance. But today, we stop and remember them in another and even higher way. Just as when we stop by a quiet battlefield cemetery—white crosses row after row. Or just as when we pass near a memorial to a sunken ship with Americans entombed below the murky waters. Or just as when we visit the hushed and sacred places of our history—places where men and women have given their lives in a painful moment of total sacrifice—Concord Bridge, Gettysburg, Shiloh, The Alamo, Chateau Thierry, Guadalcanal. Just as then, today we remember the spirit of those with whom we have shared pride and enthusiasm, with whom we have forged values and memories, with whom we have shared the brotherhood of growing up together and spending our maturing years together. Today we call for a deeper remembrance than the mere physical presence of Aggies who have passed this way. Today, we rededicate ourselves to the higher meanings of the endeavor we shared with them. The endeavor which now we must carry on because we have been granted a little more time, a few more miles, a few more years to work with.

That endeavor is to capture in our lives, to keep the ideals, the soul of the Texas A&M spirit: SOLDIER—STATESMAN—KNIGHTLY GENTLEMAN.

*Speech title derived by editor from speech contents

Some persons would suggest that such an ideal is outmoded, that it is out of step with the decade that has been labeled the "Me" decade. They would say that such an ideal has no use to a nation comfortable under a blanket of national security and insulated by a prosperous economy. Some would regard the ideal as a hopeless throwback, for today Americans have the time and the money to explore personal awareness, to enjoy unprecedented levels of self-indulgence, to engage in a quest for personal freedoms, and to manifest in countless ways a concentration on personal fulfillment. We see the acceptance of religious cults, of reliance on psycho-therapies, of drug dependence, of family dissolutions, and of a general trend toward material ends at all costs.

### SOLDIER—STATESMAN—KNIGHTLY GENTLEMAN.

Such words would appear to have no place in our times. Yet, as we look ahead, we cannot escape the signs that the next few years will demand changes in our lifestyles of recent years. The next few years will force the stark realization that the challenges our nation faces are as great as those which have confronted any other age of Americans. The challenges are real, and they relate directly to the lives, the attitudes, the careers, and the day-to-day comforts of our people. All Americans are likely to be affected—but A&M's men and women will be called upon once again in greater measure to apply their talents, to teach attitudes, to forge characters, and to make sacrifices. To keep faith with the names called at Muster, the watchwords through this period need not be reluctance nor hesitance, not fear nor abandonment—instead, they can be preparation, forging strength, and steeling ourselves for what may be one of the decisive eras in the history of modern civilization.

### SOLDIERS

A&M's men and women must be soldiers—at a minimum in the sense of expressing an understanding and a determination, if not actually bearing arms—because one of the basic realities of our time deals with our nation's international security.

The dominant facts of the international environment will take shape as it becomes more and more obvious that the Soviet Union means exactly what its leaders have been saying consistently for some years. They have said that they intend to see to it that the Western nations and their democratic systems fall before the advance of Marxism-Leninism. Now they intend to use their armed forces and covert cells to set up the conditions for the overthrow they seek.

General Sir John Hackett, a respected British military expert, has concluded that "Soviet policy in the 1980s will be one of unlimited opportunism with a wide range of possible actions and responses backed up with prepared military plans kept constantly up-to-date. The idea will be to exploit every opportunity to advance the Soviet interest, using tactical manipulation of instabilities throughout the world and national rivalries, by what they plan to be a dominant position of military strength abroad—even at the cost of damping down domestic progress within the U.S.S.R.—as a fulcrum for the lever of Soviet political and economic intentions."

The tools will be those we have seen before—only on a larger scale and in areas of the globe not exploited up to now. They will supply arms to insurgents, topple governments, encourage coups, support terrorism and kidnappings, provoke assassinations, train communist technocrats in the Third World, spread propaganda, spike animosities between nations, create internal dissension, seek control over needed materials as well as their prices, and intimidate leaders in geographically important areas of the globe with threats of force.

Our national defense attitude cannot be based on ascribing benign or passive motives to the Soviets and their allies. It is very clear that using the lever of their unprecedented military strength, the Soviets intend to create instabilities throughout the world and then keep the United States immobilized and pinned down by the threat of an unfavorable direct military confrontation. As long as we allow a differential in military strengths, we can expect that their blatant exploitation of international instabilities will affect our ability to trade freely with other nations, and very soon, directly affect our daily lives.

The reality of the 1980s demands that A&M's soldierly traditions of preparedness, of toughness, and of duty serve to educate Americans on the need to strengthen our nation. A&M's legacy has always been one of preparing citizen-soldiers, even while preparing careers and livelihoods. To keep faith with the men and women we are remembering today, to earn our inheritance, we cannot be blind, ignorant, or indifferent, for we—like many of them—will be called upon in some way at the very minimum to express understanding in the difficult job of standing up to a power with tremendous capacity for domination as it attempts to exert control in every part of the globe.

### STATESMAN

Men and women who see their country and ask, "What is the right thing to do?" Not, "What's in it for me?" Not, "What is the expedient thing to do?" Not, "What is the advantageous thing to do?" But simply, "What is the right thing to do?"

For business, for government, for education, for the professions, for agriculture—Aggies must be statesmen—and do what is the right thing to do for the country.

There is an emerging recognition, for example, that our industrial plant as a nation is handicapped by lack of capital, by declining productivity, by disadvantages in international markets, by the sheer scale of the need to modernize, and by a continuing adversary relationship between labor, government, and industry. The implications of the continued decline of industrial capacity can be seen in the difficulties besetting the financially strapped Chrysler Corporation, whose chairman asserts that its problems are but the leading edge of difficulties that will face other automakers and indeed many other industries between now and 1985.

Lee Iacocca, chairman of the Chrysler Corporation, states: "We are the classic microcosm of the problems that affect our nation. Energy cripples us. Inflation has hit the automobile industry especially hard because of the high inflation in petrochemicals and lead productivity is down. The creativity of the company to invent new items is reduced. I never create a job anymore; everything I do is to meet a law. It worries me for all industry. There will be other cries for help." When the other problems of the Chrysler Corporation are matched with the recent decisions of US Steel, the nation's largest steel maker, to close 16 plants and release 8% of its work force of 13,000 employees, Mr. Iacocca's comments ring loudly. Chairman David Roderick of US Steel worries about the trend and suggests that our national position in steel could be as serious ten years from now as our present dependence on foreign oil. Rising costs, cheaply produced foreign steel, and huge expenditures to meet environmental standards erode the ability of many of our industries to amass the billions of dollars that will be necessary to replace antiquated plants. The task is formidable and can be accomplished only when statesmen's qualities are brought to it—men and women such as A&M's, prepared by their education and shaped by their character to look beyond the narrow interest of the short-term temptation to ask, "What is the right thing to do for the country and its future?"

The basic strength of our country has been the ability of our industry to grow and compete. Yet today we lack a cohesive national purpose to maintain our industrial preeminence. Can we still forge a clear national purpose? Can we boost and support critical growth industries? Can we create fair government standards of import protections? Can we commit the necessary research and development funds? Yes, but only if Americans realize the personal impact of continuing slippage of our industrial capacity and productivity.

Productivity is an obligation of every American, and we must invest in the future by building the skills and capabilities of every person. Spending for education and training and motivation are critical parts of our capital investment, for the skills of our people represent the most valuable capital in our national treasure chest.

One factor fueling our productivity decline is that in the past our greatest productivity gains have come from improvement in technology and equipment, and today, we are not making the investment in plant equipment and modernization to keep us ahead in the productivity race. We have always been the most idea-motivated nation in the world, always in relentless pursuit of innovation and invention. Today, it would seem that we have lost some of the zest for that quest.

Statesmen's qualities are needed in every sector of American life, and Aggies will be there to commit our talents, enhance our productivity, revive our quest for national achievements, and as we work to dismantle the hostility and the wasteful tensions between business, government, and labor. Among the names called in our Muster are men and women who have built with their hands and their brains and their energies—

they have provided the raw human power to build this state and this nation. It is our inheritance to remember that spirit and preserve it.

### KNIGHTLY GENTLEMAN

Men and women whose self-assurance is balanced by a good heart. Gentlemen and women, whose strength of character is balanced by a sense of justice. Gentlemen and women whose self-reliance is balanced by responsibility and duty. These are not celebrated attributes today. Instead, there is a pervasive sense that Americans are somehow owed comforts by some invisible grantor of privilege. The net effect of that sense of being owed by someone else is that there has been a decline in the individual commitment to excellence, discipline, and accomplishment. But the reality is that there is no person, no institution, no invisible grantor that owes, that is able to pay all those perceived debts without cost.

The dawning of the recognition that everything must be fought for and earned is an important fact of life. In every field, the American ability to endure, to set out on a difficult course and master it, will be challenged.

It may well be on the very personal recognition that nothing just falls in place automatically, and that everything must be produced by someone, that the fate of the United States, and indeed, Western civilization depends. Clearly, this recognition must be balanced by a continuing commitment to fairness, to opportunity, and to openness in our society; but the fundamental fact that echoes from the lives of those whose names are called at Muster is that for everyone who relaxes from the pursuit of excellence for our nation, someone must pay, and in time, we all would pay. That faithful calling of the Muster, the long unbroken ranks of the Corps, the willing presence of Aggies in every place that there is work to do—these gentlemanly traits have little to do with heroics, but everything to do with duty.

### SOLDIER—STATESMAN—KNIGHTLY GENTLEMAN.

These are A&M ideals that have their roots in our most revered traditions of the past; but they grow to full strength when they are needed in the present. These are A&M ideals that are the bedrock of the beliefs in our souls; but they spring into action in our hands and bodies when duty calls them forth.

These are A&M ideals that reverberate from the roll call of names called at Muster; but they can be given the sincerest tribute only when we who can, choose to live them. The truest respect we can give today in remembering the spirit of Muster is to preserve it. To live it. To be there. And we will—because like the man in the famous poem by Robert Frost—while we may be distracted and dissuaded from time to time, we know why we are here and what we must do. The woods may indeed be "lovely, dark, and deep." But together with the spirit of those whose names echo in here today—even though they may not be here—we have an unmistakable bond of spirit, and we together "have promises to keep and miles to go before" there can be any thought of sleep.

# Frederick McClure '76

*1981—G. Rollie White Coliseum*

Fred McClure '76. Photo from editor's collection.

Frederick Donald "Fred" McClure was born February 2, 1954, in Fort Worth. In high school he was Texas state president of the Future Farmers of America and later served as FFA national secretary. He was a special summer White House intern in 1975, and during his senior year at Texas A&M, Governor Dolph Briscoe appointed him to the State Advisory Council for Technical-Vocational Education. He was Texas A&M student body president, speaker of the Student Senate, a Rhodes Scholarship state finalist, and a member of the Singing Cadets. McClure graduated summa cum laude in agricultural economics, receiving the Brown Foundation–J. Earl Rudder Outstanding Student Award. In 1981 he earned a law degree from Baylor University School of Law, where he was president of the Student Bar Association.

After practicing law in Houston, he joined Senator John G. Tower's office as legislative director and legal counsel. He was a managing shareholder of Winstead Sechrest & Minick, managing director of Public Strategies Inc., and Government Affairs Staff Vice President for Texas Air Corporation. He served as associate deputy US attorney general, chairman of the Board of Visitors of the US Naval Academy, and a member of the National Civil Aviation Review Commission.

After serving as special assistant for legislative affairs to President Ronald Reagan and assistant for legislative affairs to President George H.W. Bush, McClure became a partner in the Washington, DC, office of Sonnenschein Nath & Rosenthal LLP, specializing in public law and policy strategies. In 1995 he was appointed to a six-year term on the

Texas A&M University System Board of Regents, serving two years as vice chairman. He served on the US Secretary of Energy's Advisory Board and the boards of the George Bush Presidential Library Foundation and the Cotton Bowl Athletic Association, which he served as chairman for four years.

He was recognized as a Texas A&M Distinguished Alumnus in 1991, was a vice president of the Association of Former Students, and served on the board of the 12th Man Foundation. He was on the Select Committee on the Corps of Cadets and on the Academic Task Force of A&M's Target 2000 Project. In 2012 McClure was named executive director of the George H.W. Bush Presidential Library Foundation at Texas A&M. Four years later he became executive director of leadership initiatives in the Office of the Provost at A&M.

## "The Signs of the Times"

Indeed, it is a pleasure and an honor for me to have been asked to participate today in the greatest of all Aggie traditions. As my best friend, also a member of the Class of 1976, put it, Aggie Muster distills all of the Aggie traditions into one single ceremony which emphasizes the very best of the Aggie Spirit. Words are inadequate for me to use in expressing my gratitude for your extending the invitation to me to present the 1981 Muster address at this, the largest Aggie Muster in the world! When I stood on this stage as Aggie Muster chairman on this day in 1976, little did I realize that five years later I would have the opportunity to present the Aggie Muster Address, and for this honor I am grateful.

In a rather indirect way, I began preparation of this speech on December sixth upon receipt of the invitation from the Muster Committee. I wasted no time in calling my parents, who were as elated as I.

Since 1969, when Future Farmers of America caused me to start making speeches, my family has had sort of a family joke about my speech-making. During that year, my first, my second, indeed my fifteenth speech was entitled "The Signs of the Times." As the ensuing years passed, whenever I would mention an invitation to my father, invariably he would say, "Son, are you gonna talk to them about the signs of the times?" Over two thousand speeches later, when I called my parents on December 6th, my father repeated the question and we all laughed at this bit of family folklore.

On December eighteenth, I visited my father, and he brought up the subject of Aggie Muster during our conversation, indicating to me his plans and his desires and his wishes to be here today. Again, he posed the age-old question and made serious efforts—this time to let me know that he was not joking; that he thought the speech would be appropriate for this occasion because it focuses on the future and our roles, individually and collectively, in that future. Despite the fact that Aggies join together in meeting halls the world over on this day to answer "Here" for those Texas A&M men and women whose death prevents their answering Roll Call, the Aggie Spirit compels, even forces, us to look ahead; to push onward; to be whatever in the world we want to be, so long as we are the best at it that we can possibly be.

Today, this ceremony means much more to me than any Aggie Muster I have ever attended. It means so much to me because there is one other person who, in my view, was the finest non-former student Aggie on the face of this earth and whose name should be added to Roll Call.

You see, at the time, I did not realize the importance of that conversation with my father on December eighteenth. That conversation about Aggie Muster was among the last words which we shared, for three days later he unexpectedly died and joined those whom death has taken from our ranks, but whose memory lives in our hearts.

So, today, Aggie Muster means so much more to me than it ever has before! For the first time I can understand and I can sympathize with the grief and suffering which accompanies the loss of a loved one; of a friend. Thus, during my remarks today, I am committed to accomplishing two basic tasks. Although my father's desire to be here today cannot occur, I am going to once again on this day, as I have oftentimes in the past, heed his fatherly advice. I am not going to dwell on the lives of those who have preceded us but focus instead on the future and our responsibilities in that future. Secondly, with your indulgence, I will glean the wisdom from my father's last words to me and take a forward look into the "Signs of the Times."

In the sixteenth chapter of St. Matthew, a group of Jewish leaders asked Jesus to teach them about the times in which they lived. He answered, "Can you not understand the signs of the times?" In other words, don't you know what today is all about? Maybe we should ask ourselves the same question. How well do we understand the signs of OUR times?

Many years ago I discovered an excellent description of twentieth-century America while leafing through Charles Dickens' great novel, *A Tale of Two Cities*. Its opening paragraph precisely describes America in the year 1981.

> It was the best of times; it was the worst of times. It was the age of wisdom; it was the age of foolishness. It was the epoch of belief; it was the epoch of incredulity. It was the season of light; it was the season of darkness. It was the spring of hope; it was the winter of despair. We had everything before us; we had nothing before us.

Now, on the one hand, there are many things around us which indicate that these are indeed the best of times. I watched on television when man first landed on the moon in July of 1969. I watched on television the Apollo 13 lift off from Cape Kennedy. In a few days, that same spacecraft developed serious problems thousands of miles out in space. Fortunately the crew, because of their superb training and their technological know-how, safely recovered their crippled craft. We've flown on jet planes that can fly across the face of America at speeds of over 700 miles per hour. Many of us watched our American hostages return [from Iran] to Frankfurt, getting their first glimpse of freedom in 444 days. We, as well as over 30 million people, saw their arrival as we sat in the comfort and safety of our own homes. Our brilliance as a nation and as a people seemingly say that, yes, these are indeed the best of times—the best times in our history.

Yet, despite our progress, we are not freed from HUMAN problems that are as old as man's existence. Though we have learned to control so much knowledge and uncover so many mysteries, we have not yet learned how to control ourselves. You see, America is plagued by greed, racial tensions, crime, inflation, discontent, and individuals who are not willing to accept the responsibilities of being an American—the same problems that have destroyed great nations throughout history.

You have heard from revolutionary groups that America must be torn down and rebuilt if we are to solve our problems. Have our problems become too big for us? Must discontent, hatred, greed and racial tensions be the lot of so great a nation? Is it impossible to reverse our problems? Can we not change America without first destroying it?

Stretch your imagination just as far as you can—what will America be like in ten years; in twenty years? Will she be greater or will our problems have overcome us?

Though there are those who say America is dying, I say we must fulfill our obligations to continue to fight to strengthen America. Though there are those who say that America has no hope, I say that there is hope for those of us who want it badly enough. Though there are those who have said that the American dream will never become a reality, I say we have not failed to reach that dream until we have quit trying. The American dream will become a reality when each and every individual has an equal chance to see it come true in their own individual lives.

But, to make that dream come true in our lives we must be willing to make the sacrifices; be willing to give of ourselves; to accept the responsibilities which accompany the freedoms afforded each of us by our Constitution and our Bill of Rights.

Indeed, you—we—we're lucky. We are lucky because we have had the chance to attend this great University and be totally filled with that thing called the Aggie Spirit. Although it is oftentimes difficult for us to put into words which can be communicated to others what that Aggie Spirit actually means, others who see us know what it is.

You see, it's that intangible quality that makes hundreds of our fellow Aggies gather on a day like today to remember those who are not here, to answer Roll Call. Many of those who have been honored during Aggie Musters for the past 78 years were those who stepped forward and accepted responsibility. Indeed, the very first Muster was to commemorate those who had given their lives. As the years have passed, other individuals who have given their lives as well have been honored. But, there is one very important thing which we must not and cannot forget—it is not necessary, my friends, that we give our lives. The only sacrifice that is required is for each of us to give the very best that is in us; to be the very best of whatever we are; to do whatever we want to do, yet making sure that whatever we do, we're the best at it! And that, my friends, is what it means when we say that we are Americans. That is what it means when we say that we are Aggies.

There is an unbelievable and intangible quality which fills students and former students of Texas A&M. They are the types of individuals who wish not to be spoon-fed, wet-nursed, entertained or recognized for recognition's sake only. Aggies are dedicated to assuming their full share of responsibility for this world in which we live.

Unless we gear our minds and our souls to this type of positive thinking, to develop a fervor for the untried and for the unexplored, we will be depriving this country and this world of its greatest and perhaps its most valuable resource. How else will America and Americans meet the challenge? We must raise ourselves from our despair, from our powerlessness, from our fears, and our frustration. We must stand up and be counted, giving this nation the extraordinary energy, strength, and commitment that will imprint an indelible stamp on the pages of history. And, in my view, there are no greater Americans than Aggies who are prepared to accept this challenge and overcome those things which indicate that these are the worst of times. If we do these things, we will be fulfilling the legacy which has been left by those whom we honor today. We will be making the worthwhile lives which they spent on this earth even more meaningful and even more valuable.

Archibald MacLeish said "America was promises." And its promises have always motivated us—self-fulfillment, freedom, independence, service, a decent living. The promises of pleasure, of a life beyond mere drudgery, of being new, young, in the forefront of an adventure, on top of things. The "inalienable rights" of life, liberty, and the pursuit of happiness. These dreams, these purposes, brought millions to America's shores, and inspired newcomers to expand this country's industry, its trade, its borders, its wealth, its influence. Individualism, success, happiness, involvement: are these worthwhile goals? I ask you, are they too self-centered, too trivial, too little concerned with the real problems—goals only rarely attained? Is this dream still valid? Or was it ever real in the first place?

You may possess all the ability in the world, but the one thing which overrules ability is attitude. Examine leaders in history, those individuals that people will follow. They won't wait to see how smart he is or how smart she is; they assume that a leader is smart. Nothing can compete with a positive attitude! It is not your aptitude but your attitude that determines your altitude in life.

It's the controlling force in every phase of life. It's the one factor which accounts for the defeat of champion teams by nothing teams. It accounts for the losing or winning of a war. It accounts for some men becoming tycoons while others remain insignificant nothings. It accounts for Cassius Clay defeating virtually every fighter he encountered. When he screamed that he'd knock out an opponent within four rounds, the opponent was only concerned with hanging on for four rounds, not fifteen!

You see, whether we live in a have or have-not nation, or community, the greatest wealth each of us has is himself—his ideas and ideals, his talents and energies, his nerves and his muscles. And by sharing the qualities of our living with others, we impart to them the most precious of our possessions. You have within your power the ability and the attitude to do great things; to make meaningful and lasting contributions to this world in which we live; to be whatever you want to be, and to be the very best at it! But, my friends, it takes commitment—to ideals, to purpose and to meaning. We can easily forgive a child who is afraid of the dark. The real tragedy of life comes when men and women are afraid of the light. If we are to lift ourselves from this morass, we must shift our sights from the superficial to the sacrificial—from these problems that indicate that these are the worst of times.

Paraphrasing Grantland Rice's well-known quote, "When the Great Scorekeeper comes to mark against your name, it will not be whether you have won or whether you have lost, but how you played the game."

There exists a commercial with which many of you are no doubt familiar, which says that "you only go around once in life, so do it with all the gusto you can!" Well, I'd like to change that up just a little bit— you only go around once in life, and, my friends, if you do it right—if you do it right—once is going to be enough! History will judge us not by what we say today, but by what we do tomorrow—not by the promises we make, but by the promises we keep.

I am growing weary of hearing people clamor for their rights, even though I am one who has chosen to enter the legal profession. I want to see people who are willing to stand up and clamor for the responsibilities which accompany those rights. This is what it means to be an American! This is what it means when we say that we are Aggies, and are filled with that intangible Aggie Spirit which has been around for over one hundred years. Responsibilities abandoned today will return as more acute crises tomorrow!

If you understand the signs of OUR times, you will understand what it's all about and the role you MUST play in assuming your full share of responsibility for this world in which we live. It is because others have assumed their share that we enjoy the freedom which affords our gathering here as others do around the world on this day.

To be free is to know how to embrace those who came before us, while reaching out to those who will follow. To be free is to succumb, over and over again, time and time again, to the demands of responsibility—to believe that the decent idea will eventually triumph over the indecent one; that the rules that apply to you apply to everyone else.

All a person can do in this life is to gather about him his integrity, his imagination, his individuality and this great gift of freedom from our Founding Fathers—and, with these ever with him, out front in sharp focus, leap into the dance of experience.

We must reach high for freedom. We must plant our own seeds and then tend them or the amber waves of grain will wither in the drought that we have inflicted upon ourselves. We must accept the fact that the potential of the people is worthless—worthless—unless we all work together to make the United States truly united.

Democracy with all its complicated structure cannot exist without a proud national will. When patriotism dies, then begins the burial of a nation.

Indeed, we gather here on this day, as do thousands around the world, to answer "Here" for those whose death prevents their answering Roll Call. And in so doing we re-dedicate ourselves to the essence of the

Aggie Spirit; we accept the most worthwhile challenge of life—being of service by assuming our full share of responsibility.

And, as my father so forcefully told me during that last conversation, by accepting this responsibility we focus on the future, and on our roles in that future. We only go round once in life, and if we do it right, once is going to be enough.

Let me ask you—do you insist on standing when the flag passes in front of you? Was that old shiver and tear still there when this great Texas Aggie Band sounded the Star-Spangled Banner? If they were not, then Silver Taps for many things you loved will continue to echo—and echo—and echo until those tragic notes are too faint to muster anymore.

# William B. Heye '60

*1982—G. Rollie White Coliseum*

William B. Heye '60.
Photo from editor's
collection.

William Bernard "Bill" Heye Jr. was born March 3, 1938, in San Antonio. He was cadet colonel of Texas A&M's Corps of Cadets his senior year and graduated with a degree in electrical engineering. He served three years as a US Air Force project officer developing reconnaissance equipment. Following his release from active duty, he followed the advice of A&M's longtime Memorial Student Center director J. Wayne Stark '39 and earned an MBA with distinction at Harvard University in 1966.

Joining Texas Instruments, he directed semi-conductor manufacturing in Taipei, Taiwan, that grew from 900 employees to 4,000 in just three years. As president of Texas Instruments Asia Ltd. in Tokyo from 1978 to 1979, he was responsible for TI's semiconductor business in the Asia Pacific area. After that he was vice president and general manager of the TI Consumer Products Division and president of Varco, Inc. As vice president for manufacturing at Mostek, Inc., he expanded the firm's DRAM (Dynamic Random Access Memory) capacity in plants in Malaysia and Ireland. From 1991 until 2004, as president and CEO of SBE, Inc., Heye directed operations that designed and manufactured infrastructure products for Cisco, Motorola, HP, Nortel, and Lockheed Martin. The company added iSCSI (Internet Small Computer System Interface) storage connectivity, enabling remote backup storage over IP networks. He served on the boards of SBE and Ten X Technology, Inc.

Heye and his wife, Joan, were Aggie Parents of the Year in 1986–87 and founding members of the Texas A&M Chancellor's Century Council and the development council for the Bush School of Government and Public Service. He founded and was chairman of the Corps of Cadets Development Council and served on A&M's College of Medicine Advisory Council. In 1991 he was recognized with the Texas A&M Distinguished Alumnus Award.

## Quality = Spirit and Leadership*

It's an honor to be here on this occasion of significance to all Aggies. As I talk today, I will be mentioning some of the events of my life, and I'd like to introduce the person who's shared these with me, the person who's been my wife since my senior year at A&M, Joan.

I have been associated with A&M longer than most of you in this auditorium have lived. It's funny . . . you know you've been out of school awhile when they start asking you to make speeches. Or they stare extra hard at the class number on your ring, or they say "What was your class, again?" It's obviously normal to be in a class of the 80s or maybe even the 70s but dating back to my year of 1960—that's something.

This difference of 20–25 years is known as one generation. I am aware of all this because Joan and I have our own next generation at A&M. We have two sons at A&M today. Bill, who is a junior and first sergeant of Squadron 10, and Pat, who is a freshman in Squadron 3. We have 2 more children at home, a daughter and a son—both of whom are candidates for A&M.

In order for you to understand a little of where I am coming from and why I say some of the things I do today, let me explain some of my background.

My wife and I have always been on the adventurous side, and we made a decision early on that within reason we'd take chances on new opportunities that came to us. In addition to that, we have been extremely fortunate.

We have moved our family 18 different times. We have been in 15 different apartments or houses. We have lived with our family in two countries outside the US—Taiwan and Japan. We have traveled extensively in the Pacific area—Australia, Singapore, Malaysia, Thailand, the

*Speech title derived by editor from speech contents

Philippines, Hong Kong, Korea—through Europe a number of times, and around the world several times. We have been fortunate in that not only have we traveled together but our four children have accompanied us on many of these.

It's a fact that once you start this process, it keeps going. Since learning of my selection as Muster speaker in late December, I have made notes for my speech today as I traveled—in January on a 747 crossing the Pacific en route to Japan—in February crossing the Atlantic en route to France.

When you've been out of school for a number of years and attended many Musters in different places, there are certain aspects of it that are of significance to you. One of the most moving experiences for me occurred not at a formal Muster ceremony, but during the month of March 1974 in the Philippines. Let me explain.

I know many of you have read the story and have seen the pictures of the Aggie Muster outside the Malinta tunnel on Corregidor during the Second World War in April, 1946. In fact, the 1978 Muster speaker at A&M was Colonel Tom Dooley '35, one of the survivors of Corregidor back in 1942. As the situation deteriorated in the Philippines, General MacArthur left Corregidor by PT boat on 11 March. Bataan fell in April, and Corregidor was due to hold out for only 15 more days past Muster day in 1942 before it was surrendered to the Japanese.

In 1974, my family and I had the opportunity to take a family trip to Corregidor during the time we were living in Taiwan. We found the island of Corregidor, in the middle of the Manila harbor, had remained amazingly untouched, uncommercialized, and uninhabited through that time thirty-one years later.

As we stood on the same spot at the end of the tunnel where the 1946 Muster had been held, history seemed to scream at us. My youngest son John, who was then six, to this day has vivid memories of all of the island of Corregidor.

I thought that was a very moving and very strange feeling until the next day when we went to the American Memorial Cemetery in Fort Bonifacio outside the city of Manila. In this cemetery are 17,000 white crosses under which American and allied dead are buried. Their names are individually listed in an open, semicircular colonnade in the center of the cemetery. The battles in which they died are depicted in murals on the floor and on the inner faces of the colonnade.

There were gardeners in the distance tending the grounds, but we were the only visitors to the memorial that day. Staring out at the sea of white crosses—in every direction as far as the eye could see—history was again screaming at us. You could feel your insignificance and the insignificance of any one individual. Yet you could almost feel the resolve that the large group generated. You were not an individual, but were part of the power of the being as a whole.

Standing in the midst of those crosses, in that foreign but strangely familiar land, I was poignantly reminded that there is no more powerful force in the world than that of a group bonded together in common cause.

That, my fellow Aggies, is what I think Muster does for the sons and daughters of Texas A&M each year—it reminds us of our potential for accomplishing many things with the power available to us in groups.

One of the things that I think deserves our attention is the subject of my talk tonight. That subject is quality. The quality of things. The quality of life. Quality means doing things right. It means high standards, high expectations. It means accepting only the best.

Before I get into quality in more detail, let me fall back 25 years to set the stage of where quality fits into your lives—you, the students.

Twenty-five years ago, here in G. Rollie White Coliseum, I sat where you now sit. Twenty-two years ago, I stood where I now stand, on this stage. On the first of these occasions, I was an entering freshman and was sitting through one of those bewildering orientation sessions. In the second, I was the Corps Commander addressing the new incoming freshman class.

This last week, I looked at my notes from that speech in September 1959 and found two items that I emphasized. I made the point that a person could receive a degree from any college but they could receive strong leadership training only from Texas A&M. I stressed that although their first year would be an extremely difficult one, they would gradually learn that the Aggie Spirit, the glue that binds us together, would allow them to do things that they never really thought were possible. That by the time Final Review came in May (and here you have to remember the Corps was still compulsory for all entering freshmen back in those days), that they would be proud to shake the hands of their Aggie buddies from all classes and then they would realize the significance of the words, "there's a spirit that can ne'er be told; it's the Spirit of Aggieland."

It was true then, and it is still true today. Two of the values you receive that are unique to A&M are the Spirit and leadership.

The first of these, the Spirit, really translates into teamwork. Teamwork must be experienced in order to be learned. It comes not from a book but from doing. It takes practice and it takes work. It is real. It is important that it be learned as early in life as possible because the successful people in the world know that teamwork is essential to accomplishing anything but the simplest tasks.

Regarding leadership, by the time you graduate from A&M, you will have learned more about your own capabilities as a leader. Although there is much talk today about achieving higher efficiencies, of automating production, of "let's get the computer to do it," the relationship between people is still the single most important determinant of any organization's success. The role of the leader in making this relationship between people work for the good of the organization is clear. If the leader is good, the organization is successful in achieving its objectives.

Leadership is all well and good, but the leader must know where he is going. He must have values that guide him through uncertainty. Change is one of those uncertainties. People always seem to worry about change, but they needn't. There is a useful way of looking at change that borrows the terms of music.

In music, there is a bass clef and a treble clef. The notes of the treble clef generally carry the melody, while the bass determines the beat. The melody or the treble varies throughout a given selection, while the bass remains a relatively constant repetition. In my way of looking at change using these terms, the bass clef is equivalent to shared values and can be thought of as the spiritual fabric.

In an illustration close to home, I think I could describe some of the changes that have occurred at A&M over the last 25 years in these terms. The bass clef of values, tradition, and excellence in education has remained amazingly constant over the years. I see this as I am exposed to activities at the university through my two sons. On the other hand, the melody or the treble clef has changed frequently over time, as it must. Changes that fall into this category would include such things as changes in the length of hair, the non-compulsory Corps, and the opening of the university to women in 1971.

We now have run full circle back onto quality. Quality, I would submit, must be part of your bass clef of values.

You, today's students, are our future leaders. You have been exposed to teamwork, to spirit, and you have been trained as leaders.

But you must adopt values to guide you. How can you lead if you don't know where you're going? Quality is one of those values so powerful that its application shapes lives. Quality is a sine qua non. Or since most of you no longer take Latin, putting it into today's terms—you really shouldn't leave home without it.

Quality has amazing attributes. It doesn't need a description, because people recognize it when they see it. To understand it is to apply it. There's really no such thing as medium quality. You either have it or you don't.

Quality today has a global aspect. That we are no longer isolated is an understatement. If your understanding of quality is confined to a US-only version, you're in trouble. More on this later.

Let's get more specific on what quality means—let's bring it closer to home.

Recently during the course of business at Texas Instruments, I had the occasion to listen to Mr. Will Willoughby, deputy chief of the US Naval Materials, Reliability, and Quality Assurance organization. I don't know when I've met someone with as firm a grasp of his subject or more conviction of the righteousness of his cause. He had a simple definition of quality. He said that quality was what you accept. Let me repeat that. He said that quality was what you accept. Whatever you accept becomes your standard. He illustrated this with some examples.

The United States has one of the highest crime rates in the world. There are many places where people fear to be in the streets, and others where people fear for the safety of their homes. Any time we decide as a country we don't want this, we can change. Our judicial system reflects what we tolerate. You get what you accept.

Drunk driving. Sixty percent of the highway deaths in this country are a result of drunk drivers. What do we do about it today? Not much. Sometimes, maybe a slap on the wrist. It's an easy problem to fix, however. A simple change in the law that stated that anyone ever caught driving while intoxicated would never drive again would fix the problem. No ifs, ands, or buts. Do we have enough support to do that? You get what you accept.

It's not as though solutions to these two problems have not been put into place by other countries. I have lived in places where life was quite different. In Taiwan it was a criminal offense to possess a gun. This was strictly enforced, and there were no crimes of violence committed with guns. There were no guns.

In Japan, you could expect to see a roadblock set up by the police in any night of the week on any street. Every driver was subjected to a simple Breathalyzer test on the spot through the open window of his car. No questions were asked, and there were no exceptions. Those persons failing the test were immediately removed from their vehicles and taken to a waiting police van for further observation and confirmation, a process that could take hours. The result—not only no drunk driving but very little driving after drinking whatsoever. No one wanted to take the chance.

The people in Taiwan and the people in Japan accepted these measures. They got what they accepted. Their expectations and their level of acceptable quality in these areas are different from ours in the United States.

Political corruption is another problem we tolerate. "Abscam" [an FBI sting operation in the late 1970s and early 1980s] was not an isolated case. It's been said they won't go back and do it again for fear of who else they'll catch. Political misconduct is in the papers every day. Look at the recent Oklahoma county road commissioners scandal. More than 115 past and present commissioners from Oklahoma's 77 counties have been convicted. In 14 counties, every single commissioner was found to be on the take. Closer to home, the grand juries are just now starting into Texas territory. What happened? This didn't start yesterday. It appears to have been going on for several generations. It happened because you and I said it's alright. We're getting in spades what we've accepted for years.

This country has forsaken quality for quantity. It's a cancer eating at us from within. US manufacturers were spoiled and complacent when no one was there to compete with them—when they competed with themselves. If the Japanese hadn't come along, we'd still be buying junk.

There was a time when quality was available to us. Mass production came along, however, and quantity became important. Had to run those production lines at high volume. Even with mass production, it's been clearly shown, however, that when you achieve quality you get significantly higher productivity as well. That would help the US return to a net producing nation again.

Did you know that today we export more raw materials compared to our own exports of finished goods? Do you know what that makes us? A colony is defined as a nation that exports raw materials and imports finished goods.

Does this bother you? Quality is what we accept. The system has not failed us—we have failed the system.

It's encouraging to note that some changes are occurring. Your buying habits are now indicating more of a quality awareness. Japanese goods cost more, but that is what you are buying. You are voting for change with your pocketbook, and it's being heard.

On a more personal level, quality is caring. Caring for small things as well as large. When you go to visit a company's offices, or another school's campus, or someone's home, have you ever failed to notice how they keep their grounds or their yard? Was the grass cut and trimmed; was trash and clutter lying about? Of course you noticed. Everyone notices. What have you done for your school today?

Quality has larger elements. Those of you that have read *The Agony and the Ecstasy* [by Irving Stone] know that Michelangelo was first and foremost a sculptor. He got roped into painting the ceiling of the Sistine Chapel by Pope Julius II and started on this with a group of painters he employed. He immediately saw that he couldn't maintain his standards with that arrangement and let the group go. He restarted it entirely on his own—a decision that cost him four years of his life. He did it all for one reason—he felt that even if he disliked the task, he had committed to do it, and he would do it better than anyone had done it before.

Earlier, I mentioned the global aspect of quality. In the last couple of years, the United States has gone through much breast-beating as it discovered this global characteristic and the telling effect that quality can have as a marketing tool. The walls of the Fortress America market came tumbling down as people opted for higher-quality goods.

What's the significance of this to you as students, as leaders? You must ask yourself the question—how can I tell what the real standard of quality is if I don't know what's going on in the rest of the world? You'd better ask the question, because it's clear that some of our present leaders never asked the question.

Too many people in the US have been smug, complacent, and satisfied. Not only have they not made an attempt to travel, to learn a foreign language, to understand what was going on in other countries—they didn't care.

The lesson is clear. The person aspiring to top leadership must realize the significance of this global aspect of quality. This now translates into the broadest definition of quality. It means an understanding of product quality—yes. But it means more—much more. It means an understanding of other countries' people, their culture, their values. It means a willingness to accept the good parts of their way of doing things.

This, then, is the ultimate expression of the concept of quality. It is a value that must be a part of the bass clef of every one of you personally. Applied on a constant basis, it will profoundly affect your direction the rest of your life.

In closing, let me leave you with one last thought. As you run off and accomplish all these good things, you will be getting caught up in the most busy period of your life. Many of you will also be starting families at the same time. My suggestion is that you not neglect the application of quality to your own relationship with your family. The person who conquers the world but fails his family has missed the most basic tenet of what we have been discussing tonight. Remember that not only are your children a genetic copy of you and your wife or husband, but that their actions and their accomplishments are another and possibly more important reflection of you. It all fits together. I wish you success.

# Haskell M. Monroe

*1983—G. Rollie White Coliseum*

Haskell M. Monroe.
Photo from editor's
collection.

Haskell Moorman Monroe was born March 18, 1931, in Garland, Texas. One of only nine campus Muster speakers who did not graduate from Texas A&M, Monroe completed his BA and MA coursework in history at Austin College in 1952 and 1954, respectively. He went on to receive his PhD in history from Rice University, where he studied under one of the leading historians of the Civil War period, Professor Frank E. Vandiver.

In the fall of 1959, Monroe joined the faculty of Texas A&M. His special fields of study and teaching were the antebellum South and the Civil War period. While an associate professor he was active in campus committees, as a speaker, and as a publisher of many articles. Monroe was awarded the Association of Former Students Faculty Distinguished Achievement Award in Teaching in 1964. He edited the *Papers of Jefferson Davis 1808–1840, Vol. 1*, which was published in 1971.

After serving as assistant graduate dean (1965–68), assistant vice president for academic affairs (1972–74), and dean of faculties (1974–77), Monroe was named associate vice president of academic affairs in 1977. As dean of faculties, Monroe chaired the Centennial Committee, which coordinated activities to celebrate Texas A&M's 100th birthday in 1976. In 1980 he was named president of the University of Texas at El Paso. From 1987 to 1992, he was chancellor of the University of Missouri.

It is interesting to note how often fate crossed the career paths of Monroe and his former mentor, Professor Vandiver. Monroe had been considered for the position of president at North Texas State University in 1979, but Vandiver was ultimately selected. One year after Monroe left

Texas A&M in 1980, following twenty-one years of dedicated service, Vandiver became the nineteenth president of Texas A&M University.

Monroe died November 13, 2017.

## What Kind of Aggie Are You?*

Two months after he became US President, Harry S. Truman wrote his wife: "Things have changed so much it hardly seems real. I sit here in this old house listening to the ghosts walk up and down the hallway. The floors pop and the drapes move back and forth."

Today, I don't hear ghosts, but I must note the changes and remember twenty-four years ago, almost to this day, when I proudly drove up from Houston, a hopeful graduate student looking for a job. I had driven fast that morning, because the department head phoned to describe a vacancy in the history department and wondered if I could come for an interview soon. I asked him if three hours from the time of the phone call was soon enough. Much has changed here since that interview, but the truly essential qualities of A&M have remained constant: That ain't no dog—that's Reveille; $5.00 for a ticket to the chemistry final—good bull is still good bull.

In 1963, this newly re-named institution had slightly more than 8,000 students—all male. All freshmen and sophomores—except veterans and those with physical handicaps—enrolled in compulsory military training. Meanwhile, those same students scored slightly below the national average on entrance examinations. The vast majority majored in agriculture or engineering. Business and education were only departments.

As a member of the committee which recommended adding the symbolic word "University" to the title of this school; that compulsory military training be abolished; that admission requirements be increased; that women be admitted; that all applicants for admission be judged only on the basis of their academic record, without regard to race, color, creed, or any other condition; I am very proud to recall the splendid record of progress here since those sometimes traumatic

*Speech title derived by editor from speech contents

changes. I need not remind you that now the student body is marked by unusual ability, that the scope of the institution from agriculture to zoology has broadened, but that the change in scope is much less than the marvelous increase in the quality of these programs. The number of National Merit Scholars here has gone literally from 0 to 438 in twenty years, while research volume has soared upward. Yet, the Corps of Cadets remains strong, still the largest outside the military academies, and no other band can excite as many chills of delight as when the bugle rank begins the Aggie War Hymn.

Perhaps we historians reminisce too much, but I hope it is appropriate on this occasion to ask you the question I received in Fort Worth, after assuring a Muster audience that their alma mater was making rapid progress. As always, I asserted that all good things about A&M had been preserved—even strengthened—and the bad things were being eliminated. When I concluded my remarks, an elderly man jumped up and inquired, "What kind of an Aggie are you?—you didn't even go there." I responded that I was an Aggie by choice and he shot back: "What the hell does that mean?"

I told him that when I had first come here, I had two other opportunities, and in the years since had been offered employment elsewhere. Yet, on each occasion I had chosen to remain at A&M because of the opportunities here for me. Then I added, "But I understand some people didn't have that choice." By this time the inquirer was smiling. "In the fall of '28," he noted, "my father called me into the front room of our farm house and said, 'Son, you can stay here on the farm and pick cotton this fall or go to College Station and maybe they can straighten you out.'" We had a good laugh, but his question has remained with me, and I now ask: "What kind of an Aggie are you?"

What does it mean to claim an association with this place? Or, more importantly, what does it mean for the rest of our lives for us to have been here? I have learned that because of my twenty-one years of service on this faculty, many people assume that I attended class here. Like you, my life has been changed by my experiences here, certainly, but I was never enrolled officially—yet I am deeply proud to claim my ties of affection here. Whether that entitles me to be an Aggie or not is something I leave for others to judge. I am proud and will always be proud of that circumstance. Early in 1980, I tried to summarize that pride when I responded to the last question from the Regents of the [University of Texas] System where I am now employed. The oldest member of that board asked tersely, "I guess Aggie blood is maroon. Can you change the color of your blood?" I quickly professed my pride in Austin College where I attended as an undergraduate, Rice where I received my PhD, and A&M where I had worked happily for twenty-one years. I told him that if I was selected to be the president of the university where I now serve, I thought I could add to that number love for another institution—but take nothing away from any of the three. At that point another Regent, an Aggie by the way—Class of '46—came to my rescue. He said that as a physician, he always noticed that when a first child was born to a young couple, they acted like they could never love anything else as much as they loved that baby—until their second child was born. I told the other Regents that his thoughts completed my answer.

After you leave this campus, you will always remember Muster, Bonfire, and Silver Taps, plus all of the other traditions which make this institution truly distinctive. Surely you will ponder their meaning for you—no matter what class, age, or relationship with the University. I believe that these traditions help us remember the many fine individuals we have encountered in our years here—to remember the joy of their company—but more importantly, the quality of their character and their effects on our own lives.

Eleven years ago today, I had the honor of escorting the provost of Columbia University to Muster here. He was on campus to deliver memorial lectures honoring President Earl Rudder. Very much against his desire, he came with me, fearing that this was some pep rally or undergraduate hijinks. Then, as he witnessed the outpouring of emotion, and particularly as the roll was called of those who now were present only in the heartfelt memories of those who answered—please recall that was the era when many young men went almost directly from this campus to the battlefront in Vietnam—as he listened to that tragic recitation of what was in fact a casualty list of Aggies lost in Vietnam, he announced, "Now I understand that this ceremony is a time of rededication to the values not only of Texas A&M, but of the United States of America."

This ceremony has been held in many other places. In Guion Hall, an auditorium which stood where Rudder Complex is today. Later on the lawn of the MSC [Memorial Student Center]—the only occasion when no one worried about walking on the grass. I have spoken to Musters in an open air pavilion near the surf at Corpus Christi, a marvelous seafood restaurant in Mobile, a beer hall in Kerrville, over boiled crawfish in Lafayette, and the Officer's Club at Carswell Air Force Base in Fort Worth. Perpetuating Aggie traditions at Dallas, Houston, New Orleans, Beaumont, McKinney, Tyler, San Antonio, and McAllen, where they gave the speaker three crates of delicious grapefruit. No matter how Musters vary, they are all alike. Young and old come to pause, renew acquaintances, exchange pleasantries, and concentrate on what this school has meant to them.

Texas A&M produces individuals who try to make the world better by accepting it as it is and then working from within for improvement. Many others start by questioning everything, as if they believe it is best to tear the world into shambles and then rebuild from its ruins. Surely Aggies are not the only ones to believe that trust is a vital human quality. I suspect that attitude comes partially from the land grant heritage, which began here in 1876 with a lonely building on an almost treeless plain marking the ridge between the Navasota and the Brazos Rivers. Even the bricks in that building were a local product, for the little gully in front of the President's home produced clay for the bricks in that first building. Occasionally, as the Physical Plant Department digs another trench near Sully's statue, a few of those bricks can be seen underneath that soil. But it is not the soil, the bricks, nor the water that shapes us here—it is people. Men and women who have helped to make us what we are. I have my special list of men and women—some here today physically—others only in my grateful memory. Surely, you, too, have such a list.

Perhaps the most important point that I make today is to emphasize that the success of our efforts after leaving College Station is the true purpose of Texas A&M. You and I need not tell someone about A&M

and what it means to us. We illustrate it clearly with our habits, values, and accomplishments. Muster is a time to remind us of that mission; to recall in our memories the qualities of those who have preceded us here as examples so that we may look ahead and renew our personal goals of determination. We know that Muster is generations old. It has been held in foxholes, battleships, prison camps, office buildings, and no doubt more than we might suspect, in the solitary loneliness of men and women isolated from their friends and loved ones on this day. Still, today, we the living and the healthy, quietly pause together to reaffirm our determination that our lives will properly reflect what this institution has meant to us and that we will carry with us wherever we go the values of this blessed place. Blessed because so much has been given by so many to make it possible for us to be here: here to hope and to dream of what we can contribute to progress. As we do so, we remember those we have loved so deeply, as their names are recited, that God's blessing will be upon them, as we hope it will be upon us and upon this University.

As you go away in a little while, please recall that Texas A&M will need your concern and your support, so that others may come here and enjoy the same pleasures and opportunities which we have encountered. We are part of an endless maroon line which for 107 years has marched nobly toward high achievement, thoughtful concern for others and the defense of freedom. No doubt, in the years ahead each of us will face times of personal stress and private trial. When doubt is about to encircle us, I hope that each of us can call forth the bugle rank of courage to step forward from the north end zone of our hearts—to sound those clear notes of our personal war hymns of courage and skill born here.

Thus, if my hopes are fulfilled, when our race is run, we will hear the supreme compliment for our lives—for many will recall our works and answer "Here" on our behalf. If we are not willing to accept this challenging pattern for our lives, we will not be keeping faith with those loving souls whose memories we honor as the purpose of Muster; but if we are determined to mark our lives with a full measure of effort, an unceasing concern for those around us, and a bountiful supply of faith as found in the lives recalled today—then, and only then, are we worthy to proclaim so proudly the spirit which "can ne'er be told, the Spirit of Aggieland." It is that spirit that we must never allow to wane, for it will make us uncommon people who try harder, achieve more, and never are content with less than our best efforts. Perhaps that spirit cannot be told—told fully in words—but it can be demonstrated all our lives if we remember the meaning of our years here together.

What kind of an Aggie are you?

Proud and grateful, Sir.

# Jack M. Rains '60

*1984—G. Rollie White Coliseum*

Jack M. Rains '60. Photo from editor's collection.

Jack Morris Rains was born November 23, 1937, in Waco and graduated from Thomas Jefferson High School in Port Arthur in 1956. He received a BA in business administration from Texas A&M in 1960 and went on to earn his law degree from the University of Houston College of Law in 1967. He was admitted to practice before the Supreme Court of the United States.

He was a founder and chairman of the board of 3D/International from the late 1960s until 1987. In 1993 he helped found Houston's Tanglewood Bank.

Rains has a long record of public service on the board of trustees of the Baylor College of Medicine and the University of Houston Law Foundation. He was chairman of the Texas Veterans Land Board, a director of the Houston Livestock Show and Rodeo, and founding chairman of the Harris County–Houston Sports Authority. He served Texas A&M as a vice president of the Association of Former Students (1975–78) and as a member of the President's Council (1984) and the Target 2000 Project Committee (1981–84). He was the Texas secretary of state from 1987 to 1989.

In 1983 Rains received the Outstanding Alumnus Award from the University of Houston Law Alumni Association, and in 1984 he received the Outstanding Aggie Award from the Houston A&M Club. In 1987 he was inducted as a Distinguished Alumnus of Texas A&M University.

He joined the Texas-based law firm of Gray, Reed & McGraw.

# A&M's Strong Maroon Line*

Muster is a tradition that affirms for the entire family of Aggies, for the world, the enduring nature of our spirit. It is a celebration of the values, ideals, principles, and virtues characteristic of which every Texas Aggie is, first, a beneficiary, then a donor.

The Muster ceremony symbolizes the essence of the Aggie Spirit: commitment to our nation, state, school, but, most of all, to one another, to mankind. It is a commitment to service. Muster is a celebration of life, of love, a ritual that affirms to us and demonstrates to all, there is no end to Texas A&M's maroon line.

What is this maroon line? It is this century's march of a long column whose beginning certainly preceded the founding of Texas A&M. In fact, it stretches back in time to the dawn of civilization.

The forebears of this century's Aggie maroon line are the defenders of civilization, those who made possible man's freedom to progress. They were the Greeks who fought and died at some forgotten pass; the centurions who defended Rome's far-flung empire; the knights who protected the church and civilization during the Dark Ages. In America they were the minutemen of Concord, the defenders of the Alamo, the heroes of San Jacinto.

Our forebears placed service above self; their commitment to an ideal was greater than their commitment to self, even to the point of death. They were the men and women who led the march of civilization. They stand out in history as exemplary triumphs of the human spirit. Texas A&M's strong maroon line springs from such stock.

Just as Texas A&M was first established with teaching, research, and service as its triad of responsibilities, so, too, our early graduates quickly embraced the tradition of service: service in peace, service in war. In war, the choices are clear. That unwavering maroon line has answered every call of our nation since the Spanish-American War. Our campus is graced with memorials to those whose commitment was total.

No words are more inspiring than the citations for conspicuous gallantry of the Aggies awarded the Congressional Medal of Honor. Those

*Speech title derived by editor from speech contents

descriptions of epic heroism are displayed in our Student Center, itself a memorial [and later in the Sam Sanders Corps of Cadets Center]. It is appropriate that today we recall why it is called the "Memorial Student Center." The dedication reads:

> In humble reverence this building is dedicated to those men of A&M who gave their lives in defense of our country. Here is enshrined in spirit and in bronze, enduring tribute to their valor and to their deep devotion. Here their memory shall remain forever fresh—their sacrifices shall not be forgotten.

The Aggie tradition of service to country is well established.

Muster was at first a gathering of Aggies to honor the heroes of San Jacinto, to celebrate the birth of Texas. During World War II, the gathering became "Muster" and attained a magnificence that catapulted the tradition and A&M to national, then international prominence. Following Pearl Harbor, dramatic measures were required. Aggies en masse answered the call to arms. America's military preparedness was inadequate. The Japanese sneak attack had devastated our Pacific fleet; our nation was vulnerable.

The enemy now controlled the Pacific. Our troops were virtually isolated, hopelessly outnumbered, tormented by the knowledge there was little hope for relief or resupply. It was America's darkest hour.

Despite a valiant defense, Bataan fell; the few surviving forces retreating. They dug in and braced for a last-ditch stand on the island fortress of Corregidor. The Japanese were relentless; bombs and shells rained down incessantly. The situation was hopeless—it was only a matter of time.

In the Hell of that siege, on April 21, 1942, twenty-seven Aggies, including General George F. Moore, Class of '08, gathered and celebrated San Jacinto Day. The din of battle did not dampen the spirit of those brave men. They sang A&M songs, recounted their days on campus, and toasted the Texas heroes of 1836. The comradery of their Muster was interrupted by a Japanese attack. [For the unembellished story of Corregidor in 1942, see the 1978 Muster address by Col. Thomas Dooley '35.]

Less than two weeks later, Corregidor had fallen. Those twenty-seven Aggies were either dead or prisoners of war. Those defenders of Corregidor, of America's honor, members of a proud maroon line, joined the heroes of the Alamo, of San Jacinto. Their place in history is secure.

Texas A&M's heroes of Corregidor became everyone's heroes. They were saluted by the Texas legislature, hailed on the floor of Congress, and embraced by a proud nation. Their courageous gathering, a celebration of ideals and an act of brotherhood staged in the face of impending destruction, immortalized Muster.

The following year the cadets on the College Station campus sent out the call. All A&M men were to "Muster" on April 21. The term "Muster" and the tradition swept the nation. That 1943 Muster was carried via radio to the nation and the world, broadcast to the thousands of Aggies serving in the Armed Forces overseas.

As the names of the heroes of Corregidor and other battles were read, comrades answered, "Here," declaring that our ranks remained full, that A&M's strong maroon line would not be thinned, not be defeated. The nation was inspired. That Muster clearly demonstrated to a beleaguered world what Texas Aggies were about.

What has since evolved as A&M's greatest tradition has been analyzed and interpreted by many. James Pipkin, Class of '29, speaking to a Muster audience in 1951, observed:

> Doubtless each of you experienced feelings like mine, though other faces and other years may have risen up before you. We do this because we share in a great tradition, greater than the single memories of any one of us. And though years pass, faces change, visible appearances alter, the spiritual core of that tradition remains unaltered and undiminished.

Muster is shared values, common experience, dedication to purpose, and willingness to sacrifice for the common goal—that is our wellspring. Dwight David Eisenhower addressed the Homecoming Aggie Muster on an Easter morning in 1946. The general reflected on the agony of the war just ended. He recalled the terror, the exhaustion, the human sacrifice. He took that opportunity to commend the contribution of A&M's valiant maroon line to the hard-won victory.

In his remarks, General Eisenhower praised the role of the citizen-soldier, noting his reward for service:

> This reward is the respect, esteem, and love of his associates. . . . Such a man is a stranger to resentment from his men. They accord—they demand for him, a position before the world that comes only to those who have rendered honest service to their fellows.

While General Eisenhower spoke of the reward for leaders in time of war, it is the same in time of peace.

Each day of our lives, we are faced with choices: to shirk responsibility, to flee, or to stand, to do our duty. The test is perhaps as dramatic, as dangerous as the Hell confronted in war. More likely, the choice will be as simple as to discharge a duty of citizenship—to vote.

To vote; is that so important? Consider the alternative. To fail to exercise our rights leaves the decisions to others, decisions that are critical to our republic. Single acts combine to determine our destiny. The sacrifice of our brothers demands that we exercise our rights as free people.

The A&M tradition of military service, through both World Wars, Korea, and Viet Nam, is legend. And it continues today. The maroon line circles the globe protecting freedom.

Muster began seventeen hours ago in the Pacific and will conclude following Muster in Hawaii. As the sun circled our globe, ceremonies were held in Asia and the Indian Ocean; in the Middle East and the Mediterranean; in Central America and the Caribbean.

Men and women of A&M serving today on active duty participate in those ceremonies. They serve the cause of freedom as surely as did the heroes of Corregidor.

There are many ways to serve, however, other than the military. The men and women of A&M have compiled a distinguished record of unselfish service to their fellow man. For over a century we have been the farmers who feed you, the doctors who heal you, designers and builders shaping the environment, teachers shaping tomorrow's leaders. We are leaders today. We turn the wheels of commerce, expand man's knowledge, extend his frontiers. We perform the countless variety of tasks that make civilization possible; our experience, enjoyable and rewarding. And, yes, perhaps most importantly of all, we are mothers and fathers. We are Aggies; we are good citizens. We are what's right about America!

Recently, I attended the dedication of a building here on campus. It was named in honor of an Aggie whose service to others is an example for us all. The speaker at that dedication ceremony had served on the Board of Regents with the Aggie being honored, knew of and recounted his unselfish service, his commitment to the University, to all Texas.

The speaker reminisced of the many battles the two Regents had joined in behalf of the University. He closed by honoring his comrade with a quotation from Shakespeare's *Henry V*. It is appropriate today:

> We few, we happy few,
> We band of brothers;
> For he today
> that sheds his blood with me
> shall be my brother.

Those two were as surely brothers as any Aggie is to another who shares such experiences.

This story is important for two reasons. First, both men, by virtue of their tireless service, are examples in the finest traditions of Texas A&M. But of even greater importance, it illustrates clearly the requirement for membership in the A&M family. While the speaker was a Regent, he was not an Aggie in the strictest sense. He holds no degree from Texas A&M University. However, his service, his commitment to the University, his willingness to "shed blood with his brothers" have made him as much an Aggie as anyone could ever hope to be.

The speaker, like so many others, has by his commitment, by his choice, become an Aggie. So too have professors and staff, moms and dads, friends and spouses, all who embrace our ideals, share our values, match our commitment, adopt our traditions.

The speaker, a naturalized Aggie, honored his brother. We, in turn, are honored and strengthened to have that individual and so many others like him join A&M's growing maroon line.

We gather today, Aggies all, to recall our past, to strengthen our ties, to honor those who have passed before us, those who have shed their blood—our brothers. We come today to affirm our commitment, our love for this place and all that it represents. Primarily, we celebrate our love for one another, for those of us present today and those present in our memory. We are one company.

In a moment we will call roll and, in the hush, all will be present. As taps sounds, reach out. Take the hand of your brother. Physically form a bond, a strong maroon line.

While taps sounds across this and every Muster, a tear may fall. It is no time for sorrow. For somewhere a bugle sounds recall. United again, we fall into formation. That strong maroon line marches on!

# Lt. Gen. Ormond R. Simpson '36

*1985—G. Rollie White Coliseum*

Lt. Gen. Ormond R. Simpson. Photo from editor's collection.

Ormond Ralph Simpson was born March 16, 1915, in Corpus Christi. At Texas A&M, he was a member of the Aggie Band, one of two school buglers, and commanded the infantry regiment. A Military Honor Graduate, he was commissioned a Marine second lieutenant.

In a military career spanning three wars, he commanded every Marine formation from an infantry platoon to a reinforced division of 35,000 in Vietnam. During the last two years of World War II, he participated in the liberation of the Philippines and assisted in planning for the invasion and occupation of Japan. He commanded the 1st Marine Regiment in Korea in 1953–54.

As a brigadier general, he was assistant commander of the 3rd Marine Division in Okinawa and led the Marine Expeditionary Brigade during the 1962 Laotian Crisis. In 1965–66 he commanded the 2nd Marine Division at Camp Lejeune, North Carolina. Promoted to major general in 1966, he headed the Marine Corps Recruiting Depot at Parris Island, South Carolina, for a year before commanding the 1st Marine Division (reinforced) in Vietnam in 1968–69. Then, for two years, he commanded the Marine Corps Supply Center. As a lieutenant general, he served as director of personnel and deputy chief of staff for manpower at Marine Headquarters until his retirement in 1973.

Simpson's decorations include two Distinguished Service Medals, the Legion of Merit with three gold stars, the Bronze Star, and the Navy Commendation Medal.

He served as assistant vice president for student services at Texas A&M and head of the School of Military Science from 1974 to 1985.

For two decades, he welcomed each fish class with a presentation on the Aggie Code of Honor and lectured extensively on leadership and the art of command. The General O. R. Simpson Corps Honor Society was formed in 1980. When he retired in 1985, the Main Drill Field at Texas A&M was named in his honor. In 1988 he was inducted as a Distinguished Alumnus, and in 1993 he was inducted into the Corps of Cadets Hall of Honor. Simpson died November 21, 1998.

## "So You Think You Are a Texas Aggie?"

*President Ronald Reagan was tentatively scheduled to deliver the 1985 campus Muster address. Lieutenant General Simpson agreed to stand in for him if he was unable to attend. A special feature of this Muster was the presentation of the US flag made by American POWs at the end of World War II by the widow of Jerome A. McDavitt '33, the ranking American officer in the Japanese POW camp at Cabanatuan and a member of the Corregidor Muster group in 1942.*

For anyone associated with Texas A&M or who has ever been associated with this great institution, Muster is a very special time. As the world turns, the observance of Muster spreads across the globe with probably the last tonight in Hawaii or possibly aboard some Navy ship in the far Pacific. No one else does anything like this. This follows because we are not quite like anyone else. It is altogether fitting that the largest Muster should be here on this campus. For this is where it all started—the wellspring of the Aggie spirit.

Muster is a time of remembrance—and a time of reflection. My comments address the latter.

So you think you are a Texas Aggie? Of course you do, and you instantly resent any implication that you might fall short.

After all, you say:

Here I am at campus Muster . . . and I come almost every year.

I am currently enrolled—or am a former student.

I go to football games, stand up all the time and yell like mad.

I go to basketball games. When I do, I remember to take a copy of the "Batt" [*Battalion*, the student newspaper] to hold up in front of my face when the visiting team is introduced.

I never miss a midnight yell practice at Kyle Field.

I know the words to the "Spirit of Aggieland"—well, most of them at least.

I sometimes say "Howdy" to people I meet on campus.

I stay off the grass at the MSC [Memorial Student Center] and holler at anyone who steps on it.

I have some t-shirts that say "TAMU," some that say "Texas Aggies."

I write letters to the "Batt" complaining about parking in particular and KK's in general. ["KK" was a slang term for "Kampus Kops," the A&M police force.]

I always spell texas university with lower case, not capital letters.

My Dad, who is a real "Old Ag," has a maroon jacket and comes to all the home football games wearing it, along with a cap that says "Aggies."

I go to the "Chicken" [the Dixie Chicken, a restaurant and bar] regularly and to the "Hall of Fame" [a dance hall] every Thursday night.

Some of us have senior rings that prove we are really Texas Aggies!

Is that enough to satisfy you . . . ?

Well, not really. None of these, taken singularly or as a group, make a real Texas Aggie. I would call them accoutrements. They are symbols, not the real substance of a true Aggie.

In my view, there is a great deal more to being a Texas Aggie than mere symbolism. I think it starts with a set of standards—surely not exactly the same for everyone—but all with a common thrust. This includes many things.

Among them:

You are aggressive and play to win, but you never cheat—not yourself, not the other person, not the organization.

You have a wholesome respect for others and for their personal dignity.

You accord this not only to your friends but to acquaintances and indeed to all with whom you deal, even though some, by their actions, may not seem to warrant it.

You work as long and as hard as is necessary to get the job done, not only to the complete satisfaction of your superiors but to your own. You do not recognize an "8-to-5 syndrome."

You are confident without being cocky, proud without being arrogant, competent without being overbearing, considerate but never subservient, steadfast but not stubborn, humble in victory, gracious in defeat.

You are imaginative and creative. You are not afraid to leave the crowd and make your own way alone if the rewards are those that you really want and the odds of gaining them are reasonable. If you stumble and fall, you don't look for someone to blame. Rather, you pick yourself up and carry on.

You are always your own person—never anyone else's.

You are proud of your school and its worthwhile traditions—Muster, Silver Taps, 12th Man—but you spend no time bragging about this to others who could not possibly understand unless they have been a part of them. All this is summed up in a single word—integrity!

I believe integrity is the basic building block for the Aggie Spirit in any real Texas Aggie.

Being a Texas Aggie is not of the flesh—but of the spirit. In a very real sense, it is a "state of mind."

We all know or have read about alumni who have made very generous monetary gifts to the university. They have provided funds for Sul Ross Scholarships, Presidential Endowed Scholarships, Endowed Professorships and even Endowed Chairs. In making these very significant gifts, they have said something to the effect, "I want to give something back to the school that gave me so much."

I have not discussed this with any of these people, but I am of the opinion that their gratitude is not necessarily for a splendid education in, for instance, engineering or agriculture, though that certainly is part of it. I rather believe it is prompted by something far less tangible. I think it is because while here they learned the necessity for self-discipline and a set of standards somewhat as I have outlined. I think they learned and never forgot the true meaning of integrity.

It is fair enough for you to ask me, "Do you really think you live up to all these things—all of the time?" My reply must be, "Not at all; as a mortal person I make at least my share of mistakes. But I recognize the standards and I try. It is the best I can do."

And this is what A&M expects of you—to recognize the standards and give it your best try. In short, A&M expects you to be a person of absolute integrity—to be a real Texas Aggie.

This Aggie spirit is both your heritage and your challenge. Make the most of it!

Good Luck.

# A. W. "Head" Davis '45

*1986—G. Rollie White Coliseum*

A. W. "Head" Davis '45.
Photo from editor's
collection.

Alfred Webb "Head" Davis Jr. was born December 21, 1924. He graduated from the A&M College of Texas in 1945 with a degree in general business. He went on to earn a law degree from Southern Methodist University School of Law in 1950.

He was senior partner in the Bryan law firm of Davis, Stacy, Lohmeyer & Davis.

He served on the board of directors of the Association of Former Students in 1960–61 and from 1979 to 1984. He was president of the Association of Former Students in 1983. He also served as a trustee of the Association of Former Students Student Loan Fund and a board member of First City National Bank of Bryan. He was named a Distinguished Alumnus in 2003 and inducted into the Corps of Cadets Hall of Honor in 2005.

Davis died January 13, 2005.

## What Is a Great University?*

The opportunity to deliver a campus Muster speech comes but to a few. Though not likely, it is possible that, in the coming years, upon my brow shall rest the laurel leaves of victory, but never again from mortal hands will a greater honor be bestowed on me. I am fully cognizant of this privilege that is beyond measure and the duty imposed thereby.

I shall ever be grateful to the Muster Committee for selecting me from among many others better qualified, and especially do I thank Susan Aycock, Michael Alston, and Wendy Wayne.

*Speech title derived by editor from speech contents

If you believe that there is an inexhaustible source of strength from above yielded to us through prayer, and I know you do, perhaps you should now invoke that strength in my behalf just as I am doing, for, you see, compared to my present emotional state, the Aggie 12th Man Kickoff Team, just before the kickoff, is as calm as a babe in its mother's arms.

How often does one hear the word "great" used, at least by the faithful, as a descriptive adjective in referring to this University? It seems to me that this word has no rival in frequency of use by us in extolling the qualities of Texas A&M. I assure you, one of the first things I was told when I was a freshman here in 1941 was, in essence, "Fish Davis, lemme tell you something—this is the greatest college in the world, and if you don't believe this, we can help you outta here—the same way you came in." These words began and concluded my orientation. The same statement, phrased a bit differently, is commonplace today. You can be sure that in 1941 I agreed with this premise because the sophomores told me to. Today I agree because I know it to be true.

Just what is a great university? I am not sure I can answer that precise question, but I can state with absolute certainty those things which a great university must possess.

A great university must have:

A Great Faculty
A Great Student Body, and
Great Facilities.

This triad, or union of three, begins, as a matter of law, with the faculty, is embellished by the students, and is crowned by facilities.

An attempt at enumerating the accomplishments and stature of the Texas A&M faculty would not only be impossible, it is unnecessary. Suffice it to say that this faculty of 2,170—73% of whom hold doctoral degrees—recruited and assembled from all parts of the United States and even the world, teaching and researching in 76 departments and 11 colleges, adorned with citations, awards, and recognitions from industry, government, and their peers, is able and distinguished, and is devoted to teaching, research, and extension.

Thus, the first requirement for Greatness is in place.

The college catalog in 1941 stated as the only requirements for admission to Texas A&M College that the prospective student had to be sixteen (16) years of age, a high school graduate, and free of contagious or infectious disease. Having graduated in the third quarter of the 1941 Class of Wichita Falls Senior High School, these requirements presented no problem for me. It is true, however, that the third quarter situation did very soon thereafter present some very real problems.

Times have changed and today, on this campus, there are 33,000 students from all over the world who have met and won significant challenges in important endeavors, and all have achieved remarkable results on the Scholastic Aptitude Test. There are a total of 625 National Merit Scholars on this campus. Those of us here today who are not students recognize and take pride in the knowledge that we are surrounded by a host of verifiable geniuses.

Thus, the second requirement for Greatness is in place.

The commitment of the people of Texas, the blessing of the Permanent and Available University Funds, and the wise and judicious actions of regents and university administrations have afforded Texas A&M physical facilities that can legitimately be described as Great. This is not to say, however, that improvements, changes, and additions are not needed. Such are needed and are receiving attention, as demonstrated by construction now in progress on this campus aggregating in cost $75,000,000.

Suffice it to say, this speaker finds substantial improvement when comparing the present to, say, Mother's Day 1942. Then, there being no suitable place, a typical visit with one's mother occurred as she sat in a 1936 Ford and her Aggie son propped a leg on the running board.

I submit the third requirement for Greatness is in place.

These qualities just mentioned are truly indispensable, and a university cannot achieve greatness unless all three are a reality. But, standing alone, they do not constitute the Texas A&M you and I describe as Great and of which we are so justly proud; for, based on this standard alone, there is a great university in every state, and in many states there are more than one. Yet, you and I know that in the entire world there's no other university such as Texas A&M.

If the statement just made is accurate and defensible, and I believe it to be, what is the basis for its truth? The basis for such truth is that at Texas A&M there is a "spirit that can never be told."

In 1925, when Marvin H. Mimms, Class of '26, wrote the immortal words of the "Spirit of Aggieland" and set them to the marvelous music of Colonel Richard C. Dunn, he captured the essence of Texas A&M for all the ages.

> Some may boast of prowess bold
> Of the school they think so grand,
> But there's a spirit can ne'er be told
> It's the SPIRIT OF AGGIELAND.

"Spirit" in this context means vital force, frame of mind, desire, and essential character, and it is inextricably intertwined with esprit; therefore, it also means loyalty and attachment to the group of which all Aggies are members.

If Texas A&M has this vital force, and esprit that can ne'er be told, different from any other institution anywhere, and I know it does, then what is its source—from whence does it come? Incontrovertibly, it comes from our devotion to and our assiduous observance of our traditions. No other source is possible.

The Bonfire symbolizes the burning desire of every Aggie to beat Texas. This tradition has grown from meager beginnings until it is quite an engineering feat; it demonstrates in its present practice an unbelievable amount of devoted time, leadership, and ingenuity; and is attended by thousands of people. To build and attend the Bonfire with fellow Aggies, and to hear the band and stirring speeches, creates an attachment to the group that can never be told.

With roots that extend back to E. King Gill and the Dixie Classic of 1922, where the Aggies prevailed in one of the greatest upsets of all time, the Twelfth Man tradition, a phrase first used by Harry W. "Red" Thompson ['21], a yell leader of the time, says to the world that Aggies are ready and eager to enter the fray for the honor and glory of the University and the Maroon and White. And it creates an attachment to the group that can never be told.

E. J. Kyle stated that Silver Taps was first observed in 1898 and such was probably for Lawrence Sullivan Ross, that soldier, statesman, and knightly gentleman, Brigadier General of the Confederate States of America, Governor of Texas, and President of the A&M College. Silver Taps demonstrates today, as it ever has, the parting tribute of the affection of the student body for a fellow Aggie. It's right and it's proper and it creates an attachment to the group that can never be told.

The design for the A&M ring has remained essentially the same for decades, and the constancy of this design is regarded as absolutely imperative.

Generally, college rings are purchased from the jeweler on the corner, where desire for ownership and the purchase price are the sole requirements. Not so with the A&M ring. Here one must have acquired 92 hours of college credit, and meet other requirements, and purchases are made from one authorized source, where credentials are checked.

Several years ago Mrs. Davis, my incomparable Genita, who has endured three generations of Aggies (her father, her husband, and her children), decided without my knowledge that I needed a new A&M ring. Following procedures, she saw the ring clerk, who, by design or otherwise, exhibited my academic record to her. I got the ring, but the self-professed myth of *summa cum laude* has been forever dissolved. Genita determined I had graduated donium–justum–barilus, which, translated, means "done—but just barely."

The ring, once earned and obtained, is worn with honor and pride which creates an attachment to the group that can never be told.

Jack Fritts, Class of '53, one of the truly great Presidents of the Association of Former Students, stated to the Class of 1982 at commencement ceremonies, "You are and always will be—Aggies." A true statement if ever one was made, for you are never quite finished with A&M and A&M is certainly not ever finished with you. This concept is the foundation of the greatest alumni organization in the world, presently led by Ted Pitzer, Class of '50, of Dallas. Support of Texas A&M by her former students is unexcelled, and the reason is that something good happens to students while they are on this campus and, unlike the nine lepers in the 17th chapter of Luke, our former students return to give thanks and it creates an attachment to the group that can never be told.

Lord Moulton said, "The measure of a civilization is the degree of its obedience to the unenforceable." So measured is the greatness of the student body of a university, and the university itself. By unenforceable observance of our traditions, we reaffirm for ourselves and proclaim to the world, through symbolic gestures, the essential values of Texas A&M—honor, respect, pride, fidelity, constancy, devotion—a fighting, indomitable spirit, and love. Most of all, love, for love is the predecessor of tradition and is, therefore, the essence and first tradition of Texas A&M. And it creates an attachment to the group that can never be told.

So it is that today we have assembled, in the character of Texas Aggies, to celebrate, if you please, one of the greatest of our traditions: That time dedicated to recalling the fidelity of that little band at San Jacinto 150 years ago, and, additionally, to honor the memory of those Aggies who now lie beneath the silent clods of the valley, they having made their journey to that distant country from whose bourne no traveler returns.

This, too, is right and it's proper, and, when taken together with our other traditions, all fit together with exact nicety, and the clear and undeniable result is a spirit that can never be told and thereby a Texas A&M that not only is great, but a Texas A&M that is indescribably different and clearly better than the best.

A first impression might indicate that all this can be accomplished and this esprit acquired and nourished with little or no effort. Such is not the case. Life at A&M, as well as life after A&M, has never been easy.

It was not easy when students lived in tents and carried their own firewood and water, and it was not easy to muster on Corregidor.

Today it is not easy to maintain the academic excellence that is required and at the same time:

> Devote a significant portion of one's time to a military organization; or
>
> Find time to devote to student government and professional societies; or
>
> Participate in intercollegiate athletics; or
>
> Participate in the Texas Aggie Band or Singing Cadets without a scholarship and without a school of music; or

Earn all or a portion of one's college expenses as a great majority of Aggies do.

And it is not always easy and convenient to observe and keep our traditions:

To struggle through the mud and the night to build a symbol of the burning love and devotion to Texas A&M University;

To attend Silver Taps to honor the loss of a member of the Texas Aggie family;

To hold a midnight yell practice in the rain;

To stand throughout a ballgame;

To hold a yell practice after a loss at Kyle Field.

These things involve more than what's required, and they occur when it's least convenient and the most difficult.

Notwithstanding the foregoing, life at Texas A&M has been glorious for one hundred and ten (110) years simply because, however unexplainable, for those who persevere, the struggle becomes the victory.

It is best stated in the words of Marquis James in his biography of Andrew Jackson:

To those who fight for it daily
Life has a flavor
the protected never know.

For my own benefit and in allegiance to our deceased classmates whose memory we revere and whose loss we now deplore, the admonition is vigilance which mitigates against complacency.

Santa Anna, because of superior numbers, thought Houston could not and would not attack him. He pursued Houston across the Colorado to the Plain of St. Hyacinth. Complacency set in and it was too late for Santa Anna, when he discovered during his siesta, that he had chased Houston until Houston finally caught him.

Complacency can play no part in the matter of our traditions. The future is always mortgaged, which requires repayment. My classmates, living and dead, would say, "Press on—Keep our Traditions—Gig 'em, Aggies," and so would yours. Fortunately, this matter, at any given time, is squarely in the hands of the student body of this great and different University, and it couldn't be with a better guardian. For such reason, Texas Aggies everywhere take comfort in the sure and certain knowledge that at our beloved Texas A&M there will forever be "A SPIRIT THAT CAN NEVER BE TOLD."

My prayer is that I have been found deserving of this honor that has been conferred and that I merit the confidence that has been reposed.

Thank you so very much.

# Robert L. Walker '58

*1987—G. Rollie White Coliseum*

Robert L. Walker '58.
Photo from editor's
collection.

Robert Lowell "Bob" Walker was born January 20, 1936, in Victoria and graduated from high school in Spur, Texas. He earned a bachelor's degree in marketing from Texas A&M, a master's in education from Pepperdine University, and a PhD in educational administration from Texas A&M.

He began his career in educational fund raising at Pepperdine University in 1959. A decade later, he became associate executive director of Texas A&M's Association of Former Students, where he directed the association's annual giving program. In 1972 he was named director of development for Texas A&M University and the following year took on added duties as executive director of the Texas A&M University Development Foundation. Walker served as the university's vice president for development from 1978 until he retired in 2008. He held the James W. Aston Endowed Chair of Institutional Development and taught a graduate course in institutional resource development.

Walker was instrumental in establishing Texas A&M's Visitor Information Center, creating an endowment program for professorships and chairs at Texas A&M, and implementing the university's President's Endowed Scholarship program. Under his leadership, the assets of the Texas A&M University Development Foundation grew to more than $150 million.

# What Is the Aggie Spirit?*

Mr. President, distinguished platform participants, Muster Committee, ladies and gentlemen, and students of Texas A&M University.

It is such a great honor and privilege to be your speaker on this occasion. My work as a fund raiser takes me to visit Aggies all over the United States, and literally all over the world. It is always exciting to see the Aggie Spirit still living in our graduates many years after they leave the campus.

It has been said that, "God gives us memory so that we can have roses in December." People can always live in our hearts, can't they? They never die unless we forget them. Isn't that really what Muster is all about—remembering people we love?

Often, I am asked, "What is it with you Aggies? Why are you so loyal to your school? Why do your former students give so much and why do they seem to care so much about Texas A&M University?" Well, that's what I would like to talk about tonight. It's the Aggie Spirit.

Do we have the Spirit because we have better buildings, better laboratories, a larger campus? Do we have the Spirit because we have smarter students or a better-trained faculty than anyone else? The former students might say that the reason A&M is so great is because we went to school there. The faculty might say it's because we teach there. Those of us in the administration might say it's because of our leadership. I contend that it may be some of all of the above. The bottom line is this. The real reason we're all here today is because of you—the students of Texas A&M. Without you, we have no reason to be here. We have no reason for dormitories, classrooms, laboratories, parking lots, faculties, or administration. Once you have the students, then it's important to have a faculty that cares, and I contend that the faculty, along with the students, make up the two hidden ingredients of the Aggie Spirit. It's because of the good impressions that you, the students and the faculty, make on visitors, on former students, on corporate leaders, on foundation directors that motivate them to want to

*Speech title derived by editor from speech contents

invest in Texas A&M. You students have no way of knowing the good impressions you make on our visitors when you speak, when you're friendly, and when you're helpful. Faculty members, your willingness to go the extra mile to help students succeed makes the difference. The interaction between faculty, students, and visitors is special. Let me illustrate.

In September of 1974, Dr. Ned Ellett of the College of Veterinary Medicine called me to say that he wanted me to meet two ladies that were here to pick up their dog. Their dog had surgery in the Small Animal Clinic. She had a damaged knee comparable to a football injury—cartilage damage in the joint. Their dog was a Pug, and her name was Puggie Poo. They went on and on about how happy "Miss Puggie" was to be at Texas A&M and how friendly the students were, how devoted and competent the faculty was. Looking across the table at me when we were having lunch, the lady said, "Mr. Walker, Miss Puggie would like to make a gift to Texas A&M." I looked at Dr. Ellett. He was not laughing, so I didn't laugh either, and I said, "That would be marvelous." That afternoon, they brought by a check drawn on the account of Miss Puggie Poo with her address and phone number. It was a check for $1,000 made out to the College of Veterinary Medicine's Small Animal program for little people and signed by Miss Puggie Poo's paw print off of an ink pad. When I was asked that week by the President how things in Development were going, I said, "Dr. Williams, they are going to the dogs."

I tell you of this incident because it's the faculty and the students that are making good impressions on people. They were the motivating force behind the good public relations that had been created with these ladies. The rest of the story was that these ladies' attorney later called and said that they were doing some estate planning and hopefully a sizable gift would come to Texas A&M.

When I was asked to implement the President's Endowed Scholars' Program, one of the first Aggies I called on was H. B. Zachry '22. After I had explained the scholarship program to Mr. Zachry, I said, "Mr. Zachry, could you fund a President's Endowed Scholarship?" He said, "No, but I'll fund two."

Last week, I talked with a faculty member who's making plans to make a gift of real estate worth more than $400,000 to Texas A&M,

because as he said, "I believe in the people on this campus." There is a present faculty member who just keeps on giving each year to establish an endowed professorship. Recently, a former student who hadn't given much in many years sent us a check for $20,000 when he was asked to contribute to a fund in memory of Dr. Charlie Crawford, one of his former professors.

The parents of an out-of-state Aggie sent $1,000 last year when their son graduated. They did this in honor of a faculty member who had gone out of his way to help their son when he needed assistance.

Another letter I received was from a man in Brooklyn, NY who is not an Aggie and had no relationship to any Aggie. I quote, "About a year ago, I had a short visit at College Station and enjoyed your hospitality. Because of the fine impression that your students made, I find myself wanting to learn more about Texas A&M. Any brochures concerning its past, present and future would be appreciated. Also, any programs that interested parties can contribute to financially for deserving students, I would be glad to receive."

When you students leave here and look back through the years, such as the Class of '37 and as all those who have preceded you often do, you'll remember SCONA [Student Conference On National Affairs], standing at football games, Bonfire, Midnight Yell Practice, the Corps of Cadets, the dorm you lived in, intramural sports, the band, the MSC [Memorial Student Center], the Singing Cadets, the Ross Volunteers, the clubs, the outfits, but most of all, you'll remember your fellow Aggies that were a part of those organizations. People and our relationship with them is what is really important to us. No person is poor when they have good friends who care. As Aggies, we're rich indeed because we're surrounded with people who care. Most of us are Aggies today because of the trust we had in some relative, friend, or teacher who cared.

There are nearly 100 members of the Class of 1937 here celebrating their 50th anniversary. Why do they come back to the campus? It's not because of the buildings. Most of them are gone or changed since they were students. It's because of their classmates. It's because of the close bonds they developed while living on the campus. It's because of the faculty that made an impression on them as they studied, as they played, as they worked on this campus. Some of your lifelong friends are sitting beside you here tonight. Who knows—your future wife or husband may be in the next class or organization that you become a part of.

When I read names like [Ford] Albritton, [Wofford] Cain, [John] Blocker, [Harold] Dunn, [Sterling] Evans, [J. W. "Cop"] Forsyth, [Michel] Halbouty, [E. J.] Kyle, [C. E. "Pat"] Olsen, [Chester] Reed, [Earl] Rudder, [G. Rollie] White, [Jack] Williams, [Royce] Wisenbaker, and [H. B. "Pat"] Zachry—they're only names. Yes, they are buildings or places, but there's a great story behind each, and how, as a former student, each cared about providing for the future and making an investment in you, the students of Texas A&M. Cop Forsyth from the Class of 1912 said to me 15 years ago, "All of us who are former students of Texas A&M have received more than we'll ever give back. We owe a debt we can never repay." He would often thank me for asking him to give to Texas A&M.

One day in 1972, I received a telephone call from an attorney. He said, "Mr. Walker, I have a client who wants to know how he can leave some money to A&M." His client turned out to be Mr. Walter W. Lechner, Class of 1914. Mr. Lechner and his wife had plans to leave their estate to another university in Texas, but because of a demonstration against that school by faculty and students, Mr. Lechner said, "I want my assets to go to Texas A&M where I have confidence in the faculty and the students." Today we have Lechner Fellowships and more than $10 million has been received with more coming from oil income provided by Mr. Lechner's estate because he saw something in students and faculty that he admired. What we do as faculty and students can hurt as well as help our University.

Many years ago, I received a phone call from Dr. Dick Creger in the Poultry Science Department. He invited me to meet a man who had worked for the department for 28 years. We met in the Poultry Science pavilion with chickens and animals all around. This gentlemen dressed in worn-out khakis and an old straw hat handed me an envelope and said, "There, Mr. Walker, I want to give that to A&M." I opened the envelope and there was $42,000 in certificates of deposit. With the raise he received that year, he was making $5,000 a year.

He lived very modestly so that all of his money possible could go into a scholarship fund. His plan was to have $50,000 available to help students, because he said, "I've been cleaning up after these chickens for students because I love Aggies. Aggies are special and I want to help them in the future." We didn't take his money because it was his life savings. Through his will the money will come to A&M for scholarships.

Ladies and gentlemen, I could keep on telling you stories about Aggies who care, who are investing in you the students, who want A&M to be the special place it is because they believe in all that you stand for. I salute you, the faculty members, for the great job you do in showing that you care about students and your willingness to give of yourself so that they might succeed.

Although Muster has a lot to do with memory, we should remind ourselves in the words of Samuel Johnson, "The business of life is to go forward." We cannot allow our memories to master us, to stalemate us with grief, or "what might have beens," or our own personal mistakes or shortcomings. Our task is to build even greater lives with greater influences, having learned from the spirit of those great Aggies that have gone on before us. After you graduate and become former students, you will look back and remember—the Aggie Spirit is people and the impressions they made on your life. [The quoted lines below are from Virginia Scott Miner's "Brief Valentine."]

They say that once each seven years,
All things are made quite new.
A thing I dare dream false—
Lest there be change in you.
For I have grown very fond of all your funny ways—
And merely ask that you remain the same
Throughout all your days.

Thank you and God bless you.

# Gerald D. Griffin '56

*1988—G. Rollie White Coliseum*

Gerald D. Griffin '56.
Photo from editor's
collection.

Gerald Duane Griffin was born December 25, 1934, in Athens, Texas. After earning a BS degree in aeronautical engineering at Texas A&M in 1956, he served four years in the US Air Force.

He spent more than twenty-five years with the United States space program at government agencies and in private industry. He was lead flight director for the *Apollo 12*, *Apollo 15*, and *Apollo 17* manned spaceflight missions; director of the Lyndon B. Johnson Space Center; and deputy director of both the Hugh L. Dryden Flight Research Center and the John F. Kennedy Space Center. In the private sector he held senior engineering posts with Lockheed and General Dynamics.

During the flight of *Apollo 13*, Griffin was scheduled to lead the lunar landing team in Mission Control. When the landing was canceled after an oxygen tank explosion, he led one of the teams of flight controllers responsible for the safe return of the astronauts. He was a technical advisor for the movies *Apollo 13*, *Contact*, and *Deep Impact*.

Upon leaving NASA in 1986, Griffin was president and CEO of the Greater Houston Chamber of Commerce before becoming managing director of the Houston office of Korn/Ferry International, a world-wide executive search firm, in 1989. He is a fellow of the American Institute of Aeronautics and Astronautics, the American Astronautical Society, and the British Interplanetary Society and a senior fellow of the Eaker Institute for Aerospace Studies. He served on the Texas National Research Laboratory Commission, the Texas Space Science Industry Commission, and Texas A&M's Space Research Advisory Board. He was named a Texas A&M Distinguished Alumnus in 1985 and inducted into the Texas A&M Corps of Cadets Hall of Honor in 1996.

## Meeting the Challenge of the Future*

I know that many of you hear from time to time, from many speakers at many events, that they are very honored to be appearing before you. I want you to know that, tonight, I really am honored to be here. I consider where I am at this very moment to be one of the greatest honors anyone can ever receive.

I would like to add my congratulations to the Class of '38 on your 50th reunion. Your class and those classes very close to you carried a terrific burden in World War II and you carried it very, very well. We're very proud of you. Well done.

Fifty years, that's hard to think about. My 50th reunion will be held in the year 2006—sounds like a space odyssey. That's only 18 years from now, and I intend to be right here on campus to celebrate it. It's really not that far away when you think about it. The kids that will graduate in that year from college are already three years old. One of them is my grandson, Brad, who is here tonight. With some luck, I'm going to watch him walk across this stage or another like it in about 18 years plus about a month to get his A&M diploma. And you notice, I said "A&M." That's part of my standard brainwashing technique. Now, that's if he can finish in four years. Brad, I want you to know, that's a vanishing breed at Texas A&M, so you have a real challenge.

Tonight we celebrate Aggie Muster. The back page of your program tells the history of the Muster, and I'm not going to go into it in great detail here. But there is a point I would like to make, and it's been made already, that I believe that everyone would agree that Muster is the most important recurring tradition for all Aggies, no matter where they are on this planet. This solemn, but not sad, occasion is a unique day for everyone associated with A&M to renew their commitment to the Spirit of Aggieland. That's what we're here for, and I hope my few remarks tonight will help you renew your own commitment.

*Speech title derived by editor from speech contents

Normally, I don't think it's too good to dwell too much on the past, but I'd like to take a short glimpse backward, because I think it'll set the stage for some later comments.

You know, we are associated with a very interesting institution with a very interesting history, and a turbulent one at that. It was more than 125 years ago, 1862, that President Abraham Lincoln signed the Morrill Act establishing land grant colleges. It took fourteen years just to get the doors open at the A&M College of Texas after that act was signed. And what an on-again, off-again beginning we had. Thomas Gathright, our first president, was asked to leave in 1879 over a dispute with the faculty and problems with management of the Corps of Cadets. In 1883, things got so bad that the presidency was completely abolished and a faculty chairman was appointed to run the college. Things got better when Lawrence Sullivan Ross became president in 1890; in fact, things got so good and so calm that under his Presidency we played our first football game and beat Ball High–Galveston 14-6 [later research revealed that A&M's first football game was against Texas in 1894]. However, in 1908, it almost came apart again. The school almost closed. That was the year of the Great Strike of the Students, over then-president Henry Harrington.

Some interesting charges were brought against Harrington, and I'm going to quote a couple of them for you, because I think it tells you about the turbulence of the time. Harrington was accused of "being of high temper, domineering disposition and quarrelsome to the faculty and students." He was accused of using "profane, abusive and vulgar language." He was charged with "engaging in fist fights with both faculty and cadets." He was charged with "committing a murderous assault with a shotgun against a student." The interesting final charge was that "he was not in touch with the student body." Well, Harrington finally resigned in August of 1908, and A&M has been on the move ever since.

A&M progressed slowly for the next several decades, but the winds of change blew strongly in the late '50s and early '60s. A profound change occurred in 1963: The Agricultural and Mechanical College of Texas became Texas A&M University and women were allowed to enroll on a "limited basis." In 1971, only 17 years ago, A&M's doors were finally opened to all students, male and female. Since that time, A&M's

progress has been unparalleled among major institutions of higher learning. And we can look back to those changes of the '60s and '70s that allowed A&M to reach new greatness, and we're still improving.

With that brief chronology, let's lay some world events alongside A&M's history. A&M was born in the aftermath of the Civil War. It witnessed World War I, World War II, the Korean War, the Vietnam War, and other skirmishes around the world. During its history, A&M has seen and participated, from the beginning, in the development of such things as the automobile, the airplane, agricultural technology, oil and gas exploration and production. We've seen the splitting of the atom, we saw space flight from its infancy, computers, and now, today, biotechnology. What's next? Texas A&M has played, or is playing, a major role in every one of these advances and, more importantly, through its entire history A&M has produced many more than its share of people with unexcelled capabilities and unexcelled leadership qualities.

I entered Texas A&M in September of 1952. I was here four years. Yes, Brad, I made it in four! I was in the Corps, I graduated and was commissioned in '56, as Sharon said, and I spent four years flying in the Air Force. From the day I entered Texas A&M, I knew something was different about this place. I know students here hear this a lot, but those of us who are getting a little older, we say we can't remember what happened yesterday, and that's true, but we can remember what happened a long time ago. Well, I can remember my first day at A&M vividly. It was hotter than blazes, I was scared to death, but my fondest memory is of my first commanding officer. His name is John Whitman, he's from Marble Falls, he majored in petroleum engineering. I don't know where John is today, but he had to be eight feet tall. He was shined and pressed to absolute perfection. He exuded leadership, he commanded respect. I would've followed him anywhere, and I would today. John Whitman is just one example of what I would experience through four years of A&M and four years of the Air Force, and that is leadership by Aggies.

That experience continued right into my career in the US space program. There were many Aggies involved then, as there are now, in that program. Throughout my years at NASA, there was Aggie after Aggie in positions of major responsibility. It was great to be director of the Lyndon B. Johnson Space Center in my last assignment and, although

I'm gone from there now, I'm glad to report that another Aggie, Aaron Cohen, Class of '52, is now the Director of the Johnson Space Center.

The early space program was different than it is now. It always has been and always will be a somewhat risky business; we were not expected to be perfect, and we made plenty of mistakes in the early days. But we learned from our failures and we were allowed to press on without a lot of wailing and gnashing of teeth. We also had a clearly stated objective: To get to the moon within the decade of the '60s, and we did it. We were young; we didn't know the words "can't" and "maybe." The words we chose to use most of the time were "go" and "yes." In my years in Mission Control during the Gemini and Apollo programs, my strongest memory is that we were full of confidence and the confidence that I brought to that scene, I can tell you unequivocally, was something that I brought from my years at A&M.

There's also one anecdote from the Apollo program that I can really trace to A&M, and I have to tell this. I was the lead flight director on Apollo 12; that was the second flight to the moon, the second landing on the moon. On Apollo 11, Neil Armstrong and Buzz Aldrin had landed in the Sea of Tranquility, a relatively flat place, and we picked that because it was a relatively flat place to land. On Apollo 12, we went to a more rugged terrain, and we had a very precise landing to make because we wanted to get close enough to a thing called the Surveyor Spacecraft, which had been sent up unmanned about 7 years before. We wanted to take pieces off of it and bring them back to Earth and analyze what that lunar environment had done to it in those 7 years. The flight had Pete Conrad as a commander, Dick Gordon and Al Bean, all good friends of mine today.

The flight began very dangerously. We were hit by lightning about 50 seconds after lift-off, and it knocked everything off in the spacecraft. Thank goodness the launch vehicle kept working, and we got on into Earth's orbit. After much gnashing of teeth and working, we got the systems turned back on and checked everything and, although we delayed one revolution to head for the moon, we said let's go for it and we did. I might add, the rest of the flight went very well after that. Pete Conrad and Al Bean got in the lunar module and landed on the surface. Sure enough, they landed very close to the Surveyor Spacecraft.

They got out, they got their pieces off of it, came back and went to sleep. Now, it just happens that Al Bean is a teasip. When I went home that night, I told Sandy, "I've got to do something for him." Everything was going so well at that point! Our usual practice was to awaken the crew with music, so I brought a record to the communications people the next morning, had a tape made, and we woke them up to a very loud rendition of the Aggie War Hymn! Now I use this story to indicate that Aggies in positions of leadership have all kinds of advantages. In this case, at least from a space perspective, I think we have the ultimate "gotcha" on the teasips.

Well, the winds of change never stop blowing, and it's howling a gale in Texas today. We are in a swirl of economic problems that will challenge our best efforts for several years to come. The Texas economy of the past was resource-based almost in its entirety. We literally, for our first 150 years, lived off the land: oil, gas, and agriculture. These resource-based industries are going to be very important to the future of Texas, but the Texas economy of the future will depend much on knowledge-based industries. Texas A&M University, with its education and research, will play a major role in providing the knowledge that Texas will require. A&M will again meet the challenge for the future.

But other winds of change are important to consider, too. A&M is unique, but the magic qualities that set A&M apart from other great universities are becoming fewer in number and harder to maintain. I believe that all Aggies need to think about the future of our traditions that make us unique. I don't want to be misunderstood here. Former students don't dictate A&M traditions. Students on campus, right here in College Station, determine A&M traditions. They maintain them, discard them, or start new ones. But I humbly submit there are some worth saving forever, and I offer them to you now. One, is speaking—just a simple "howdy." Two, the concept of the 12th Man, always ready to help the Aggie cause. Three, the Corps of Cadets and their famous Fightin' Texas Aggie Band. Four, Silver Taps. And Five, Muster. As we recognize our fallen comrades tonight with the roll call, it's important to reflect on what Texas A&M means to each of us. A&M is not a place; it is a spirit; it's a way of life. I'm sure that all of you feel that Spirit with pride tonight.

Texas A&M University—ain't it great! Thank you.

# Chet Edwards '74

*1989—G. Rollie White Coliseum*

Chet Edwards '74. Photo from editor's collection.

Thomas Chester "Chet" Edwards was born November 24, 1951, in Corpus Christi and attended Houston's Memorial High School. He graduated from Texas A&M University in 1974 with a bachelor's degree in economics and received the prestigious Brown Foundation–J. Earl Rudder Award, presented to A&M's top graduates. From 1974 to 1977, he was legislative and district aide to US Congressman Olin E. "Tiger" Teague '32. He earned a master's degree in business administration from Harvard Business School in 1981 and worked for the Trammell Crow Company.

Edwards was elected to the Texas Legislature as representative from the Ninth Senatorial District in 1982. He was named one of *Texas Monthly*'s "Top Ten Legislators," Senator of the Year by the Texas Youth Commission, and one of "Five Outstanding Young Texans" by the Texas Jaycees. He compiled a 99.7 percent voting record during his first term in the Senate.

He was instrumental in the passage of the "Super Tuesday" Presidential Primary Bill and is credited with producing a compromise workers' compensation reform bill passed in 1990. He is noted as a champion of consumer rights and a watchdog on utility rates. He chaired the Senate Nominations Committee, setting tough but fair standards for appointees, and the Sunset Advisory Committee, where he demanded efficiency and responsiveness from state agencies.

Edwards served in the Texas Senate until 1990. He was then elected to the US House of Representatives, representing Texas' Eleventh Congressional District from 1991 to 2005 and the Seventeenth District from 2005 to 2011.

# The Meaning of Aggie Muster*

Today, friends, families and strangers all across the world share a sacred, common bond.

Why? Because we are the Aggies—the Aggies are we.

Think with me about the meaning of these:

Fish Camp, Corps of Cadets, Reveille IV, Aggie Band, MSC, Singing Cadets, Twelfth Man, Ross Volunteers, Bonfire, Final Review . . . Silver Taps.

These great traditions—these lasting legacies—are the building blocks of the Aggie Spirit. It is that Spirit that binds us together, one to another.

Never is that spirit more present, more heartfelt, than at Aggie Muster.

What is the meaning of Aggie Muster?

Today, we honor those who once shared that special spirit that only Aggies can understand.

By paying respect to their lives, we learn a deeper respect for life itself.

By sharing the loneliness of their families, we learn we are not alone. We are all part of a special family.

By recognizing their time on this earth is now gone, we learn how precious each moment must be.

I am reminded of a poem I found as a freshman at A&M. It is called "A Small Moment" [by Jean W. Brown].

> This time will become but a small moment in life's scheme of
>     things.
> But what I have invested here—of myself, of my time, of my
>     thoughts—
> Will become a part of what I am to be, and what I have to give and
>     how I am to grow.
> Therefore, let me not misuse or misjudge this small moment.
> Rather, let me give it all that I have, And take from it all that it has
>     to offer me.

---

*Speech title derived by editor from speech contents

What is the meaning of Aggie Muster?

It's a celebration of "a spirit that can ne'er be told."

Friendship, leadership, honesty—respect for our past and commitment to our future—caring, can-do attitudes. The Aggie Spirit is all of these and much more.

The Aggie Spirit is embodied in the lives of those who have touched our lives. To me, it is the unselfishness of Wayne Stark, the courage of General Earl Rudder, and the patriotism of Congressman Olin "Tiger" Teague.

It is on their shoulders—their sacrifices—that you and I now stand.

Most of you never met Congressman "Tiger" Teague, Class of '32. His life exemplified the Aggie Spirit.

Born in Mena, Arkansas, he had never enjoyed the luxury of indoor plumbing until coming to A&M. He worked his way through college.

In World War II, he fought in defense of our great nation. It was in the forests of Germany that he nearly lost his life.

While still on crutches, he returned home and ran for Congress. Why? So that other young men might not have to suffer the ravages of war.

As the most decorated veteran ever to serve in Congress, he limped with a shortened leg and a 17-pound shoe—permanent scars from his service to country.

Tiger Teague knew seven presidents, but he always remained an humble man. He dearly loved Texas A&M.

In his death, as in his life, he taught me a valuable lesson. I shall never forget that cold January day in 1981. Amidst the countless white crosses in Arlington National Cemetery, the black, riderless horse symbolically carried Congressman Teague to his final resting place, overlooking the Lincoln Memorial.

At the very moment this great Aggie was being laid to rest in the quiet stillness of Arlington, I heard an uproar off in the distance. Thousands of citizens celebrating the newfound freedom of 52 Americans who had been held hostage for so long in Iran. The hostages were being given a tumultuous welcome as they rode to the White House. It was a celebration of freedom. As I looked down at Tiger Teague, a man who had dedicated his life in war and peace to preserve our freedom, I realized, more than any textbook could tell me, that freedom and opportunity are not free. Aggies such as Tiger Teague have given much for you and me. Aggies such as you in the Class of 1939 [celebrating their 50th anniversary on campus].

So, what is the meaning of Aggie Muster?

Perhaps it is this: As the beneficiaries of those no longer with us, we must be good stewards for generations yet to come. We must be the best we can be and make the most of those brief moments we have here.

Until that Muster candle is lit for us some day, as Aggies we should give something of ourselves to make a better community, a better country.

How do we honor our Aggie comrades today? With candles, yes. With spirit, yes. But, also listen to these words from Gettysburg:

> But in a larger sense we cannot dedicate—we cannot consecrate—
> we cannot hallow—this ground. The brave men, living and dead,
> who struggled here, have consecrated it, far above our poor power
> to add or detract . . . It is for us the living, rather, to be dedicated
> here to the unfinished work which they who fought here have thus
> far so nobly advanced. . . ."

As we say goodbye, as we honor our fellow Aggies now gone, I would send with them and leave with us this message. It is not my message, but it touches on the Aggie Spirit.

This was the message of a 7-year-old Hispanic girl I met just over a year ago. At the time she was fighting a battle against cancer, a battle she was not sure she would win.

She was poor and needed help finding medical care. A card she sent to me said this in Spanish: "Cuando morimos, dejamos todo lo que tenemos y nos llevamos todo lo que dimos." In English: "When we leave this world, we leave behind all that we have and we carry with us all that we have given."

To those Aggies who have given so much to us—softly, call the Muster.

# M. L. "Red" Cashion '53

*1990—G. Rollie White Coliseum*

M. L. "Red" Cashion '53.
Photo from editor's
collection.

Mason Lee "Red" Cashion was born November 10, 1931, and raised in the center of the Texas A&M campus, where his father was general secretary of the YMCA. He married the former Lou Burgess in 1952 and graduated from A&M with a BBA degree in 1953. After serving in the US Army, he established a charcoal manufacturing business in 1955. A year later, he entered the insurance business as partner in a general agency. The agency merged in 1966 to form Anco Corp., which he served as chairman of the board.

Cashion is a past president of the Bryan–College Station Chamber of Commerce, the Brazos County Industrial Foundation, and the Brazos County Association of Independent Insurance Agents. He was chairman of the board of the Region VI Education Service Center and has served as guest professor of insurance at Texas A&M University.

He was a football referee for high school and college games, most notably in the Southwest Conference. With the National Football League from 1972 to 1997, he refereed over 500 games, including Super Bowl XX and Super Bowl XXX. After retiring, he continued to train new NFL referees in the art of keeping the game interesting and exciting. Cashion was easily identified with his enthusiastic drawl of "First dowwwwwn!" A past president of the Professional Referees Association, he was inducted into the Texas Sports Hall of Fame in 1999. He was named a Distinguished Alumnus of Texas A&M in 2003.

## Aggie Spirit—Live It, Share It, Give It*

Today, Aggies all over the world gather for the 1990 Muster. I am indeed honored to have the privilege to be the 1990 Muster speaker.

The Muster Committee is to be congratulated and complimented on all of their efforts. I have certainly enjoyed working with Sharon Brunner and her entire committee in the preparation of this program.

My memories of A&M are basically divided into three periods. First, as a child growing up in the middle of the campus of an all-male school. The second period is my years as a student trying to get an education and get out and join the world. The third period is as a former student and resident in the community watching the changes as our college emerged into one of the world's great universities.

During each of these periods, many changes have occurred; changes which have benefitted us all. Traditions have changed during these years, just like everything else.

Most of you do not remember the traditions and requirements of hitchhiking for a fall Corps Trip to Houston or Austin. If you "up-streamed" before the designated point on the road, it would get you many hours on the bullring.

The YMCA published a small card that listed the proper requirements for hitchhiking.

I remember my parents opening their campus home to student girlfriends and family because there was no place to stay on busy weekends. I remember the student who had two dates arrive on the campus for the same weekend! One stayed at our house. He told both of them that he had to go to work part of the weekend, as many of the students did in those days, and he would pick up one date and be with her for a while and then take her to the house and say that he had to go to work and go meet the other date. He sure was happy when Monday rolled around!

I remember walking to the swimming pool by all of the faculty houses that occupied where we now sit as well as where the Memorial Student Center is presently located. There is a marker just north of John Koldus'

*Speech title derived by editor from speech contents

house on the campus [the vice president's home on Throckmorton Street] commemorating these early families in the life of A&M.

As a student, I made little impact on A&M, although it made a big impact on me. One of the great changes during that time was the emergence of the Memorial Student Center and its importance in student life.

Since graduation, the changes to A&M are too numerous to count. Under the leadership of Perry Adkisson and Bill Mobley and their predecessors, progress and changes continue at an unprecedented pace. Physical construction alone this year could exceed 100 million dollars.

And I will tell those that are students today, many more changes will be made. When you return to the campus—one, five, or twenty years from now—there will be change. There may even be a few more oak trees.

Over the years, A&M has meant much to Texas and to our country. A&M's significance is more important today than ever before. In time of need, A&M has responded with its people, its resources, and technology.

In time of war, A&M has furnished more officers than any other school.

In time of peace, the research at A&M has led to countless improvements and additions to our daily life.

Following the wars, our greatest contribution has been the development of leadership. Former students of A&M are leaders at every level of business and public service in Texas and throughout our nation.

Today, A&M again has the opportunity to be in the forefront in its role to lead Texas.

Texas is beginning to emerge from several years of downturn. I truly believe the largest single factor in aiding this recovery is the ability of Aggies and Aggieland to convert the technical innovations and leadership training developed on the campuses to practical application in our everyday lives and commerce. The nation is looking to Texas to provide leadership in social and economic development and Aggies will make sure this occurs.

One thing has not changed. This is the Aggie Spirit. The Muster is the symbol of what Aggie Spirit is all about.

From the few who gathered on Corregidor, to the thousands who gather today, the opportunity to Muster and celebrate the Aggie Spirit is one of our greatest traditions. It renews a fire in all of us. The Aggie Spirit affects a lot of people. Faculty, staff, students, former students, family, and friends can all get caught up with the spirit.

Aggie Spirit is that special bond that ties us together in all our endeavors.

James Pipkin, Class of '29, speaking at Muster [in 1951] observed:

> Doubtless each of you experienced feelings like mine, though other faces and other years may have risen up before you. We do this because we share a great tradition, greater than the single memories of any one of us. And though years pass, faces change and visible appearances alter, the spiritual core of that tradition remains unaltered and undiminished.

With the Spirit goes an obligation. To the faculty and staff, we are not looking for someone who just wants a job. If you don't have something to contribute, you will never understand what the Spirit is all about. To the students, you must learn not only the academics, but you must learn about your fellow man. His or her needs, cares, concerns, and wishes are just as much a part of the searching process as Chemistry 101.

And to the former students, you have an obligation. It is easier for you to get a job and it is easier for you to get a promotion and it is easier for you to win an election than for someone without the Spirit. This is because those before you have done their part to make life easier for you. Your part is to make life easier for those who follow. Perhaps we should alter John Kennedy's inaugural remarks to say "Ask not what A&M has done for you, but what can you do for A&M."

And to the friends and family: you, too, get caught up in the Spirit. Your role is to share it with all those with whom you come in contact. You must make an effort to understand the Spirit.

The Aggie Spirit,
You must Live it—to Understand it
You have to Share it—to Feel it
And most of all

You have to Give it—in order to Receive it!

As we call the roll for Muster, some will be sad for the loss of a loved or close one. Greater than sadness is the celebration of what they have meant to us and why we answer—"Here." For the Muster is a celebration for all those who contribute to the Aggie Spirit. Please, as the roll is called, grab the hand of a friend.

A previous Muster speaker [Jack M. Rains '60 in 1984] ended by saying: "While taps sounds across this and every Muster, a tear may fall. It is no time for sorrow. For somewhere a bugle sounds recall. United again, we fall into formation."

For you to honor those whose names we call, take the Aggie Spirit— Live It, Share It, and Give It, until we meet again next Muster day.

Thank you, Good Luck, and God Bless You.

# Adm. Jerome L. Johnson '56

*1991—G. Rollie White Coliseum*

Adm. Jerome L. Johnson '56. Photo from editor's collection.

Jerome LaMarr "Jerry" Johnson was born September 21, 1935, in Houston. He attended Texas A&M for three years before leaving to earn a commission as a naval aviator. He is the first Texas Aggie to hold four-star rank in the US Navy and the third Aggie to achieve this rank in the US armed forces. He retired July 21, 2000, after two years as vice chief of naval operations (1990–92). He also served as commander of the Second Fleet and commander of NATO's Striking Fleet Atlantic (1988–90). At sea, he commanded Attack Squadron 27, the combat stores ship USS *San Jose*, the aircraft carrier USS *Coral Sea*, and Carrier Group Four. As the longest serving naval aviator on active duty (almost thirty-eight years), he was designated as the navy's "Gray Eagle." His awards include the Legion of Merit, the Distinguished Flying Cross, and the Bronze Star.

Following retirement, he was president and CEO of the Navy–Marine Corps Relief Society until June 2003. He was also board chairman of the Military Officers Association of America (2002–4) and on the boards of several corporations and nonprofit organizations. He graduated from the Naval Postgraduate School and earned a doctorate in strategic intelligence from the Defense Intelligence College.

Johnson has served as chairman of the board of directors for Smiths Detection Inc. and Smiths Interconnect Inc.; vice president of Wärtsilä Defense Inc.; trustee for the National Museum of Naval Aviation at Naval Air Station Pensacola, Florida; and member of the board of advisors for the Jewish Institute for National Security Affairs.

# Leadership Is a Duty*

I am honored to be here on this day which is so very important to all Aggies. What a great privilege to share in this unique and heartfelt traditional tribute to our departed friends, loved ones, and heroes.

As we know, Muster first began in 1903 to commemorate both Sam Houston's victory at San Jacinto and to remember the Aggies who departed during the previous year. In 1836, Texans had courageously stepped forward to establish and defend the newly formed Lone Star Republic. The battles they fought against overwhelming odds are etched into the fabric of our history. Goliad, the Alamo, and San Jacinto helped form Texas and represent the ideals of service, duty, and sacrifice that continue today in our great nation. Among my favorite studies in my early years was the history of Texas. It is inspirational reading, as is the history and faith of our nation's founding fathers.

As we gather together this year, the recent memories of Operations Desert Shield and Desert Storm are still fresh in our minds. Texas, and this nation, mobilized in support of the Gulf War with the dedication we've come to expect from the sons and daughters of San Jacinto. Tens of thousands of Texans served in the armed forces, Texas industry surged to provide us with the weapons to do the job, and the port cities of Texas loaded fifty-four ships with millions of tons of equipment for over three divisions bound for action in the Middle East.

Texas Aggies once again went into harm's way to defend freedom; and once again some of our number paid the ultimate price. Among them: Major Richard M. Price, United States Air Force, Class of '74, died when the cargo plane he was flying in support of Operation Desert Shield crashed in Germany. [Former Reveille mascot handler] Lieutenant Danny V. Hull, Class of '81, United States Navy, died when the helicopter he was piloting crashed as his battle group was conducting amphibious exercises in the Arabian Sea. First Lieutenant Thomas C. Bland, Jr., Class of '86, United States Air Force, disappeared on 31 January when his AC-130 gunship crashed into the Persian Gulf.

*Speech title derived by editor from speech contents

These men were doing what they loved to do—serving their country—flying—enjoying the thrills and challenges of life. They, and their families, deserve our utmost honor and respect. They are truly heroes in the finest tradition of our great university.

Such selfless dedication is not new for Aggies. The Class of '41 [holding their 50th anniversary reunion] here today can tell you of the contributions made by their classmates and the other 18,000 Aggies who served in the Second World War. Around the Simpson Parade Field are 55 oak trees, in memory of Aggies who gave their lives in the First World War. At the Memorial Student Center we read the inscription: "John 15:13—Greater love hath no man than this, that a man lay down his life for a friend." Duty, leadership, and sacrifice have always been the hallmark of Aggies who have served in our previous conflicts. Members of Class of '41, we're very proud of you gentlemen; you are great role models for us all.

Where do we get such fine young people?

Today, Aggies are serving proudly in the Navy, Marine Corps, Army, Air Force, and Coast Guard. When I was a fleet commander, I had the chance to visit and operate with various units of the fleet, Marine Corps, Army, and Air Force. In every organization I visited, in every ready room, flight line, and command center, I was privileged to see bright, energetic, and highly motivated young men and women. The services have been blessed with the best recruits and young officers we've ever had. They want to do a good job, they want to learn, they want to contribute, and they are more than willing to work hard to be part of a winning team. They are there, in every corner of the globe, providing proof of this country's commitment to freedom. It's a pleasure to know that no Aggie serving our country stands alone; they are joined together today all over the world to commemorate our great university, our insurmountable pride, and the loss we share for those who have departed our ranks.

On February 24th this year, our valiant servicemen and women wrote another chapter in our history. This tremendous victory was brought about because, from the earliest deliberations, the leadership of this country was convinced of our need to protect the sovereignty of an ally. President George H. W. Bush, as Commander in Chief, made heroic decisions; our representatives in the Senate and House held a courageous vote in support, and we were inspired by the great military and civilian statesmen: Defense Secretary Dick Cheney and General Colin Powell. Above all, victory was the result of a national consensus. America relearned the principle that first you commit the government and the people, then you commit the troops. Saddam Hussein's aggression was answered by a coalition of nations resolved to maintaining freedom.

Before this war, many in this country wondered if the American dream might be only a fragile and naive fantasy. We had watched the physical dismantlement of the Berlin Wall and wondered if it was a result of anything we had done, or had communism only buckled under the weight of its own distorted ideology? We were victorious in the cold war, but many asked the questions: Did we still have the strength, the wisdom, and the confidence to defend our principles? Did we still believe in the power of free men to do what was right?

Those questions were unequivocally answered last month on the day President Bush announced to the world the liberation of Kuwait. As we begin to study the lessons learned from Operations Desert Shield and Desert Storm, the most important point is clear already—despite the dire predictions of some that America was in decline, soon to be eclipsed by other powers. It is now clear that the United States emerged from Operation Desert Storm with the tremendous responsibility of being the world's only superpower. No other nation can move the machinery of war anyplace in the world—unchallenged, to deter aggression in the defense of freedom. I emphasize the word and the mission of our armed forces: deterrence. I'm not saying we are a superpower in the spirit of national chauvinism. Whatever glory there is in world leadership is not enough to pay for the burdens. Leadership is a duty, not a privilege. We depend—as do our friends—on a global community of free and peaceful nations; but that global community also depends on us for leadership—on our vigor, our power, and our dedication to the traditions of justice.

As a maritime nation, we are further dependent on freedom of the seas to import raw materials and export the quality industrial products to keep our country strong and vibrant—freedom of the sea and international commerce will remain fundamental to our way of life.

Here at home, tough challenges still lie before us, in our communities, in our economy, and in the way we take care of our own. These challenges are real, but not insurmountable. As a result of the tremendous success in Operation Desert Storm, I sense a renewed spring in the nation's step, a sense of the possible, an awareness that patriotism and high ideals are not just for the simple-minded and the innocent, but for anyone who cares to make this world a better place. I believe that America is rediscovering those values on which Aggies have built their reputation since 1876. Think how our spirit surges when we hear Lee Greenwood's words in the song ["God Bless the USA":] "I'm proud to be an American."

By no means are our values limited to geo-politics and military strategies. Texans have always been in the forefront of technology and research, and Texas is a historically vital link in the transportation and communication lifelines of America. Aggies in industry, research, education, and government are committed to the same ideals and are leading the way to a bright future. The problems we face within this country require the same leadership and commitment that were mobilized to check the aggression of Saddam Hussein. Texas Aggies are part of the solution because they are responsive, even in this sometimes cynical age, to the time-proven principles that forged our state and made this country the world leader it is today. The sense of commitment and hands-on leadership that Texas A&M instills is exactly what America needs. In the finest traditions of our university and its rich history, we are called to serve. And we will!

Tonight, let us again renew our commitment to Aggie ideals of unselfish service to community, country, and humanity. The base of Lawrence Sullivan Ross' statue reads, "Soldier, Statesman, Knightly Gentleman." The words are not just a description of a great man, but an inspiration and goal for all Aggies to strive for. More importantly, they are a fitting epitaph for our departed. The many heroes who, as in the past, we honor tonight, helped make us, and America, what we are. We have that same responsibility to shape the future. We can do no less, in the honor of those who have gone before us. Thank you for being here tonight to honor our comrades. God bless you all, and God bless America.

# Frank W. Cox III '65

*1992—G. Rollie White Coliseum*

Frank W. Cox III '65.
Photo from editor's
collection.

Frank Wallace Cox III was born April 4, 1943, in New Boston, Texas. He was head yell leader his senior year at Texas A&M, on the Corps staff, a member of the Ross Volunteers, and first sergeant of Squadron 2 in A&M's Corps of Cadets.

During the Vietnam War, as a captain in the US Air Force, he served as commander of a Strategic Air Command Minuteman Missile combat crew. Following the war, he was a personnel staffing specialist for a 6,000-employee organization and managed one of the largest employee involvement programs in the federal government. In the latter job, he trained over 3,000 managers and students in several states. He is the founder of Source of Success, a management consulting firm that has trained 25,000 government, civilian, professional, and volunteer workers. He authored *I Bleed Maroon* along with manuals on leadership and teamwork. He also composed a poem entitled "AGGIELAND—Why I Love Her So," which he recites at the end of his speech.

## Where Else but Aggieland*

*Frank Cox was introduced by Seth Dockery, Aggie football player and subchair of the Muster Speaker Selection Committee. Seth was about six feet four in height and weighed about 220 pounds. Frank was five feet seven and weighed about 150 pounds. Frank called Seth back up to the podium to stand by him for a minute as he started his speech.*

*Speech title derived by editor from speech contents

Seth, I really appreciate all you said about me, but I'm wondering why you didn't tell them about my being an all-American linebacker at A&M and about all those grand-slam home runs that I hit in the bottom of the 9th inning against the 'sips to beat them out of the championship?

Seth, as you know, there are a lot of students on campus who get us mixed up all the time. I just wanted to clear it up once and for all: he is Seth and I am Frank. The easiest way to tell the difference is, I'm the one with the muscles.

Thanks, Seth. Seth Dockery—dedicated Christian, graduate student, involved Aggie, member of the fightin' Texas Aggie SWC Champion football team. I bet his momma is proud of him! As well she should be. As each of yours are of you.

Wow—where has the time gone? Class of 1942—heroes of World War II (the war to end all wars, we thought)—defenders of freedom. Can you believe it's been over 50 years since you stepped off that train at West Gate and stepped onto the hallowed grounds of Texas A&M, the greatest university in the world?

It's hard for me to believe that it's been over 30 years ago when I was sitting right over there along with fish Bickham and fish Pounds and 5,000 other burr-headed, khaki-clad Aggies at "All College Night." Scared to death. Wondering what in the world we'd gotten ourselves into. The head yell leader jumped up on the stage and pointed right at us. I could have sworn he was pointing at me when he said, "Hey, you! You ain't gonna make it!" I said, "Wow, it's true, seniors do know everything." Then he said, "I want you to look at the man on your left and the man on your right, because they ain't gonna be here at the end of the year!" I glanced over at fish Pounds and fish Bickham and said to myself, "I don't know about them, but I can tell you one thing for sure, I ain't even gonna be here at the end of the week, much less the end of the year." But I was! I'm so glad I stayed. Johnnie, Herb, I'm glad you stayed. Clyde, Cliff, Darryl, Steve, Rob, Dan, Mark, John, Liz, Cristy, Tracey, Brigett—I'm thankful you stayed. And each student and Aggie here today, if I knew your name, I'd call it out because each of you is so individually important to Texas A&M. I'm glad you stayed. I'm glad I didn't quit. I would have missed out on the greatest years of my life. I would have missed out on meeting you, on being here today to thank you.

Are there any campus cops here today? Aw, yes. I know you KKs ["Kampus Kops"] have a thankless job and I just wanted to let you know how I appreciate the attention you always give me when I come back to campus. [*Pulling a campus parking ticket from pocket.*] That's not all. [*Pulling another parking ticket from pocket.*) You always make me feel like I'm a student again. So, on behalf of all the students at Texas A&M, I say, "Thank you—Not!"

I'd like to ask all present Aggie students to please stand. Yes, all present-day students. Silently stand for just a minute. There they are— America's best, the cream of the crop!!

These students are active every day in the more than 600 student or- ganizations on campus. Doing something worthwhile. My family and I have had the opportunity over the past few months to get to know several of you in a way we would never have expected this time a year ago. You have blessed us.

I would be amiss if I did not mention the Muster Committee. You'll never know how much your letters and words of encouragement have meant to us. You have always treated us with great kindness and love and care. You are Aggies in the truest sense of the word. And though some of you may not have been on the "official" Muster Committee, you are still an integral part of Muster if you handed out a "Muster card" or if you invited a friend to come to Muster or the mere fact that you are present here today—that makes you a part of Muster. And though some of you may not have been "officially" selected as a mem- ber of the "hospitality committee," you are carrying out the tradition of Aggie hospitality each time you say "Howdy" or greet a stranger or give directions to a visitor on campus. You are the Aggies. Thank you; you may be seated.

My mother wants to thank the speaker's selection committee. She thinks y'all have great judgment and deep wisdom as evidenced by your selection. Hey, I've never known my mother to be wrong. After all, she was born on April 21st. Happy birthday, Mom!

I also want to thank Jennie Brisco, who has done such an outstand- ing job as Muster chair, and Seth Dockery, the "puny" one I introduced you to before, and Greg Riels, mascot corporal and first sergeant of E-2 next year, for that 8th day of January when you came to New Boston with Reveille to ask me to be the Muster speaker. The word spread like wildfire that the Aggies were in town. The newspaper came over to do an article; people were taking pictures and getting autographs and shaking their hands and petting Reveille. It was the biggest event in New Boston since 1955. That's when a young singer named Elvis Presley came to town in a pink Cadillac singing "You ain't nothin' but a hound dog." Well, the Muster Committee didn't have a pink Cadillac, but Elvis didn't have "Miss Reveille, Ma'am." I'll take Reveille any day.

I especially want to thank the Class of 1942. We've all enjoyed getting to know you as you were roaming about campus today. Some of you played on that 1939 national championship football team. But much greater than that, as a class, as one, you all stood together on May 16, 1942 and raised your right hand and swore that "I will support and defend the Constitution of the United States of America, against all enemies, foreign and domestic . . . So help me God." And He did and you did. You were all called to active duty the next day. More than 100 of your fish buddies, the ones you studied with, cried with, laughed with, lived with, prayed with for four years, would never return to the shores of America. They gave their lives, their all—for you and for me, so that we might have a place such as Texas A&M to attend. Thank you, Class of '42.

One, Turney W. Leonard, won the Congressional Medal of Honor. Several became brigadier generals. Two of you, J. B. "Dick" Hervey and Richard "Buck" Weirus, became executive directors of the Association of Former Students. Two, Dick Hervey and Manny Rosenthal, have been honored with the Distinguished Alumnus Award [Weirus would be named a Distinguished Alumnus in 1993]. You are our heritage. You carried the torch brightly. You held the banner high. You are our heroes! We will never forget what you have done! We will never forget, for we are the Aggies!

And of course, I want to thank the family and friends of those Aggies who have passed away. Most of them we did not know personally. They may not have been as famous as a Randy Matson or an Earl Rudder, yet they are just as important in making Texas A&M what it is today.

Whether they were your grandfathers, fathers, sons, daughters, sisters, or brothers, we love and appreciate each of them. We are here to celebrate their life. We are here not because it's April 21st and that's what Aggies do on this day. We are here because of what started Muster in the first place—because of the love, care and concern of Aggies for their fallen comrades. My desire for you is that you may experience the "peace that passes all understanding." That you may know more than the 12th Man who came down from the stands. Even that you may know the one man that came down from God himself. May you be comforted by God's own spirit. God bless you. We love you.

And of course we want to thank the defenders at Corregidor. All of the 26 brave Aggies who, along with General George F. Moore, "stood tall" in the midst of battle and heavy enemy fire. We are proud of the five of you left—especially the one who is here with us today—Mr. Urban Hopmann, Class of '39. For us, you gave your best in the true Aggie fashion and spirit. We won't forget—for we are Aggies, the Aggies are we!

Aggieland—how special, how different!! Let the Harvards, Yales, Berkeleys, Rices, and tu's come to A&M to learn how a university should be run; to learn what type of graduates should be walking across their graduation stages. Let the military academies come and look at the Corps of Cadets of Texas A&M. Let them follow the Aggie Corps around for a day or two and discover why one of their own, General George Patton said, "Give me an Army of West Pointers and I'll win a battle. But just give me a handful of Texas Aggies and I'll win the war." [This quote, created for a T-shirt, has never been confirmed.]

While these other schools preach liberalism and socialism—we'll make leaders and patriots.

While they stress "I," and "What's in it for me?" We ask, "Can I help you" or "Can we work this out together?"

They worry about whether it's "politically correct"—we just worry if it's just plain ol' correct.

While they think and discuss—we'll join forces and "just do it."

While they think they can do it on their own—we say, like the motto of our football team, "lean on me!"

While they like "Silence of the Lambs"—I like "We've Never Been Licked."

They can have their Madonnas and Jane Fondas—as for me, I'll take you—the Class of '42!

While they fret over their rights—we'll concentrate on responsibilities.

While their university presidents go to conferences and talk of their "world class SAT and ACT takers"—our president, Dr. William H. Mobley, can talk of our world class students, leaders, organizations, traditions, and accomplishments. He can talk about the Aggies. [*Turning to President Mobley:*] "Bill, Seth said I could call you Bill today, do you really get paid for doing this? Wow!—What a cush job!

We are a world class university. We are the Aggies!!! Come, sit at our feet—learn from us.

Yes, we are already "world class." Don't let anyone tell you different. You are the cream of the crop. You are the best. If there be a student, if there be a professor, if there be an administrator, if there be a regent who thinks we need to become like one of those other institutions; to change, to diversify; then I am here to tell you that Highway Six still runs both ways. Why change when you're the best already? Don't they know that's what got Adam and Eve into trouble in the first place? They were trying to become something less than what they already were. You are the best. "Some may boast of prowess bold, of the school they think so grand, but there's a Spirit can ne'er be told, it's the Spirit of Aggieland."

Wow—how fortunate we are—where else could the Class of '42, '65, '92 and '95 and '98 come together with one purpose, one love, one desire? Only Aggieland!

Where else would they change the date of an accounting test for 1,500 students? Thank you, professors. Where else would they change the time of a ball game, so that the baseball team could come to Muster? Thank you, Coach [Mark] Johnson. Where else would they cut football practice short so the team could participate in Muster? Thank you, Coach [R. C.] Slocum. Only in Aggieland. Where else would they send the basketball coach, Coach [Tony] Barone, who's never even been to a Muster, to go speak at a Muster in Chicago? Only Texas A&M. And don't you leave us, Coach Barone! We're going to build that sports complex. Texas A&M has been trying to get the state officials in Austin to approve the construction of a "special-events center" for several years, but seem to be blocked at every turn by the state committee. It has been a source of controversy for some time and is bogged down in the political process. All we need to do is get the Bonfire committee, the yell leaders, the red pots, the Corps of Cadets, the non-regs, the 12th Man and the former students together and we'll have it built, be playing in it and beating the 'sips before those folks in Austin even know we've begun!!! We'll build it and we'll come!

Why—because we are the Aggies!

Where else but in Aggieland—

Do they build the world's largest Bonfire to show our love for our school?

Do they have a 12th Man willing to stand throughout the game to show our willingness to do our part?

Do the students turn out all the lights and silently walk to the middle of campus on a cold and dreary Tuesday night to stand and honor the life of a departed fellow student as we do in Silver Taps?

Do people, such as you, take off work and travel hundreds of miles to muster together with 10,000 other Aggies to pay respect to those comrades who have passed on, as we do today?

Only at A&M! Why? We are the Aggies!

Where else does a student have the opportunity to be totally involved in every area of life—physically, mentally and spiritually—as we do at Texas A&M University? Oh sure, physically we can't all be a Randy Matson. Why, I couldn't even carry a shot-put 70 feet, much less throw it that far. But each can grow physically at A&M.

And mentally, there is no question that Texas A&M is one of the great academic universities in the world. And I'm glad to know that when you fail a course, you don't quit, you just change majors like we used to.

And of course I would be lying to you, I would be cheating you, if I didn't tell you there is a spiritual side of life that cannot be ignored. How sad it would be if you broke every athletic record at A&M or had a 4.0 GPA and yet left here without knowing what life was really all about. That's why it is always so uplifting to me and my family each time we visit the campus and walk about the grounds and see many of you wearing scripture shirts or shirts with your Christian club represented on it! You are a blessing to us. My favorite shirt is the one that has "Jesus" on the front and "whoop" on the back. I thank you and admire you for your boldness. God bless you.

I am not a rookie, I didn't jump off the turnip truck yesterday, I've been around the block a few times. I fully realize that there may be some of your even here today who have not yet come around to the understanding of what I am talking about in this area. All I ask of you is that you take my words in the same spirit in which they are given—and that's in a spirit of love, concern and care for you!

So, what am I saying? Get involved! Aggies are A&M! You are A&M! Do it all! Meet as many people as you can. Make as many friends as you can. Because, before you know it—you'll blink, turn the corner, take a breath, pick up a leaf and you'll be saying, "Wow—where has the time gone?"

When it is time for my Muster's call, my last thoughts will be of Jesus and family. Yet, welling up from the inner recesses of my heart and mind will be thoughts of my days at Aggieland.

> Marching to the cadence of the drum and bugle corps.
>
> Watching "Old Glory" flapping in the breeze with a chill running up my spine and a tear down my cheek.
>
> Listening to "The Spirit of Aggieland" and the "War Hymn."
>
> Thinking of the seven Congressional Medal of Honor winners and the Class of 1942.

I will be thinking of the Aggie POWs—like James Ray, Class of 1963, who was a prisoner of war in Vietnam for over 6 years. And do you know what he says got him through those hard times? His faith in God and the lessons he learned at A&M and in the Corps of Cadets. James Ray, we won't forget! We are the Aggies! No! We will never forget! I will think of those who've given their all on the battlefields of Germany, the waters of the Pacific, the sands of Iwo Jima, the hills of Korea, the jungles of Vietnam, the deserts of Iraq. I will think of you—you—you!

AGGIELAND
"WHY I LOVE HER SO"

You ask me why I love her so,
Absorb this poem and then you'll know.

Have you listened to the clinking of spurs on the senior's boots;
Or sought out the history and legends of the Aggies' family roots?

Have you watched the Band and Corps outside the famed old dorm,
Assemble and "dress right dress" until a straight line is formed?

Have you ever noticed when "Old Glory" is unfurled,
How a sense of victory and pride does about them swirl?

Have you felt the firm grip of their strong handshake?
Have you wondered where we find these young men to make?

Have you watched the 12th Man stand throughout the game,
Always one for all and all for one; each different, yet all the same?

Have you listened at "Silver Taps" when the RV rifles blast the night,
And the deadly silence is broken as the birds take off in flight?

Have you been present when the "Muster Roll" they call,
For those who've passed away, one by one 'til they've called us all?

Elephant walk, Bonfire, Corps Trips and Midnight Yell too,
Where do they find the study time and yet all this do?

Have you stood at Final Review for the senior's last march-by?
Have you seen them salute their friends with a tear in their eye?

Have you considered the Aggie thousands who lived and fought and
   died,
So that you and I, in freedom, can enjoy all of America's pride?

It must come from somewhere, deep within,
The same spirit and devotion that causes us in life to win.

Why, we've won at Austin, Corregidor, and Iwo Jima, too,
And in Korea, Vietnam and Desert Storm—we always do!

Don't you know? Haven't you seen or heard?
We're the Aggies, the Aggies are we—true to our word.

Well, I have! Why I've been there for it all!
And I'll remember it yet, even past my own Muster's call!

Why it's Aggieland—where I met my best and life-long friends,
The ones who've loved me in spite of my failures and my sins.

It's where I've always most longed to be!
Yes, it's Aggieland, there for you and for me.

If it weren't for Heaven, Aggieland is where I'd want to spend eternity,
There with my family & Aggie buddies, who, except for Jesus, have
    been the closest to me.

Now, do you see why I love her so?
You should! It's all over me! It's that Maroon Aggie glow!

Long after you've forgotten me and the words we've heard today, you
will remember the lighting of the candles, the digging-in of the heels of
the RV [Ross Volunteers] firing squad, the roll call.

You will remember Muster! You'll never be the same!

Some ol' Ag summed it up—"When I am finally alone, in the shadow
of my days, I will hear a mustering of Aggies and the echo of my name."

I will treasure this moment that you have given me all my days.

Thank you! God bless you! God bless Texas A&M! Gig 'em Aggies!

# Jack G. Fritts '53

*1993—G. Rollie White Coliseum*

Jack G. Fritts '53. Photo from editor's collection.

Jack Garner Fritts was born February 1, 1932, in Austin and earned a bachelor's degree in animal husbandry at Texas A&M. He was president of the Association of Former Students in 1982 and a key figure in initiating plans for construction of the Clayton W. Williams Jr. Alumni Center. He also served as chairman of the building committee that had gifts and pledges in hand to pay for the $7 million structure on the day it opened in 1987. He was instrumental in establishment of the Richard "Buck" Weirus Spirit Award program, which honors some fifty students annually for their contributions to student life at Texas A&M. He also served on the executive committee of Texas A&M's Target 2000 Project and participated in the founding of the Texas Aggie Credit Union. He was owner of Sentry Realty Service and worked with Workers Compensation Group Administrators, Inc.

Jack Fritts originated the candlelight ceremony that is now an integral part of Aggie Muster. He first came up with the idea when he lived in Lubbock and then made the ceremony a part of the Capital City A&M Club program when he moved to Austin. In 1983 he spoke at the first and last Aggie Musters held on April 21 by crossing the International Date Line. Fritts was named a Distinguished Alumnus of Texas A&M in 1987. He died May 31, 1997.

# That Certain Feeling*

I wish to thank each member of the Muster Committee and especially the speaker selection subcommittee for the invitation to be the speaker for tonight's Muster. My mother asked me to thank the committee, and she is sorry she couldn't make the trip tonight. She and my younger sister, Mary, are watching this tonight via satellite in Buda, Texas. My brother, Bob, who lives in Houston, wanted me to tell you that he attended t.u., and that while there he learned enough to send his daughter to Texas A&M.

I have received a lifetime of joy in being involved with Texas A&M and have received my share of honors for that service. None of those honors mean more to me than being asked by a committee of student Aggies to be your speaker tonight.

I know and have known a lot of Aggies—and let me tell you something, Old Army—the students serving on this campus Muster Committee are among the finest Aggies I have ever met. One of the committee members is from Croatia! Now, how in the world can she explain the Aggie Spirit to her fellow Croatians, when we can't even explain it to our fellow Texans?

I told Meredith Minnick that if it seems that I get choked up during my talk, to just ignore it. I'm not really emotional, just still going through puberty.

There are forty students serving on the Muster Committee, and they range from fish to fifth-year seniors. Working with this committee is not an event, it's a lifetime experience! One of the ways they try to make the speaker feel at ease is to write letters of encouragement to him prior to Muster. I wish I could read each of those letters to you, but time will not permit. But I will share excerpts from some of them without revealing the writer's name. The letters were personal and I did not get their permission to read any part of their letters.† Here is what some of them had to say about Muster:

---

*Speech title derived by editor from speech contents
†Permission from each writer has now been obtained to use the quotes along with the editors' names.

I'm a first generation Aggie and I'm not exactly quite sure what to expect on April 21st." (Kimberly Greebon '96)

My boyfriend encouraged me to become a part of this exceptional group and, needless to say, it's been one of the biggest highlights during my undergraduate years. I have learned so much about the pride and commitment Aggies have for one another. I am very thankful to be a part of this incredible university. (Happy B. "Berry" Von Dohlen '92)

My first experience with Muster was in 1990 when I was a freshman and we honored my father. I was so moved by that experience that I wanted to help other families ease their pain by letting them know that a whole body of Aggies cared very much about them. (Monica Lehmann '93)

I attended my first Muster ceremony in 1990 during my freshman year. It was an experience that I will always remember. It finally made me truly understand what it really means to be an Aggie. I finally understood the depth of the Spirit of Aggieland. (Erin Joyce '93)

When I received the phone call that I had been selected to the Muster Committee, I was filled with one of those 'unexplainable Aggie feelings.' I feel that this is the biggest honor that I have ever received. To honor those who have passed before us is a spiritual way of saying, 'until I see you again!' We all lose people who we feel are extensions of ourselves and I am ready to do whatever it takes to comfort those who are at a loss by helping to heal them through Aggie Muster! (Thomas C. Marcotte '93)

There is something special about this place, something that knocks on every heart, opens it, and fills it with love, pride and spirit, not found anywhere else. (Jasenka Borzan '95)

My grandfather, Class of 1946, will be honored at this year's campus Muster. My whole family will be here for the occasion. I'm really hoping Muster comforts my grandmother—this will be her first Aggie Muster. (Jenifer Hall '94)

Last year I had the honorable task of lighting the first candle for the roll call. Lighting that first candle was one of the most fulfilling experiences of my life. I was never so proud of myself, never so proud of my university, and never so proud of being an Aggie as I was at that time. (Amy B. Wilcox '93)

I had never attended a Muster until the one my freshman year, and it really touched me. It made a permanent mark on me of how strong the bond is between all Aggies, regardless if it is your best friend or someone you never knew. The bond between myself and Muster was made even tighter my junior year, when I had the privilege of firing in the Ross Volunteer volley during the ceremony. I will never forget standing at present arms with my rifle during the playing of Silver Taps while the woman right in front of me cried and cried at the loss of a loved one. (Joel R. Cantwell '92)

Let me tell you this, Old Army, don't you worry about these Aggies, for you can be assured that they will honor and protect the traditions of Texas A&M with as much fervor as any of us!

The committee gave me the opportunity to read a collection of speeches which have been made at campus Musters dating back to 1946 when General Dwight Eisenhower was the speaker. Maybe they wanted to give me inspiration or humble me and, if so, they succeeded on both counts. I am now included, rightly or wrongly, on a list with some of the greatest Aggies who ever existed. I thank the committee!

What is a muster? According to Webster's, it is "a gathering together." Some synonyms are assemble, congregate, gather, group, marshal, rally. The history of Muster has been discussed tonight, so I won't repeat what's already been said. I'll just tell you that Texas Aggies chose April 21st as their day to muster, restore old friendships, honor their fallen comrades, renew the spirit that can ne'er be told, and celebrate the day Texas won its independence. Our friends at that university to the west celebrate Texas independence on March 2nd, which is the day Texans declared their independence. We Aggies celebrate the day Texans won their independence. Therein lies another basic difference between two great universities, one of which still knows how to play the game of football!

And speaking of football, for the first time in our history, we played twelve regular season games and went 12 and 0! Our everlasting thanks to Coach R. C. Slocum, his staff and those student athletes who helped us walk a little taller, a little straighter and with a little more pride.

The Aggie Muster is also a day to renew friendships, remember the days we shared at this university, or as A. W. "Head" Davis, Class of 1945, who served as a great president of the Association of Former Students, would say, "reflect on those times we spent on the post." This time-honored tradition we call Muster is carried on admirably by the students at Texas A&M. Why? Maybe it is because they care—they care about their friends and this family called a university. We do not know when the roll will be called for each of us, but I can assure you that it will be, and when it is, let our comrade or a member of our family answer the call.

Whenever we talk about caring for others or service to others, we must include the members of the Class of '43 in our discussion. According to Jack McMahan, a member of that class, they won the big war all by themselves. They did so with a loss of ten percent of the members of their class. They have seven members who attained flag rank in the military, four who have received Distinguished Alumnus awards from Texas A&M, and one, Ford Albritton, of the Albritton Tower fame, is one of very few men who has ever served our university as president of the Association of Former Students, a member of the executive committee of the Twelfth Man Foundation, and as a member of the Texas A&M Board of Regents.

The Class of '43 is celebrating its 50th reunion this week and they will soon be inducted into the Sul Ross Group, which includes former students who graduated at least 50 years ago from this great university.

Earlier, cadet Greg Riels talked about the Medal of Honor winners of the Class of '43. Let me tell you about the first Aggie killed in Vietnam, Captain Byron Stone, Class of 1960, who while at A&M was in my old outfit, "A-1" or, as we called it, "A-Infantry." Byron went through jump school and Ranger school and was serving his country with distinction when he was sent to Vietnam. The Distinguished Service Cross that Byron's parents received was accompanied by a citation that read, "Undaunted by extremely heavy enemy gunfire, Captain Stone completely disregarded his own safety and bravely exposed himself to the full force of violent enemy attack to cover the withdrawal of friendly troops. He demonstrated fortitude and perseverance by holding his position for one hour and forty minutes while annihilating a great number of enemy troops. Despite the overwhelming onslaught, he covered the withdrawal of the friendly forces with outstanding effectiveness and continued his courageous efforts until mortally wounded."

Some of the words used to describe Byron Stone and those Medal of Honor winners, who served so well and gave their all, were—responsibility, perseverance, fortitude, heroic, gallant, tradition, courageous, fighting spirit, valor—the kind of words we can use to describe the Spirit that can ne'er be told, words which we can apply to the men and women of Texas A&M.

What could those men have been able to accomplish in their lives had there been an alternative to that type of combat and they had survived the war? Suppose they had served in the time of Desert Storm, when our vastly superior technology saved thousands of lives. When President George H. W. Bush (wouldn't he have made a great head yell leader?), who fought alongside many Aggies in World War II, made one of the toughest decisions he faced as President of these United States and sent our troops into battle, the whole nation stood solidly behind him. I know that history will be very kind to Barbara and George Bush, for he was truly one of our greatest presidents. The fact that many Aggies played pivotal roles in Desert Storm speaks well for the alumni of this family called a university, and we mourn those that were lost.

It is a shame that the price we have to pay for liberty and freedom is often someone else's life.

My favorite verse from the Bible, which also happens to be the inscription on the dedication plaque gracing the Memorial Student Center, is from the Book of John, Chapter 15, Verse 13: "Greater love hath no man than this, that he lay down his life for his friends." Captain Byron Stone and those ninety-one Aggies in the Class of '43 who gave their lives for their friends know that particular verse.

I hesitate to mention those in the Class of '43, who I consider friends and who have had an impact on my life, but I am going to and, if those I leave out will forgive me, I must mention Dick Hidell, Jack McMahan,

Phil Bible, Brian Snider, and Willie Zapalac—all from Austin; Bum Bright, General Mike Cokinos, Frank Litterst, Caddo Wright, Cam Fannin and Judge Raymond Fuller. (That's his name, he's not really a judge.) All great men, tried and true! Each endowed with an ample supply of the Spirit that can ne'er be told!

No other university produces graduates who have the opportunity to become friends with so many of their fellow graduates over so many different class years as we Aggies do.

At a recent meeting of the Capital City A&M Club, we had Aggies in classes from 1930 to 1992, men and women. Sixty-two years of graduates, and all with that one common bond—they were fighting Texas Aggies!

Let me tell you about some of my experiences as a fish. After World War II, many Aggies came back to Texas A&M to finish their education which had been disrupted by that global conflict. So many in fact, that the university was overflowing. No major construction had been done the previous four years so the facilities were stretched to the breaking point. Does that sound familiar, Dr. Mobley? In 1946, the administration decided to send the freshmen classes for the next four years to the old Bryan Army Air Base or, as the elaborate brochures described it—the Texas A&M College Annex. A "unique learning experience," is what they said, where there were plenty of dormitories, classrooms and drill fields! Each Aggie in the Classes of '50, '51, '52, and '53 spent two semesters living with 19 other men in army barracks, sleeping in bunk beds and, with your "old lady" or bunkmate, sharing a small table for a desk. We had to go to another barracks to take a shower, shave, or use the toilet facilities. We drilled on the airstrip and dined in a real old-army mess hall. Our favorite recreation was avoiding contact with wetheads [sophomores] and having water fights among ourselves.

The headquarters barracks was next to mine, and the bugle stand was at the headquarters. That bugler was drowned out nearly every morning at 6:00 a.m. by those who would have preferred to sleep in. And talking about wetheads, my side of the first few conversations I had with them went something like this.

"My first name is what?" "What is a 'whip out?'" "I'm supposed to hit a what?" "I'm supposed to call you Mister?" "What do you mean, I can't say I don't know?" "What in the world is a bull ring?" "You mean I have to stand up for the whole game?"

When we wanted to go somewhere for a weekend, we got out on Highway 21 and hitchhiked! Very few fish had cars, and buses were too expensive. Some of you may remember the Aggie Lines we had for hitchhiking from one city to another. When we were ready to go somewhere, we went to a specific location in that town. We took our place in line and waited to work our way up to the front and hitchhike. We dared not go "upstream" [to cut in front of the line], but we were welcome to go "downstream" if we wished. Many times, I spent hours hung up in Caldwell or Hempstead or Navasota or Hearne, trying to get to Austin, Houston, Dallas, Fort Worth, or Waco. Unable to catch a ride.

Despite all that adversity, those four classes have consistently been among the leaders in contributions of time and money to the Association of Former Students and to this university.

I've got to take this opportunity to tell you about the best tea-sipper [Aggie slang for a University of Texas student] who ever lived. Yes, there are some good ones. The best of them all is my brother-in-law, Calvin Collier of Pearland. My outfit's favorite place to go on weekends was Houston. Calvin and my sister, Doris, housed more Aggies during my four years at this university than the Aggieland Inn! One Friday night before the Corps Trip to Houston, nine of us slept in the living room of their one-bedroom, one-bath apartment. Besides that, they even let us use their only car.

Out of about 2,000 of us who started in 1949, only 849 finished their commitment. For those who persevere, adversity becomes victory. Live that life again—never! Savor those fond memories—forever!

Bonds of friendship are developed through our relationship among and with people who have common interests and that friendship is nurtured through effort and practice. As Head Davis ['45] said in his [1986] speech at a campus Muster, the friendship developed at Texas A&M becomes an "attachment to the group," an attachment with the "Spirit that can ne'er be told." That attachment is profound, because we never stop making new friends! One of the best ways to acquire and develop Aggie friendship is through active involvement with the Association of Former Students—undeniably the best alumni organization in the world, with World Class leadership among the staff of that association. What a special place they have created at the Clayton W. Williams Jr. Alumni Center, staffed with special people who care about Texas A&M.

Some friends may pass and others may fade, but the friendships we develop because of our common bond leaves us with more friends than we started with! Take some time and make an effort to honor your friends as you would like them to honor you!

There are a lot of people in the world with many good traits—those who care about honesty, integrity, have faith in their God, care about family, about their state and nation. But only here at Texas A&M, do we put it all together in one common bond—that Aggie Spirit—the Spirit that can ne'er be told.

It's that certain feeling you get when the Fightin' Texas Aggie Band plays the National Anthem or "The Spirit of Aggieland."

It's that certain feeling you get when the band steps off on "Hulla-baloo."

It's that certain feeling you get when the Singing Cadets sing "The Twelfth Man."

It's that certain feeling you get when you hear Reveille barking at a basketball game.

It's that certain feeling you get when you see Parsons Mounted Cavalry following the Band.

It's that certain feeling you get as a student and they call your name as a winner of the Buck Weirus Spirit Award.

It's that certain feeling you get when you attend Silver Taps on campus and witness members of the student body honoring one of their own.

It's that certain feeling you get the first time you go home wearing your senior boots or when you march up Congress Avenue on Thanksgiving morning.

It's that certain feeling you get when the ring clerk hands you your Aggie Ring.

It's that certain feeling you get when the Bonfire, on which you worked so hard for so many hours through rain, mud and cold, is blazing as a symbol of your undying love for this family called a university.

It's that certain feeling you get when you march at Final Review and you turn this university over to the juniors.

It's that certain feeling you get when you finally walk across the stage of Jolly Rollie and get that piece of paper, called a diploma, which tells the world that you finished what you started!

It's that certain feeling you get when you've worked long, hard hours on the Muster Committee, and the night finally arrives and in spite of all your worries, everything comes off picture perfect.

It's that certain feeling you get when they say "softly call the Muster" and you have a final opportunity to honor those friends and family members you loved so much!

It's no wonder that others do not understand why we love this family called a university so much! As Garth Brooks said in one of his songs, "Our lives are better left to chance—I could have missed the fame, but I'd [have] had to miss the dance." You have to live the life of an Aggie, or live with one, as my wife, Gaye, and my two daughters have, to acquire that certain feeling—the Spirit that can ne'er be told!

We are gathered here tonight to honor over one hundred Aggies, young and old, men and women, by answering the roll and lighting a candle in remembrance of them. Let's weep for them once more tonight and then spend the rest of our time on this good earth celebrating their lives!

May the good Lord bless and keep you and may he grant us this simple prayer—may the Spirit of Aggieland live forever!

# Andrés Tijerina '67

*1994—G. Rollie White Coliseum*

Andrés Tijerina '67.
Photo from editor's
collection.

Andrés Anthony Tijerina was born December 12, 1944. A native of Ozona, Texas, he was an assistant professor of US and Texas history at Texas A&M University–Kingsville at the time of his Muster address. He previously served as program manager for the Texas Department of Commerce and was publisher and owner of the *Austin Light*; group communications manager for Motorola, Inc.; and executive director of the Texas Good Neighbor Commission. He flew 150 combat missions with the US Air Force in Vietnam, earning the Air Medal and the Distinguished Flying Cross.

Tijerina holds a bachelor's degree from Texas A&M University, a master's degree from Texas Tech, and a PhD from the University of Texas. Following teaching stints at Texas Tech, UT Austin, UT San Antonio, and Texas A&M–Kingsville, Tijerina joined the faculty of Austin Community College as a professor of history.

He authored *A History of Mexican Americans of Lubbock* and edited *Human Services for Mexican American Children*. His Vietnam War memoirs were published in the final volume of the Time-Life Book series *The Vietnam Experience*. His memoirs are also included in the volume entitled *A War Remembered*. His books *Tejanos and Texas under the Mexican Flag* and *Tejano Empire: Life on the South Texas Ranchos* were published by Texas A&M University Press. He edited Andrés Saenz's *Early Tejano Ranching in Duval County* and coedited Elena Zamora O'Shea's novel *El Mesquite*. His works have been recognized with the Presidio La Bahía Award, the Kate Broocks Bates Award, and the T. R. Fehrenbach Award.

Tijerina is a Fellow of the Texas State Historical Association. His writings have appeared as chapters, articles, and book reviews in journals ranging from the *Southwestern Historical Quarterly* to the *American Historical Review.*

## Becoming a Texas Aggie*

I would be remiss if I did not acknowledge first that it is I who am honored beyond words to have the privilege to address you on this proud and solemn occasion of the Aggie Muster. It is good to be back at Aggieland, back with my fellow Aggies. And I can truthfully say that I have never seen so many Aggies in my life. To see so many young energetic faces; to see the Cadet Corps again. It has got to be the highlight of my life. But I did not come here to be honored; rather I came, as you, to pay due respect and honor to the legions of Texas Aggies who have gone before us, who have paid the price before us to make this day possible.

I would like to dedicate my remarks today especially to the Muster families, to the Class of 1944—my own Birthday Anniversary Class— and to the fallen Texas Aggies everywhere, in whose honor we meet today.

I beg your permission today and your patience in allowing me to be very personal in my remarks. For I can only share with you my own personal experiences. I have not commanded armies. I have done nothing to compare to the great Aggie names that we all revere. I did get degrees from Texas Tech and Texas University, but those only gave me a diploma. At A&M, I took a diploma, and I became a Texas Aggie.

And I'd like to talk to you today about what it meant in my life to undergo the transformation of becoming a Texas Aggie. I'd like to reflect on the unique Aggie Spirit of inclusiveness that opens its doors equally to all on the basis of merit. At the same time, I think it is necessary to remember that as loyal Ags, we also owe a debt of gratitude, of service to contribute to this great institution and its traditions. And

*Speech title derived by editor from speech contents

finally, I will address the tradition of the Aggie Muster as the culmination of this transformation process and indeed, the final step in the
Aggie Spirit of unity.

I was the youngest in a small family of four after my father left us
when I was about five years old. My mother was left with the responsibility for my sister, Sylvia; my brother, Albert; and me. She coped
for a while, holding down two jobs. But she became ill, and had to be
hospitalized for an extended period of time. Sylvia, Albert, and I lived
with different relatives. We stayed with my grandparents, or an uncle
and aunt to pick cotton in O'Donnell, then we would move to another
cotton field in Miles. Once we lived in a garage among the tractors; another time we spent the winter in an old boxcar that was parked in the
middle of a cotton field. Albert and Sylvia and I slept on a pile of straw
covered up with big comforters; no doors, no lights, no windows—just
a big sliding door. We missed a lot of school in those days.

The experience made us appreciate school, and it made us appreciate
each other, especially when my mother rejoined us. We all worked hard
to make a home together. Our little family developed strong bonds of
love and loyalty. Indeed, it wasn't until I took a sociology course in
college that I learned that we were poor.

It was us four against the world, because, even then, segregation
was still pretty blatant. We weren't allowed to go into swimming pools,
the theater, barber shops, restaurants. Each of us lost friends because
at some point in our relationships, they would tell us their parents
wouldn't permit them to have Mexican friends.

I know the low-income Anglo kids from across the tracks had problems
too, but racism was an additional burden for us as Mexican-Americans,
over and above the social and financial problems.

I went through the school system, watching my friends dropping
out, leaving only a few Hispanics in high school. I actually began to
think I was a Mexican. I mean, I knew I was born in the United States,
but even some teachers called us Mexicans. By the time I finished high
school, I felt I had graduated despite my teachers. When I came to
A&M, my brother Albert was a junior in the band. I still expected to
encounter discrimination. Instead, I quickly began to experience the
Aggie transformation.

My first day in the dorm room, I almost picked a fight with my Anglo roommate. I walked into my room to find this tall, blond Anglo; yellow hair, blue eyes, pink skin—the works! I told him that I didn't ask to be with a white man, and I knew he sure didn't ask for me. But that if he ever tried anything with me, by golly, he was going to have to fight one mean Mexican. And this guy just looked at me in amazement. I said, "You know what I'm talking about. You're white and I'm Mexican." Then he said, "I just came here to be an Aggie like you." That shocked me like a slap across the face, to think that any Anglo could see me as a Texas Aggie, something that he could look up to. That was the first time I had ever been perceived as something other than a Mexican.

For Aggies, above all else, identify themselves as Texas Aggies, and the measure of acceptance at Texas A&M is not how white you are, nor even how wealthy your parents are. The seniors used to tell us, "Don't bring us your high school rings and jackets. Earn your Aggie Ring."

My roommate for three and a half years, Jim Ross Davidson ['67] from Poteet, accepted me as a Texas Aggie without question. We learned together, Roommate and I. We became equally proficient in doing push-ups and whipping out. Oh yes, we sometimes studied books. Jim Ross saw me as an Aggie. And I always wanted to be like him, an Aggie.

I could see now why Albert loved A&M. Albert was Class of '65, a distinguished student on a math scholarship. He was a student senator on Corps Staff, President of the San Angelo West Texas Hometown Club, and Combined Band Head Drum Major of the world-famous Fightin' Texas Aggie Band. That's my outfit. Oh yes, and Albert was an RV [Ross Volunteer]. Albert was the Corps bugler, and every time I hear Silver Taps today, I can't believe it isn't Albert, still leading the Silver Taps bugle team at the top of the Academic Building.

I remember one Sunday afternoon in 1965. Albert and I were sitting in the open window of his dorm room, legs hanging out, talking about the inevitable tour of duty we were going to do in Vietnam. I said, "I can't believe that we're going to do it. There are plenty of people who aren't going to go, and I don't think that you and I should go off to a war and get killed for a society that treated us the way it has. Why should we go and fight for this country? For people who have done nothing but discriminate against us and mistreat us and try to cheat us every step of the way. They've abused us and our family. Why should we go and die for these people?"

Albert thought awhile. He was only one year older than me, but he was much smarter. He wasn't just smart. Albert was wise. He's the reason we came to A&M in the first place. So finally Albert said, "No, we're not. We're not going to fight for those people." I jumped right in: "Right."

"No," he said, "We're going to fight for those people who did let us into schools. We're going to fight for the teachers who did help us and did reward us when we did well. We're going to fight for the Aggies and the people who gave us scholarships, who let us into a major American university. And we're going to fight for those people who defended our rights and allowed us to grab at the big American pie. These are the people, and these are the institutions we're going to fight to defend.

"The commission you and I are going to get is the same commission George Washington held, and he didn't stop to ask if this is the right war. You and I are going to defend the same principles in the Constitution that he did—liberty and justice for all.

"And when we come back, Andy, you and I are going to fight side by side. You're going to be a Ph.D. and I'm going to be a lawyer, and we're going to whip all those people who are abusing other Americans. We're going to defend and strengthen this nation."

That was the last time I ever doubted what I was going to do in life. It was a mission that we had, and that's what I went to Vietnam with. It would be easy for us to say that this was not the right war. But we both went, merely to do our duty. And incidentally, I still believe that America went into that war for the right principles—liberal media notwithstanding. Mistakes were made, but everywhere I went over there, I saw Texas Aggies doing their duty and paying the price. And I will never apologize for that.

Albert and I were both Air Force pilots. He also earned the Distinguished Flying Cross and the Air Medal. But I lived to wear mine. Albert was killed in action over Northern Laos. We lost him. We lost his Aggie Ring, and a promising young American. This world hardly got to know Albert. They didn't know he was going to be a lawyer. I often thought Albert was too big for this world.

But I soon heard that the San Angelo A&M Club now had a scholarship in his name. Then I learned that Albert's name was on a plaque at the old quad where we lived on the campus. And I began to realize that A&M could not forget Albert, because he was a Texas Aggie. That's right, the Aggies knew Albert. Some of them on this very stage knew him better than I did in some ways. He was an RV, Class of 1965. And the Aggie Muster is the one place where I could go and hear his voice answer—along with the men of Corregidor—"Here. Still Fighting."

Albert was not too big for A&M. Because he is part of what we are doing today. He is just another one of the many Ags we will always remember in the A&M tradition. Because that's what the Aggie Spirit does to you. The Spirit of Aggieland embraces the student. It is an inclusive spirit that fulfills all the promise of this land of the free. I am proud to see that as large as our great university has grown, we still have the 12th Man Spirit on campus.

In the last few years, a national TV audience has marveled at what we at Aggieland knew all along—that every one of us wants to get down on the arena floor, and fight for A&M; that at Aggieland, we stand for the 12th Man for four quarters, regardless of the scoreboard; because at A&M, the 12th Man isn't just a legend. E. King Gill spoke at the campus Muster my freshman year. He wasn't a myth; he was just another Texas Aggie, paying the price.

The Spirit of Aggieland is a meritocracy. It is an inclusive culture that is open to Hispanics, African Americans, women, rich, and poor. A&M does not ask a person to deny their heritage, but to achieve new heights. Indeed, it does not ask a person to quickly shed even their old prejudices, only to judge and act by new standards—fair standards based on merit, on service, and on universal human values.

I can't say that my Aggie buddies did not come to A&M without old prejudices. But I can say that A&M was the first place I ever went to where I was always judged on my merit with no regard to my ethnicity, color, or income level. You may not believe this, but A&M was once a poor boy's college.

A&M nurtured our talents and developed our leadership skills. Of all the Texas Aggies that I knew to be of Hispanic heritage here as a student, all of them received distinguished honors at A&M. Many of them went on to achieve distinction after graduation. I wish I had time to name them and tell you about how many there were, but frankly, no one was counting. We were not Hispanics or blacks or Anglos. There's only one kind of Aggie, and that's a Texas Aggie.

And in all the time I was a student, I never once experienced an act of racial discrimination. I never once saw a Hispanic or a black demeaned or denied in any way on the basis of ethnicity. I'll admit that some Old Army Ags grumbled about women being admitted for the first time. I never saw or heard such protests about African Americans, who were first admitted during my senior year.

And I might add that even my Old Army buddies have come around in the last few years, as they have called to tell me to be sure and watch their daughter on TV, marching with the Corps or the Aggie Band. They've learned to concede that change in the form of gender inclusion is the better part of the university's growth. Diversity has been healthy. It has provided a broader base for understanding, cooperation, and acceptance—all in the Texas Aggie Spirit. If we can revere our Aggie Mothers, surely we can accept our Aggie sisters.

The women of A&M have marched in step, and amply demonstrated that the Aggie Spirit does not distinguish in gender any more than it does in race, wealth, or social status. To the women of A&M—welcome to the Aggie Spirit. And I enjoin you—embrace it in all its tradition, in all its responsibility. It will embrace you as it did your Aggie brothers.

The Aggie Spirit transforms and changes your life forever. It makes you part of that magnificent fighting spirit of San Jacinto. It binds you to Texas Aggies everywhere, Aggies of the Class of '44 and Aggies of the Class of '94. What a great honor it is to share common bonds with Aggies who served this nation in combat. To claim an undying kinship with the names that now consecrate the Review Field, the flags around Kyle Field, and the Memorial Student Center. They paid the price. And now it is our turn to pay due respect, and to pay our price full measure as Texas Aggies.

I realize now that, on that day before Albert went to Vietnam, he was no longer talking to me as his little brother. Albert was a Texas Aggie senior, and he was charging me with the same recall to service which all Texas Aggies have answered. In his words, Albert spoke for all

Aggies, and his charge was not limited to any one ethnic group. It was national in scope, and it identified the Constitutional principles. The Texas Aggie senior was passing the torch.

And so I now charge you to be mindful of the price to be paid for freedom, for the Aggie name and the Aggie pride. The Spirit of Aggieland is the sum total of the human costs that have been paid in excellence, in dedication, and in combat for that high station that A&M holds among military schools; for the leadership it continually displays in higher education; for the respect it commands in a cynical world; and for the blood that Texas Aggies have shed for international peace.

President Dean Gage, I know you guard your recruitment and enrollment figures carefully. And, of course, I would like to see more Mexican Americans on this campus. I would hope that the doors of A&M remain equally open to all Texans and those who have a burning desire to become Texas Aggies. Let them know that the Spirit of Aggieland is an inclusive culture, but make them know that we have our standards; for the Aggie record of excellence has not come cheap. I might add that I was glad to note today as I approached the campus, that Highway 6 still runs both ways.

Students are coming to A&M in unprecedented numbers to share in the Aggie pride, to obtain a valuable diploma, and to wear the A&M name. But they should not come to this university simply to inherit the legacy; for pride is not a commodity to be bought for the price of a college tuition. It must be earned.

After all, students don't come here for just a degree, just another diploma. If that's all they wanted, there are many other state-funded colleges that can give that. They want the A&M name and the Aggie pride. And we must remind them of the costs that have been paid to make A&M that great institution.

A&M was not built on hallowed ground; it was built on agricultural farmland. A&M is not a great institution because of state funding, but because of the respect for its honored traditions. It wasn't state funds that made the MSC a memorial. It's the remembrance of those Texas Aggies who gave their lives and knowingly chose to make the supreme sacrifice.

We have traditions at A&M that must be preserved. And we have institutions. The "Fighting Texas Aggie Corps of Cadets" is not just an ROTC unit. No other Texas university could have sent an entire senior class after Pearl Harbor to be commissioned en masse into the officer corps. The Corps, Mr. President. The Corps, ladies and gentlemen. The Corps must be preserved at Texas A&M. I don't know the statistics, but I'll bet that the majority of Texas Aggies have not gone through the Corps. In our hearts, however, the Texas Aggie Corps of Cadets will always be the "Keepers of the Spirit."

For those who like the A&M name, let them respect it. Let them respect the Memorial Student Center. Let A&M keep its doors open to the poor boys and girls of the state, but teach all students the price for the Spirit of Aggieland. At A&M, we respect tradition—in our memorials, as in the Aggie Muster. Enduring respect for the A&M tradition is the Spirit of Aggieland.

I am amazed to see how much of the old small-college atmosphere the campus has retained, despite the tremendous growth. It proves that A&M can take its traditions intact into the next century. I hope so. But as I began coordinating with the members of the Aggie Muster Committee, I did ask them about one tradition that was my most cherished memory of A&M. I asked them, "Does Silver Taps still capture the Spirit in its farewell to a fallen Aggie?" Because—of all my memories—that was the one most sacred.

As I remember, all the lights go dim across the entire campus at retreat, around 10 PM on the night of a Silver Taps. I don't know why, but it seems there was always a cloud ceiling over our heads at Silver Taps.

From all corners of the campus, the students walk silently from their dorms to the square in front of the Academic Building. They don't say a word as they walk over the grass, between the buildings, and onto the square around the statue of Old Sully. For a few moments, they crowd around, waiting, meditating.

Then, the Ross Volunteer rifle squad marches down one of the broad sidewalks to the center of the square. The metal taps click in perfect unison in the slow, deliberate funeral cadence. Click. Click. Click. Click.

They halt. Take position. At a hushed command, they cock the bolt action rifles for the first volley. You know it's going to be loud, but your nervous system is never quite ready for that crack of thunder. Boom. And about the time you catch your breath again—Boom. And boom.

Three rifle volleys shake the air, and all of a sudden the Academic Square seems like an enclosed room, echoing the thunder, back and forth within the walls, and bouncing back off the overcast sky. The echo shocks the trees, rustling the dry leaves down onto the square. Rifle smoke rises to meet the overcast sky. And a large flock of pigeons and doves always flushes from around the eaves of the Academic Building, and starts up to the sky. They fly overhead, circling for their bearing; then like the wisp of a cloud, they melt silently into the heavens. As the doves disappear, the bugles sing the first notes of Silver Taps to say goodbye to the departing soul of a dear friend.

The Aggie Muster holds within it all of the solemn grace of Silver Taps. But more. Because in the Aggie Muster, there is an answer to the roll call. In this way, the Aggie Muster is the final step in the Aggie Spirit of unity.

We accepted them within our ranks as Texas Aggies when first they came. Their only admission requirement was that they have a burning desire to be a Texas Aggie. They chose to stand with us, united as Texas Aggies. They shed their youthful objects, and took up higher goals, broader ambitions, and nobler principles. They knew the price of defending those principles. They learned, as Texas Aggies, to respect those who had already paid the price. And they accepted the commission to answer the recall, to fight for and to respect, in the A&M tradition, the Spirit of Aggieland. And now that they have passed on from our world, we will remember them. We will call out their names on April 21 at the Aggie Muster. And the Aggie Spirit will speak for them.

# Lee J. Phillips '53

## 1995—G. Rollie White Coliseum

Lee James Phillips was born September 21, 1931, in San Antonio. He retired in 1994 after service as a senior lecturer and undergraduate advisor in Texas A&M's Department of Industrial Engineering. He was a US Army aviator for five years after graduating from Texas A&M with a bachelor's degree in electrical engineering. Following employment as a field engineer and commercial manager for Texas Electric Service Company, he joined the faculty at Texas Tech University, where he also served as assistant dean of engineering.

Lee J. Phillips '53. Photo from editor's collection.

he held various administrative positions at Texas A&M from 1976 to 1988 before joining the industrial engineering faculty. He served as faculty advisor to Corps of Cadets Company F-2.

When A&M mascot Reveille IV was retired in 1984, she went to live with Lee and his wife, Joanne. In 1994 an A&M fish camp was named in his honor.

## The Ties That Bind*

For an Aggie, it doesn't get any more meaningful than this: the Fightin' Texas Aggie Band, the Singing Cadets, the Ross Volunteers, Reveille. The reunion Class of '45 and the relatives and friends of those Aggies we honor tonight. It's great to be with Aggies here and all over the world, and I am honored to be a part of this Campus Muster.

My Aggie heritage began with my uncle, Calvin Daniel Thompson. His love of and pride in this school so impressed me that when I entered public school I had no doubt that I would go to the Agricultural

*Speech title derived by editor from speech contents

and Mechanical College of Texas and be an electrical engineer. I'm therefore extremely proud of the fact that my daughter, Lee Anne '78, and my son, John Calvin '79, chose to continue the line. My prayer, of course, is that my grandson, Jaime Brandon, will be a member of the Class of 2008—or thereabouts.

There is one member of my family that does not have a class year after her name. In our days, women didn't enroll in A&M. That is not to say they didn't come to A&M. Joanne probably logged as many miles between San Antonio and Aggieland as I did. We had just moved to Bryan in the middle '70s when we had Reveille and the mascot corporal over for a visit. As they were leaving, Joanne said, "Don't ever question my maroon blood. I never said a word when Rev jumped on my new sofa." So I like to refer to her as an "Aggie in a class by herself."

It will be 20 years next September that the phone rang at our home in Lubbock, Texas. It was Colonel Tom Parsons who said there was a new mascot at A&M and that the Lubbock game would be her first away from home. She needed a place to stay. That phone call started a wonderful relationship with the Reveilles and the members of Company E-2 that exists today, and Joanne and I are proud to be considered a part of their campus family.

When we learned that Rev IV would be retiring and staying with us, it suddenly dawned on us that the kids had been gone for several years and we were getting pretty comfortable—there being only two of us around the house. We realized that her arrival would mean there would have to be some rules and restrictions. I'm proud to report that Rev had not been with us for more than two weeks before Joanne and I had learned the rules and what the restrictions were!

The Class of '45 knew "the" [original] Reveille. In fact, they were instrumental in having her certified as a general in the K-9 Corps. In an effort to raise money for the war effort, the War Department set up a program so that if you wanted your pet to be a private in the K-9 Corps it would cost a few bucks, a sergeant would cost a few bucks more, and a captain would cost some real money in those times. So, of course, the Aggies had to see to it that Reveille was a general.

Some of the Class of '45 was still around in January 1944, when Reveille died, and they started the tradition of burying our Reveilles at the north end of Kyle Field where she could always see the scoreboard. I can't tell you how many visitors, prospective students, and friends I have taken to the Reveille graves, had them read the plaque, then turn, look through the portal, and see the scoreboard. One person said, "You people have so many traditions that mean so much to you. No wonder you are so proud!"

Around the end of 1943, most of the Class of '45 had left for war, and they returned with interesting experiences. As a class prepares to return for its 50th reunion, the Association [of Former Students] sends an information sheet for them to fill out. For the Class of '45, there were two items on that sheet that were of particular interest to me—military service and honors and awards received.

I found that they participated in operations from the Battle of the Bulge to the Battle of Leyte Gulf. Their jobs ranged from "jeep jockey" to general. One member of the class was the first American to meet up with the Russians at the Elbe River in Germany. One noted he had spent 48 months in combat, and under honors and awards he said, "I survived." One respondent characterizes this entire class. He was a member of the 8th Air Force flying B-17s out of England. He said, "Bad day over Berlin. Missing in Action. After jump, walked through Poland and Russia [to get to American lines]." For honors and awards, he said, "Being a Texas Aggie." This is the character of the Class of '45.

Of course, the class had character and had its characters. One member of the class listed all of his accomplishments in the military, all of his battle experience, and under honors and awards he entered: "I spent more time on the bull ring in a wool uniform than anyone else in my class!"

And speaking of characters, a Muster wouldn't be complete if we didn't mention P. L. "Pinky" Downs. He was an Aggie's Aggie! He was a member of the Class of '06 and told folks he majored in "conversation." But he always wanted the best for his Aggies. He spent 10 years on the Board of Directors for A&M, and it was during his tenure that it was decided to build an indoor swimming pool. Pinky found out that another school had just built an indoor pool, so he drove over to the other campus and found that the dimensions of their pool was 60 feet wide and 90 feet long. When he got back to A&M, he was horrified to find the proposed dimensions of our pool were the same—60 feet by 90 feet. At the next directors meeting, even though the plans were ready to go out to bid, Pinky insisted the pool be lengthened by 10 feet. The directors were pretty unhappy with Pinky's proposal, and one said, "Why in the world do you need that extra 10 feet?" Pinky was a little reluctant to tell them the real reason, so he said, "Well, the boys are gonna want to play water polo and they gotta have room for the horses." I went over to the pool, which is named for Pinky—the P. L. Downs Natatorium—and asked Martha Nix, the pool manager for the past 13 years, if she had heard that story. She said, "I don't know about the story, but I do know our pool is 60 feet wide by 100 feet long! And I'll tell you something else. Every pool used in competition has eight swimming lanes. Now you go up to the balcony and count the number of tiled lanes in this pool." [There are nine.] So Pinky got the biggest and the best.

In thinking about the Class of '45 returning to the campus, I tried to think of what the Class of '45 had in common with the Class of '95. One thing that comes to mind is that they didn't graduate in four years either. On the other hand, I would probably say the thing we all have in common are our traditions—those beliefs and customs Aggies have handed down from generation to generation—time-tested, value-proven conventions that underlie that certain spirit.

You see,

> We have all stood as the 12th Man.
>
> We have all worked on Bonfire (although I only remember working on one per year). [The Bonfire stacks collapsed in 1957 and 1994, but each was rebuilt in a few days and lit on time.]
>
> We have all experienced Silver Taps. You have stood where I have stood and where the Class of '45 has stood and where Aggies have stood since 1898 in solemn, silent tribute to a fallen comrade. Therefore, we know your feelings on those occasions and we can identify as Aggies.
>
> And now we Muster as Aggies have done since 1883.

These traditions are the ties that bind—they provide a means of communication—a common language. For example, in a proper setting such as Kyle Field, if I held my hands over my head to form an "A," every Aggie knows we are going to do the "Aggies" yell, and they "pass it back" and then "hump it." Did you ever stop to think what that language sounds like to someone that's not an Aggie?

And if I made a fist and stuck my thumb in the air, everyone knows we're going to do "Gig 'em"—well, almost everyone. Gotta tell you a story. Back in the late '70s, the nation decided we were about to run out of fossil fuel. It looked like we were going to freeze to death if we didn't start conserving energy. So everyone got geared up to teach energy conservation—A&M included. The problem was, that while we certainly had the expertise on campus, we didn't have enough qualified people to go out to our businesses and industries and show them the techniques. Well, we got lucky. We found a young man who had just moved into the Arlington area who had done research in solar energy and wind energy and could do all the calculations needed to figure how to reduce energy consumption. The only problem I could see was that he was not from A&M. But we were desperate and he was good. So we set him up in an office in Arlington, got him some meters and some forms and, since we wanted him to work the Dallas/Fort Worth area, we got him one of those beautiful flat white University cars with the black lettering "TEXAS A&M UNIVERSITY" on the side. He was mighty proud of that car! One day he called to say he had had an interesting experience and thought he had better check it out with me. He said he was in downtown Fort Worth, stopped at a pedestrian crossing when a man jumped in front of his car and just stuck his thumb "right in my face." "Well," he said, "I didn't know what he meant, but I figured if it was good enough for me, it was good enough for him, so I just shoved my thumb right up against the windshield too. He just smiled and walked away." James said, "Do you think I did okay?" "James," I said, "you did great and you sure could have done a lot worse."

Well, we can communicate and if we can communicate, we can solve problems. And we will always have problems. Just ask Student Body President Brooke Leslie how her 12 months went trying to get 42,000 Aggies going in one general direction. Or ask Association of Former Students President Jim Creel how his job is going trying to get 180,000 former students together. For that matter, there's our University President—he's got Aggies, former students, plus 5,000 faculty and staff and 6,400 Aggie Moms to keep on a track. His cup runneth over. It reminds me of the story told about Haydon Boatner.

Colonel Boatner was Commandant of the Corps of Cadets when I was in school. He was recalled to active duty during the Korean conflict, made a general and sent to Korea. When he reported in, General Mark Clark had a difficult situation on his hands. It seems the United Nations forces had been placing the Communist prisoners on an island by the name of Koje—it was known as Koje prison island. They put so many prisoners on the island that one day we woke up to find that the prisoners were now the guards and the guards were prisoners. Naturally, this was not only embarrassing but dangerous, and General Clark wanted it straightened out right away. So after explaining the situation to General Boatner, he asked if Boatner could handle it. Boatner replied, "If they don't have a former students association or a mothers club, I don't see the problem." He probably spoke from the heart, but I think we should all try to work together with our president and our leaders to keep this the great place that we love.

And none of this is to try to imply that the traditions that tie us together make us all the same. Our generations are different. Probably you are saying thank goodness. So am I. So are the members of the Class of '45. It seems we're all pretty happy with our generation. But we are different. Just look at our taste in music:

The Class of '45 was singing "The Boogie Woogie Bugle Boy of Company B."

My class was more sophisticated. We were singing "Mairzy Doats and Dozy Doats."

And then there's the Class of '95—you are either singing "You Never Even Called Me By My Name" or "Hold My Hand" by Hootie and the Blowfish.

But guess what, Aggies! There is one song on which we can all agree, and it is "The Spirit of Aggieland," played by the Fightin' Texas Aggie Band. When we sing it tonight, let's remember those who have sung it for the last time in Aggieland, for if they were to stand in judgement of your stewardship of our traditions, they would surely say, "Well done, God Bless, and Gig 'Em Aggies."

# E. Dean Gage '65

*1996—G. Rollie White Coliseum*

E. Dean Gage '65. Photo from editor's collection.

Errol Dean Gage was born October 24, 1942, in San Saba, Texas, and received his bachelor's degree in veterinary science from Texas A&M. He served as A&M's interim president in 1993–94 and had been senior vice president and provost for three years. He joined the A&M faculty in 1969 after teaching small animal medicine and surgery at Auburn University and the University of Tennessee. He headed A&M's Department of Urban Practice and Small Animal Clinic before moving into full-time administrative service. He is a Diplomate of the American College of Veterinary Surgeons and was named a Distinguished Alumnus of A&M's College of Veterinary Medicine in 1991. He served as director of the Center for Executive Development in A&M's College of Business Administration and was an adjunct professor in the Department of Management. Gage has published over 70 scientific papers, contributed to five textbooks, and given more than 150 papers and presentations to professional, scientific, and educational associations. He provided valuable advice and guidance to the Campus Muster Committee and continued counseling students at every opportunity.

## "The Meaning of M-U-S-T-E-R"

I have a Muster message for you this evening which I pray you will remember and will have an impact on your life. I hope that we communicate much better than the California patrolman did with the driver of a convertible on the San Diego freeway. The patrolman saw this guy driving down the freeway during the morning rush hour with the top down and a dozen penguins in the back seat. Knowing that a traffic hazard was being created, the patrolman pulled the guy over and instructed him to get off the freeway and take the penguins to the San Diego Zoo. The next morning, the officer saw the guy on the freeway again and with all twelve of the penguins in the back seat, but this time wearing sunglasses. Again, the officer pulled the guy over and asked him, "Didn't I tell you yesterday to take those penguins to the zoo?" The man answered, "That's right, officer, and they had such a great time at the zoo that today I'm taking them to the beach." I am confident that you and I will communicate much better this evening.

On April 30, 1939, the great Hall of Fame baseball player, Lou Gehrig, told the assembled crowd in Yankee Stadium in New York that he was the luckiest man on the face of the earth. On April 21, 1996, I stand before you, this assembled crowd, with the humble feelings that I am the most blessed man on the face of the earth. I have been blessed in life with a wonderful wife, Kathy. We are blessed with two wonderful Aggie daughters and two Aggie sons-in-law. My being an Aggie and having served in many leadership roles on this campus are irreplaceable experiences and memories. However, the honor to be Campus Muster speaker is one of the most meaningful blessings ever.

To all the wonderful students on the Muster Committee, I will forever be grateful for this honor and for your many cards and letters of encouragement. You have my personal respect and admiration for all the hard work you have done for Campus Muster 1996. May our friendship never end, as you have given more to me than I could ever give to you. I have watched you live the Spirit of Aggieland and the meaning of Muster.

I am not here to reminisce about the past or how it was in the good old days of Ol' Army when I was a student. It is not that I don't recall those days. I do remember them well, and they will forever be imprinted on my mind and in my heart. Why, I still remember the central laundry on campus where students sent all their dirty clothes to be washed. We each had a laundry number stamped on all of our clothes. Mine was GX2095.

My goal this evening is for you to remember Muster 1996. I want to share from my heart what I believe to be the true meaning of Muster. Thomas Jefferson said, "I like the dream of the future, more than the history of the past." For us to dream of the future, we must remember and learn from the contributions of those of the past. If not, we may not have a future. We are here to answer the roll call for those who cannot be here themselves, because they have already answered God's call on their lives. We celebrate life during Muster because of the lives that others have lived before us. These are lives lived for us so that we may fulfill our vision and dreams of a life of freedom and liberty. May our vision and dream of the future be dedicated to those whom we honor at Muster and to our Heavenly Father who has given each one of us a life to live.

Fifty years ago today, April 21, 1946, some 130 Texas Aggies returned to the small Philippine Island of Corregidor for Muster, just seven months after the surrender of Japan and the end of World War II. To that assembled group of brave Aggies, General Douglas MacArthur sent this historic Muster statement: "In this hallowed soil lie the mortal remains of many men who here died that liberty might live. Among the bravest of these brave men are the sons of Texas A&M, unable themselves to answer this year's annual Muster. It is for us, therefore, to do so for them. . . . to answer in a clear and firm voice." My friends and fellow Aggies, this is our reason for being here today. It is for us to answer in a clear and firm voice for those unable to answer this year's annual Muster. To you members of the Class of '46 and to the veterans of the 1946 Corregidor Muster, we pay special tribute this evening. You are our heroes and our defenders of freedom and liberty. Without you and those who served with you, the history of the dreams we now enjoy could never have been lived.

Fifty years ago today, April 21, 1946, there was another historic Muster just a few hundred yards from where you are now seated. It was on Kyle Field. It was the Victory Homecoming Muster where General of the Army Dwight D. Eisenhower was the keynote speaker to a crowd of over fifteen thousand people. Aggieland was much different in those days. College Station didn't have the Hilton Hotel or many places to stay. Guests could stay in the dorm for twenty-five cents a night. Some twenty-nine Aggie generals who had commanded during World War II were awarded honorary doctor of laws degrees. Over nine hundred Aggies gave their lives to God and country in World War II, and a special Roll Call and Silver Taps were observed in their honor. It was only fitting that this special Homecoming Muster was held on an Easter morning. There could be no greater Sunday to remember the sacrifice of life given so that others could live. We often take our freedoms for granted, but they did not come cheaply nor without sacrifice. They came at a high price. We must never forget the ultimate sacrifices given so that we may live as a free people today. Perhaps, it can best be said, as it is inscribed on the wall in the Memorial Student Center and taken from John 15:13, "Greater love has no one than this, that he lay down his life for his friends."

This evening, I want to ask you a very personal question, "What does Aggie Muster mean to you?" Muster is not a time to mourn death, but a time to celebrate life itself. Muster is the most solemn and sacred of all Aggie traditions, but it is a time of joy and happy remembrance. Those who have gone before us are those whose lives have touched ours. May we do the same for those who come after us. May we expect no less of ourselves.

Muster cannot be explained. Muster must be experienced. The word, "Muster," is a military term meaning to assemble for inspection, to gather, to discharge from service or to conduct a roll call. For us, it means to softly call the Muster and to answer for those who are absent for the first time since the last roll call. But, this evening, I want to look at the deep and profound meaning of the word, "Muster." May we never be the same for sharing this time together.

The word Muster has six letters. I want to share what I believe each letter represents individually and what each contributes to the whole meaning of the word Muster. The first letter, "M," represents Memory. For it is truly the memory of those who are absent that has brought us together. For every name called and for every candle lit at Muster, there is the memory of an Aggie's life. It is the memory of how they touched our lives, how they loved us, and how they sacrificed for us. These are the reasons why we celebrate, more than we mourn. As we light a candle for each of the absent this evening, ask yourself a question, "Is my life one which lights a light in the lives of those around me?" Do we let our light so shine that others see the One in us who is the Giver of all light and life? In the true Muster spirit, our goal should be to share and spark a little light in everyone we touch in life. Our memory of those whose lives we celebrate this evening is nothing less than our past experiences with them. We must live life to its fullest and leave a memory for others to follow because we were a person of faith and integrity who helped point the way before them. Life is like a field of newly fallen snow. Where we choose to walk, every step will show.

The second letter in Muster is "U," which stands for Unselfishness. Aggies are known for being unselfish and loyal and for helping other Aggies in need. No greater evidence is portrayed of Aggie unselfishness than the 12th Man, Aggie Bonfire, the Big Event or the March to the Brazos. However, these are traditions which only reflect the unselfish heart for others and characterize the true Aggie Spirit. How can we ever repay the sacrifices of those whom we honor this evening or those who gave their lives on the tiny island of Corregidor or other foreign lands in past war? Unselfishness is part of being an Aggie and is part of what life is all about. It is placing the good of others before our own interests. A hundred years from now it will not matter what our bank account was, the type of house we lived in, or the kind of car we drove. But, the world may be different because we were important in the life of another person.

I personally knew two Aggies whom we honor tonight. One was older and one was younger—a senior student. One demonstrated unselfishness to me when I was a young boy. The other was a recipient and later a giver of the unselfish Aggie Spirit of acceptance and family. Dr. Russell Benson, DVM, Class of '47, was an Aggie veterinarian who unselfishly encouraged me to dream and achieve my goals. No one from either side of my family had ever gone to college before me, but he unselfishly took time to inspire me that I could do it. He was the veterinarian in my home town who made a difference in the lives of many young men and women. He was an unselfish Aggie who invested in the lives of others.

Danny Long, Class of '96, was killed this past year in a tragic car accident going to the wedding of a friend in San Marcos. Only a few weeks before his sudden death, Danny had been in our home for a Bible study for college students and had shared his experience at Texas A&M. Danny told how he was never accepted in high school, but how the Aggies had so unselfishly accepted him and given him a home in the Aggie family. He made the most of it by unselfishly giving of himself to others and achieving success. Danny had a heart for others and showed it by how he lived. Muster reminds us that we too must be unselfish in all that we do and in how we live. No one of us lives only unto ourselves.

The third letter in Muster is "S," which represents Spirit. It is the Spirit of Aggieland. It is the spirit that can ne'er be told. It is the spirit that can only be experienced by having attended Texas A&M. It is the spirit that has brought us together this evening to remember the absent. It is the spirit of the Corps and student body. It is the spirit of the 12th man, Aggie Band, Silver Taps, the Ross Volunteers, Bonfire, Elephant Walk and "Howdy." Texas A&M has changed and will continue to change over the years, but the Spirit of Aggieland and that for which it stands must never change. The Aggie Spirit is both our heritage and our future. It means that no one of us will ever be forgotten and that our lives will forever be remembered. The Aggie Spirit will always burn brighter because of Muster. Muster is what keeps the Aggie Spirit alive and the Aggie Spirit is what keeps Muster alive.

But, spirit is much more and is really what gives our life and being and purpose. It is something inside that is real and meaningful. Spirit is lighting a light in others and passing it on. It must be experienced to be real and alive. I have the Aggie Spirit inside, but I have another Spirit inside which makes the real difference in life. I am not ashamed to tell you that I also have the eternal Spirit of the Living God in my heart which makes Muster a time to reflect more deeply on the real meaning of life. The Aggie Spirit is alive and well and will be personally felt as the candles are lit to remind us of the spirits of lives who are absent this year.

The fourth letter in Muster is "T," which must clearly represent Tradition. Tradition may not always be understood by those on the outside, but it is respected and admired. Tradition can only be passed on by those who have experienced it. Since 1883, Muster has been a tradition which has outlived those who have already experienced it. No ceremony, event or activity can more fully represent Aggie tradition than Muster. Muster brings all traditions together because our lives are touched by all of them collectively over the years. Tradition is something to be protected and passed down from one generation to another. The tradition of Muster is also different because it recognizes the sacredness of life itself. It is a tradition of principle and virtue which reflects that life is larger than we are. It reminds us that we are here on earth for only a short while. To softly call the Muster evokes emotions so deep that the word tradition seems hardly capable of describing it.

To think that this ceremony is being repeated in more than 400 places around the world is beyond the comprehension of other universities. Perhaps, it is just because we do care more about each other and are often reminded of the importance of family, which was the first institution God established on this earth. Think of your own family's traditions. Is not the tradition of Muster similar and equally meaningful? Aggies are family and Aggies keep traditions.

The fifth letter in Muster is "E," which represents Enthusiasm. Enthusiasm is what keeps traditions alive. Enthusiasm is to tradition what spirit is to the soul. Ralph Waldo Emerson once said that nothing great is ever achieved without enthusiasm. It is contagious and represents what we call a "can do" attitude. Attitude is what we say to ourselves and is what others see and hear in us. It is our manner of acting, feeling or thinking that shows our disposition. It is our behavior toward another person or situation. Our life is a reflection of our attitudes. Research has shown time and again that success is correlated to an attitude of enthusiasm, not education, family, money, background or even intelligence. The world is full of people who have wasted their education, intellect and God-given talent through a bad attitude. Aggies like to take on the competition and play to win with a "can do" attitude.

Muster reminds us to be enthusiastic about life and to invest our lives in something which will outlast us. We are all here for a purpose, just as those we honor today lived out a purpose in their lives. We are to find what is in our box, to make it a priority, and to live with an enthusiasm that touches the lives of those around us. Enthusiasm must have substance and be for the right cause. Muster should remind us that our enthusiasm must be for those principles, virtues and truths in life which make Aggieland great. Our enthusiasm must be for that spirit that can ne'er be told.

The last letter in Muster is "R," which represents Responsibility.

Responsibility is the often forgotten part of freedom and liberty. I dare say that we would not be here this evening if it were not for the responsible actions of those who have gone before us. Aggies have always accepted responsibility and answered the call of duty. Muster is the personal reminder of what responsibility really means. To be responsible is to be answerable or accountable for our own behavior and actions. It is to be dependable, reliable and trustworthy. It is one of several paths, and it distinguishes itself from the others because it is the right path, and the only one upon which you will never get lost. In life, it is linked to integrity. Integrity is what we are when we think no one is looking. It is character and being true to our word and our obligations. It is the Aggie Code of Honor. Look at the word responsibility. It is "response" and "ability." It is our ability to choose our response. Our ability to respond is determined by what we are on the inside and our respect of life itself.

We live in a world where responsibility is a vanishing virtue and where people do not want to accept responsibility for their own actions. The "R" in Muster must remind us that we are responsible for our own actions and that our actions do impact those around us. We are responsible for the one life which has been given us to live. No one can live it for us, any more than we lived the lives of those whom we honor this evening. We have a responsibility to put our lives together, with God's help, in such a way that the world cannot devour us.

I am reminded of the young father and his five-year-old son. The young father came home from work very tired and worn out. He simply wanted to relax and rest in his favorite recliner and to read the paper and watch the evening news. The young son wanted to play and kept after the father to do so, but the father was too tired. He thought about something that would occupy the young boy's time for an hour or more. He got a picture puzzle from the closet and instructed the little boy to go to his room and put it together. To the father's great surprise, the young boy was back within ten minutes. The father asked, "How could you have finished that puzzle; it was a picture puzzle of the whole world?" The little boy answered, "I know, Dad. But, you must remember that on the other side of the picture of the whole world was a picture of a little boy. I simply put the little boy together and the world took care of itself."

Is this not our responsibility, to put our lives together in such a way to make a difference in the world?

If Muster is not a responsibility given each of us to respect life, then it is meaningless. It is our personal responsibility to protect and respect Muster for the lives of those for whom we dedicate it. Many of you will light a candle this evening in memory of a personal loved one. But, may all of us assume our responsibility with one clear and firm voice to softly answer "Here" for those unable themselves to answer this year's annual Muster.

I return to my original question to you. What does Aggie Muster mean to you? From my heart, I have shared what it means to me. The six letters in Muster have great meaning and comprise a word so rich in meaning that we pause each April 21 to remember life itself.

The meaning of Muster is personal and sacred to every person who has experienced it. May it live in our hearts forever as we reflect on what it really means:

**M**emory of Aggies who have gone before us.

**U**nselfishness to help others in the Aggie family.

**S**pirit that can ne'er be told and of life itself.

**T**radition that keeps the spirit alive and passes it on.

**E**nthusiasm for what makes Aggieland great.

**R**esponsibility to those absent for us to answer, "Here."

You cannot imagine what a great honor this has been for me to share in this Muster ceremony with you. I leave you with an appropriate challenge and prayer which I hope you will personally take to heart:

I am only one, but I am one;

I cannot do everything, but I can do something;

What I can do, I ought to do;

And, what I ought to do, by the grace of God, I will do.
[paraphrased from Edward Everett Hale's "Lend a Hand"]

There you have it. . . . the meaning of Muster.

# H. Bartell Zachry Jr. '54

*1997—G. Rollie White Coliseum*

H. Bartell Zachry Jr. '54.
Photo courtesy of the
American Road &
Transportation Builders
Association.

Henry Bartell Zachry Jr. was born August 21, 1933, in Laredo, Texas. After earning a bachelor's degree in civil engineering and serving three years in the US Air Force, he joined the world-wide construction firm founded by his father, H. B. "Pat" Zachry '22. He worked in numerous capacities on foreign and domestic projects and attended the Management Development Program at Harvard Business School before being named president of the company in 1965. He was named chairman of the H. B. Zachry Group, Inc., which includes Zachry Construction Corporation and the Zachry Foundation.

Zachry served on the board of the Southwest Research Institute and was chairman of the San Antonio branch of the Federal Reserve Bank of Dallas. He was general chairman of the San Antonio–area United Way and served on the boards of the Texas Department of Corrections, the Texas Air Control Board, the Texas Research League, the Southwest Foundation for Biomedical Research, and the Alamo Heights Independent School District. He served on the Texas A&M President's Advisory Council and advisory groups with A&M's Civil Engineering Department and the Texas Engineering Extension Service.

He was named a Distinguished Alumnus in 1997 and inducted into the Corps of Cadets Hall of Honor in 2001. Bartell and his father are the only father-son pair to share these honors. He was also named an Outstanding Alumnus of A&M's College of Engineering.

Zachry's gifts to the university include two endowed General Rudder Corps Scholarships and inspired the formation of the Corps of Cadets Leadership Excellence Program. He funded two President's Endowed

Scholarships in memory of his father, and along with his family, company, and foundation he has created faculty chairs, professorships, and fellowships and funded many scholarships for exceptional civil engineering students.

## What Can I Do for A&M?*

My personal road, which began in Laredo, Texas, in 1933, has always had a sign post that read "A&M Ahead." My father saw to that, but the rare privilege of being here this evening was not on the map, and it is one of those events in my life that I will cherish always. I am deeply honored, and I am especially grateful to the Muster Committee, a group of dedicated young men and women who have been so supportive and who have embraced fully the important tradition of Muster.

It is absolutely fitting for Aggies to pause and briefly reflect on a single life, and then collectively celebrate the lives of all those absent Aggies for whom voices will answer "Here," because, in so doing, we honor them and all who preceded them—Aggies who can no longer in this life gather for a Muster.

Moreover, it is a celebration, as well, of the Aggie Spirit that resides permanently in the hearts of all Aggies—young and old—but especially for those gathered here and around the world for Muster on this 21st day of April. Muster is also a time to reinforce that special bond between Aggies that is unique to Texas A&M.

On this day in 1836, the battle at San Jacinto won Texas its freedom to go forward as a republic, but for us today and at every Muster, it is a reminder of the opportunities we have been provided and the obligations we have incurred living under a flag of freedom. It is a reminder, too, of an extraordinary, broad learning experience at Texas A&M, the cost of which others have largely borne. It is a debt we owe that we can attempt to repay by what we do with what we learned and what we might in turn do for A&M.

General Douglas MacArthur put it succinctly in addressing students at West Point in 1962 when he said, "Duty, Honor, Country—those

*Speech title derived by editor from speech contents

three hallowed words reverently dictate what you ought to be, what you can be, what you will be."

*Texas Monthly* is not a magazine that I read regularly, but I have a new favorite writer by the name of Paul Burka. I find little to dispute in his recent marvelous article about A&M. In it, he concluded that the decision in 1963 to permit co-education, reached by the Board of Regents with Sterling Evans as chairman, marked a new beginning, and it was made possible because General Earl Rudder, Class of '32, was president. This, I believe, but I also believe "Old Aggies" are not liabilities but assets and that the years before 1963 were years of positive growth that laid the foundation for what A&M was to become.

General Rudder came to A&M in 1958 and became president in 1959 when my father was chairman of the board. My father had also been a member of a prior board that sought and selected a president who they were confident would bring the necessary leadership and courage and character to enable A&M to fulfill its proper place of leadership and academic education to meet the needs of our state and nation.

Ironically, Sterling Evans graduated from Uvalde High School in 1917, and my father graduated in 1918. They were lifelong friends, as Mr. Evans reminded me just a few weeks ago. Both cared for their school, and they served two years together on the Board of Regents. Being from the classes of 1921 and 1922 [at Texas A&M] clearly identifies them as "old school" or, better yet, "old Army." Yet they had a dream, a vision if you will, of raising their school to new levels of greatness, while still maintaining the traditions so dear to all Aggies.

Aggies do love their school and, because Aggies love their school, differences are resolved toward the central best interests of making it a better place to serve the future needs of Texas. Change comes indeed, but it is tempered by the involvement of thousands who want to preserve the values they share and believe should remain a part of A&M.

Traditions spring from enduring values. New ones develop; some old ones fall into disuse—but, in sum, they contribute to the shaping of leadership and character and are, therefore, part and parcel of an education here. Like duty and service to your fellow man, they become core values, too, that are nurtured at A&M.

There is a story about a Mississippi River boat captain who had a young boy as a passenger. As the captain maneuvered his boat around a sand bank, almost invisible, the young boy asked how the captain knew where the sand banks were. The captain replied, "I don't know where they are, but I do know where the deep water is." The deep water is making this campus and where we live a better place.

I was a member of the Class of '54. Because I was in the Corps of Cadets, I cannot imagine A&M without this dimension. It remains not a relic of the past but an important dimension at A&M of potential military service to our nation and the preservation of freedom.

Recently, I had the distinct privilege of visiting several military installations and an aircraft carrier during training exercises. On a flight deck you sort of stand a little taller, seeing the flag of the United States of America and the service of a volunteer military protecting and projecting a democratic nation. It was a thrill for me to observe and appreciate a strength of our nation and know with a measure of confidence that A&M was here, too.

We have with us the Class of 1947—a class originally composed of 900 members. Seven hundred members of that Class of '47 remain on the Association [of Former Students] rolls today and 180 of those are here with us tonight. Many actively served in World War II and an entire class was deeply touched by that war, where a number of them lost their lives. Many knew Korea and Vietnam and other conflicts as well. As they pause to reflect about old friends when the roll is called at Muster, they are especially aware that service to our country in times of war and peace continues to be a core value from which traditions have evolved. It endures here at A&M.

But for all Aggies, whether their service is in the armed forces, government, community or for a neighbor, reaching out is a way of reflecting the Spirit of A&M.

Today A&M is a source of pride to our state and to all Aggies. One can almost accept that philosophy from the cow country: "Them who can brag without lying, let 'em brag." It is an incredible university— truly beyond any credible vision when that decision to include women was made in 1963.

I believe that decision was predestined. Consider this: Alexis de Tocqueville, a French aristocrat, came to America in 1831. He traveled all across the nation and made observations about American society. His observations produced a study called "Democracy in America." One of those declarations was, "If I were asked to what the singular prosperity and growing strength of America ought mainly to be attributable, I should reply 'to the superiority of its women.'" How then could A&M grow and prosper without such a vital element to project its purpose?

The Class of 1997 has 6,392 students, 3,103 of which are women . . . A class that continues to reflect core values while adding to traditions and elevating academic performance . . . A class that will preserve the deep roots that are A&M.

Just as a decision in 1963 preserved the past and opened a new door to the future, later this year another door will be opened as the Bush Library ushers in a new and exciting window to the world. "Be bold and mighty forces will come to your aid" must have been the vision that inspired those who have made it happen. President Bush served his country in the armed forces in time of war. He has served our country in government in both peace and war. He is a president who, in the eyes of the world, provided the leadership of his country to support a victory in Desert Storm. He is a president who brings to A&M his distinguished record of service to his country and to his fellow man. That record of service, integrity and leadership is a statement of our values. Here on campus, his regular presence will provide a new dimension and a new era for A&M—through a library for study and research, classes with lectures including those by the President and others of national stature, and, significantly, an international center with its interaction of visitors from all over the world, here at the invitation of the President. It epitomizes a lofty reach for A&M as it integrates a global perspective in expanding academic excellence while preserving its fundamental philosophies but, as in the words of the poet Robert Browning, "A man's reach should exceed his grasp or what's a heaven for?"

Students come to A&M for different reasons, but they are Aggies before they leave. As incoming students, some might wonder "what can the school do for me?" As Aggies, they ask "What can I do for A&M?" It is not an application of the Golden Rule, but a love of values and tradition working its way into the bloodstream of all Aggies.

If there is any doubt about the Aggie Spirit being alive and well, let me dispel that with the words of Chinh Hung Vu, an Aggie from the Class of '95, whom I met at a student leadership conference:

> Is it the bark of Reveille, or the Roar of the Twelfth Man?
> Is it the soft call of Muster, or the beat of the Aggie Band?
> Maybe it's the Silence of Silver Taps as darkness draws us in!
> Maybe it's the Final Cannon Shot as the Good Ags Win!
> Sometimes it's the Wildcats as each class yells out loud.
> Sometimes it's the MSC as we live as Aggies, proud.
> Mostly it's the People as Aggies we'll always be.
> Mostly it's the Love of Aggieland that everyone can see.
>
> Definitely it's the Aggie Pride that's felt by us all.
> Definitely it's the Spirit at Muster's final call.
> There is a Spirit, a Spirit that can ne'er be told.
> The Spirit grows within us as our Aggie lives unfold.
>
> The Spirit of Aggieland is too strong in all of us to let it go untested.
> We stand proud not to instill the Spirit in everyone that we meet,
> but to bring out that Spirit that lies within us all!
> That's what being an Aggie is all about!

The Aggie Family is indeed alive and strong. Our values and traditions, our pursuit of academic excellence are secured by a dedicated student body, faculty, administration and former students. Our school can continue to be conservative without being restrictive, moral without being judgmental, intellectual without being exclusive. Changes will come, but A&M must continue to reflect the broad educational experience all of us found at "the school we think so grand."

# Gene Stallings '57

*1998—Reed Arena*

Gene Stallings '57. Photo from editor's collection.

Eugene Clifton "Gene" Stallings Jr. was born in Paris, Texas, on Texas Independence Day, March 2, 1935. He was All-State in football and basketball at Paris High School. He earned All-Southwest Conference honors as an end under Texas A&M Coach Paul "Bear" Bryant and was a tri-captain of the Southwest Conference Champion football team in 1956. He received a bachelor's degree in physical education.

After six years as an assistant to Bryant at Alabama, he returned to Aggieland as the youngest head coach in the nation. In 1967 he was chosen Senior College Coach of the Year as his Aggies beat Texas 10-7 to win the Southwest Conference title and defeated Alabama and Bryant 20-16 in the Cotton Bowl.

During his fourteen seasons as a defensive assistant with the Dallas Cowboys, Dallas won seven division titles, three conference championships, and one Super Bowl. In 1986 he was named head coach of the St. Louis Cardinals. The next year the franchise moved to Phoenix. In 1990 he became head football coach at the University of Alabama. His Crimson Tide compiled a 52-10-1 record, winning four SEC titles and the 1992 National Championship, earning him National Coach of the Year recognition.

He received the National Boys Club Alumnus of the Year Award in 1982 and was named Dallas Father of the Year in 1983. He and his wife, Ruth Ann, received Abilene Christian University's National Christian Service Award. The Stallings Center at the University of Alabama opened in 1993, ministering to children under the age of five with disabilities. He wrote *Another Season: A Coach's Story of Raising an Excep-*

*tional Son,* a book chronicling the challenge of raising a family with love and tenderness while guiding football teams to achieve their best.

Stallings was named a Distinguished Alumnus of Texas A&M in 2000. He served on the Texas A&M University System board of regents from 2005 to 2011.

## Doing the Very Best You Can*

Thank you, Brian, I am always quite amused when I am introduced. Truth of the matter is, I WAS the youngest head football coach in the nation, age 28, and I was the youngest fired at age 35. That shows that there's not a whole lot of distance in between the outhouse and the penthouse, and I've been in both of them.

It is really, really a pleasure for me to be here. Dr. Bowen, all of the distinguished guests, the members of the Muster Committee, Class of '48, and the loved ones who later on we will softly call to Muster. What a pleasure it is for me to be here. What a pleasure for my family. I know I can't introduce everybody and I have children and grandchildren, but I do want to introduce two people while I'm here. My wife, Ruth Ann, we've been married some 40-odd years, and my little boy John Mark, if y'all would stand up.

I'm a little nervous up on this stage. I hadn't coached the St. Louis/ Phoenix Cardinals long and we had a governor in the State of Arizona by the name of Rose Mofford. Rose asked me if I would go with her to Yuma and speak on "Yuma Says No To Drugs." There were about 5,000 people in the audience, and most of them were above us and we were down sort of on the floor on a platform like this.

There was a curtain behind me, and a guy called me up to the podium to ask me a question and then I went back and sat down. I noticed my chair was out ahead of the governor's a little bit, and I didn't feel comfortable with that, so I scooted my chair back. When I did, I went off the back of the stage, and I threw my arms back and hit the gov-

*Speech title derived by editor from speech contents

ernor right up side the head. I knocked her back, and she was in an unladylike pose with her legs sticking up and 5,000 people looking at her and her eyes rolled back in her head and I said, "Good Lord, I've killed the governor."

I started tapping her like you see them do on television, and her little old eye wiggled, and I knew then she wasn't dead. I didn't really know how to address a woman governor in this situation, but I knew I had to say something, so I looked at her and I said, "Honey, you okay?" Well, the headlines the next day said, "New Coach Makes Hit on the Governor."

I know the Singing Cadets are back there, and I love the Singing Cadets and the great Aggie Band. When I was coaching here, I loved "The Ballad of the Green Berets." When things would be going bad out on the field, the Aggie Band would strike up "The Green Berets."

I had the privilege last night of having dinner, along with Ruth Ann and some of my grandchildren and my daughter, with the Muster Committee. These 40 youngsters, students here at Texas A&M, are a really delightful group. I would say that for each of the past 35 days I've gotten a handwritten note, a sweet handwritten note from one of the members of the committee saying how they were looking forward to this particular day. They were looking forward to all of the people coming back to campus, and they were welcoming me with an opportunity to come back. And how I appreciate that. I mentioned that to them last night. When you talk about quality, we have quality here at Texas A&M.

I love the traditions of Texas A&M. How many times I've had the privilege of saying that. You know, when you are a student you are sort of involved in the traditions, but when you get away from here, you will appreciate the traditions. The older we get, the more we think about what used to happen. As I reminisce a little bit about some of the traditions at Texas A&M, I think about the Bonfire. I used to love the Bonfire. I would go out in the cutting areas and I would spend some time with the people who were hauling the logs in. And when I was a player and I was a coach, we would go to the Bonfire. Invariably, somebody would get up and go over "The Last Corps Trip" [by Philo H. DuVal Jr. '51].

It was Judgment Day in Aggieland
And tenseness filled the air,
All knew there was a trip at hand,
But not a soul knew where.

Assembled on the drill field
Was the world-renowned Twelfth Man,
The entire fighting Aggie Team
And the famous Aggie Band.

And out in front with Royal Guard
The reviewing party stood;
St. Peter and his angel staff
Were choosing bad from good.

First he surveyed the Aggie team
And in terms of an angel swore,
"By Jove, I do believe I've seen
This gallant group before."

"I've seen them play since way back when
And they've always had the grit;
I've seen 'em lose and I've seen them win
But I've never seen 'em quit."

"No need for us to tarry here
Deciding upon their fates,
'Tis as plain as the halo on my head
That they've opened Heaven's gates."

And when the Twelfth Man heard this
They let out a mighty yell,
That echoed clear to Heaven
And shook the gates of Hell.

"And what group is this upon the side,"
St. Peter asked his aide,
"That swelled as if to burst with pride
When we our judgment made?"

"Why sir, that's the Cadet Corps,
That's known both far and wide,

For backing up their fighting team
Whether they've won or lost or tied."

"Well, then," said St. Peter,
"It's very plain to me
That within the realms of Heaven
They should spend eternity."

"And have the Texas Aggie Band
At once commence to play
For their fates, too, we must decide
Upon this crucial day."

And the drum major, so hearing
Slowly raised his hand
And said, "Boys, let's play 'the Spirit'
For the last time in Aggieland."

And the band poured forth the Anthem
In notes both bright and clear
And ten thousand Aggie voices
Sang the song they hold so dear.

And when the band had finished,
St. Peter wiped his eyes
And said, "It's not so hard to see
They're meant for Paradise."

And the Colonel of the Cadet Corps said
As he stiffly took his stand,
"It's just another Corps Trip, boys,
We'll march in behind the band."

Silver Taps. You know Silver Taps is something special for us. I can remember as a student, we would see that flag flying at half-mast, and
we would go over to the Academic Building where the flags flew, and
we would go up and read about one of our fallen comrades. On a certain day, at a certain hour, around 10:15 at night, all the lights on the
campus would go totally dark. Everybody is making their way toward
the Academic Building and all you could hear were footsteps. There
would be somebody in pajamas, there'd be somebody in a suit, there'd

be somebody in blue jeans, there'd be somebody in a uniform—and we would all assemble at the Academic Building.

Very quietly you would hear the Ross Volunteers and when I listen softly, I can hear their feet as they're coming and they were marching out, 21 of them, and they would give the 21-gun salute. Six members of that great Aggie Band would play Silver Taps. They'd play it three times and then we'd all go back. We'd go to our dorms, go to our homes, and not a word was spoken. Not one word was spoken. You talk about tradition; that's tradition.

Then, it's the Aggie Ring. Those of us can remember getting our Aggie Ring. I love my Aggie Ring. I remember when I graduated and my mother and daddy gave me a little teeny-weeny diamond to put in my Aggie Ring, and that was sort of a tradition in those days and I was so proud of that.

I'm coaching at Texas A&M a few years later and I get this letter. It says, "My name is Josh Sterns. I'm 87 years old and I'm trying to put a ring collection together for Texas A&M. We're trying to have a ring for each class and we want your ring for the Class of '57." I sat down and I wrote Mr. Sterns a letter that said, "Dear Mr. Sterns, I really appreciate that. I love what you're trying to do, but I want to keep my ring."

About two weeks later, I get this letter and it says, "My name is Josh Sterns. I'm 87 years old and I'm trying to put a ring collection together for Texas A&M. We're trying to have a ring for each class and we want your ring for the Class of '57." I sat down and I wrote Mr. Sterns a letter that said, "Dear Mr. Sterns, I received your letter and I think it's a great idea. I appreciate what you're trying to do, good luck to you, but I want to keep my ring." About two weeks later, I get this letter and it says, "Dear Coach Stallings, my name is Josh Sterns . . ."

Anyway, we wrote like that back and forth, and finally we won the Southwest Conference Championship, and we beat Alabama in the Cotton Bowl and you can't imagine how good I'm feeling. I'm in such a good humor and I get this letter, and it says, "Dear Coach Stallings, my name is Josh Sterns. I'm 87 years old and I'm trying to put a ring collection together for Texas A&M. We're trying to have a ring for each class and we want your ring for the Class of '57. I'm trying to do something for A&M before I die. What in the world have you ever done for Texas

A&M?" When he said that, I took it off and put it in a box and mailed it to him. There is something about that ring.

There's also something about standing up at the games. You know the reason you stand up—because you're ready to go in. You never know when the coach is short-handed. I've been short-handed from time to time and that's what standing up is all about.

You know, King Gill was the original 12th Man and they needed him, so now all the Aggies stand up and they are basically saying, "If you need me, Coach, I'm ready." That's a great tradition. Where else in the world do they do that—stand up throughout the whole game and say to the coach, "I'm ready"? It's the traditions that are super, super important.

Final Review was a big tradition. I loved Final Review.

Kissing our dates after we scored. When I was a coach here, we didn't score much and I got a little pressure. I would get notes from time to time.

Muster. There is something very special about Muster. It gives us an opportunity to remember our fallen comrades. We gather together once a year, we say something about our friends, we renew old friendships, and then we softly call the roll and someone says "Here." I was thinking about all the Aggies that have died in the war. The hundreds, and perhaps thousands, that have given their lives so we would have an opportunity to attend Texas A&M a free man or a free woman.

I couldn't help but think a little bit about the Congressional Medal of Honor winners. It's Horace S. Carswell, Jr. '38; Thomas Fowler '43, 2nd Lt. US Army; William George Harrell '43, Sgt. US Marine Corps; Lloyd Hughes '43, 2nd Lt. US Army Air Corps; George Keathley '37, Sgt. US Army; Turney Leonard '42, 1st Lt. US Army; Eli Whiteley '41, 1st Lt. US Army.

In reading about these men, I kept reading this kind of phrase: "He gave his life in a supreme effort to save all members of his crew . . . He exemplified the high traditions of military service when he gave his life . . . His grim fortitude and his great valor and his great fighting spirit, against almost insurmountable odds, reflected the highest credit upon himself in the finest tradition of the United States military . . . His heroic decision to complete his mission regardless of the consequence and the utter disregard to his own life . . . His gallant execution of his decisions . . . His supreme courage and inspiring leadership and his fighting spirit enabled our forces to hold off the enemy attack."

Over and over and over and over. There's just something special about these people. It's something about the student that died. It's something special about A&M.

You know that at A&M right now we have over 41,000 students. The Class of '48 didn't have very many. When I went through school here, we didn't have a whole lot. And now 46 percent of those 41,000 students are female. We've got over 2,400 on the faculty and over 80 percent have their doctorate degree.

We've got over 700 National Merit Scholars right here at Texas A&M. We've got the world's largest band. We've got over 2,000 in the Cadet Corps. We've got over 5,200 acres of campus with over 100 buildings. We have some of the largest schools in the world—agriculture, business, geosciences, vet. medicine, and so forth—right here on our campus. And yet, when we really boil it down, we have the friendliness of just a regular university.

We've got the George H. W. Bush Library right here on Texas A&M's campus, and in November, when we had the opening ceremony, we had every living President, with the exception of President Reagan, and then his wife Nancy Reagan was here. Lady Bird Johnson was here representing President Johnson. Probably the greatest assembly of people in the world—right here on the Texas A&M campus.

I can't keep from reminiscing about when I came to Texas A&M for the first time and I was living in Hart Hall. We were all in the Cadet Corps and I'm in "B-Athletics," and we would have to fall out and march to chow in the rain. The year wasn't too good. We had a coach by the name of Ray George and we didn't win too many games, so they let him go at the end of the year.

They said that somebody by the name of Paul Bryant was coming to Texas A&M. I didn't even know who he was. But, it didn't take long before I knew who he was. He took us off to a place called Junction. We went out in two buses and came back in one bus about half full. We had had all that write-up about going to Junction with the new coach and everything was going to be great. We couldn't wait!

We were finally playing a game against Texas Tech, and I asked Ruth Ann to come down, and I got her a flower and put her up in a room. This is a big deal. And we lose the game 41-9. Coach Bryant called us all up and said, "You don't deserve any women. Texas Tech players will have all the women. I want you in your room and in bed by 11:00 p.m." We played at night, and this was about 10:00 p.m. and our dates were out there waiting for us and we had to just run by them and wave at them.

We went to practice on Monday. You know you never practice in game gear. You never practice on Kyle Field. You just don't do that. You play on Kyle Field and you practice in practice gear. The manager went running around, and he told us that Coach Bryant said to put on your game gear and go out on Kyle Field. I didn't like the sound of that! We put on our game gear and, I can see us now, we were all sort of just walking around. Out on the field, by himself, was Coach Bryant. He was singing "Jesus Loves Me." I can hear him now. I said, "Oh, me."

We decided we didn't want to get beat 41-9 anymore as a result of that particular practice. There wasn't any loosening up and shaking and exercising. Coach Bryant called us all over and said, "Men, when the game was over the ball was on the 19, and we're going to take up where the game left off."

I remember that same football team a couple of years later, when we were playing Rice in 1955. We were behind 12-0 with only three minutes left to go in the game and we won the game 20-12. I remember just a little later [in 1956] when we go to the University of Texas and the Aggie team had never defeated the University of Texas in Memorial Stadium. Jack Pardee and some of the rest of us were having a great game and, all of a sudden, winning the championship for Texas A&M for the first time in a long time.

I remember coming here as a coach. I lived over in the MSC [Memorial Student Center], and I would walk across to G. Rollie White [Coliseum]. What a great experience it was to be able to come back and coach. Those are some good memories. I can remember coaching a team that started off losing four games in a row. Then they won seven in a row and won the championship. That's what Texas A&M is made out of.

I can remember things not going too good for me later in my career and I was fired here at Texas A&M. The seniors in the Cadet Corps came to my house, and they were out in the front yard and in the side yard and the streets. Somebody knocked on my door, and there were all the seniors of the Cadet Corps showing their appreciation and their regard. That's Texas A&M.

You know, sometimes we sort of live in the past. I can remember Barlow "Bones" Irvin, Athletic Director. You think you've got facilities here; we didn't spend a dime for anything, but he's one of the reasons you've got what you've got. He saved that money, and he wanted things to be good for Texas A&M.

I remember some of the spring games when the Old Army ROTC and the Air Force ROTC used to play. That was a big deal. I was coaching one of those games and the only good player I had got kicked out. I changed his number and sent him back in. I shouldn't have done that. I didn't think anybody would recognize him, but the guys on the other team did. That was a mistake.

I can remember some of those hitchhiking days. I couldn't wait to get to get out there and hitchhike back to Paris, and I couldn't wait to hitchhike back to A&M.

Pinky Downs . . . J. E. Loupot . . . Tom Harrington. Chancellor Harrington, what a gentleman he was. I can see Chancellor Harrington now when he would come to watch us practice from time to time. General Earl Rudder . . . Homer Norton . . . Dr. Carl Landis. We had a military professor by the name of Cochise. We called him Cochise—didn't know what his name was—he looked like Cochise to us . . . John David Crow, the names just go on and on and on. It's the Congressman Teagues, it's the Senator Gramms. Those are the memories of Texas A&M, but you know things don't just happen. Texas A&M just didn't get good all of a sudden. It takes a while.

While I'm coaching at the University of Alabama, I'm watching the girls gymnastic team, and you can't believe how good these girls were. We were competing for the National Championship there at Alabama and they were on the balance beam and that balance beam wasn't this wide [holding up his fingers]. I just couldn't believe how they were flipping and hopping and jumping and carrying on.

I nudged the guy sitting beside me, and I said, "Hey fella, I bet you half the men in this room can't even get up on that thing. Look what those women are doing." I just couldn't believe how good they were, and as I was watching these women compete I had a little flashback.

All of a sudden my mind sees Mary Lou Retton trying to win a gold medal for the United States in gymnastics. There's never been a woman to win a gold medal in the United States in gymnastics and Mary Lou Retton was close. Now it comes her time and I can hear the commentator say that she is going to need a perfect "10" to win the gold. He said you can't have a perfect 10, it's impossible. She's going through her routine, and it was good, and all of a sudden she dismounts. It is a perfect dismount, and she gets a standing ovation, and everybody is clapping and cheering. The television camera goes to Mary Lou Retton, and then it goes to the audience, and then it goes to the judges, and it eventually comes back, and they hold up a "10." A perfect "10."

They were interviewing Mary Lou Retton a short time later and they asked her how could she do that. Under all that pressure, with thousands in the arena and millions watching on television and now all of a sudden you perform a perfect "10." I loved her answer. She said, "Well, I've done that routine over a thousand times." That is preparation. She had done it over a thousand times, and now she is called upon to perform under pressure, and she's able to do it because she's done it over and over and over again.

I was on the plane yesterday flying in, and there was a student who turned around and asked me, "Coach Stallings, have you got any words of advice for someone who is fixing to graduate and go into the world?" I said, "I sure do. Make your boss look good. Whoever hires you, you make him proud that he hired you, and you do the very best you can and you work hard and you make him look good." Somewhere along the line we've got to understand that.

When a player would come to the University of Alabama, one of the things I would tell him was that education was the key. I'd say, "Son, I wish you'd get your degree. You've got to get your degree. You've got to get your education. I want you to get a championship ring if you possibly can, because that's important to an athlete. I want you to perform as well as you can possibly perform. I want you to leave here with a work ethic, because I know the importance of a work ethic." I think that's one of the things Texas A&M will do with its students and when they graduate, they will go out and develop a work ethic. Somewhere along the line we have to have appreciation.

I'm coaching for the Dallas Cowboys a few years ago, and we've got 13 rookies that made our team, and we're sitting around that table trying to come up with a goal for the Dallas Cowboys that year. This is what it was: "To have a genuine appreciation for the contribution that everybody makes." That said, in our way of thinking, that the offense appreciates the defense, the defense the offense, the player the coach, the coach the player, the player to have an appreciation for the trainer that kept him on the field, and the equipment man that kept him in good gear.

When that year was over, if we could have a genuine appreciation for the contribution that everybody made, we thought we could win. The last game we lost that year was the Super Bowl. Because we learned to have a genuine appreciation for the contribution that everybody made.

All of my coaching career, I have always appreciated a great player, but I've loved the second team player. The guy that just wasn't quite good enough. I had an appreciation for him because his job wasn't to play; his job was to get somebody ready to play. If you would ask me right now who I had the greatest appreciation for at the University of Alabama, I would probably say the lady that kept our building clean. Her name was Ben—I called her Charlie—I don't know why, she just looked like Charlie to me. You can't imagine the visitors I had and the traffic that would come in that building, but it was always spotless because it was her job to keep the building clean.

It's an appreciation for the contribution that everybody makes. All of a sudden things began to make sense.

Friendships. We at Texas A&M develop friendships. I read the other day what friends are all about. Friends are somebody who when things don't come out right, he comes right in. When none of your dreams come true, he is there. He never looks for your money, except when you've lost it. He never gets in your way, except to clear it out for you. Nothing is more important to him than to make you look important.

When you get turned down, he turns up. When you get cornered, he's in your corner. He never insists on seeing you except when nobody else will. When you're taking your bows, he's bowing out. You can do anything with his friendship with the exception of buying or selling it. He just asks you to earn the privilege and the right to be called a friend. I love that.

There's just something about having a friend, having a good friend. There's something about doing things right. There's something about being a Texas A&M graduate and doing something right. It's having appreciation. It's having no regrets. It's doing the very best you can with what you've got.

And, in closing, I leave you with the poem "If" by Rudyard Kipling. Kipling is writing this poem to his son and he's trying to tell him what to do and he says,

> Son,
>
> If you can keep your head when all about you
> Are losing theirs and blaming it on you;
> If you can trust yourself when all men doubt you,
> But make allowance for their doubting too;
> If you can wait and not be tired by waiting,
> Or, being lied about, don't deal in lies,
> Or, being hated don't give way to hating,
> And yet don't look too good, nor talk too wise;
>
> If you can dream—and not make dreams your master;
> If you can think—and not make thoughts your aim,
> If you can meet with Triumph and Disaster
> And treat those two imposters just the same:
> If you can bear to hear the truth you've spoken
> Twisted by knaves to make a trap for fools,
> Or watch the things you gave your life to, broken,
> And stoop and build 'em up with worn-out tools;
>
> If you can make one heap of all your winnings
> And risk it on one turn of pitch-and-toss,
> And lose, and start again at your beginnings
> And never breathe a word about your loss;

If you can force your heart and nerve and sinew
To serve your turn long after they are gone,
And so hold on when there is nothing in you
Except the Will which says to them: "Hold on!"

If you can talk with crowds and keep your virtue,
Or walk with kings—nor lose the common touch;
If neither foes nor loving friends can hurt you;
If all men count with you, but none too much:
If you can fill the unforgiving minute
With sixty seconds' worth of distance run,
Yours is the Earth and everything that's in it,
And—which is more—you'll be a Man, my son!

In my way of thinking, Kipling is saying you do the best you can with what you've got. Then you'll reach the age of 75 and 80 and 85 and 90 with no regrets. We've laughed a lot and we've helped somebody else. We've helped build a home for the handicapped child. We've helped send some money for the unwed mother. We've sent somebody else's child to college with the exception of our own and we feel like we've done something.

That's what Texas A&M people do. They feel like they've done something and now all of a sudden we lose a comrade, so we gather in a room such as this to pay our respects and a little later, somebody will say, "Let's softly call the Muster."

Thank you.

# W. Mike Baggett '68

## *1999—Reed Arena*

W. Mike Baggett '68.
Photo from editor's
collection.

William Mike Baggett was born November 8, 1946, in McLennan County. An A&M yell leader his senior year, Baggett graduated with a degree in accounting. He earned a Bronze Star in Vietnam as a US Army first lieutenant. After earning his degree at Baylor Law School in 1973, he served as a briefing attorney for Texas Supreme Court Justice Price Daniel Sr.

He would serve as chairman and CEO of the Dallas law firm of Winstead, Sechrest & Minick, with more than 200 attorneys in Dallas, Houston, Austin, and Mexico City. He also was on the board of Frozen Food Express. He has headed the Dallas Bar Association, been a trustee of the Dallas Bar Foundation, a Fellow of the Texas Bar Foundation, and on various committees of the State Bar of Texas. His legal publications have been cited as authority by ten appellate courts, and he tried more than fifty commercial trial court cases, recovering some $600 million for his clients.

He was chairman and CEO of the Cotton Bowl Athletic Association and served on the Texas Higher Education Coordinating Board. The governor appointed him to the Joint Select Committee on the Judiciary. In addition to serving as president of Texas A&M's Association of Former Students in 1987, the Dallas A&M Club, and the Texas Aggie Bar Association, he was chairman of the Texas A&M Foundation and class agent for Texas A&M's Class of '68. He served on Texas A&M's College of Business Development Council and the board of the 12th Man Foundation. In 1996 he received the Outstanding Alumni Award of A&M's College of Business and in 1998 was named a Distinguished

Alumnus of Texas A&M University. He was inducted into the Corps of Cadets Hall of Honor in 2012.

## Character, Leadership, Teamwork, Emotion*

Howdy! This is a great day in Aggieland, around our state, and around the world. This is the day of the greatest Aggie tradition—Muster.

As your Muster speaker, I hope to do better than a recent legal speech I gave to lawyers. After my speech, I walked the hall outside the room where I gave the speech. A member of the audience was talking on the phone to her office. She did not see me in the hall. She told her office that she did not like my twang or accent, and that I told too many corny jokes. Except for that, she did learn some things. I will try to go slow on the corny jokes and I assume you don't mind my Aggie accent.

Muster is very special: Aggies gathering together with reverence, respect and appreciation, we answer for our departed Aggie family and rededicate ourselves to service.

I will never forget my Muster in Vietnam—Aggies mustered together from all over Vietnam. I drove my jeep—with "Gig 'Em Aggies" painted on the front—from my compound between Saigon and Cambodia to Bien Hoa. After Muster I drove alone along Highway One and through the field back to my base camp. As I was driving, I thought about a very special Muster, a great tradition, and what probably was the most dangerous trip of my life: My base camp did not understand, but I did—it was Aggie Muster.

Aggie Muster celebrates those who place service above self. Aggies are first beneficiaries and then donors. I am humbled and honored to participate in Campus Muster.

Muster is a celebration of the Aggie family.

Michele, Class of '98, now completing her master's degree in accounting as a member of the College of Business Fellows program and a Pi Phi, applied for Muster Committee as a sophomore.

---

*Speech title derived by editor from speech contents

She wrote in her application: "Higher education is an important priority, but at Texas A&M we are taught values, camaraderie, and support for each other. Muster honors those who have gone before us, who had a similar allegiance to each other and their university. Aggies initiated that special camaraderie to each other and the university. That relationship is maintained and strengthened over the years through Muster because it brings the Aggie experience full circle. Muster is the embodiment of the Aggie Spirit."

Michele became a member of the Muster Committee for three years. She gave back to A&M, with her fellow Muster Committee members, and lifted Muster and A&M and Aggie Spirit to newer heights, just as this current Muster Committee is doing. Thank you, Muster Committee.

York, Class of '96, a member of the Ross Volunteers firing squad at Muster, former president of the A&M student body, and now in law school at the University of Chicago, during his busy law school academic days, joined the Chicago A&M Club. He worked on the Muster in Chicago. Realizing that York recently graduated from an involved A&M experience, the president of the Chicago A&M Club asked York what they should do for a Muster speaker. York responded, "Get a member of the Aggie family that speaks from the heart."

Jo, Class of 1968 from Baylor University (a time when A&M did not admit females), is the mother of York and Michele. Although not an Aggie by education, she understands, teaches, and builds the Aggie Spirit.

Michele, a second-generation Aggie female; York, a second-generation Aggie in the Corps; and Jo, an Aggie by choice—all reflect the larger Aggie family. They reflect the breadth, preservation, and growth of the Aggie education and the Aggie Spirit. They reflect the multi-generational Aggie family. They are my daughter, Cary Michele Baggett, my son, Carl York Baggett, and my wife, Jo Baggett.

Why did I, as a potential first-generation Aggie, choose A&M and the Aggie family?

One word: pride.

I say that Aggies are proud of who they are, proud of what they do, proud of who they do it with.

I did not know or understand the source of that pride, but I liked it and I wanted to be a part of it.

What is the source of that pride? Education and Aggie Spirit.

Education: Academic excellence is the base.

A&M has come a long way. As Gerald Griffin, Class of 1956, recalled in a prior Muster speech that the president of Texas A&M was removed from office in 1883, the presidency was abolished, and a faculty chairman ran the college.

Lawrence Sullivan Ross later became president, and things got better when A&M played its first football game and beat Galveston Ball High 14-6. [A&M's first game was a loss to Texas 38-0; Ball High was the second game.]

There has been substantial progress since that first football victory.

A&M has been and is a hot school for prospective students.

Despite enrollment restrictions for several years, A&M is 4th nationally in the number of students at 43,389—almost half of which are women.

Speaking of women, I remember marching to President Rudder's home protesting admission of women and the Corps becoming non-compulsory. As a fish in the Corps, I was encouraged to march several consecutive nights. After about three days of this activity, at about 1 or 2 in the morning, standing at attention, so tired I really was not concerned about these worldly issues, I regained consciousness long enough to suddenly wonder—why was I protesting going to school with women? I liked women. I also realized that not all higher education students longed to be in the Corps—to march on the president's home and stand at attention for hours protesting a school with women. A&M dealt with these worldly issues as only Aggies would do—we maintained our great traditions, Aggie Spirit, and we broadened and improved our student body.

The current student body of men and women, cadets and students, now includes over 700 National Merit Scholars. The average SAT score is 1160, 100 points higher than the national average.

The Corps of Cadets has 2,200 members, including the largest fish class since 1987.

More than 80% of the 2,400 faculty members have doctorates.

A&M is 9th nationally in research at $367 million in 1998.

A&M's 5,200-acre campus is among the largest in the nation.

The campus has more than 100 buildings, with a combined value of more than $1 billion.

The new George H. W. Bush Presidential Library attracted over 250,000 visitors in its first year of operation.

Recently, the A&M Foundation completed a very successful capital campaign with the goal of raising $500 million over five years. At the time of the campaign announcement, the $500 million goal was the largest ever undertaken by a public university. We exceeded the goal and raised over $600 million.

A&M currently is in the closing stages of Vision 2020 to establish goals and guidance for recognition as a top-10 public university—to prioritize future capital campaigns and ensure continued academic progress.

Education is the ticket to opportunity. A&M is providing those opportunities in an ever changing economic and more technical and global environment.

If you read previous Muster speeches over the years, they reflect reverence for those who sacrificed and gave their lives for freedom; recollections of world military confrontations World War I, World War II (which many of our honored Class of '49 participated in and vividly remember), Korea, Vietnam, and Desert Storm; national questions of war and morality; and the Cold War with Russia.

Aggie education and Aggie Spirit have survived these changing times; they have flourished and continued to grow.

What is this Aggie Spirit that is above and beyond academic education?

"There is a spirit can ne'er be told."

It is not a 60-second sound bite or an immediate personal gratification.

Another quote from Cary Baggett's Muster Committee application says: "Things you do at A&M are not easy. It takes great effort to learn, appreciate and preserve traditions that have been passed down from our predecessors. You must work at things that are not easy to obtain. The very reason they mean something is because they are not easy and must be worked for. That is what it is all about. It is worth it, if you pay the price."

It cannot be bought; it must be experienced and earned.

It is both our heritage and our future.

When I was president of the Association of Former Students in 1987, I spent some time with the president of the Texas Exes. He was also a lawyer. Close to the end of our joint terms, he asked me (and told me not to tell anybody that he had asked), "What is this 'Aggie Spirit,' and how can Texas get it?" I told him that it is something that is built over many years, and the University of Texas will never have it.

Aggies think and act like owners. They accept both opportunities and problems—theirs and others'. They leave a place, a time, an experience better than they found it.

Aggie Spirit is something that you understand over time and know when you experience it, but when somebody asks what it is, it is hard to describe. "There is a spirit can ne'er be told."

Aggie Spirit is that pride that says once an Aggie, always an Aggie. We are never quite through being an Aggie.

Aggie Spirit reflects at least four broad categories:

> character
>
> leadership
>
> teamwork
>
> emotion

Aggie Spirit starts with and is founded upon personal character.

To obtain the American dream, the Aggie dream, you must be willing to make sacrifices, be willing to give of yourself, and to accept responsibility.

It is not necessary for all of us to give our lives. What is necessary is for all of us to do our best in war and peace, and to be the best at what we do.

Aggies are uncommon people who try harder, achieve more, and are never content with less than their best effort.

Discipline is, in the long run, self-interest—foregoing short-term pleasures in favor of a little more hard work, perhaps a little more research, more practice in your profession. It leads to long-term success.

Aggies come early, stay late, and do what is necessary to get the job done.

Aggies have strong job commitment. Commitment empowers you, making you more valuable. Commitment is a gift that Aggies give to themselves.

Aggies are fixers, not finger pointers.

Aggies are men and women who ask what is the right thing to do—not "What's in it for me?"

Aggies do what is right, regardless of the consequences.

Aggies do what is right when they don't have to, and when nobody is watching.

Aggies are willing to give more than they receive.

Aggies are willing to give without expectation of receiving something in return.

Character is fulfillment, knowing you did your best and the right thing in the long run, not seeking immediate self-gratification, and appreciating your best effort at whatever task you pursue.

Character provides the base for leadership. To lead is to serve. Lead by example.

Leaders follow the same advice they prescribe for others.

Leadership is being willing to do whatever you ask somebody else to do.

Leadership is recognizing and appreciating the contributions of others, no matter how large or small.

Leadership is being a good listener.

The following is Aggie Field Scovell's [Class of 1930 and father of the Cotton Bowl] short course in human relations and Aggie leadership traits:

The six most important words:

I admit I made a mistake.

The five most important words:

You did a good job.

The four most important words:

What is your opinion?

The three most important words:

If you please.

The two most important words:

Thank you.

The one most important word:

You.

The least important word:

I.

Leadership guides and empowers others to do their best. Character provides the foundation for leadership, leadership provides the guidance for teamwork.

Aggies are "true to each other as Aggies can be."

Aggies are willing to give more than they receive. For many, giving more than they receive makes them all stronger than they would be individually. Give a little, gain a lot.

The Aggie team is enthusiastic—nothing great is achieved without enthusiasm.

As you have heard, I am a lawyer, chairman, and CEO of a law firm of over 230 lawyers. Lawyers are great examples of the need for teamwork. Lawyers are well-educated and highly motivated individuals. Lawyers view themselves as "stand-alone warriors." Stand-alone warriors are lonely and cannot experience their full potential if they do not join with others to be part of a team.

We are all stronger together than we are alone.

Our law firm message—one I learned from my A&M experience—is "We strengthens Me."

Lawyers don't understand where our teamwork message comes from. They certainly don't know and would not acknowledge that it is based upon Aggie teamwork, but they like it, appreciate it, and it works.

Team attitude overrides individual ability.

The first three components of Aggie Spirit—character, leadership and teamwork—form the foundation for pride—for the emotion of pride.

Aggie Spirit is saying "Howdy," being friendly, and being helpful.

Aggie Spirit is that certain feeling you get:

When the Aggie Band plays the national anthem;

When the Aggie Band plays the "Spirit of Aggieland";

When the Aggie Band plays the "Aggie War Hymn";

At Midnight Yell Practice;

At Silver Taps;

At Bonfire;

At Final Review;

At graduation; and

Today at Muster.

Aggie Spirit:

Makes you feel good;

Makes you smile—on your face, in your head and in your heart;

Makes you stand tall;

Makes you proud of who you are;

Makes you proud of what you do and who you do it with.

It makes you proud to say "Once an Aggie, always an Aggie."

"The spirit can ne'er be told" is alive and well in the hearts and minds of all past and present Aggies and is growing for future Aggies.

# Randy Matson '67

*2000—Reed Arena*

Randy Matson '67. Photo from editor's collection.

James Randel "Randy" Matson was born March 5, 1945, in Kilgore, Texas. After working in a stock brokerage and then in athletic fund raising at West Texas State University, in 1972 he became the Annual Fund director for Texas A&M's Association of Former Students. He served as executive director of the association from 1980 to 1999, helping lead the renowned alumni organization through two decades of the greatest growth in its history. As executive director, he worked with twenty association presidents as well as six A&M University presidents (including two interim) and was closely involved with the planning and construction of the Clayton W. Williams Jr. Alumni Center. In 1997 he was recognized by Texas A&M's faculty and students with the Distinguished Achievement Award for his contributions to the university.

Matson has been an A&M legend since he broke the world shot-put record in his sophomore season at Aggieland. That same year, 1965, he became the first man to break the 70-foot barrier. The following year he lettered in basketball at A&M. On April 22, 1967, in Kyle Field, he made his greatest all-time shot put of 71 feet 5½ inches. He had won a silver medal with a throw of 66 feet 3¼ inches at the 1964 Olympics in Tokyo and then set a new Olympic qualifying record of 67 feet 10½ inches before winning the gold medal with a throw of 67 feet 4¾ inches at the 1968 Olympics in Mexico City. He was awarded the Sullivan Award in 1967 as the outstanding amateur athlete in the nation. Matson was named a Texas A&M University Distinguished Alumnus in 2001.

## Traditions Set Us Apart*

Thank you. I really appreciate that support. This is a pretty awesome experience, standing before about 13,000 people. I've been in front of bigger crowds before, but I was wearing short pants and didn't have to say anything. To be honest, I prefer not saying anything, but since I can't put a shot or play basketball anymore, I guess I'll have to talk this time.

Aggies have always given me tremendous support, whether as an athlete or as Executive Director of the Association of Former Students. I remember how in 1968 at the Olympics in Mexico City, I received a telegram with 5,000 names on it from the student body of Texas A&M. I remember carrying that telegram in my bag on the field in case I needed it for encouragement. The athletes from other schools couldn't believe that the students would do something like that, but I told them, "It's nice, but you don't have to go back and face those 5,000 Aggies if you lose!"

Also, I might add that the last person I saw in the stands as we marched onto the field to compete was General Earl Rudder, President of Texas A&M, and he didn't say, "Good luck." He said, "Win!" And when he told you to do something, you tried very hard to do it.

It is a great honor for me to be a part of the 2000 Campus Muster. I was surprised and honored to be asked by the Muster Committee to speak, and tried to talk them out of it. I told them I had a commitment to speak at Muster in Amarillo and, quite frankly, felt they could get someone better. I even gave them names of Aggies I know who would be great. After twenty-seven years with the Association of Former Students, I had kind of developed the ability to do a head and shoulder fake and get out of things, but here there was no escape for me with the Muster Committee. Now, I kind of promised not to say anything about the young people on the committee, and I won't directly, except to say that the experience of working with them has been one of the most rewarding of my 27-year career at Texas A&M. Over the years, I had started to wonder if we are replacing some of the great Aggies from

*Speech title derived by editor from speech contents

our past, like H. B. Zachry '22, C. C. "Polly" Krueger '12, Earl Rudder '32, and Jack Fritts '53. If these young Aggies on the Muster Committee are indicative of our new generation of Aggies, then I now believe our greatest days may be ahead.

I was so blessed in my career at the Association to have known former students like these I have mentioned. Another great Aggie comes to mind on this occasion—Richard "Buck" Weirus '42, who preceded me as Director of the Association. Buck was my mentor. He knew more Aggies than anyone, and he loved Texas A&M. I remember one time when Buck was about to have major surgery and called me into his office. He was working on his pallbearer list and wanted to know what I thought. I told him I was surprised to see the list of names, because I thought some of them were people that he didn't even particularly like. Well, he agreed, but said they had given A&M a lot of money and might give even more! He was going to be a fundraiser for A&M right to the end! As you know, the name of Buck Weirus is synonymous with spirit, which is why there is an award named for him. Buck loved the traditions of A&M and understood how important they are in the heart and the history of this university.

Traditions are what make us different from other schools, other people. The great tradition of Muster is the one of which other schools are most envious. In my 20 years as Executive Director of the Association, I attended meetings of alumni directors from all the major universities in the country, and they all wanted to know about this thing we call Muster. How could we get tens of thousands of our former students together, essentially at the same time, on April 21, at some 350 locations across this state, nation and around the world? It is hard to explain to someone who is not an Aggie—like trying to explain what the Aggie Spirit is. You have to experience it. They don't understand that the love for A&M is something former students take with them when they leave campus, and it increases with the years. My friends in the Class of '50 who are being honored tonight know how that feeling can grow over the years, and it is the reason they are here tonight.

I was fortunate in my just-completed career to see real Aggie Spirit in action through the 20 former students with whom I was privileged to work when they served as Presidents of the Association of Former

Students. I consider them among my heroes in life. Without exception they were dedicated to giving back to A&M above and beyond what would be expected. They all loved the school, they each had different talents, and they would do whatever was asked of them.

I want to single out three of these great Aggies—three who are no longer with us, because I never attend a Muster that I don't remember them and what they have done. And since that is what Muster is all about, I want to tell you just a little about each of them.

Ted Pitzer '50 died late in the year in which he served as president. He was instrumental in the successful planning and construction of the Clayton Williams Alumni Center. He had built several buildings for his company, and he understood what was involved in constructing a major building. Unfortunately, he developed an aggressive cancer while president and underwent experimental treatment in Memphis, Tennessee. We were at a critical stage of the project, and he asked our consulting architect and me to come to Memphis. We did, and it was between very painful treatments we would work on the building plans. He never complained, because it was so important to him to serve A&M.

Richard Williford '55 was president in 1989. He lived in Tulsa, but it was so important to him to come to A&M whenever he was needed that he learned to fly and bought his own plane. After serving on the Association's Board, he went on to become a trustee for the Texas A&M Foundation. He was on his way to College Station for a Foundation event, when his plane went down, and he was killed.

Jack Fritts '53 was my president in 1982. In the '70s Jack lived in Lubbock and instituted the candle-lighting ceremony which has become part of virtually all Musters today. Jack loved the A&M students and came up with the idea to recognize students who served others. Thus, we have the Buck Weirus Spirit Awards, a highly prestigious award on campus today.

Jack also loved Muster and even made two Muster speeches at the same time in two different countries, by crossing the international date line in traveling from New Zealand to Hawaii. Texas A&M has lost some true friends in these three, as I have, and I very much miss the wise counsel each gave me.

We all have those we remember who touched our lives in some way, and when they are Aggies, they are part of us, even if we didn't know them personally. Just as the Class of '50 has carried on the Muster tradition, so now will you students of today. As you leave the university, you will want to ensure that this tradition will be just as revered by future students. Musters away from campus are different from this one on campus in the way they give Aggies a chance to get together and enjoy fellowship with each other. The further away from campus, the more important that aspect of Muster becomes. Over 27 years, I have been the Muster speaker in 27 different places: from San Diego to Washington, DC, from Laredo to Anchorage, Alaska. When you are living in Alaska, it really means a lot to be able to get together and talk about A&M. It is a bond that you have in common. That part of Muster is different when you live in Harris County with 30,000 Aggies. And that is where the Campus Muster is different. It is obvious 13,000 of us Aggies didn't get together to talk about our college days, except maybe those in the Class of 1950. The main purpose of the Campus Muster and what has become the focus of all Musters is to come together and remember those students and former students who are no longer with us. Muster is our way of saying to our classmates and fellow Aggies that they will not be forgotten. We will have roll call tonight and light candles for our comrades in over 350 locations around the world.

This year, Muster is even more important and more meaningful to all Aggies. The Bonfire tragedy on November 18, 1999, marks the worst day in the history of our university, when we lost 12 Aggies and had 27 injured. That day will never be forgotten by all Aggies and by our university. Out of that time of pain and mourning by families, friends, classmates, and fellow Aggies came a spotlight on our school unlike any we had ever experienced. Others saw how Aggies cared and reached out to one another, how the traditions of A&M supported us through this time of sorrow. Still others saw that there is so much more to these Aggie traditions than just words or rote activities.

These traditions set us apart from others and gave us support and strength in a time of great trial. Even older former students, like me, saw that students today have the same strong feelings for each other that we had. Out of that terrible tragedy came a new and stronger bond between the past and today. On behalf of former students everywhere, I want to say we are so proud of what we saw in you that day.

So, as we come to that time for which we have gathered tonight, we think of the families who have lost sons and daughters, brothers and sisters; and the classmates and friends who have lost valued relationships. And we want each of you to know that we will never forget those who have left us.

We are here to demonstrate our remembrance and to pledge that none of you shall be forgotten, as long as there are two Aggies left in the world.

I think it would be appropriate at this time for me to use the words of Bill Moss '51, past president of the Association, whenever he concluded a talk to a group of Aggies, quoting the words of the immortal P. L. "Pinky" Downs '06: "God bless you, Texas Aggies!"

# Joe E. West '54

## 2001—Reed Arena

Joe E. West '54. Photo from editor's collection.

Joe Earl West was born March 8, 1932, in Woodward, Texas. The former Aggie yell leader retired in 2000 after eighteen years as a clinical pathologist with the Texas Veterinary Medical Diagnostic Laboratory. Following a twenty-two-year career as a US Air Force veterinarian that took him across the nation and to Europe (retiring as a colonel), he practiced in Illinois and helped establish the Mississippi State University College of Veterinary Medicine. He joined the diagnostic lab, an agency of the Texas A&M University System, in 1982. West earned a DVM degree at Texas A&M, a master's degree in radiation biology at the University of Rochester, and a PhD in comparative pathology at the University of California at Davis. He authored or co-authored more than forty scientific or professional articles. He has been named Texas Veterinarian of the Year and was presented the President's Awards of the Texas Veterinary Medical Association and the Texas Academy of Veterinary Practice.

A past president of the Brazos County A&M Club and the National Capital A&M Club, West was instrumental in establishing A&M's Association of Former Yell Leaders and served as co-class agent for the Class of '54. He has served Texas A&M and the Association of Former Students in numerous capacities and is active in community affairs. He and his family cared for A&M mascot Reveille V for five years after she was retired in 1994. West was named a Distinguished Alumnus in 2011 and inducted into the Corps of Cadets Hall of Honor in 2014.

# A Spirit Can Ne'er Be Told*

Good evening and Howdy!

Thank you for choosing to participate in this cherished tradition, Aggie Muster!

What a special evening at Texas A&M University! We are here in Reed Arena as a part of the Aggie Family, to celebrate and perpetuate the great tradition of Aggie Muster, joining some 400 other Musters throughout this state, nation and world.

Since the early days of Aggie Muster, it has been tradition for a speaker to "share a few words," as a part of the ceremony. As an Ol' Ag, I stand before you tonight with deep humility. I thank the Muster Committee for this unimaginable honor. My cup runneth over with blessings and I share these words from my heart!

"There's a Spirit can ne'er be told; it's the Spirit of Aggieland!"

Tonight, I will begin with some brief history of Aggie Muster, well-documented by John A. Adams Jr. '73 in his book, *Softly Call the Muster*, then relate some personal experiences about Muster and about our Honor Class of 1951, share some impressions about you, our current students, and then close with some thoughts about the traditions you take with you, including wearing the Aggie Ring and attending Aggie Muster.

Members of our Honor Class of 1951 and others here tonight have attended many Musters over the years, sometimes in far-away places and occasionally under difficult circumstances. However, for you freshmen, the Fightin' Texas Aggie Class of '04, this may be your first Aggie Muster. Texas Aggies all over the world are sharing in this honored tradition, and as we think of them, from my personal experience, they, too, are thinking of us, often referring to the Campus Muster, respectfully, as the "Big Muster." So, ladies and gentlemen, fellow Aggies and guests, we are joined tonight by the indefinable, but real Aggie Spirit, as we assemble to honor the Class of 1951, and to reverently remember those no longer among our ranks, but whose cherished memories will live within our hearts forever!

*Speech title derived by editor from speech contents

As you know, we celebrate Muster on San Jacinto Day, April 21, which commemorates Texas independence. Although dating to the late 1800s, Aggie Musters gained momentum and participation in the early war years beginning in 1942 and 1943 in the Pacific and European theaters. A memorable Aggie Muster was held on April 21, 1942, on the Pacific Island of Corregidor, known as the Rock. Even though the island was being shelled relentlessly by the Japanese, under these indescribable conditions, General George Moore, Class of '08, a former Commandant of Cadets at Texas A&M, and the 24 other Aggies "mustered" in spirit, holding true to the tradition. Days later, Corregidor fell to the Japanese, and the surviving Aggies unfortunately became a part of the infamous Bataan Death March, marked by atrocities and "man's inhumanities to man." News of the 1942 and 1943 Aggie Musters received national and international attention and brought great credit upon the State of Texas and Texas A&M. In the fall of 1942, General Douglas MacArthur, Commander of the Pacific forces, paid tribute to Texas A&M because of the bravery and courage of Aggies who fought for our freedoms.

As the Muster tradition evolved, Mr. E. E. McQuillen '20, then Executive Secretary of the Association of Former Students, urged that on April 21, wherever there are two or more Aggies, they would meet, recall their times on campus, renew friendships, and remember those whose footsteps and voices were no longer heard.

In 1946, General Dwight D. Eisenhower was the speaker for Campus Muster held at Kyle Field. As former Supreme Allied Commander in Europe in World War II, and US President-to-be, he came to praise Texas A&M for the distinctive contributions made by A&M men to the allied victory. Texas A&M provided more officers than any other college, university or military academy, and General Eisenhower gave credit to the ROTC program for the leadership and courage displayed by Texas Aggies, including the seven recipients of the nation's highest award, the Congressional Medal of Honor. You may have seen these honored Aggies' pictures and descriptions of their gallantry in action in the Memorial Student Center and in the Sam Houston Sanders Corps Center.

My first Aggie Muster was as a fish on April 21, 1951, when the Aggies in our Honor Class were seniors. It was held during the day on the front lawn of the new Memorial Student Center, across from Simpson Drill Field. Some of you were at the ceremony this afternoon which celebrated the 50th anniversary of the dedication of the MSC.

It was during my early Corps of Cadets experience that I realized there was something different about Texas A&M. I respected the discipline and accountability, the structure, the pride of accomplishment of an outfit as a result of the hard work of its members, all striving to achieve something greater than themselves.

For me and my classmates, you members of the Class of 1951 were outstanding. You held positions of leadership that are now held by many of today's student leaders. You were sharp, and you had our undivided attention, and you communicated your great expectations of us—regularly! The juniors and sophomores, Classes of '52 and '53, knew that, too. You all were our mentors and an excellent leadership team. That was when Kyle Field was only one level, when there were only 7,000 men and no girls, and very few of us owned cars—and definitely no parking problem.

It was the learning, yes, from upperclassmen, and participating in traditions that helped make me a Texas Aggie. Remember Yell Practice on the steps of the YMCA and the Grove including "Pinky" Downs '06, Silver Taps, hitch-hiking to Corps Trips in Austin, Dallas, Fort Worth and seeing our Aggie Sweetheart from the Texas State College for Women [now Texas Woman's University], known as Tessieland, presented at halftime at the A&M-SMU game in Dallas. You will recall that afternoon we saw your classmate, All-America fullback Bob Smith, set a long-standing Southwest Conference rushing record of 301 yards in 29 carries to beat the Mustangs in a hard-fought battle in the Cotton Bowl.

After graduation and commissioning, you members of the Class of 1951 bore the brunt of combat in Korea and for many, subsequently, in Vietnam and other conflicts. I know several of you and am familiar with some of your successes. You include architects, attorneys, many CEOs, Past Presidents of the Association of Former Students, "aces" in the skies of Korea, general officers in the armed forces, Parents of the Year at Texas A&M, Chief of the Army Veterinary Corps, Rookie of the Year in the National League, author of the "Last Corps Trip" poem, influential members of the 12th Man Foundation, recruiters and fund raisers for the Corps of Cadets.

During a memorable outfit meeting of our fish Squadron 8 in Dorm 15, near Sbisa [Mess Hall], one evening in the fall of 1950, our Commanding Officer told us, "Men, you have to aim high to hit high." In addition to your sustained giving back to Texas A&M through the years, as was stated earlier, this weekend you gave 24 Sul Ross scholarships in memory of the 24 classmates who gave their lives for the freedoms we enjoy tonight. Your class has obviously "hit high." I personally know of no finer examples of Former Students and the Aggie Family than the Class of 1951. Thank you again for your many remarkable contributions to our University, state, nation and world.

"There is a spirit can ne'er be told; it's the Spirit of Aggieland!"

My experiences at Musters have included attending one with only one other Aggie, fulfilling the requirement of "two or more . . ." Several years later, while on assignment in Washington, DC, I was honored to participate in the National Capital A&M Club's April 21 Wreath Laying Ceremony at the Tomb of the Unknowns at Arlington National Cemetery. The Musters in Washington were always made special by the highly decorated World War II veteran, Aggie Congressman Mr. Olin E. "Tiger" Teague '32, who arranged for our Musters to be held in the Cannon House Office Building on Capital Hill.

In the mid '70s, Aggie Musters at Ramstein Air Base, Germany, Headquarters of US Air Forces in Europe, a part of NATO, were unique. They were held under conditions of high tension during the Cold War between East and West, with our F-4 and F-15 jet fighters within a short flying time to the Berlin Wall. For the Berlin Wall to come down in my lifetime, much less to have a section of it on our campus at the beautiful George H. W. Bush Library, could not be imagined at the time—great testimony to our national leadership. Yes, that was the former Navy Lt. George Bush who fought in the Pacific in World War II, was shot down, rescued, and became our Commander in Chief and one of our greatest US Presidents. He had that section of the Berlin Wall put there, on our campus.

During the early 1980s, I enjoyed participating in the Aggie Muster at the newly chartered Golden Triangle A&M Club at Mississippi State

University, assisted by a recent graduate who was new with the Association of Former Students, Porter Garner III, Class of 1979. As you know, he is now the Association's Executive Director and is speaking at the Tyler Muster.

Since returning to Aggieland in October 1982, I have been honored to speak at Aggie Musters with A&M Clubs across Texas, including at a South Texas ranch near Pearsall; at a restaurant in Bandera, with my parents, sister and two Aggie brothers, Dale '57 and Milton '61, attending; to one held in a church in Kaufman; to the more formal Musters in Dallas and Fort Worth. Each Muster is always unique, but all have a common thread—meeting old friends, making new friends, remembrance, reverence for life, and re-experiencing the Aggie Spirit and the comradeship we enjoy—all honoring Texas A&M University.

"There is a spirit can ne'er be told; it's the Spirit of Aggieland!"

These memorable experiences along with my work at the Texas Veterinary Medical Diagnostic Laboratory, an A&M System agency, and the College of Veterinary Medicine, have been rewarding. My contact with Texas Aggie students, including with many of you here tonight, has been especially gratifying.

Most of you here tonight are students and, from my perspective, you are among the best, the brightest and most caring in America. You represent our future, integral to Vision 2020, promoting even greater excellence, and you are key to the continuity of the Maroon Line and the perpetuation of the Aggie Spirit and traditions like Aggie Muster. Since my return to Texas A&M, I have been privileged to work with Aggies in diverse areas, including the Corps of Cadets, student body, former students and with traditions, including Reveille, Yell Leaders and enjoying many others including the Aggie Band, RVs [Ross Volunteers], Aggie athletics, and occasionally working with Aggie Moms.

In March 1994, the Mascot Company E-2 surprised my family and me with the retiring of Reveille V to our home. She immediately chased our cat, Skeezix, out of our house and quickly established herself as the ranking member of our five-companion animal household. Now I know some of you are wondering—Yes, she even tried to sleep in our bed! Reveille V was an important part of the Aggie connection during those special years, 1994 to 1999. My family and I are so grateful.

In 1997, I was involved with several others in chartering the Association of Former Yell Leaders of Texas A&M University. Now we Ol' Ags have noted a few changes in signals and motions for several of the yells, and a few changes in the uniform over the years; however, today's yell leaders, with high time demands from their numerous activities, show the same pride in leading and inspiring the 12th Man and represent our University in an outstanding manner.

Veterinary students I was privileged to work with have impressed me by their enthusiasm, depth of knowledge and diversity of interests in our great profession.

Service to others and giving back are hallmarks of today's Texas Aggies. I commend you students on the positive impact you are making on our Bryan–College Station community. Several thousand of you helped clean up our community during the recent annual Big Event. You also collect and donate large sums of money, approximately $100,000, to the local March of Dimes, including funds raised from tomorrow's Corps of Cadets March to the Brazos. These, along with homes built by your local chapter of Habitat for Humanity, are but a few examples of your commitment to your fellow man, also reflecting, in my opinion, your caring parents and your caring administration.

I have met you when you come speak to the College Station Noon Lions Club; I see you on your way to classes taught by some of the nation's leading educators, often authorities in their fields, including recipients of highly prestigious national and international awards. I have seen you in committee meetings, as hosts to the Ol' Ags returning for Aggie Hostel, in numerous activities in Student Affairs, and the Student Recreation Center. I always enjoy my brief dialogs with you and you return my "Howdy" and friendly greeting. Some of you come from afar, including Norway, Ecuador, and India. As Texas Aggies, you help give our University its solid international stature. With each encounter, all of you reassure me about the future of Texas A&M and the Aggie Network.

Others of you here tonight know many of these students whom I have been describing, for they are your children, grandchildren, or other relatives, many belonging to a long Maroon Line. Some of you are, as I was, the first Aggie in your family.

As students at A&M, we grow close to all our traditions, including Silver Taps, Bonfire, Midnight Yell; but I have found two traditions that will always be close to your heart: wearing your Aggie Ring and attending Aggie Muster.

Your Aggie Ring symbolizes your hard work, pride in accomplishment and your affiliation with this remarkable University; it will be your instant connection with other Aggies and friends of Texas A&M, occasionally at the most unexpected times and places. Many stories are told about our Aggie Ring.

A friend of mine in the National Capital A&M Club, Lt. Cliff Chamberlain '40, was speaker at the 1945 Aggie Muster. Captured at Corregidor and a survivor of the Bataan Death March, he told about his 999 agonizing days as a Japanese prisoner. With tears in his eyes he told how the Japanese took his Aggie Ring. He said, "They stole my ring, but they could not steal the right or honor of wearing it." After the Muster that night, the Muster Committee took up a collection to purchase a replacement ring which was later presented to Lt. Chamberlain. On February 17, 1988, he died wearing that Aggie Ring.

"There's a spirit can ne'er be told; it's the Spirit of Aggieland!"

The second tradition you will continue forever is the one we celebrate tonight, Aggie Muster. Muster defines who we are as Texas Aggies, representing honor, integrity and service to our fellow man and to our nation.

Many words describe Muster, including tradition, remembrance, family, reunion, and comradeship. In addition, I believe that Aggie Muster is also an expression of love and compassion.

There are five brass plates at the entrance to the Memorial Student Center with the names of the 916 Aggies who gave their lives in World War II. On these plates is inscribed the scripture, John 15:13—"Greater love hath no man than this, that a man lay down his life for his friends."

Mr. James Pipkin '29, Muster speaker in 1951 when our Honor Class were seniors, said: "We do this because we share a great tradition, greater than the single memories of any of us. And though the years pass, faces change, visible appearances alter, the spiritual core of that tradition remains unaltered and undiminished."

Ladies and gentlemen, Aggie Musters for April 21, 2001, are now complete in Saudi Arabia, Uzbekistan, Germany, and Washington, DC; in progress in Tyler, Dallas, and La Salle County; and will soon be held in Seattle and the Whidbey Island area, and Hawaii. Tonight, the Aggie Family is connected over this state, nation and world, as we honor with reverence this cherished tradition.

In closing, I ask you to show love and compassion to others, to wear your Aggie Ring proudly and to continue to choose to participate in Aggie Muster, wherever you are!

"There is a Spirit can ne'er be told, it's the Spirit of Aggieland!"

Softly call the Muster . . . !

Thank you, God bless and Gig 'em!

# Gov. Rick Perry '72

*2002—Reed Arena*

Rick Perry '72. Photo from editor's collection.

James Richard "Rick" Perry was born March 4, 1950, in Paint Creek, Texas. While growing up, he attained the rank of Eagle Scout. At Texas A&M, where he earned a bachelor's degree in animal science, he was elected yell leader his junior and senior years.

The fifth-generation Texan, Perry flew C-130 tactical aircraft in Europe and the Middle East during his tour of duty in the US Air Force from 1972 to 1977.

After serving two terms as Texas agriculture commissioner and three terms as a state representative, he was elected lieutenant governor of Texas in 1998. He became the first Texas Aggie governor in December 2000 when Governor George W. Bush was elected president of the United States. A year later, he announced his candidacy for his first full term as governor (which he won in November 2002). He was reelected three times to become the longest-serving governor in Texas history.

Perry was named a Distinguished Alumnus of Texas A&M and inducted into the Corps of Cadets Hall of Honor in 2002.

## Freedom Is Not Free*

I am deeply humbled and greatly honored to join with you today on the hallowed grounds of this campus to commemorate the 2002 Aggie Muster.

*Speech title derived by editor from speech contents

With the rising of the sun over the Far East, until its descent over the Hawaiian Islands, we, the men and women of Texas A&M, gather once again to Muster.

As a school rich in tradition, no tradition is more sacred, or more meaningful, than Muster.

But there is one other tradition I am mindful of today that frankly I feel compelled to mention. It has been a source of controversy, and I feel like it is time I addressed it straight on—I support the new tradition of the Aggie Governor.

Living behind the Orange Curtain, in the shadow of the t.u. tower, can be a difficult duty. But being the First Family of the greatest people on earth—the people of Texas—is the highest of all honors.

And, President Ray Bowen, not that I am one to say "I told you so—," but if the Dean of the Vet School back in 1970—Dr. A. A. "Double A" Price—could have foreseen the future, he might not have been so quick to tell me after four semesters that I was better suited for a degree in animal science.

Hey, we all peak at different moments in life—those of us south of a 3.0 GPR are just late bloomers!

This year's Muster, like each one that has preceded it, is bittersweet. Today, we are honored to be joined by those who have suffered great loss. A classmate, a friend, a loved one has passed from this earth, and left a void in our lives that can never be filled. Today, the Aggie Family shares our grief and our sorrow.

And we also share your joy. For the years they walked among us, they illuminated our lives. Though they are no longer here to share a laugh, a smile or a tear—as we light a candle in their memories, we know that they are alive in the hearts and souls of the living.

Muster not only commemorates the lives of the recently passed, but it reminds us of the heroism—the courage—the unconditional love that has defined the Aggie Spirit for one hundred twenty-five years.

Sixty years ago today, the Muster tradition grabbed the heartstrings of freedom-loving people. With the published words of a war correspondent, an incredible story traveled halfway around the world about 26 Texas Aggies, led by General George Moore '08, who paused to observe the Muster tradition on the besieged island of Corregidor.

With heavy hearts for 10 of their Aggie buddies who had perished on "the Rock," and with the uncertainty of their own fate, that band of Aggie brothers stiffened their resolve in defiance of tyranny, mourned the loss of their classmates, and celebrated the unique bonds of loyalty forged at a place called Texas A&M.

Tonight, among the roll call for the absent, you will hear the name of Tull Ray Louder, Class of '41. He was in the Philippines that fateful day in 1942. Fifteen days later, he was captured and forced into 40 months of slave labor that he survived alongside a fellow Aggie POW.

Tull Ray Louder, like many of the men on Corregidor, is no longer with us. But as sure as they stood together that fateful day, the Aggie Spirit carries on!

General Douglas MacArthur spoke with great authority when he stated in September 1942, "Texas A&M is writing its own military history in the blood of its graduates."

In this hall today are some of the men who have lived those words. Their senior yearbook states they arrived in Aggieland on a "sweltering Sunday afternoon in early September, 1948—1,500 strong—from cities and towns all over Texas and the Southwest. We were tall, short, fat, thin, some cowhands, some city slickers, many farmboys, but all were green and all were scared to death by the whole thing."

More than 50 years later, they are not filled with fear, but fond memories. They have lived full lives, and with pride can look back and know they left a lasting imprint on the world.

Three of them have been recognized as Distinguished Alumni, nine attained the rank of either Admiral or General in the armed forces, and many have succeeded in the world of private business, and given generously to private causes and this university.

As they celebrate their 50th reunion, their ranks are thinner not only because of age, but because of heroism.

Sixteen of the classmates with whom they spent the best four years of their lives—sixteen fellow cadets with whom they marched—with whom they shared moments of turmoil, tears and laughter—would perish as the United States fought for freedom in Korea.

Years later, three more friends would perish in Vietnam.

The honored Class of 1952—you have given so much since that last march around the drill field at Final Review. You have contributed to a better world by standing up for freedom. And, if I might, I would like to ask all of the members of the Class of '52 to please stand, or if you can't, to raise your hand in the air, so we can pay you proper tribute.

Thank you. May God bless you and keep you safe the rest of your days.

As sure as the members of the Class of '52 stood before us today, the Spirit of Aggieland is alive and well.

When I think about my 52 years on this earth, I am drawn to individuals who have spanned several generations of Aggie lore, and who are testaments of the Aggie Spirit.

I think about Gene Overton, a classmate of James Earl Rudder in 1932. He was the first individual to take me to the grounds of this campus as a young boy from the country. Until I arrived here in 1968, he was my connection to Texas A&M. A man of principle, a leader of vision, Gene Overton was my scoutmaster, and as strong a testament of Aggie values as I ever experienced.

Gene Overton is no longer with us—but he lives on in the form of the Aggie Spirit.

I think about Jack Nagle ['43]. Some say I had a lot in common with Jack—he was a yell leader and a bit of a hell-raiser. In fact, the administration got so tired of Jack's antics that they invited him to leave for the Second World War before finishing the required coursework.

On the day that he packed his bags for good, he went to Kyle Field, where he scooped up a handful of dirt and placed it in a Bull Durham pouch for safekeeping.

Jack went off to flight training, and eventually the war. When his plane went down over Belgium, Jack's lifeless body was found, and on his person was that pouch of Kyle Field soil that he kept as a reminder "of the school we think so grand."

Jack Nagle is no longer with us—but he lives on in the form of the Aggie Spirit.

I also think about a giant of a man in more than one way—George Shriever ['69]. At six foot six, George was as intimidating a presence as anyone I met that first week as a fish. He was my commanding officer.

I remember when my dad dropped me off in the loving hands of

Squadron 6 on that hot, humid August day in 1968. We toted my foot-locker up to the dorm, and then Dad went outside and he grabbed ol' George by the arm, pulled him under a tree out in the quad and he gave him a simple message: "Make a man out of him."

I had the good fortune of living in the room next door to George—sometimes in his room under the bed. At any hour of the night, George and Roger Matson would knock loudly on the wall, and I knew that was my signal to come running. He may have needed his shoes or brass shined—or he may have just wanted me to sing him to sleep that night. Whatever George needed, I did—I was his fish.

Four years later, after George Shriever had done two tours of duty in Vietnam as a pilot, we were both sent to Dyess Air Force Base. I ended up being his co-pilot in a C-130 as we flew to destinations around the world.

George and I shared Muster together—just the two of us—somewhere over the Eastern United States at flight level 2-4-0 on April 21st, 1975.

He was a grand fellow, a big ol' teddy bear, and one of the hardest things I have had to do in quite some time was show up 12 days ago at that service, and pay my last respects to a wonderful husband, a proud father, and a great Aggie.

George Shriever is no longer with us, but he lives on in the form of the Aggie Spirit.

You see, they were from the Classes of '32, '43, and '69—but they were all cut out of the same cloth, because the values taught at Texas A&M transcend time.

The first lesson you learn at A&M is to take care of your fish buddies. If one of you fouls up, you all fouled up. The joys and sorrows, you share together. You are as strong as your weakest link.

There's a reason for that—you are part of a cause greater than self.

For generations, Texas A&M has been creating leaders like Gene Overton, Jack Nagle and George Shriever. They are the individual parts that make the Aggie Spirit whole—and they departed this campus forever changed, and ready to make a difference.

Some wonder why we Aggies get so absorbed in this institution. As long as there is a Texas A&M where young men and women are taught the lessons of leadership, and trained to make a difference for their fellow man, we who once walked its grounds will have a love for her that does not fade with the years, or ebb and flow with the times.

Neither the passage of time, nor the evolution of progress, can dim the enthusiasm or temper the love the former student feels for Texas A&M.

Before the doors of this institution ever opened, the Spirit of Aggieland was alive in the hearts and souls of all who love freedom. It rode shotgun with a Texas Ranger by the name of Lawrence Sullivan Ross, who would one day fight to keep the A&M College from being placed under the control of the University of Texas.

It was alive 166 years ago today as the forefathers of Texas Independence marched across a field next to the San Jacinto River and delivered a crushing defeat to Santa Anna's army.

It lived in the heart of a country boy from Brady—James Earl Rudder '32—who would lead a group of Army Rangers up the hundred-foot cliffs at Pointe du Hoc on D-Day—June 6, 1944.

With each new generation, a new verse is written, and the same chorus is echoed. When our nation calls, Aggies answer. When freedom is jeopardized, Aggies fight. And, when danger draws near, Aggies run to the sound of guns!

On the Austin memorial that bears the names of dozens of Texas Aggies—the Korean War Memorial—there are four simple profound words chiseled into its face—"FREEDOM IS NOT FREE."

In the sunken hull of a ship called *Arizona*—in a quiet field overlooking Omaha Beach—in hundreds of places of burial where white crosses and Stars of David line up, the remains of the war dead rest in eternal peace, telling all who will listen—"freedom is not free."

In the dawn of their lives, and at the calling of their nation, they sacrificed their dreams for ours.

They loved freedom so much that they were willing to pay any price, bear any burden for it.

During two World Wars and in Korea, Vietnam, the Persian Gulf, Aggies have paid that price by answering the call of duty.

In the tragedy that befell this nation on September the 11th, three more would give their lives as terrorists inflicted unprecedented harm.

Texas A&M would also play a critical role in training the members of Texas Task Force One, who participated in search and rescue at Ground Zero.

In chapter and verse, page after page, the story of Texas A&M tells of men and women who have answered the high calling of service to their fellow man.

And the greatest measures of that sacrifice are the names etched in brass on memorials to the dead. Each stands as a tribute to enduring love, and they collectively speak of the great legacy of sacrifice.

During times of conflict, Texas A&M has sacrificed one thousand, one hundred and ninety-one of its own.

One of those names is that of Joe Bush. Joe Bush preceded me as a yell leader by six years.

When the traveling rendition of the Vietnam Wall recently came to Austin, I went one day to see it and to find his name. On the grass below, I placed a piece of Corps brass.

I think about the great pleasures in life that Joe Bush would not experience: the blessing of growing old with someone he loved—seeing his daughter, Robin, graduate from this institution—the opportunity to live in peace and prosperity.

He traded that one tragic day—February 10th, 1969—so a child in Southeast Asia could live in freedom.

I believe Alfred Lord Tennyson was writing about men like Joe Bush when he asked the question, "When can their glory fade?"

One thousand, one hundred, ninety-one brave souls who once walked this campus . . . who once studied in these buildings . . . who once had dreams of a full life, and of growing old—when can their glory fade?

We who live in freedom today have but one answer. NEVER!

Theirs was the greatest gift—but they gave it so you and I would not have to. So my question to the current students here today—the "Keepers of the Spirit"—is this: What will be your gift to this world?

Will you rejuvenate the life of a child from a broken home as a teacher or a mentor? Will you work in a lab searching for the cure for a deadly disease, or on a new gene therapy that will change lives?

Will you serve your neighbors and community as a police officer, a firefighter, or a volunteer at a soup kitchen?

Will you serve your country by proudly wearing the uniform of our armed forces? Will you serve in public office, or take an active role in a community of faith?

By attending this great university, you have been afforded the opportunity of a lifetime and the chance to make a meaningful impact on the world around you.

In an era when we are told to "Look out for number one," Texas A&M teaches you a very different lesson: Look out for others.

In a world full of takers, Aggies are called to be givers.

As you seek success, do not misplace your sense of wealth. Prosperity in the absence of virtue is emptiness.

The nicest house on the block, a sports car, a large bank account— they are all poor substitutes for fulfillment. Living well means making a difference.

How do you know if you've got the right stuff? How do you know you've got the stuff it takes to live up to the Aggie legacy? Well, ask yourselves a few questions.

When the lights on the campus go dark, and Silver Taps is played, does it still bring chills?

When you join 80,000 strong at Kyle Field in a rendition of the "Spirit of Aggieland," do the eyes still mist over?

When you think about that tragic November—that morning in 1999, does your heart still ache? [This is a reference to the collapse of the Texas A&M Bonfire in which twelve Aggies were killed.]

When you hear the words of the Aggie Code of Honor, does it remain a sacred covenant in your heart?

And, if you ever lose faith—if it ever becomes a climb that's just too steep—if hope has all vanished, and your will is weak—look for inspiration from the Hall of Aggie Heroes Past.

You see, they too had doubts—they too wondered if their lives or their deaths would make a meaningful difference. They too suffered failures and pains. But they never gave up. Aggies never do.

We fight on to the last—we honor our state and nation—we live and breathe to make this world a better place—and we always remember who we are, and where we come from.

Because "We are the Aggies, the Aggies are we." And may it ever be!

Thank you, God bless you, and God bless Texas A&M.

# Edwin H. Cooper '53

*2003—Reed Arena*

Ed Cooper '53. Photo from editor's collection.

Edwin Hanson Cooper was born September 3, 1930, in Hays County. Upon graduation from Texas A&M, he served two years of active duty in the US Army's 2nd Armored Division, including service in Germany. He was assistant county agricultural agent for Travis County and a specialist in wildlife conservation for the Texas Agricultural Extension Service. He was a special assistant to Texas A&M presidents J. Earl Rudder and Jack K. Williams; A&M's director of Civilian Student Services; and director of admissions.

On September 1, 1972, Cooper was appointed Texas A&M University's dean of admissions and records. During his fifteen years in this position, he signed diplomas for 90,121 graduating students.

On June 1, 1987, he was appointed director of A&M's Office of School Relations, responsible for the university's undergraduate recruiting program. He took a leadership role in establishing the University Outreach Program. He served as coordinator of special projects in the Office of University Relations for three years before retiring from Texas A&M after thirty-seven years of service.

With former *Texas Parks and Wildlife* magazine chief photographer Leroy Williamson, he established Cooper-Williamson, a freelance writing and photography firm. He also spoke professionally on topics ranging from Texas Hill Country humor to setting priorities in life. In 2002 he published *How Life Stacks Up*, stories and observations gleaned from his life experiences, and in 2013 he published *Forty Years at Aggieland*.

# Manifestations of Spirit*

President Gates, when my colleagues and I in the Class of '53 were students, there was something we called "Old Army." And now we are Old Army.

Being here with you tonight is one of the finest honors I've ever had. I appreciate it.

Texas A&M was born in 1876 while US Grant was President of the United States. It was the year Alexander Graham Bell invented a ridiculous contraption called the telephone.

In his local history of A&M College, Austin E. Burgess, Class of 1915, tells of conditions on campus in early days, and I quote:

> The campus was such a wild waste that it was not considered safe for children to be out at night. The howling wolves furnished every night—and all night—a scary serenade. On one occasion a wild animal wandering over the campus threw the whole community into a frenzy of excitement. An alarm was given, and the whole battalion of some thirty students and professors (Imagine that—the professors) turned out for the hunt, but in the high weeds of the campus the beast easily escaped. We learn from other sources that deer were frequently seen on the campus, and that wolves sometimes stuck their noses in the door of what was then used as the mess hall.

1876 was also the year Aggie Spirit had its birth. It was born of toughness. Tents provided the only housing. Students had their own axes to cut wood for their wood stoves. There was only lantern light for study. Long drills and fistfights occurred to settle differences and to command discipline. With newborn spirit, toward the end of that year, the wolves sniffing around the mess hall simply meant that the cooks were doing something spectacular for dinner. The feelings of terror were gone.

To survive under such conditions, you had to have a few good friends. People you could lean on when the going got rough and tough—and to

*Speech title derived by editor from speech contents

celebrate with when occasional good times were had. And someone to stand beside you with emotion when traditions began to emerge.

Aggie Spirit is built on traditions that seem to grow in power as time goes by. Physical challenges have been replaced with academic and other types of challenges. Spirit is all inclusive. Whoever you are at Aggieland, wherever you are from, you are welcome to join the world's greatest fraternity, bonded simply by Spirit. It is as real as life itself.

Primarily because of this Spirit—while at A&M and in life ever after—there is an intense desire among Aggies to do things right, and with vigor. Because of this, the world has a high level of expectancy about A&M and its Aggies. When things don't go right, there is shock and disappointment. It makes the headlines.

Let me share with you four brief manifestations of Spirit which shall always linger in my mind:

First of all, have you ever heard of Florence, Texas? It's just south of Killeen and in the golden triangle created by Oakalla, Prairie Dell, and Andice. Now you know where it is.

Eli Whiteley '41 was from Florence, Texas. In World War II, he served as a first lieutenant, US Army in the 3rd Infantry Division, at Sigolsheim, France. He earned the Medal of Honor, and he was one of seven Aggies to win that high award. His citation reads:

> While leading his platoon on 27 December 1944, in savage house-to-house fighting through the fortress town of Sigolsheim, France, he attacked a building through a street swept by withering mortar and automatic weapons fire. He was hit and severely wounded in the arm and shoulder; but he charged into the house alone and killed its 2 defenders. Hurling smoke and fragmentation grenades before him, he reached the next house and stormed inside, killing [2] and capturing 11 of the enemy. He continued leading his platoon . . . until he reached a building held by fanatical Nazi troops. Although suffering from wounds which had rendered his left arm useless, he advanced on this strongly defended house, and after blasting out a wall with bazooka fire, charged through a hail of bullets. Wedging his submachine gun under his uninjured arm, he rushed into the house through the hole torn by his rockets, killed 5 of the enemy and forced the remaining 12 to surrender. As he emerged to con-

tinue his fearless attack, he was again hit and critically wounded. In agony and with one eye pierced by a shell fragment, he shouted for his men to follow him to the next house. He was determined to stay in the fighting, and remained at the head of his platoon until forcibly evacuated.

A manifestation of spirit plus other mysterious forces overtook Lt. Whiteley, possessing a feeling against all odds. He became a quiet, gentle professor of agronomy on this campus. The first day I met him, I noticed that one eye was artificial. I didn't ask him why, and he didn't tell me why.

Dr. Gates, those members of the Class of '53 assembled before you tonight entered the Agricultural and Mechanical College of Texas in September 1949, having been admitted under these strict requirements: Must be at least 16 years of age. Must have graduated from high school. Must be free of infectious and contagious diseases. We came in quickly because we heard that the next year they were going to require that we be able to read, write and do simple arithmetic.

Had the admissions staff adhered strictly to those requirements, the group before you tonight would be much smaller, and you would likely have a different Muster speaker.

They assigned our entire fish class to a year of hard duty at Bryan Air Force Base, which had been closed in 1946 due to lack of a war. Our campus was called "The Annex." They lovingly refer to it now as the Riverside Campus. We didn't even know a river was there.

My classmates and I remember the fall of 1949 as the time when 100 was the magic number. The temperature was 100. The humidity was 100. We recorded 100 inches of rain, or so it seemed. And the laundry staff—I guess they were mad at us—doubled up on starch, causing us to fear that our uniforms would break apart if dropped.

Twenty of those gentlemen out there and I were assigned to Barracks T-161, a structure we will never forget. Once we glanced inside that tar-paper structure when we were moving in, we posted guards at the doors—there were only two doors—to prevent our parents and girlfriends from peeking inside that dismal place, for fear of immediate transfer to another school.

Tough as it appeared, the 20 of us decided to give this new life a try.

Not one student in T-161 owned a car. We were stranded six miles from the exotic nightlife of downtown Bryan and couldn't even get there. Bugle calls over the PA system signaled us when to arise, when to eat, when to be quiet so we could study at night and when to sleep. After a full day of classes, 100 of us practiced and marched as members of the Aggie Fish Band. Those exercises began to establish close friendships and reliance upon one another.

If we didn't march too well, Col. Adams, the band director, would simply take our mouthpiece and say, "Cooper, when you learn to march, I'll give you your mouthpiece back." So, we learned to march.

The same feelings we had in the Fish Band magically arose across the Annex. The toughness of life there became a challenging joke we began to take in stride, along with a certain amount of pride. Our Aggie Spirit was born.

And though we may have been academically challenged due to less than stringent admission requirements, the Class of 1953 Remembrance that you just listened to indicates that in life after college, there was a degree of success achieved. I can only conclude that the special love and admiration we developed for this school and for each other—somehow inspired pride and accomplishment throughout our lives. This class is another manifestation of spirit.

And then, memorable words from President James Earl Rudder— whose challenge to all was "commitment": "For Aggies, the difficult we do immediately; the impossible takes a bit longer."

About moving the president's home to the south side of the campus, facing east, in 1965, he said: "The sun will shine on A&M every day, and I want to be the first one to see it." He saw that sunshine and directed this University toward excellence at every level.

Then, from Randy Matson's Muster speech in the year 2000:

> I remember how in 1968 at the Olympics in Mexico City, I received a telegram with 5,000 names on it from the student body of Texas A&M. I remember carrying that telegram in my bag on the field in case I needed it for encouragement. The athletes from other schools couldn't believe that the students here would do something like

that, but I told them, "It's nice, but you don't have to go back and face those 5,000 Aggies if you lose!"

Also, I might add that the last person I saw in the stands as we marched onto the field to compete was General Earl Rudder, President of Texas A&M, and he didn't say, "Good luck." He said, "Win!" And when he told you to do something, you tried very hard to do it.

My wife and I were there, and we saw him win the gold medal—one of the big thrills of our lives. I was standing right beside General Rudder trying to take a picture of that handshake. A manifestation of spirit with commitment from one great Aggie to another.

My fourth manifestation of spirit—In 1985, General O. R. Simpson, Class of 1936, was the campus Muster speaker. Listen to his challenging words:

> . . . being a Texas Aggie . . . starts with a set of standards—surely not the same for everyone—but all with a common thrust. This includes many things.
>
> Among them:
>
> You are aggressive and play to win, but you never cheat—not yourself, not the other person, not the organization.
>
> You have a wholesome respect for others and for their personal dignity.
>
> You accord this respect not only to your friends but to acquaintances and indeed to all with whom you deal, even though some, by their actions, may not seem to warrant it.
>
> You work as long and as hard as is necessary to get the job done, not only to the complete satisfaction of your superiors but to your own. You do not recognize an "8-to-5 syndrome."
>
> You are confident without being cocky, proud without being arrogant, competent without being overbearing, considerate but never subservient, steadfast but not stubborn, humble in victory, gracious in defeat.
>
> You are imaginative and creative. You are not afraid to leave the crowd and make your way alone if the rewards are those that you really want and the odds of gaining them are reasonable. If you stumble and fall, you don't look for someone else to blame. Rather, you pick yourself up and carry on.

You are always your own person—never anyone else's.

... All this is summed up in a single word—integrity!

I believe integrity is the basic building block for the Aggie Spirit in any real Texas Aggie.

Being a Texas Aggie is not of the flesh—but of the spirit. In a very real sense, it is a "state of mind."

So now I have shared with you four manifestations of spirit which I cherish: Eli Whiteley, the Class of 1953, President Earl Rudder, and General Ormond Simpson, US Marine Corps, Retired.

To the honored families and friends of those whose names will be called tonight, I propose these thoughts for you: Perhaps Muster is the defining moment in the long maroon line of spirited tradition. Muster binds us together in ways that only members of the Aggie family can understand and comprehend.

At this particular Muster, a beloved member of your family or a dear friend is being remembered, both in joy and in somber dignity. It is my hope that during this sacred ceremony, the arms of Aggie love will embrace you as never before. And that it will be an experience so touching that its memory will never diminish.

This evening when the roll is called for our departed Aggies, someone will answer "here" for each name called. This signifies that their presence is felt, perhaps more strongly than ever before. It means that in no way will they ever be forgotten by family, classmates or friends. And it means their Aggie Spirit will endure forever—along with that of all here tonight.

May God continue to bless each of us, this magnificent University, our leaders and the United States of America!

Thank you.

# Jon L. Hagler '58

*2004—Reed Arena*

Jon L. Hagler '58. Photo from editor's collection.

Jon Lewis Hagler was born May 28, 1936, in Harlingen, Texas, and graduated from Texas A&M University in 1958 with a BS degree in agricultural economics. As a student at Texas A&M, he was active in a number of student organizations; he was a Distinguished Student, a Ross Volunteer, and the cadet colonel of the Corps of Cadets. From 1958 to 1963, Hagler served as an artillery officer in the US Army. Following his service to our nation, his education continued at Harvard University, where he received a master's degree in business administration. He was named a Distinguished Alumnus of Texas A&M in 1999 and inducted into the Corps of Cadets Hall of Honor in 2003.

After graduate school, Hagler entered the investment management business. He was an executive officer of a large mutual fund complex, helped to found two independent investment firms, and served as chief investment officer of the Ford Foundation. He is a partner in the investment firm Grantham, Mayo, Van Otterloo & Co., LLC, in Boston. He has also served on the boards of several other firms and organizations.

Hagler has served Texas A&M University as a co-chair of both the Vision 2020 Executive Committee and Advisory Council, a board member of the Association of Former Students, and was named trustee emeritus of the Texas A&M Foundation. Jon and his wife, Jo Ann, were the lead donors to the headquarters of the Texas A&M Foundation, which is named in his honor. His contribution to the Foundation Excellence Award Scholarship program provided scholarships for 100 freshmen at Texas A&M University. He was also co-chair of the foundation's One Spirit One Vision campaign.

## "The Spirit's the Thing"

I want to begin by expressing my thanks to the student Muster Committee for inviting me to be tonight's speaker. It is a great privilege for me, and I hope that I will not disappoint them. And let me be the first to thank members of the Muster Committee publicly for all your work to ensure that the great tradition of Muster remains strong.

As I tried to prepare this speech, I also wanted to thank the members of the Muster Committee for their many letters of encouragement, and the staff of the Association of Former Students—the organization that has done so much and has been so important to the Muster tradition and involved in so many other good works on this campus—for the card signed by all of you.

Finally, I must pay tribute to the 50th Reunion Class of 1954. Congratulations on all you have accomplished and on your support for A&M. I could make a remark about how you taught the three classes that preceded me to instruct us in humility, but I won't.

We live in trying times, and this is a solemn gathering. However, George Bernard Shaw once said that "life does not cease to be funny when people die, any more than it ceases to be serious when people laugh."

So, I wanted to share a story about a Marine stationed in Afghanistan who recently received a "Dear John" letter from his girlfriend back home. It read as follows:

Dear Richard,

I can no longer continue our relationship. The distance between us is just too great. I must admit that I've cheated on you twice since you have gone, and that's not fair to either of us. I'm sorry. Please return the picture of me that I sent you.

Love,
Nancy

The Marine, with hurt feelings, asked his fellow Marines for any pictures they could spare of their sisters, girlfriends, ex-girlfriends, aunts, cousins, etc. In addition to the picture of Nancy, Richard included all the other pictures he had collected from his buddies. There were 57 photos in the envelope along with this note:

Dear Nancy,

I'm so sorry, but I can't quite remember who you are. Please take your picture from the pile and send the rest back to me.

Take care,
Richard

This day, of course, has special significance for the Texas A&M family. It is, in these words from *Softly Call the Muster* by John A. Adams Jr. '73: "a time-honored day of reflection and celebration of those initiatives and gallant acts that have made Texas and America a place of independence, freedom, and peace." It is also, of course, a celebration of the lives of those we've lost and the fellowship of the entire Aggie family; a day of remembrance, of reverence for life, and of re-experiencing the Spirit of Aggieland.

I won't spend much time on the history of Muster, since the Muster Committee has done an outstanding job illuminating that. I will begin in 1946, after the conclusion of the greatest war in my lifetime and perhaps the greatest of all time—so horrific that it is estimated that probably some 45 to 50 million people lost their lives. In 1946, Aggie Muster was held in Kyle Field as part of a three-day Victory Homecoming celebration of banquets and reunions. The Muster speaker in 1946 was the Supreme Allied Commander in World War II and future President of the United States, General of the Army Dwight Eisenhower. It was Eisenhower's first stateside speech after the war, a clear tribute, in Eisenhower's words, to the "magnificent contribution made by A&M" in gaining the Allied victory in 1945. In case you have forgotten, A&M provided more officers in World War II than any other college, university, or service academy in America.

So, as we gather again today in remembrance and reflection of all Aggies who are no longer with us, it is entirely fitting that we celebrate the bravery, the dedication, and the selfless devotion to duty exhibited by those lost in battle. They were certainly true to the Spirit of Aggieland.

Each of us has our own understanding of the Spirit, depending on when we were here or those circumstances which caused us to find it. My understanding of the Spirit may vary from yours. Perhaps we have also encouraged a notion that the Spirit is something unexplainable to others, or even to ourselves. Tonight, I wish to give you one old man's thoughts on the roots of the Spirit.

On the opening day of this university in October of 1876, Governor Richard Coke committed Texas A&M, the first public university in this state, to "the cause of a liberal, scientific, and practical education." He also said this to those assembled on that day:

> Let your watchword be duty, and know no other talisman of success than labor. Let honor be your guiding star in your dealings with your superiors, your fellows, with all. Be true to a trust reposed as the needle to the pole. Stand by the right even to the sacrifice of life itself, and learn that death is preferable to dishonor.

And so, on the very first day of this place, the foundation was laid for the Spirit of Aggieland. A great education—liberal, scientific, and practical. Duty. Labor. Honor. True to a trust reposed. Stand by right, even to death.

This Spirit of Aggieland is the heritage of all Aggies. It is an elemental force, because it asserts such elemental and fundamental values. It applies to those in the Corps and to those not in the Corps. One hundred percent of the respondents to the feasibility study for the current *One Spirit, One Vision* capital campaign said that the Aggie Spirit was either "important" or "very important" in their lives.

Governor Coke gave us a good charter. He understood this was an educational institution. He didn't say anything about political beliefs. He didn't say anything about religious beliefs. And he added those elements which should distinguish all of our graduates: Duty. Labor. Honor. Trustworthiness. Stand for what's right even if the consequences are severe.

These words are beacons of insight into the Aggie Spirit today just as they were in 1876. The need for graduates who exhibit those characteristics is certainly no less today than it was in 1876.

The uniqueness of Texas A&M is its Spirit. In addition to our demanding academic programs, our large student body, and a heavy involvement in research, teaching and service, we are the ones who also have "a Spirit that can ne'er be told."

To repeat myself: The Spirit begins with a commitment to the enhancement of the lives of students and graduates with the multiple benefits of a good education. A good education should help one earn a living, but it should also help make us better citizens and help us to master ourselves as the challenges of life unfold. The uniqueness of the Spirit is the uniqueness of Texas A&M; both are about all three of these elements.

We celebrate our history and we value our traditions, as we should. Yet today this university is much more than those early wonderful and important stories of courage, sacrifice, camaraderie, duty, commitment, and tradition. We have among our 43,000 students some 600 National Merit scholars, over 3,000 students from over 100 nations, and roughly the same level of research as the very best universities in the country. We offer about 100 undergraduate and about 235 graduate or professional degrees, and we have nationally ranked programs in Education, Business, Engineering, Agriculture, Chemistry, Geosciences, and Nautical Archeology.

There are many examples of this University's production of citizens and leaders. Given our history, the easiest statistics to come by are those of our graduates in the armed forces. About 9,000 Aggies served, and almost 1,000 died in World War II. The sons and daughters of this proud university have continued to answer the call to service in all subsequent wars. Some 4,000 Aggies served in Vietnam. The last time I looked, there were about 50 pages of messages and pictures from Aggies in Iraq on the AggieNetwork.com, and about 150 pages of messages of support from those at home.

I'm told that, in total, almost 1,200 Aggies have died in the service of their country. And already we know that Captain Ernesto Blanco-Caldas '98 and first lieutenants Jonathan Rozier '01 and Doyle Hufstedler III '01 have made the ultimate sacrifice in Iraq for their beliefs, on our behalf.

The Aggie family has also produced seven winners of the Congressional Medal of Honor, ten Aggie Aces, 224 general officers, and six four-star generals. And, of course, our reach has broadened far beyond the military. We have [produced] and are producing educators and architects, engineers and agriculturalists, college presidents, chancellors, and provosts, Congressmen, Governors, Mayors, and captains of industry. Perhaps most importantly, we are producing leaders in communities all across America. No one can ever doubt that the Spirit includes a commitment to citizenship.

There is a large element of leadership in all of this citizenship. The Spirit has always asked us to get beyond ourselves and our selfish interests and be true leaders. That's what you should expect from the graduates of a great land-grant university.

The Spirit says mastering ourselves is the key to meeting the never-ending challenges of life. It asks us to take responsibility for ourselves and our actions. That is a prerequisite to true leadership. It asks us to value humility and to despise hubris. It asks us to take the time to discern right from wrong, to think independently, and then to do something about it—to be willing to follow our conscience.

The Spirit also tells us that this should be a welcoming place for all, no matter the wealth of their parents, the color of their skin, their ethnic background, or the locale of their origin. It was the Spirit, I believe, that provided the environment for my friend Hector Gutierrez to become the first Hispanic Corps Commander in 1969, thirty-five years ago, and for my friend Fred McClure to become the first black person to become President of our student body almost 30 years ago.

But I think that the real story of the Spirit is that it is about character and integrity. These are two unchanging constants in an ever-changing world. Character and integrity are behind the correlations of Aggies to citizenship and leadership.

Because we are concerned about character and integrity, we are always trying to get better. Of course, mastering growth and change is not an easy challenge. I am sure you appreciate the inherent tension between valuing our traditions and respecting the past, yet being able to embrace change that is good for the institution. Let me illustrate with the words of a former A&M President:

I do not believe every student who enters this institution should be required to take military science. . . . The sooner this fact is realized by the governing authorities of this institution, the better it will be for the cause of education in Texas.

The Board of Directors has seen fit to exclude all women from this institution. . . . I am convinced that coeducation is preferable.

You probably think I'm quoting Earl Rudder. No, these are the words of departing President W. B. Bizzell in 1925.

Earl Rudder has a unique and admired place in A&M history for many reasons. The most important, in my opinion, were his character as an individual and the fact that it was his administration that finally accomplished coeducation and a non-compulsory Corps for A&M, almost 40 years after Bizzell's letter.

Rudder valued what we had been and what we are, but he also had a willingness—a determination, in fact, to embrace change for the good of the institution. In his history of our university, Henry Dethloff said this: "Rudder restructured, revitalized, and revolutionized the institution. He built a university where a college had been."

Rudder understood that the Spirit includes a commitment to try to do the right thing, even if it is not comfortable. He knew that we needed coeducation and a non-compulsory Corps to fulfill our great land-grant educational mission. He was at odds with a large component of our former students at that time who felt we served our mission and tradition best by remaining the same—all male and all military. We were at a crossroads; our potential for becoming a better educational institution was at stake.

We now find ourselves at another crossroads. As we have grown from under 10,000 students to over 40,000, the level of support from the state has diminished sharply, especially in the last decade. This has led to larger and larger class sizes, difficulty in retaining our best faculty, and a relative deterioration in our physical plant.

Vision 2020 is, in my judgement, our generation's response to the challenges of change.

In the fall of 1997, confronting these realities, President Ray Bowen proposed—in the tradition of Earl Rudder—that we adopt a new goal, a vision of striving "to be one of ten best public universities in the nation by the year 2020, while at the same time maintaining and enhancing our distinctiveness."

I want to read that to you again. That's the goal of Vision 2020, "to be one of the ten best public universities in the nation by the year 2020, while at the same time maintaining and enhancing our distinctiveness."

Very early in 1998, President Bowen asked me to serve as Co-Chair of the undertaking. For the next eighteen months, the two of us and about 250 other people worked hard to develop Vision 2020. The report we produced has effectively been the "case statement" the university is using to raise $1 billion of private funding for A&M; so far I'm told as of this morning, we have commitments for about $750 million.

Some have questioned whether Vision 2020 means the end of A&M's uniqueness. Some worry that we are trying to mimic Berkeley or Harvard. As one who worked hard on Vision 2020, attended every meeting, helped to write and rewrite the final report, I think I know what Vision 2020 is and what is in the report. It is an ambitious vision of some things we can do to get better at our mission without impairing that which is unique about this institution. "Creating a culture of excellence" is the subtitle of the report. This is a report about how to strengthen the institution and the Spirit, not diminish either.

Let me just read six of the twelve imperatives of Vision 2020:

> Improve our faculty.
>
> Enhance our undergraduate education.
>
> Enrich our campus.
>
> Demand enlightened governance and leadership.
>
> Attain resource parity with the best public universities.
>
> Meet our commitment to Texas.

Those are not conspiratorial efforts to undermine the Spirit of Aggieland, they are assertions that the Spirit deserves increased efforts to overcome declining state support and still get better.

Vision 2020 is about this institution's commitment to the enhancement of the lives of students and graduates with the multiple benefits of a great education. Vision 2020 is about finding new and better ways of making our graduates not only well-educated individuals but whole people, capable of demonstrating for the rest of their lives the balance and leadership which the Spirit has always been about. Read the report. Pay special attention to the section on "Core Values." I think you will find it reassuring if you want the Spirit to remain a vital part of the mission of this university. We are very fortunate to have Bob Gates as Ray Bowen's successor; Bob is bringing enlightened, tough-minded and effective leadership to our university—as today's news about a new $100 million academic facility for interdisciplinary life-sciences amply demonstrates.

Our distinctiveness is the Spirit, and the Spirit has always been about education and character and leadership and integrity and honor and citizenship. It was in our early years, and it is today. And I believe that if all of us who are associated with this great university in one way or another can live up to the Spirit, then the Spirit will live on forever. It will always inspire great loyalty, but it will always be loyalty with honor. And, we will not only continue but enhance our position as one of the most distinctive educational institutions in America.

I mentioned earlier the neat letters I have received from the Muster Committee members. One of them—from Grady Wier '04—commented on how fast the year was passing and that he was beginning to believe that "it is really true when people say the older you get, the faster the years pass by." Grady then went on to say, inexplicably, "I assume that the years in your life are going by extremely slow since you are still so very young." Thanks, Grady, for trying to cheer me up!

Actually, my reflections in preparation for this evening have inevitably increased my sense of the passage of time. I enrolled as a freshman here 50 years ago this fall. "Bear" Bryant had just become our football coach when I arrived, and Earl Rudder had just taken up residence when I departed. Not even a resilient optimist like me can mistake half a century for a short interlude.

I am honored, and have always been honored, to be a part of the Texas A&M family. I feel extremely privileged to have had the opportunity to work in a variety of capacities for this great institution. I treasure the many friends and acquaintances I have met because of this university. And I pledge to those Aggies who have passed on this past year to hold the Spirit dear for the rest of my days and to continue to do every constructive thing I can to sustain and nourish it.

I hope you do not think it is impertinent of me to ask each of you here tonight to do the same.

Thank you, and softly call the Muster.

# Clayton Williams Jr. '54

## 2005—Reed Arena

Clayton Williams Jr. '54.
Photo from editor's
collection.

Clayton Wheat Williams Jr. '54 was born October 8, 1931, in Alpine in the Big Bend country of southwestern Texas and reared in his father's hometown, Fort Stockton. He graduated from Texas A&M University with a degree in animal husbandry and then served in the US Army.

Starting in 1957 as a lease broker in the West Texas oil fields, Williams drilled his first successful oil well two years later and established a series of companies involved in the exploration and production of natural gas and the transportation and extraction of natural gas and natural gas liquids. In 1987, when he sold Clajon, it was one of the largest privately owned gas pipeline companies in Texas. In 1993 Clayton Williams Energy, Inc., went public. He also moved into farming, ranching, real estate, and banking, as well as long-distance telecommunications. For six years he taught entrepreneurship classes in Texas A&M's College of Business Administration.

Williams founded the Chihuahuan Desert Research Institute. He underwrote a significant portion of the Clayton W. Williams Jr. Alumni Center at Texas A&M, was a founding member of the President's Endowed Scholarship program, and was a vice president of the Association of Former Students. In 1981 he was named a Distinguished Alumnus of Texas A&M, and he was inducted into the Corps of Cadets Hall of Honor in 1998.

In 1990, as the Republican nominee for governor of Texas, Williams narrowly lost the general election. His brief political career and his long-term commitment to the oil and gas industry, cattle ranching, and the communications business was chronicled in Mike Cochran's 2007 biography, *Claytie: The Roller-Coaster Life of a Texas Wildcatter.*

## Texas A&M Is Unique*

Howdy! . . . Come on! Howdy!

Kim, thank you so much. What a pleasure to be with these kids.

Fact is, we had a great football team at Fort Stockton. I played fullback and strong side linebacker in the single wing. They think about the Fort Stockton Panthers, "They're small but, boy, they're slow." The record wasn't all that bad. Our record was 5 and 5. We lost 5 at home and we lost 5 on the road. I guess it's not how many times you're knocked down. It's how many times you get back up that counts.

Kim also mentioned that I've had some success in business, meaning ranches, oil, gas, real estate, communications and so on. Not long ago a reporter asked me, "Mr. Williams, how do you manage to run your companies?" I said, "Well, it's not complicated. I run my companies like Christopher Columbus."

"Christopher Columbus?"

"Yes. Do you remember, when he left Spain, he didn't know where he was going. When he got over here, he didn't know where he was. When he went back to Spain, he didn't know where he'd been. And he did it all on borrowed money."

That's the way it goes.

One other thing I must share with you. When Jack Fritts '53 and some of the former students came to Midland and asked me, would I help with the alumni building, I felt honored and flattered and got emotional and started tearing up. I accepted, delightfully. And at that time oil was $28 a barrel. In 1987, the last big payment came due; oil was $10 a barrel, and I started crying again.

President [Robert] Gates, we thank you so much for your leadership, your courage, your vision. We're glad you're here.

General [John] Van Alstyne ['66], thank you for your leadership of the Corps of Cadets. Thank you and [Joseph H.] "Doc" Mills for your

---

*Speech title derived by editor from speech contents

research and your help with this talk I'm making tonight. And I say to the 2005 Muster Committee, it's been a delight being with you kids.

Singing Cadets, it's always great to have you. You were great in Midland, and you were better tonight.

I see the Class of '55 is here tonight and looking well. I extend congratulations from the Class of '54 for having made it now for 50 years after graduation. It's obvious we trained you well, or you would've never made it this far. I extend special greetings to the family of my friend Gordon Tate '55.

Of course, when I was a student here, my best grades were not in English. But, one thing my English prof did tell me has stuck with me to this day: One thing—the word "unique." There's no such thing as very unique, or sort of unique, or extremely unique, or kind of unique. Something either is or it is not unique. In all the world, there is no other word like unique.

Well, let me tell you, friends, Texas A&M . . . is . . . unique.

In defending that claim, let me tell you why Texas A&M is NOT unique.

It's not unique because it has great teaching facilities.

It's not unique because it has a great research program.

It's not unique because it has a fine faculty.

It's not unique because it has a football team or a large football stadium.

No: Texas A&M is unique because of the way we feel toward each other, the way we feel about our school—unique in the pride we feel about ourselves.

It is particularly unique because of these traditions that we have carried forward for so many, many years. We Aggies celebrate and maintain our uniqueness. And Texas A&M is unique because of the way its graduates have served this state, this nation, this school, and our fellow Aggies.

Aggie Muster is not just one of those traditions; it is our greatest tradition! It is one of the highest honors of my life to have been invited to speak at this campus Muster. I offer my sincerest thanks to the Muster Committee. These kids are really neat. You have paid me a compliment greater than you know.

Muster has come a long way since the early days of the A&M College, when cadets first gathered at the San Jacinto battlefield where we gained our independence from Mexico. It has continued to grow and evolve over the years.

While growth and evolution are often necessary for traditions to remain relevant, I would ask you not to become focused on the event of Muster, or the process of Muster. I would ask you to focus on the meaning of Muster. Meaning sometimes is lost as a tradition grows. I ask you to focus on what's the heart of Muster. Because the heart of Muster is the heart of Texas A&M, and the heart of the Aggie experience.

To really understand the meaning of Muster, let's look back at its origin. The word "muster" is a military term meaning to assemble a military unit; to bring its members together to fight in some emergency. For most of our history, America did not maintain a large standing army. It relied instead on raising of state militias to meet whatever emergency faced the pioneers and the settlers as the years go forward. In the Revolutionary War, we had the minutemen to face the British. To face Indians, we called in the Texas Rangers. Citizen-soldiers have been called on in our history to form their units to muster. The muster roll would be read.

Our Muster evolved from this tradition, but with a uniquely Aggie modification. The annual calling of the roll at our muster remembers all those who have departed our ranks.

And therein lies the key to what Aggie Muster is really all about. It's about people. It's about our heart. It's about remembering.

When we call the names of the departed, we remember them as individuals and as Aggies. We honor their contributions to our lives— and to Texas A&M. While we may not have known them personally, we say "here" for them in our heart because they will always be part of the heritage of Texas A&M. As these names of others' sons, daughters, mothers, and fathers are called, I ask you to think of our own sons, daughters, mothers, fathers and, yes, even our grandparents.

At the same time, Muster can be a very personal and individualized experience for each of us, because it gives us the opportunity to recall those Aggies who have had a great and direct part and a beneficial effect on our lives, but who are now among the departed.

This year, my thoughts are with all those Aggies who are defending freedom around the globe. I think of other Aggies I have known—

Aggies who are personal heroes to me and who have fought for freedom. As I think of their names and I look back, I form my own personal Muster list to be added in my heart to the names that will be read later tonight.

I'd like to share my personal list with you. And, as I do so, I ask each of you to join with me in answering "here" as I call their names.

First, an artilleryman who fought in France in World War I—my dad, Clayton Williams, Class of 1915. I say, "Here."

Next, an Aggie who shared the misery of those World War I trenches, who gave us the "Aggie War Hymn"—J. V. "Pinky" Wilson, Class of 1920. I say, "Here."

Another soldier who fought in both World War I and World War II, and whose muster on Corregidor was the impetus for the worldwide Muster tradition—Major General George Moore, Class of 1908. I say, "Here."

Many Aggies served in World War II, and many were heroes. This soldier, one of seven Medal of Honor recipients, added to the mystique of the Aggie Ring when, almost 60 years later, his class ring was returned to A&M from the German battlefield where he fell—Lieutenant Turney Leonard, Class of 1942. I say, "Here."

While there were many Aggie heroes in World War II, none left a greater heritage than this one; the commander of the Rangers who scaled the heights of Pointe du Hoc during the battle of Normandy D-Day Invasion. The President of A&M who opened the gates to our future—Major General James Earl Rudder, Class of 1932. I say, "Here."

In the Korean War, we lost a great yell leader and an outstanding role model who I looked up to as an underclassman—Lieutenant Lew Jobe, Class of 1952. I say, "Here."

I think of two Aggies whose remains were recently returned from Vietnam after so many years—Captain Carl Long, Class of 1966, and Lieutenant Donald Matocha, Class of 1967. I say, "Here."

When I think of Aggies who served in Vietnam, I think of my roommate. Bravery, Courage, 10 helicopters coming in under fire to land their troops. The first seven were shot down. My roommate was number 8, the first to successfully land in that battle—Major Jack E. Custer, Class of 1954. I say, "Here."

And my cowboy horse trader, hard-of-hearing best friend—Lieutenant Marion Baugh, Class of 1967. I say, "Here."

Aggies maintained their record of outstanding service in the Persian Gulf War. Three did not come home—Major Richard Price, Class of 1974; Lieutenant Daniel Hull, Class of 1981; and Captain Thomas Bland, Jr., Class of 1986. I say, "Here."

And the Aggie tradition of service continues. Four Aggies have been killed in Southwest Asia and Iraq since the last Muster. Their names will be called later tonight.

These Aggies on my personal list, and so many, many more, have left us a legacy of service and courage that continues to this day. As we gather here tonight, the tree of liberty is again being nourished by the blood of patriots. To remain free and independent and to bring the sacred blessings of freedom and democracy to others half a world away, America once again battles a deadly and committed enemy. And, as in the past, the extensive use of the National Guard and Reserve helping fight this battle means that nearly everyone here tonight knows someone who is helping fight the war on terror.

Not since World War II has the home front been so united in support of our troops. Our most fervent hopes and prayers go with them as they stand in harm's way. And, as with all of America's conflicts since the Spanish-American War, the sons and daughters of Texas A&M have shouldered their patriotic responsibilities, picked up the gauntlet, and joined the fray. The fighting is vicious, the privations are great, and the sacrifices are many. But, like the Aggies before them, they serve proudly. They know some will not return. They understand this may be the price of keeping their nation free and their loved ones safe, but they're there.

Now I'd like a very special young lady to join me. This is Madison Walker of Bryan, Texas. Madison is eight years old, and she goes to Harvey Mitchell Elementary. She's a competitive swimmer and an accomplished gymnast. Did I get all that right, Madison?

Now, Madison, let me just tell you what I think any one of the thousands of Aggies serving us scattered all over the world would say to you, Madison, if they were here tonight. They would say, "Madison, you go home tonight and you sleep in your bed . . . and you get up in the morning and go to school . . . and you go to gym class and you go to swimming class . . . and you study and learn all you can so that you can grow up to be a wonderful, responsible citizen in this world." And they would say to you, "Madison, don't you worry . . . because we've got the watch." Thank you very much.

You young Aggies in this audience tonight will soon have the watch. You will be challenged; you will be tested; you will be asked to give your all. This may not necessarily occur on the battlefield, but on the field of life. You may in your world be called to fight a lifesaving battle in the operating room or to advance great legal principles in the courtroom. You may find yourselves at war to save the family farm, or to save the company you work for, or keep your children from drugs. Your battleground may be in the laboratory, the classroom, or on the factory floor. The battle may even be with your own conscience. Regardless of the fields of conflict, just as Aggies before you, you will be called to fight.

In these times of crisis, will you call on all the things you learned at Texas A&M? Will you remember that you're a Fightin' Texas Aggie, and damn proud of it? Will you summon the courage to do the right thing when it is easier not to? Will you find the strength to lead where others fear to tread, and will you employ the will to fight on when others abandon the cause?

Will you remember that you have the fire of the Aggie Spirit in your heart, the strength of Aggie heroes in your souls?

Muster has made it so . . . Muster, and Silver Taps, and the 12th Man, and the Aggie Code of Honor, and all the other great traditions of Texas A&M and all the values they stand for.

Muster, then, is about remembering ideals of service before self, of honor, of integrity, of loyalty and perseverance. It's about renewing the ties that bind us to our school and to each other. It's about saying to the world that the values we hold are worth celebrating, even under enemy fire.

These things, to me, are the real meaning of Aggie Muster, and all the other ways in which we celebrate our uniqueness as Aggies. It is what brings us together year after year to stand for those who have left our ranks—and to drink once again from the well of Aggie Spirit.

My challenge to you is this:

Which one of you will be the next Earl Rudder? Who will become our next Rick Perry, our first Aggie governor? Who will be the next Mike Halbouty to find new oil fields and give back so much to Texas A&M?

Who will be the next Bum Bright to build businesses, to lead our Board of Regents and to give back millions to the school he loved?

Who will be the next Jon Hagler, who excelled in the financial world and who gave us the Hagler Building, home of the Texas A&M Foundation?

Who will be the next Jack Brown, whose building, the chemical engineering building, will be dedicated in the morning? And this man was an oilman, an innovator, an explorationist and a pioneer.

And, who will be the next "Head" Davis, a man for all seasons that we all knew and celebrated?

And, yes, who will be the next John David Crow, who gave us such rich memories from Kyle Field?

What will your contribution be to the future of Texas A&M?

# Bill E. Carter '69

## *2006—Reed Arena*

Bill E. Carter '69. Photo
from editor's collection.

Bill Edward Carter was born December 6, 1946, in Denton. He served as student body president while he was earning a degree in agricultural economics from Texas A&M. He is a certified financial planner and president of Carter Financial Management. He began his financial planning career in 1973 and started his own firm three years later. In 1980, he formed Carter Advisory Services, Inc. Carter received the Small Business Award of the Dallas Chamber of Commerce and awards from the Financial Planning Association, the International Association of Registered Financial Consultants, and the Financial Planning Association of Dallas/Fort Worth.

He was president of the Association of Former Students in 1992 and served on the boards of the Texas A&M Foundation, the Chancellor's Century Council, the Corps Development Council, the 12th Man Foundation and the Private Enterprise Research Center. He was named a Texas A&M Distinguished Alumnus in 2000 and was inducted into the Corps of Cadets Hall of Honor in 2008.

Carter has served on advisory boards for countless institutions and organizations as well as community, religious, and charity programs.

## Aggie Spirit in Action*

Howdy!

Spending this—the 124th—Muster with you in College Station is one of the greatest moments in my life. I am truly honored to have

*Speech title derived by editor from speech contents

an opportunity to share my thoughts about what unites us all—the enduring Aggie Spirit.

Thank you for the finest opportunity a former student could ever receive.

And thank you, Natalie, for that introduction. As former Secretary of State Henry Kissinger once said, "The nice thing about being so honored is that, if I bore people, they will think it is their fault."

Now, let me make it clear from the beginning: This will be a true Aggie speech—short and to the point—quite the contrast to a "tea sip" speech that makes a point here and a point there but has a lot of "bull" in between.

By the way, it's great to know that Reed Arena is now used for more than just graduation and Muster. I noticed that someone actually located the basketball goals that came with this building.

Congratulations to Coach Billy Gillispie and his [men's basketball] team and to Coach [Gary] Blair and his [women's basketball] team for reaching the NCAA tournament and adding the word "basketball" back into the Aggie vocabulary.

Forty years ago today, I was a Fish at my first campus Muster over in G. Rollie White Coliseum.

Since then, I've been at 39 Muster ceremonies—some here, some in other parts of Texas, and some in other states. I've had the opportunity to speak at many of them. But, today, it's a special honor to stand at the campus podium where so many others more qualified have stood.

It's a place occupied in 1946—60 years ago today—by General Dwight D. Eisenhower; and in 1962 by Medal of Honor recipient Eli L. Whiteley, Class of '41; and in 1964 by E. King Gill, Class of '24, the original 12th Man.

While it's an honor to stand where they stood, it is also a responsibility.

You see, every Muster speaker accepts an unspoken mission to help the newest generation of our Aggie family understand why the tradition of Muster is so important.

That's what Penrose Metcalfe, Class of '16, did for me in 1966 when he spoke during my first campus Muster.

He said that Muster is an Aggie's opportunity to renew and reaffirm their loyalty to their Aggie family and to their school, and he called Muster a "priceless legacy, left to us by those who have gone on before and whose memory we honor."

During Muster 40 years ago, I felt challenged to accept the "priceless legacy" that he described. I made the decision that day to observe the Muster tradition every year and, in doing so, to renew and reaffirm my loyalty to my Aggie family and to Texas A&M.

Today, I want to challenge you—Class of '06, Class of '07, Class of '08, and Class of '09—to do the same: to decide right here, right now, to observe the Muster tradition every year. To accept this "priceless legacy" and honor those in our Aggie family who have gone before us.

By observing Muster every year, you choose to carry on more than just an Aggie tradition. You decide to live by values that honor and preserve our unique Aggie Spirit. That's a decision for which you will always be proud.

Speaking of making a decision . . . I heard about an Aggie in Austin who decided he needed a pet. He took quite a shine to a talkative parrot in a local pet store when the store owner said, "This parrot sings college tunes."

So he took the parrot home, and, shortly after dinner that night, he fired up the Fightin' Texas Aggie Band CD to see if the parrot would sing along.

But the only songs the parrot would sing were the "tu" fight song and a song that sounded a lot like "I've Been Working on the Railroad."

After an hour of this, it got to be too much. The Aggie grabbed the bird and yelled, "Don't you know the Aggie War Hymn?" But that just made the bird sing the "tu" songs louder.

The Aggie was so irritated with the tea-sipper noise that he grabbed the bird and put it in the quietest place he knew—the freezer—and said, "Tomorrow, you're going back to the pet store!"

For the first few seconds, there was a terrible noise while the parrot kicked and clawed and thrashed. Then, suddenly, everything went very, very quiet.

At first the Aggie waited, but he started to worry that the bird was hurt. After a couple minutes of silence, he was so worried that he opened the freezer.

The bird climbed out onto his outstretched arm singing "Hullabaloo Caneck Caneck. Hullabaloo Caneck Caneck."

The Aggie was astounded. He couldn't understand what had come over the parrot. So he said, "I thought you didn't know the Aggie War Hymn."

The parrot looked up at him and said, "I decided I'd better change my tune. By the way, which 'tu' song did that chicken in there sing?"

Like the parrot, we've all made our share of decisions—some good, some bad. But the one decision you'll never regret is the decision to become an Aggie, to carry on our Aggie traditions, to live by Aggie values and to honor the Aggie Spirit.

When you decided to be an Aggie, you chose to be a link in the chain between A&M past and A&M future—between the moments our traditions and values were forged and the days ahead when those traditions and values will see our Aggie family through moments of victory and challenge.

A present-day philosopher [Michael Novak] believes that "tradition lives because young people come along who catch its romance and add new glories to it."

I say that every "new glory" strengthens the link between A&M past and A&M future.

Today, I want to talk about how you current students are strengthening that link with "new glories."

You are adding to the A&M tradition of serving others, and you are preserving the Aggie Spirit with all your actions.

Before I talk about all that you are doing, I feel compelled to reminisce for a few moments about the past.

How honored we are to have the Class of '56 with us tonight. During their time on campus, they "tore up the dance floor" to such tunes as Elvis Presley's "Heartbreak Hotel" and "Don't Be Cruel."

They watched "I Love Lucy" and "The Ed Sullivan Show," and they experienced Bear Bryant's first year as head football coach.

With 1,256 graduates, the Class of '56 was the smallest class since World War II. But let me tell you, it was the "grittiest"!

Thanks to my friend, Rod Pittman, a member of the class, here's proof. On this brick is carved the class motto: "Tough as nails, hard as bricks, we're the Class of '56."

These "gritty" Aggies left College Station to lead major oil companies or start exploration firms, like Joe Foster did.

Or they went off to direct the Johnson Space Center, like Jerry Griffin.

Or they served our nation as admirals in the Navy, like the late Foster Teague, who was captain of the USS *Kitty Hawk*, and Jerry Johnson, who is the only Aggie admiral to wear four stars.

Or they led commands in Desert Storm like Army Major General George Akin and Air Force Major General Tom Olsen.

The Class of '56 added innumerable glories to our Aggie traditions. And their service to industry and to our nation has strengthened the link between A&M past and A&M future. Thank you for your example, Class of '56. You have shown us the AGGIE SPIRIT IN ACTION.

A theme we see throughout Aggie history is the concept of "service before self." It is the idea that Aggies strive to serve their community and their country before giving any thought to personal gain.

Stepping back just a little further in history, I often think about the Aggies who served in World War II. They are part of what we now call "The Greatest Generation."

Today, it's hard for some people to believe how dedicated those Aggies were to serving others. But by the spring of 1944, everyone . . . everyone in the classes of '44 and '45 had left campus to serve their nation. My uncle, Ralph Durham, Class of '45, was one of them.

It was the "stuff of legends."

It was the AGGIE SPIRIT IN ACTION.

It is important to keep more recent Aggies in our thoughts and prayers tonight as they serve our nation in the global war on terrorism.

Today, Aggies will observe Muster in more than 300 locations worldwide. Many of them are calling the roll of our absent as they risk their own lives in the combat zones of Afghanistan and Iraq.

It's also fitting at this time to acknowledge our fellow Aggies that have served in the armed forces and have been there for our nation in time of need.

We're fortunate to have many of them with us tonight.

I'd like for all of you who have served in the past—or are serving now—to please stand so we can honor you with our applause.

During Roll Call tonight, I'll think about my uncle, Ballard Powell Durham, Class of '41. He was killed in action in 1944. His name is inscribed on the plaque at the entrance to the Memorial Student Center along with the names of 950 other Aggies who made the ultimate sacrifice in World War II.

I also will think about my dad, W. W. Carter, Class of '38, who returned from the war after serving as an Army officer in the Pacific Theater. Like most Aggies in those days, Dad worked really hard to put himself through A&M.

It was what A&M instilled in him—the values of serving others and a strong work ethic—that made our dairy farm near Decatur, Texas, successful. Together, our parents instilled those same values in my brother, Bob, Class of '63, and me.

Between all that they passed down to us and my own experiences at A&M, I received so much that, when I left here in '69, I wanted to do whatever I could to give back to my university, to my community and, ultimately, to my chosen profession.

Like you, I learned that the Aggie Spirit of service means reaching out to help others in small ways, every day.

That is the AGGIE SPIRIT IN ACTION.

It is service beyond self, yes, but there are times when serving requires MORE than just one's self—sometimes it requires the combined efforts of many.

I remember how a neighboring farmer once helped a man from town that got lost out in the country and drove his car into a ditch. He went up to the farmer's house, asking for help.

Our neighbor had a big, strong horse named Buddy, so he hitched Buddy up to the car and yelled, "Pull, Nellie, pull!"

But Buddy didn't budge.

Then he hollered, "Pull, Charlie, pull!"

But Buddy didn't move.

Once more he yelled out, this time saying, "Pull, Daisy, pull!"

And still, Buddy didn't move.

Then, sort of nonchalantly, he said, "Pull, Buddy, pull."

That's when Buddy started moving forward and easily dragged the car out of the ditch.

The man was grateful, but he was really confused. So he asked my neighbor why he had called the horse by the wrong name three times.

"Well," he said, "Buddy happens to be blind, and if he thought for a minute that he was the only one pulling, he wouldn't even try!"

Sometimes an Aggie knows that individual service alone can't achieve what a team of Aggies working together can. That was the spirit of Aggies past, and that's exactly what you current Aggies demonstrated last fall during the weeks when Hurricanes Katrina and Rita caused so much heartache.

I want to spend the next few minutes retelling how you added "new glories" to our Aggie traditions and how you strengthened the link between A&M past and A&M future when you showed the AGGIE SPIRIT IN ACTION.

On a Friday afternoon, a phone call came in to the Corps about the levees breaking in New Orleans. For the next 72 hours, 700 Cadets and the Aggie Dance Team worked around the clock transforming Reed Arena, where we are right now, into a sanctuary for potential Katrina evacuees.

They were "potential" evacuees because no one was certain they would ever arrive at Reed Arena. But that didn't stop you Aggies from setting up 300 bunk beds, bundling supplies, gathering food and collecting clothes.

After working for 36 hours with very little to no sleep, everything was ready and still there was no word about any evacuees.

At midnight Sunday, the word came: "They're here." The first bus was arriving.

Tired but now breathless with anticipation, everyone waited, not knowing what to expect. This cavernous place was whisper-quiet.

The first evacuee to enter the arena was a man with no shoes. Those who followed him had few if any belongings. Many had held on for days waiting for rescue and survived only to live in fear at the Superdome.

Five buses arrived at Reed Arena that morning, the last one at 5 a.m. The bone-weary Aggies who created this safe haven, not knowing that anyone would use it, cried tears of joy to see their teamwork bless others.

Many students on campus collected donations as part of the Katrina Aggie Relief Effort. Other students volunteered in any way they could. And during spring break, another group signed on with Habitat for Humanity in New Orleans.

When Hurricane Rita headed west, once again student volunteers provided shelter, helped with medical and child care and distributed food and supplies.

Last September, President [Robert] Gates summed up your service perfectly in a campus communication. Here's part of what he wrote:

> Our students once again showed Texas, and the whole nation, the meaning of our Aggie culture and Spirit. Where an entire campus opened its arms and its heart not just once, but twice, to those fleeing disaster. Where different parts of the University came together to help strangers from every walk of life. Where those who gave of themselves and those who received were, in different ways, changed forever. Where today's students proved the Aggie Spirit endures undiminished.

My young Aggie friends, you added "new glories" to our traditions with every minute you spent helping out, with every smile and word of encouragement you offered, with every hour of sleep you sacrificed in order to serve.

You made a difference individually and together.

You showed the world that Aggie traditions inspire your values, and your values compel you to serve.

There's that word again—SERVE. It's a tradition you students know well.

In fact, Texas A&M students have raised the bar by giving more blood during the annual blood drive than any campus in the nation.

Don't forget the March to the Brazos, a major service project supporting the March of Dimes. Or the Relay for Life that raises funds for the American Cancer Society.

And then, there's the Big Event—a tradition since 1983 and the largest student-run service project in the country.

Service to the needy.

Service to the sick.

Service to the community.

Service beyond self.

It's the A&M tradition.

IT'S THE AGGIE SPIRIT IN ACTION THROUGH YOU.

Classes of '06, '07, '08, and '09, the stories of your service and self-lessness inspire me.

In words that have sent Olympic competitors into the arena for 2,000 years: "When you endure, you bring honor to yourself. Even more you bring honor to us all."

More importantly, you bring honor to the Aggie Spirit.

Some people fear that A&M will become like other universities. But as I walk around campus, as I meet current students, as I look out at this very moment into your faces . . .

I believe the Aggie Spirit is as strong as ever.

I believe you treasure our traditions and live by our values.

You are an enduring link between A&M past and A&M future. You are, without question, the most outstanding student body anywhere, and I can't begin to describe how proud we are of you.

At this time, I want all of my fellow former students and all our dis-tinguished guests to stand and join me in honoring these incredible young Aggies—the Classes of '06, '07, '08, and '09!

Together and individually, these young Aggies are adding "new glo-ries" to our grand traditions.

Grand traditions like service before self.

Grand traditions like Muster.

Muster, as well as all our traditions, define who and what we value.

They are the means we use to pass those values from one generation to the next. Values such as commitment to our country and each other; to service and excellence; and to diligence, honor and respect.

Traditions give us a timeless connection to other hearts filled with the same passion to live with an integrity that goes beyond self, to reach out to the world around us and to make a difference in the lives of others.

The tradition of Muster allows us to honor all the Aggies we've lost in the last year, to remember them as men and women who were committed to something larger than themselves and to reaffirm their lasting presence in our Aggie family.

The tradition of Muster is very important for everyone who has lost a friend or loved one—but especially for you parents who lost your Aggie this year.

It is not in the natural course of life for children to predecease their parents. Nothing we say, nothing we do can fill your void.

However, because you are part of our Aggie family, you share a lasting bond with a caring community, now and always, and you will never be completely alone.

Muster is among the many traditions that make A&M so special to me:

> From the Chicken to Maroon Out to First Yell.
>
> From Fish buddies to Fish Camp to 12th Man.
>
> From Miss Reveille to Senior Boots to the Big Event.
>
> From Midnight Yell to the blood drive to the Elephant Walk.
>
> From Final Review to kissing after A&M scores to the March to the Brazos.
>
> From the cold chills running up and down my spine every time the Fightin' Texas Aggie Band steps off in Kyle Field, to the warm tears welling up in my eyes when I join you in answering, "Here," as we softly call the roll.

Muster is special to me because it is such a tangible way we Aggies show how much we value one another, our traditions and our university.

Like the "reformed" parrot in the freezer, we've all made life-changing decisions.

By deciding to observe Muster every year, and by honoring all our grand traditions, you and I choose to live by a set of values that guide us for a lifetime and perpetuate the Aggie Spirit forever.

You know, because of the Aggies in my family, I thought I knew a lot about A&M when I arrived in the fall of 1965.

I had been to Aggie football games, been on Corps trips, stayed in the dorm.

I knew that when you saw an Aggie Ring, there was an instant introduction and an immediate rapport.

I thought I knew what all that was about, but, I have to admit, I didn't really know what it meant until my fourth week on campus.

Life in the Corps was a challenge, and about the only good thing was getting to know the other Fish in my outfit—Spider D.

There were two Fish in particular with whom I really hit it off— George "Mack" Antilley and Horace Young.

That fourth weekend was our first "free" weekend. In the Corps, that meant you could leave campus. Everyone who could beg, borrow, or steal a ride left. My Fish buddies, Mack and Horace, were among that group.

They left on a trip from which they would never return.

The following week I attended my first Silver Taps, and I truly remember it as if it were yesterday. I remember walking out of the dorm with no one saying a word. It was a warm evening and there was a soft breeze blowing. There were some light clouds drifting across the sky, occasionally covering what was nearly a full moon.

As I stood in front of the Academic Building, the only noise that I could hear was the rustling of some leaves being blown by that gentle breeze. Then, all of a sudden, the silence was broken by the disciplined cadence of the Ross Volunteer Firing Squad as they marched sharply into place. In memory of Mack and Horace, they fired a 21-gun salute, and Silver Taps was played.

As I stood there listening to Silver Taps with tears filling my eyes, for the first time I began to understand what Texas A&M is all about . . . to understand why being an Aggie is so special.

I began to understand that "intangible"—that "intangible" that is kidded about but that "intangible" that is the envy of all.

That "intangible" is what you and I call the Aggie Spirit.

It's a way of life guided by traditions that instill in us our common values.

Because you will forever be an Aggie, you can walk a little taller, stand a little straighter and feel a little prouder. You will forever glow with the eternal Aggie Spirit—a mighty flame that will never go out.

As long as all Aggies hold in our hearts the love and respect for our fellow Aggies, for our university and for our unique traditions, the link between A&M past and A&M future will forever remain strong.

Aggie Muster. What a special tradition we are proud to observe tonight.

Muster endures, and, with God's blessing, may it forever be so.

Good night ... God bless ... and GIG 'EM!

# Brooke L. Rollins '94

*2007—Reed Arena*

Brooke L. Rollins '94.
Photo from editor's
collection.

Brooke Leslie Rollins was born April 10, 1972, in Dallas. She is the president and CEO of the Texas Public Policy Foundation, a public policy research institute based in Austin. Before joining the foundation, she served as Governor Rick Perry's deputy general counsel and ethics advisor and later as his policy director.

After graduating from Glen Rose High School, she graduated cum laude from Texas A&M University with a BS degree in agricultural development. She was the first woman to serve as Texas A&M student body president and received the Brown Foundation–J. Earl Rudder Award as the top graduate based on academics, leadership, and service.

Rollins graduated with honors from the University of Texas School of Law and spent several years as a litigator with Hughes & Luce, LLP, in Dallas, focusing primarily on complex commercial litigation. She also completed a federal judicial clerkship with the Honorable Barbara M.G. Lynn, a US federal district judge in the Northern District of Texas.

Rollins has served on the board of advisors for the Hispanic Council for Reform and Educational Options and the board of the Texas A&M Association of Former Students. She has also been a member of the Texas Lyceum and the Texas Women's Alliance.

## "In Fire, Gold Is Tested"

Good evening.

Having given hundreds, perhaps thousands of speeches in my life, beginning as a 15-year-old in the Future Farmers of America, I have stood at a podium behind a microphone many, many times before. Indeed, as Student Body President my senior year, I was asked by Texas A&M President Ray Bowen, who is here tonight, and President George H.W. Bush to speak at President Bush's Library groundbreaking. I had to think about it a little while, but I agreed to do it. It was a big moment for this small-town girl from Glen Rose, Texas, to stand on a stage with presidents (past and future), prime ministers, and governors, senators, you name it—all the bigwigs were there—and talk to thousands at the ceremony and millions on camera around the world. One might say that might be the highlight of most anyone's speaking career, certainly someone from Glen Rose, Texas. But it was not. Tonight is that night for me. Being asked by this Muster Committee, having been chosen by these extraordinary students to be part of this celebration, is something that will be at the top of my list for my entire lifetime.

They say that being chosen to be the Muster speaker is truly one of the greatest honors that any Aggie could ever receive. And this is true. I have wondered since that time last November when Thomas and his sub-committee surprised me with the invitation, "What I have done to deserve this?" I never commanded any armies; I have fought in no wars. I am not a hero by any stretch of the imagination. I have never been a mayor, a governor, a senator or a congressman. I have never won a Medal of Honor, not a Nobel prize, and no building on campus is named for my generosity. I have never run a Fortune 500 company. I am just a wife and mother of two precious little boys. In my spare time, I work for a not-for-profit organization, a scrappy little conservative think-tank in Austin called the Texas Public Policy Foundation.

The fact is I don't deserve this. I am humbled beyond words and have such gratitude in my heart for this opportunity and I could never properly express it.

But tonight isn't about me. It is about this impossible-to-define spirit that Thomas Conner '08 so aptly talked about in his introduction—our beloved University. It is about this magnificent place, and it is about those who have gone before us. Those who have "graduated with honors" in the truest sense. And indeed, I know that those whose names we will call in just a few moments are having their very own glorious Muster up above, and looking down on us with a smile and a big "gig 'em."

The Muster tradition, which began more than 100 years ago in 1903, is THE tradition at a university that is defined by its almost mythical traditions. I will note, believe it or not, that there are a handful of other schools across the country that have pretty good athletic traditions, with a student body that passionately loves their school, almost as much as we do, with a generous and dedicated former students group.

But there is no other university with a tradition like Aggie Muster. Muster is our defining moment. It is a celebration that captures the essence of the Spirit of Aggieland. It is about honoring our past, honoring our fallen comrades, honoring our country and honoring freedom. It is an occasion when Aggies throughout the world—indeed over 300 other Musters are happening right now—pause and we all remember. It is about celebrating freedom and values and family. It is about the realization that service above self is the highest calling. That the commitment to an idea is greater than the commitment to self. And that death is worth such a commitment.

I attended my very first Muster when I was a freshman here at Texas A&M and, maybe like you, I was a first-generation Aggie. My family had not attended Texas A&M. I came here from little Glen Rose, Texas. I graduated with 39 people in my class. I had more people in my freshman chemistry class than we had in the whole town of Glen Rose. My dear mother was in town trying to help me figure out if I wanted to stay on campus or not. I knew the colors were maroon and white and they had a pretty good football program, but frankly, other than that, I didn't know that much about it.

I got sort of involved my freshman year. I attended "most" of my classes. Now that I'm 35, I can say that to my parents. I'll never forget it when on April 21, 1991, we happened to be walking by G. Rollie White [Coliseum] and it was about 6:45. She said, "What is going on in G. Rollie White tonight?" I said, "You know, I think it's this tradition called Muster." She said, "What is that?" and I said, "I don't know." She said, "Do you want to go check it out?" I said, "Well, sure. What else is there to do?"

We walked in and I had no idea whether we were going to sing "Cumbaya," dance, or what it was. I just didn't know.

As soon as we walked in they closed the doors behind us. All the seats had been taken and there was some seating left on the cement stairs. A very nice and gracious young lady (I'll never forget her face) directed us to sit on the stairway that was literally directly across from the podium.

We sat on the stairway, the lights went down and, two hours later, my life was changed forever. For the first time I understood what it meant to be a Texas Aggie. I understood what it meant to be a part of something that is larger than myself.

How crazy and strange and ironic that four years, to the moment, later at Texas A&M's campus Muster 1995 I was the student body president welcoming all the students to Aggie Muster. It was certainly a time, in a couple of hours that April 21st in 1991, that really made such an impression on me.

I wonder if tonight, sitting in this vast arena, there is another Brooke Leslie, a small-town girl or boy, who came to Texas A&M only to get a degree, but will realize by the end of tonight that this place isn't just about a degree. It is about the highest calling. It is about being part of something larger than yourself. It is about service above all else.

There is a family of Aggies that, unlike myself, actually have known this Aggie secret for many, many years. The story really begins in the 1800s. A young man by the name of Mart had decided after spending a year in a Union prison camp in Chicago that it was way too cold to live up there. So without really knowing where he was going to end up, he packed his mother up and headed south. He ended up in Greenville on a blackland farm, married, had twelve children (eight boys, four girls) and raised them all on that farm.

All twelve children received college degrees. The four girls received degrees from the predecessor institutions of Texas Woman's College. Seven of the eight boys received degrees from Texas A&M. The oldest of the seven A&M graduates received his degree in 1893, and the youngest in 1921. Five of the brothers received engineering degrees, and two graduated in agriculture. The eighth brother, well, let's just say he couldn't get in to Texas A&M, so he decided to go to law school down the road a little bit. That's all we'll say about him.

Two of the brothers served in the Spanish-American War, four served in World War I, and one served in World War II.

An interesting aside to this story is that one of the brothers, Henry, Class of 1897, married one Sophie Hutson, one of the Hutson twins who attended A&M at the turn of the 19th century. Sophie and her sister completed all course work leading to a degree in civil engineering, and couldn't get a degree because A&M didn't award degrees to women at that time, and so she received her "certificate of completion." How fun I have to think it is for Sophie looking down today, when just a couple of years ago she was posthumously awarded her bachelor of science degree for civil engineering.

Another brother, Andrew, Class of 1906, was one of the four brothers to serve in World War I, serving as a Captain in the Corps of Engineers. Andrew's battalion commander was Major Dwight D. Eisenhower. Andrew ended up taking the battalion to France as battalion commander in 1918 when Major Eisenhower received another assignment.

Interestingly, Andrew also attended the very first Muster in 1903.

After the war, Andrew and his wife, Mary, settled in Dallas to raise their three sons: Andy Jr., Jack, and Albert. Andy Jr., Class of 1939, served in the Pacific Theatre during World War II, remained in the Army, and retired as a Major General and Deputy Chief of the Corps of Engineers, having overseen the construction of the Alaska pipeline. Jack, Class of 1946, had his college career interrupted by World War II and served as an enlisted man in the European theater, surviving the Battle of the Bulge as an infantryman. Al graduated in 1951 and served in Korea as a combat engineer.

What an extraordinary story of one family's service to country, and how proud I am, and grateful to my husband, to know that these Aggies in his family attended the same school that we muster around tonight. And one more thing—the family I describe is Rollins—and how proud I am to have taken their name when I married Al's son and Andrew's grandson, Mark, Class of '94.

Al and Jack are here with us tonight sitting right up there. Will you and every other veteran who is with us tonight, stand up and be recognized? It is for your service, your brother's, your late father, Andrew, his 7 brothers, and all Aggies who have gone on before us that we muster for and celebrate tonight.

Thank you. As you all know, the veterans who just stood were the lucky ones. They walked off the battlefield and walked back into their homes to continue their lives enjoying the freedom their sacrifice helped to secure. They were given another day, another year, another decade. Not all who served were so lucky.

Matt Worrell, fighting Texas Aggie Class of '94 and a proud member of Company L-1, married his college sweetheart Camille and gave the world two beautiful little boys, Luke and Jake. While in school, Matt and my husband Mark worked closely together—Matt as a redpot at Bonfire and Mark as a yell leader. The last time we saw Matt was at a wedding not long ago. I can still see him clearly in my mind, so striking and proud and handsome in his uniform. And I remember thinking that very night what a gift he was. How blessed this country was to have someone like Matt, willing to go into the darkness of night and the blackness of war to keep me safe.

He gave his life this past year while continuing the fight for freedom in Iraq. He is a true hero. And he is a fallen hero. And he, along with all the other names that will soon be called, will never be forgotten.

My friends, Muster represents the BEST of Texas A&M. It represents the best of us. When the candles are lighted, we must remember what that burning fire represents—love of man, love of school, the willingness to lay down your life for freedom. It is this that we must never forget.

I think one of the most beautiful parts of Muster, here or anywhere else in the world, is the lighting of the candle. It is this "FIRE" that so eloquently yet so simply represents what it means to be an Aggie. Indeed, IN FIRE, GOLD IS TESTED. It is the hardest times, the darkest moments, when our gold is truly tested.

In reading through almost 60 years of previous Muster speeches, I ran across some speakers who quoted President Abraham Lincoln. However, we tend to simplify things when looking backward through the lens of history. You probably knew that the South didn't think much of Mr. Lincoln at the time, but did you know the North was almost equally as disgusted? In 1864, the *New York Herald* called the president a "joke incarnated, his election a very sorry joke, and the idea that such a man as he should be the president of such a country as this, a very ridiculous joke." A New Year's Day editorial that same year opined, "The people of the North owe Mr. Lincoln nothing but eternal hatred and scorn. There are 500,000 new-made graves; there are 5,000 orphans; there are 200,000 widows; there is a bottomless sea of blood; there is the Constitution broken; there are liberty and law— liberty in chains and in a dungeon; thieves in the Treasury, provost marshals in the seats of justice, butchers in the pulpit—and these are the things which we owe Mr. Lincoln." And the worst of it, from the famous preacher Henry Ward Beecher, "Not a spark of genius has he; not an element of leadership. Not one particle of heroic enthusiasm." It's tough when the newspapers think you are a rat, but when the preachers join in, now that is a bad day.

Through these extremely dark days, Abraham Lincoln continued his battle for what he believed to be right. When, seemingly, the world was against him, the fire at its hottest, he marched on. He marched for freedom. He marched for principle. He marched for what he knew in his heart was right. And he won.

Ladies and gentlemen, we are in a battle in today's world for those same principles. We are in a battle for, at its core, what is right and true. We as Aggies, whether on the battlefields in Iraq (where tonight, my brother-in-law Sam, a captain in the US Marines, leads the Muster in Baghdad) or in the battlefield of ideas, must continue our march forward. It is when we face the deepest uphill climb that we are forced to carry on.

Freedom is a precious thing. The most precious. And we must vigorously fight for it every day—whether on the dusty plains in Iraq or on our country's editorial pages. Whether in the mountains of Afghanistan, or in the hallways of our state's capitol. Whether against tyrannical dictatorships or in our own county courthouses. We must preserve this beautiful, brilliant ideal, that our people, that Americans, that Aggies are constrained only by their own imagination, and limited only by how big they can dream.

And we must also recognize this truth: The battle for freedom is never finished. And it is by continuing that battle that we truly honor those that have left us this past year.

It is said, IN FIRE, GOLD IS TESTED. And so I challenge you, my fine Aggies—let us together make a new commitment tonight. Let us make this commitment on behalf of those Aggies whom we honor with a "Here"—for Matt Worrell, for Walker Best, for Sean Lyerly, for every name to be called, let our GOLD be tested.

In 1836, less than 200 men had their gold tested when they fought against thousands of Mexican forces to defend an ancient Christian mission on the plains of Texas. Though they died to the last man, the Texas volunteers within those missionary walls exacted such a horrific toll on the army of Santa Anna that Mexican Colonel Juan Almonte privately noted, "One more such glorious victory and we are finished."

And so they were. The inspiration of the men who made their stand at the Alamo fueled the victory that Sam Houston would lead just six weeks later on April 21st, 1836. In fact, the 700 ragged, ill-equipped Texans—who had been retreating for weeks—suddenly turned around and defeated a vastly superior force to gain freedom for Texas on this very day.

Whether it is the gold in our Aggie Rings, the gold in our hearts, or the gold in our principles—it is the fire that tests us, that makes us stronger, that reminds us why we are here. Not here in College Station on this most important of all Aggie nights—but here in this beautiful place we call America. Let tonight's fire always remind us not only of the loved ones we have lost, but of what we are called to do, indeed what we must do, to carry their legacy forward.

I will conclude tonight using a quote from another great defender of freedom—another whose gold was surely tested by many fires. Winston Churchill, speaking in 1941, encouraged the young men of his country, "Never give in, never give in, never, never, never, never—in nothing, great or small, large or petty—never give in."

Ladies and gentleman, we will indeed never give in . . . and we will never forget. Never, never, never, never will we forget. These ties that bind us, will bind us forever. Let us weep one more time for those we have lost, then spend the rest of our lives celebrating them.

My fellow Aggies, Texans, Americans. We have a rendezvous with destiny. And tonight, this Aggie Muster is proof that we will not fail.

In Fire, Gold is tested. And our gold, this Texas A&M, will burn gloriously bright forever.

Softly call the Muster, let comrade answer "HERE."

Thank you.

# John A. Adams Jr. '73

*2008—Reed Arena*

John A. Adams Jr. '73.
Photo from editor's
collection.

John Alfred Adams Jr. was born April 24, 1951, in San Antonio. He received his bachelor's, master's, and PhD degrees from Texas A&M University. He was commanding officer of Squadron 1 in Texas A&M's Corps of Cadets, a member of the Ross Volunteer Firing Squad, and a feature writer for *The Battalion* in 1974–75. He was assistant to the A&M commandant, president of the Brazos County A&M Club, and a member of Texas A&M's Centennial Committee. He served as a captain in the US Air Force.

He was president and CEO of Enterprise Florida, Inc., after serving as executive director and CEO of the Laredo Development Foundation. He counseled commercial banking and financial institutions on enhancement of market-entry strategies, export financing, and trade facilitation.

Adams chaired the US Department of Commerce Industry Trade Advisory Council from 2000 to 2005, and was on the Board Trade Alliance, South Texas Workforce Board, Space Florida, and a variety of trade and professional organizations. Adams authored eight books on international trade, economic development, and history. His awards include the Small Business Administration's National Exporter of the Year in May 1988.

His books on the history of Texas A&M include *We Are the Aggies* (1979), *Softly Call the Muster* (1994), *Keepers of the Spirit* (2001), *Texas Aggies Go to War in Service of Their Country* (2006), and *The Fightin' Texas Aggie Defenders of Bataan and Corregidor* (2016).

# "Spirit and Mind"

Welcome.

From the early stalwarts during the formative years of Texas A&M over a century ago, which included Edward B. Cushing, Dean Edwin J. Kyle, Alva Mitchell, Walter Wipprecht, Joe Utay, Mary and Sophie Hutson, and Lawrence Sullivan "Sul" Ross, there emerged the voice of A&M in the person of Marion S. Church, Class of 1905. While in the present day he has gone all but forgotten, in his era he proved to be the heart and soul and voice of vocal A&M former student groups that fought to ensure the survivability and growth of their cherished alma mater and Church lobbied all who would listen.

And in so doing, he would begin his many statewide presentations saying the following to friends and foe alike:

> A man's love has been defined under three heads—for his home, his country, and his God, but I add another category, distinct from those, yet holding a hallowed place in the hearts of every man—and that is love for his alma mater.

It was Church's intrinsic spirit and love of the A&M College of Texas and his rallying of those early students, former students, families, and friends of Texas A&M that helped bring us here today—and worldwide at some 300-plus Muster gatherings. It is likely that as [a] sophomore Marion Church took part in the cadet events on April 21, 1903 that drew attention to San Jacinto Day, bugging out to the Brazos for a swim and BBQ!

And thus, through the years, a broader worldwide Muster program, crafted by E. E. McQuillen '20 in the early 1940s following the report of General George Moore's "boys" on Corregidor, captured the imagination of the nation.

More people will Muster on April 21st in the name of Texas A&M than at any other non-sporting event by any other institution or group worldwide. The roots of the Aggie Spirit were set.

I have often wondered and researched the origins of that date, certain that it marks the embodiment of this tradition and the earliest rise of the famed Aggie Spirit.

Shortly after I was honored with the invitation to be the 2008 Campus Muster speaker, I attended an A&M basketball game in this hall, sitting right over there. Straight across from me was a Texas A&M University Foundation banner across the bottom of the scorer's table that simply and profoundly read: "Spirit and Mind."

This slogan might have been in use for a long time, but it was the first time I saw it there in glorious Maroon and White. It struck me—"Spirit and Mind." Wow, someone over there really "gets it"—so simple and so meaningful.

Most can define the "mind" portion—education, excellence, research, fostering young minds and the like, but stop by the Texas A&M Foundation or the Association of Former Students or stop a student in the MSC [Memorial Student Center] or an old Aggie tailgating before a home game, and ask them about the spirit part. What is this Spirit?

The answer is not as easy or direct. "Oh, it's just that Aggie Spirit thing." What Aggie Spirit thing? In time, most will collect their thoughts and then turn to a personal experience that connects them to our alma mater. Then the memories flow. Oh, it was Fish Camp. No, it was Midnight Yell Practice; no, when I got my Aggie Ring; no, my first Silver Taps; or that "ah-ha" moment when each of us finally thought we had it figured out.

Whatever "it" is—"it" is alive and well—in Aggieland.

For some it began with a Howdy Bib, for some it was passed down in generations of Aggie family grads and friends, for some it was being the first in the family to obtain a college education. For me, I would like to think it was the Aggie Bonfire my parents took me to in 1952. I had just turned 18 months old, but my mom and dad are convinced that something that night possibly put the burning desire in me to be a Fightin' Texas Aggie and, 17 years later to the day, my fish class in the fall of 1969 built the tallest bonfire on record—109 feet.

The Aggie Spirit is hard for those outside the Aggie sphere to understand or fully appreciate. It disarms many (where else would so many gather on the same day without a football game?).

Without a long legacy of tradition and Spirit—this would be just another stale, routine institution, marked by bricks and mortar, and not by the affinity of those who pass through its halls and the wider experience of being a part of the 12th Man. A unique place like Aggieland is hard to explain.

My "good friend" Mark Twain once noted, "Never let schooling interfere with your education." While my undergraduate grades and activities are a testament to this sage wisdom, education is of great value (at least that's what you students tell your folks, who are paying the bills). It's the Aggie experience, the friendships both here and after graduation and the fostering of that intangible spirit that will forever set us apart.

Visitors to campus, new faculty, and new administrators, and many who come in contact with your daily routine do not always "get it"— how would they without being a part of the experience? Yet in time it is heartening to see how those new to Aggieland gain a better sense of what the Aggie experience is all about. Don't change it. Be a part of it!

Maybe the current president of the Association [of Former Students], General Hal Hornburg '68, captured a piece of the Aggie experience and what "it" is when he said, "Texas A&M did not make me what I am, but it helped make me WHO I am. Texas A&M presents tremendous opportunities to forge character and develop future state and national leaders."

So, be kind, help all to understand this special place we call Aggieland. We do strive for excellence—in the class, on the field, in the hundreds of activities that drive this institution. But we should also cherish and foster the spirit of that long maroon line so many years ago which embodied the make-up that has represented the University over the past 132 years. And is so ably reflected in today's dynamic student body, as well as in the Class of '58.

We cannot Muster today without recognizing that this place called Aggieland trains and prepares our best and brightest to serve our nation in times of war and peace. We develop leaders both on and off the battlefield, and today around the world we have Aggie men and women in harm's way. Remember them; remember their families; and keep them in your thoughts and prayers that they may soon return safe and sound.

Aggie Muster today is a time of remembrance, of reflection, and of reverence; a time of sadness for those we remember and honor this day. Yet also, importantly, an abiding appreciation that we and they, those that have passed, are a part of the Aggie experience.

And so in closing, as it has been through the years, Aggies are the way they are because of what happens to them at Texas A&M. The blending of the Aggie "Spirit and Mind" is a legacy for the ages.

Gig 'em.

# Robert M. Gates

*2009—Reed Arena*

Robert Michael "Bob" Gates was born September 25, 1943, in Wichita, Kansas. He received his bachelor's degree from the College of William and Mary, his master's degree in history from Indiana University, and his doctorate in Russian and Soviet history from Georgetown University. Joining the Central Intelligence Agency in 1966, he was commissioned in the US Air Force the next year as an intelligence officer. He was an intelligence professional for twenty-seven years, including nine years at the National Security Council under four presidents.

Robert M. Gates. Photo from editor's collection.

Director of Central Intelligence from 1991 until 1993, he is the only career officer in CIA history to rise from entry-level employee to director. He was deputy director from 1986 until 1989 and served as assistant to President George H.W. Bush and as deputy national security adviser at the White House from January 20, 1989, until November 6, 1991.

He became president of Texas A&M University in August 2002, after being interim dean of the George Bush School of Government and Public Service at Texas A&M from 1999 to 2001. On December 18, 2006, he was sworn in as the twenty-second secretary of defense.

After leaving government service, in May of 2014 Gates became president of the Boy Scouts of America. His awards include the National Security Medal, the Presidential Citizens Medal, the National Intelligence Distinguished Service Medal (twice), and the CIA's highest award, the Distinguished Intelligence Medal (three times). Gates has been a member of the boards of several major firms as well as the boards of the American Council on Education, the National Association of State

Universities and Land-Grant Colleges, and the Boy Scouts of America. He was president of the National Eagle Scout Association.

## Character and Integrity*

Howdy!

It is good to be back home. My head and my work today are in one place, but my heart is in another—here in Aggieland.

Much has changed since I first arrived here as interim dean of the Bush School nearly ten years ago. Hundreds of millions of dollars worth of new academic and athletic buildings—completed and under construction—dot the campus. A vastly expanded faculty. An even larger and more diverse student body—geographically, ethnically, and culturally. New and innovative academic programs. New research programs and institutes. National and international esteem and recognition. Change is pervasive—as it should be in a great university.

But while as a great public university Texas A&M is always changing, what is it that stays the same? A&M is a unique American institution because its excellence is built on the firm foundations of time-honored and proven values—and treasured traditions.

The Aggie culture is grounded in patriotism; religious faith, however expressed; love of family; loyalty to one another; an old-fashioned work ethic; a sense of duty; the importance of service to others and to our country; and a shared belief in the supreme importance of character and integrity. It was because of these values and Texas A&M's extraordinary history of service to the nation that I came here to be president in 2002, the place where I believed I would conclude my public service.

Aggies treasure tradition even while leading in shaping the future. Texas A&M's future is bright because it is anchored in a resplendent past. This great university was built by men with rough hands, most from poor families, men who came here, often with little more than the shirts on their backs. But with the determination and the grit to succeed.

*Speech title derived by editor from speech contents

As the decades passed, they developed traditions that would forever keep alive the deep bond with each other cemented by hard work, sacrifice, sweat and camaraderie. Those 19th-century traditions—Corps of Cadets traditions . . . military traditions—remain the foundation of the Aggie Spirit in the 21st century.

Underpinning all of Texas A&M traditions is the importance of character and integrity—expressed in the Aggie Code of Honor: An Aggie does not lie, cheat or steal, or tolerate those who do. In a time when we are all aware of the social, political and economic costs of people—too often in leadership positions—who lie, cheat and steal, this university must remain steadfast in its commitment to inculcate integrity and character in every part of the campus community—and teach in every class the importance of ethical behavior.

Virtually all Aggie traditions have a common theme: the Aggie family. Silver Taps, the 12th Man, Midnight Yell, "Howdy," the Corps of Cadets, Aggie Ring, the Big Event, Fish Camp and—until the tragedy of a decade ago—Bonfire. All these traditions are about keeping alive the deep bonds of friendship and affection born here during student days—the same bonds so important to Aggies from the University's first days.

Always for me, though, Muster is the greatest of Aggie traditions. Tradition holds that Aggies gathered together on June 26th, 1883, to live over again their college days, "the victories and defeats won and lost upon the drill field and classroom." Eventually, the annual gathering evolved into a celebration of Texas independence on San Jacinto Day—April 21st. In 1922, April 21st became the official day of events for all Aggies and Muster was born. The March 1923 *Texas Aggie* urged, "If there is an A&M man in one-hundred miles of you, you are expected to get together, eat a little, and live over the days you spent at the A&M College of Texas." In 1942, Aggie Muster gained international recognition when 26 men, led by General George Moore, Class of 1908, mustered during the Japanese siege of Corregidor to remember campus friendships and honor Aggies who had died, all the participants expecting soon to join them.

Muster is an old military term, referring in an earlier age to the periodic gatherings of soldiers from far-flung units to report that they still lived, to see old friends—and to get paid.

Muster is the essence of Aggie culture and spirit. This ceremony has no parallel in any other institution in America—not in the armed forces, not in the CIA, not in business and certainly not in any other college or university.

Tonight's observance—here and in hundreds of places all over the world, including Iraq and Afghanistan—is not just to remember those Aggies who have passed away during the last year; we also reaffirm the unbreakable bond that links the newest fish to the oldest former student and, indeed, to all the generations of Aggies who have walked these treasured grounds over the past 132 years.

Muster means even more to me today than it did when I was here because of what I do now. To be honest, having been the president of Texas A&M has made being Secretary of Defense more difficult for me. For I cannot help but contrast walking this campus as president and seeing thousands of students 18 to 25 years old in T-shirts and shorts and backpacks on the way to class—and now, as Secretary, walking a forward operating base in the wilds of Afghanistan and seeing young Americans the same age as the students here but in full body armor. Or seeing them grievously wounded at Walter Reed or Bethesda or other hospitals or receiving them home one last time at Dover. They all have voluntarily put their lives on the line and put their dreams aside in order to protect your freedom to achieve your dreams.

We are engaged in two wars, and every man and woman in combat today—in harm's way—is there because I sent them. Since the hour I was sworn in as Secretary of Defense, 1,327 American men and women in uniform have been killed in combat in Iraq and Afghanistan; 10,443 have been wounded. Each of them is in my thoughts and prayers every day and will be every day for the rest of my life.

As in all our nation's wars since 1876, Aggies have served and are serving in today's wars with distinction. They remember where they came from. Listen to the words of a Class of 2000 Aggie, serving as a first lieutenant in the 101st Airborne, who emailed a friend on campus on the eve of the war in Iraq in 2003:

Currently, I am sitting in the Kuwaiti desert. My current position as an artillery battery executive officer in the 101st Airborne Division has me realizing that I will be facing combat in a matter of days. It had occurred to me today that there are several reasons why I am here, now, getting ready to do what I am about to do. I have talked to my family; I have talked to my friends. I haven't yet talked to anyone at my school.

There is something different about being here after having gone through those experiences unique to Aggieland. I know this because of the junior officers I see around me everyday, and the manner in which they carry themselves, and the manner in which they perceive their soldiers. This is an attempt to explain that, as I see it through my eyes.

A&M has a special way of putting you in your place. I certainly don't mean that in a bad way. You truly become part of something bigger than yourself, and realize the dependence each of us has on one another . . . going through the Corps of Cadets is, to this day, the hardest thing I have ever done in my life. And, to this day, it is the most valuable experience of my life. Learning that leadership is all about relationships, and trust, and values, things that many young people don't learn other places. These are invaluable lessons. As I come to understand the ramifications of what I do, that is, train to commit violence on behalf of the American people, I realize that it is exactly those values I learned at Texas A&M that I can rely on.

As sophomores in the Corps, we were always told to love our fish. If I had one thing to say to the commissionees in this year's graduating class, I would tell them, above all else, love their soldiers, Marines and airmen. My soldiers are my heroes. They come from across the country. They grew up without the benefits I had in my life. For one reason or another, they serve the people of the United States of America every day. Their daily routine and sacrifices are the bedrock and foundation of what makes this country safe. I am humbled every day by the sacrifices they make, by their hard work, and by their willingness to serve despite the circumstances. As an officer, and being allowed the benefits of an officer, they will always be my heroes.

So, as this campaign gets set to begin, I would like to thank you for what Texas A&M has gifted me. I pray that, as things begin, the prayers of the faculty, staff and students are with the brave young men and women who serve in the armed forces. A&M, as an institution, has done a great service to this country in the manner in which it serves the nation.

Again, I ask for your prayers for my heroes. Lord willing, we will all be home soon. In the meantime, I look forward to seeing my buddies on the high ground.

That email was sent six long years ago. In that time, 22 Aggies have made the supreme sacrifice for their country in Iraq and Afghanistan. Ten of them were students while I was president. I signed the diplomas of four of them, shook their hands and handed those diplomas to them, and witnessed their commissioning. For eight of them, I probably signed the paper that sent them into combat, and for nine I wrote the condolence letter to their families.

So I ask your indulgence tonight for me to call the Muster for them, for these Aggie heroes—and I ask you to rise and respond with a resounding "here" for each of 22: lest we ever forget their sacrifice:

First Lieutenant Jonathan Rozier '01

Captain Lyle Gordon '97

Captain Sean Sims '94

Captain Todd Christmas 2000

Captain Ernesto Blanco '98

First Lieutenant Doyle Hufstedler III '01

Maj. Matthew Worrell '94

Captain Sean Lyerly '98

Specialist Daniel Gomes '08

Specialist William Edwards '06

First Lieutenant Jeremy Ray '04

First Lieutenant Matthew Vandegrift '03

First Lieutenant Timothy Cunningham '04

Mark Humphries '74

Sgt. William Meeuswen '03

Chief Warrant Officer Richard Salter '85

First Lieutenant Ryan Sanders '01

Captain Blake Russell '98

Sgt. 1st Class Merideth Howard '76

Lance Corporal Luke Yepsen '08

Second Lieutenant Peter Burks '03

Corporal Christopher West '04

May they, heroes all, rest in peace and eternally in God's hands and in the loving embrace of the Aggie family.

Of all our traditions, Muster is greatest. Tears will be shed tonight for men and women most of us have never known personally. But they are Aggies, and so we mourn them and we miss them, and we remember them and we celebrate their lives.

The English poet John Donne wrote in 1624 [in *Devotions upon Emergent Occasions*], "no man is an island, entire of itself . . . any man's death diminishes me. . . ." Tonight, Aggies are diminished by our losses of the past year, but we are restored by memories and by knowing that the chain remains unbroken—that a new generation of Aggies will take their place in the long line, remembering and celebrating the past even as the University moves boldly into the future.

We stand and build on the shoulders of those who have gone before. They are our strong foundation. They are our family.

Tonight, we will answer "Here," knowing that when our time to go home comes, someone will say also for us, "Here." This is the Aggie Spirit; this is the Aggie family. Both will endure.

So, softly call the Muster.

# Maj. Stephen G. Ruth '92

*2010—Reed Arena*

Maj. Stephen G. Ruth '92. Photo from editor's collection.

Stephen G. Ruth holds a BBA degree from Texas A&M University, where he served as student body president in 1991–92, and a master's degree in organizational leadership from George Mason University. He served as an assistant professor of leadership at the US Military Academy beginning in 2003 and as commandant of the USMA Preparatory School for two years.

Ruth also attended the Infantry Officer's Advanced Courses, Combined Arms Services Staff School, Airborne, and Ranger School. He attended the Command & General Staff College and has served as British exchange officer at HQ Land Warfare Centre.

In addition to being stationed in Western Europe for three years, Ruth's tours of duty have taken him around the world, with deployments to Macedonia, Bosnia-Herzegovina, Bahrain, Qatar, and Kuwait. He conducted lectures on leadership at Beijing International MBA School, Peking University, and negotiations training in Baghdad, Iraq. He spent a year at Harvard's Kennedy School before bring assigned to III Corps and Fort Hood, Texas, in July 2016.

Ruth has been honored for his contributions to the armed services with many decorations, including two Meritorious Service Medals, four Army Commendation Medals, twelve Army Achievement Medals, two Armed Forces Expeditionary Medals, the Army Superior Unit Award, the Joint Meritorious Award, the Iraq Campaign Medal, the NATO Medal, and the United Nations Medal.

## We Are Called to Serve*

It's great to be back in Aggieland. I want to extend a special welcome to the honored families and friends of our fallen comrades. Please know that tonight you are surrounded by the Aggie Spirit and the love and support of the extended Aggie Family.

I bring greetings to our administration . . . starting with Dr. Bowen Loftin . . . and to our faculty and staff . . . the gatekeepers who guide and nurture us along the way. To our Former Students, particularly the Class of 1960—you have given us such wonderful examples of Leadership and Service.

And to students: You complete the Aggie package as the 12th Man, which is known and respected across the world.

The Singing Cadets, Women's Chorus, and Century Singers—your voices lift the hearts of thousands. The Aggie Band, you have been and always will be the Pulse of Aggieland. And, of course, the Corps of Cadets . . . Keepers of the Spirit . . . a title that is not merely descriptive but imparts Duty upon those who wear the uniform.

I come here today by way of the United Kingdom, where I currently serve as a representative of our great country and this fine institution. I have been privileged to serve in places around the globe. Everywhere I have gone, I have gone as an ambassador of freedom for the greatest country on earth, and an ambassador of the values of the greatest university on the planet.

But if you had asked me, in my fish year in the Corps, if I thought I would be here today, speaking at the Campus Muster, I might have smiled and told you, "I cogitate so, sir." But in reality, I was just hoping I would survive Mr. Joe Lyons, Cliff Coleman, Scot Joy, and the rest of the mean and nasty sophomores in D-2.

By the way, to the fish in the Corps who are almost done with that tough first year, just know that all that yelling by your sophomores is just therapy from their fish year. It's business, nothing personal—hooah!

*Speech title derived by editor from speech contents

The history of April 21st takes us back to 1836 . . . to General Sam Houston and the battle of San Jacinto. Texas A&M was founded a mere 40 years after that epic battle. Though, to the best of my knowledge, it is not recorded anywhere, the first A&M cadets undoubtedly listened to first-hand stories of warriors in that epic battle. They surely were inspired by those stories and they passed those values from generation to generation to generation.

The early beginnings of Muster were celebrations of our Texas heritage on the parade fields as well as on the battlefields of San Jacinto. What we remember from that time are the spirit and tenacity of our forefathers—spirit and tenacity that secured our independence. Spirit and tenacity that would later serve Aggies well—in Corregidor, in Viet Nam where the Class of '60 would serve, and currently in Iraq and Afghanistan. Aggies have that sixth sense that compels them to respond to the call of duty. From the entire class of 1942 who commissioned as a class and responded to the very real threats of World War II, to thousands of Aggies who responded in more modern times to the events of 9/11, to Hurricanes Rita, Katrina, and Ike, and, even as I speak, to those who are responding to the earthquakes in Haiti and Chile. I am quite certain there are Aggies in Iceland helping there, too. Aggies have always lived up to these great expectations. The theme throughout time is—when our country has faced its most difficult hours—Aggies have rushed to the forefront of duty to country, love of our fellow man, and in response to our common values of courage and sacrifice.

I was often reminded of this during the tumultuous days following the collapse of the 1999 Bonfire. Our solidarity in grief, in coming to the aid of the wounded, in comforting those who lost so much that day reinforced our common values. It shook us to our core, but it also revealed our core: decency, love, and devotion to others. That's what it meant to be an Aggie during those most difficult days . . . and that's what it means to be an Aggie in the best of days.

As we gather here for Muster, for some of you, it may be your first . . . and others may have brought a friend or colleague along . . . This is where your affection and reverence for this most sacred tradition becomes a part of your very being. Through this experience, you understand why Aggieland is so special, and why we love her so. Now as we are defending our country once again, we honor two of our Aggies who were killed in combat during Operation Enduring Freedom this past year: a recent graduate, Staff Sergeant Christopher Staats, Class of 2001, and one of my upperclassmen, Lieutenant Colonel Mark Stratton, Class of 1991.

A few weeks prior to his death, Mark made a special effort to share his Aggie Spirit and observe Aggie Muster. In an email to the *Texas Aggie* magazine, he wrote:

> Our primary mission is to develop the basic infrastructure to bring hope and self-sufficiency to the people of the Panjshir Valley in Afghanistan. Our highest priority is a roads network that we are building to connect 300,000 people to the modern world for the first time. The people in the mountains here defeated nine Soviet invasions, but they have welcomed us here to assist them in keeping out terrorists and the Taliban influences.

Mark continued to write:

> As the Commander of a Provincial Reconstruction Team and the only Aggie within 100 miles, I asked the Afghan Governor and his Mujahedeen security detail to join me on top of a small mountain to mark the occasion of Muster.

In his actions, and in sharing his story of just one year ago, Mark reminds us that it's not the size of the Muster gathering that matters; it's the Spirit in which we gather. What a Spirit! What a Commitment! What an Inspiration!

Lieutenant General James Hollingsworth '40 passed away last month. General Hollingsworth was the most decorated Aggie in the history of our school. He was also the only living person to have a statue dedicated to him on this campus.

Would you please stand? I will read their three names and ask you to respond with "Here" in our time-honored tradition.

Staff Sergeant Christopher Staats, Class of 2001

Lieutenant Colonel Mark Stratton, Class of 1991

Lieutenant General James Hollingsworth, Class of 1940

This tradition has served Aggies well through both peace and war. Each Aggie here should know that we do not take your current commitment or future sacrifices for granted. Thank you; please be seated.

Members of the Class of 1960, you have served us well. My first Full Bird Colonel was from the Class of 1960, a former Yell Leader and later a Professor of Military Science—who is the head guy in charge of the Army ROTC program—Colonel Richard Biondi. Sir, you taught me how to have an argument—excuse me, I mean a professional discussion—with a superior officer. You taught me how I must consider the bigger picture, the strategic objectives of an organization, and how I must always allow both parties to finish a "professional discussion" with their dignity and integrity intact. And you also taught me that sometimes, the best solution is simply, Salute the Flag and move out! (with a quickness!) Sir, I have enjoyed getting to know your entire family over the past 20 years. Thank you.

I also want to talk about another member of the Class of 1960, because the lessons he taught have also guided me for decades. I can recall meeting Mr. Bill Heye during my early years as a cadet. He is one of those typical Ol' Ags who visits the campus, attends a few board meetings, talks to some students, and gives some "money" to the university.

But I was profoundly impacted when I discovered that he had also been your Corps Commander. I realized that he continued to be a great role model . . . and then realized that I also wanted to be that type of a role model. I wanted to reinforce the concept that Leadership Titles are not reasons to be proud of oneself; rather, titles bestowed on us are simply non-negotiable obligations to serve your constituents, your community, and your alma mater for a lifetime! Thank you, sir.

What these Old Ags have taught me is that with Leadership comes Responsibility. I have a four-year-old son. I am already preparing him for his fish year in the Corps. I ask him, "What comes with freedom, son?" and he dutifully answers, "Responsibility, sir." Then he bear-crawls up the steps and shows his mother his four-year-old "war face." She really likes that face.

People tell me all the time, when referring to our three children: treasure the memories, they will be grown and gone before you know it. So it is with our time at Texas A&M University.

One of the great attributes of Texas A&M is that it is a meritocracy —a meritocracy full of opportunities that abound if you are willing to work hard and serve your Aggie community that has loved you so much and given you so much. And you have a constant reminder to take with you . . . a constant reminder of Responsibility, Leadership, and Service. That reminder is the Aggie Ring. Some of you received your Aggie Ring just last Friday.

Raise your hand if your ring is just five days old. A round of applause for those brand new Texas Aggies.

Now raise your hand if your ring is 50 or more years old!

Everything on the ring represents a value that all Aggies should demonstrate. On the top is a large shield, symbolizing the desire to protect the reputation of the university. The five stars on the shield refer to the continued development of mind; body; spiritual attainment; emotional poise; and integrity of character. The eagle inspires you with its agility and ability to reach great heights.

On the side, the Lone Star encircled with a wreath of olive and laurel leaves symbolizes achievement and a desire for peace. The live oak leaves represent the strength to fight for our country and our state. These are the values that current students strive to internalize and the values that former students endeavour to uphold for the rest of their lives.

By embracing this sense of Responsibility and Commitment to excellence, as individuals you will always honor the Aggies who have gone before you.

Let me conclude with some thoughts about what makes the Aggie experience so unique and the Aggie Network so special. Some call our values old-fashioned in a culture that places a premium on satisfying self. We live in a "me first" time. We are told to "look out for number one." Or "get the most out of life."

I am here to tell you that you will never live a life of fulfilment by looking inward . . . only outward. The greatest blessings in life are shared with others. They are an offering of selflessness poured out on the altar of sacrifice.

If you want true rewards, give your life in Service to others. If you want true self-satisfaction, deny yourself and take up the cause of people in need around you.

As Aggies, we are called to Serve . . . called to serve causes greater than self. We are called to serve in foreign battlefields . . . in board rooms of corporations . . . in classrooms and hospital rooms. In each setting we are sent to serve, and to be helpful to others.

We were placed on this planet to make the world a better place. We are sent here to combat evil with goodness . . . to permeate darkness with light . . . to wash away age-old hatreds with eternal love . . . to make peace among enemies.

And we never stop, and sometimes die trying, because the mission is greater than the man.

May we leave this Muster with new ties of friendship and seek new opportunities to serve. May our hearts be kindled in fellowship and also softened with sympathy for those who sorrow and suffer. Happy Muster to all of you! May God Bless Texas A&M University and may God bless the United States of America.

Thank You and Gig 'em.

# Tobin R. Boenig '95

### *2011—Reed Arena*

Tobin R. Boenig '95.
Photo from editor's
collection.

Tobin R. "Toby" Boenig was born February 19, 1973, in Seguin, Texas. He graduated from high school in a class of fifty-four in Marion, Texas, in 1991 and served as state vice president for the Texas Future Farmers of America. Enrolling at Texas A&M University, he pledged to a friend that he would concentrate solely on his classes and not get involved in anything extracurricular. That pledge lasted a couple of weeks. Toby served in many student leadership positions while at A&M that included Speaker of the Student Senate and student body president. He graduated cum laude in 1996 with a BS degree in agricultural development.

He returned to Texas A&M in June 1998 to work in the Services for Students with Disabilities Office and became manager of collegiate licensing that same year. Boenig earned a law degree at the University of Texas School of Law and went to work for the Vinson & Elkins law firm. He then served as a compliance attorney at the M. D. Anderson Cancer Center before he became vice president and chief compliance officer at the University of Texas Medical Branch.

## "Rise to the Challenge"

Good evening. It is one of the great honors of my life to be asked to participate in this evening's Aggie Muster Ceremony. April 21st is a special day for all Aggies. On this day, I have been fortunate to travel across the state of Texas to speak at numerous Aggie Musters. Never would I imagine a return trip to College Station to speak for this occasion. I feel so very blessed. It is a daunting task to capture the spirit of Muster and attempt to inspire this great crowd. I do hope to rise to the challenge.

My five-year-old son, Kieran, in the auditorium tonight, is a big super hero fan. In fact, he loves them all . . . Iron Man, Superman, Batman, but his first super hero obsession was Spiderman, and it still remains one of his favorites today. When Kieran was about three-and-a-half years old, he learned the all important lesson, that "with great power comes great responsibility." He reminds me of that quote often, and I am reminded of it tonight because I am well aware of those who have spoken on this night before me.

And even more important than that. . . I feel a great responsibility because I know what Aggie Muster means to you . . . and to all Aggies. Texas A&M is so rich in tradition.

Texas A&M is so rich in tradition, but no tradition is as important or as meaningful as Muster. At its core, Muster is about life. . . a celebration of our lives when we were on this fine campus, and a celebration of our classmates, who while they are not present in body today are present in our hearts. To those families and loved ones who are here tonight to honor their Aggies. . . we share your sorrow, and we too, mourn for your loss. We thank those who have gone before us for their contributions to their families and to our Aggie family. For it is our collective whole that makes Texas A&M the unique and special place that it is.

To the Class of '61. . . it is great to see you. This campus has seen a lot of changes from when I was a student. . . I can only imagine the changes that you have seen over the past 50 years. You are a generation that has witnessed many historical events and played such an important role in recent history. You were born the children of the "greatest generation"—the sons and daughters of the survivors of the Great Depression and the heroes of World War II. Your teenage memories are of the Korean War. . . Many of you would serve proudly in Vietnam following your time at Texas A&M. You rose to the challenges that faced you and served for God and country, and I would like to offer my sincere thank you for that service.

Your life span has also witnessed the greatest leaps in technology—the space race, the information super highway, and so many more. Your contributions have not gone unnoticed. I would also like to thank you for your contributions to Texas A&M. While my days at Texas A&M in the early and mid-1990s were, in many ways, different than yours, some things did not change when I was a student and even remain the same today. . . We are always there for one another . . . in triumph and in tragedy. That will not change. That cannot change! That's why we love this place, and that is why young men and women enroll to be Aggies year after year.

As a student at Texas A&M, I was always amazed with the numerous stories of Aggies meeting some challenge that I could never imagine. *Aggies who rose to the challenge.* It's a very humbling experience when you walk the halls of the Memorial Student Center with the plaques of the Aggie Congressional Medal of Honor winners . . . when you walk by General Rudder's statue and are reminded of his bravery at Pointe du Hoc in Normandy during World War II. Have you ever wondered what you would do in the face of some unimaginable challenge? I did. I used to wonder if I had the strength to rise to a tremendous personal challenge.

Never did I realize that I would be presented with an unimaginable challenge so soon after I graduated from college. I graduated from Texas A&M on May 10, 1996. That's right. . . for those quick mathematicians out there. I did have an extra senior year. As I was saying. . . I graduated from this fine institution on May 10, 1996. Eight days later, that great challenge in my life arrived.

Seven of us—all Aggies—decided to celebrate the end of the school year with a trip down the Guadalupe. I had been on the Guadalupe River more times than I could count—I grew up just miles away.

Texas had been experiencing a drought that caused the Guadalupe to be very slow and shallow. It didn't matter much to the seven of us. We were going to float and tell old college stories—old stories that weren't really that old.

I don't remember what all was talked about that day, but I do remember how relaxing the day was unwinding with friends. I lay on the edge of my raft, shut my eyes, and took a quick nap or siesta. When I shut my eyes, the water had looked about three or four feet deep. My eyes were shut for probably three minutes, and then I became so hot that I could barely stand it, so I rolled off the side of the raft. I didn't open my eyes to see how deep the water was when I rolled off because I knew the water was deep enough. I was wrong. The water was only about a foot deep and my raft was about a foot above the water. So I had about a two-foot fall and hit my head on a rock.

A fierce pain shot across my head. I don't think I was knocked unconscious. I tried to reach up to feel my head, but my arms wouldn't respond. Then I tried to turn over because I was face down in the water. Nothing happened. I couldn't turn over. I had no idea what was going on. I wasn't scared lying in the water at that point, but I kept thinking to myself "How am I going to turn over? Why CAN'T I turn over?" I lay in the water for a short while with my eyes closed because I didn't want to lose my contacts. I started getting scared. It was at that point that I opened my eyes under the water. All I could see was murky water and gravel... and blood.

I stayed underwater for what seemed like forever, wondering if my friends would ever come and help. Since I was stuck on the rocks, my body floated in one place while all my friends continued to tube down the river. They thought that I was joking as I lay face down in the water. But they quickly realized something was wrong. I think they might have seen blood, and that's when they knew I wasn't kidding around.

They finally came to me, and Jeb turned me over. His first reaction was "What are you doing? What's wrong?" In fact, I had no idea what was the matter.

To this day I am not sure how they got me back on the raft, but suddenly I saw these former student leaders of Texas A&M take action. Everyone had a role and understood the immediate chain of command. My duty was to shut up and listen. (Something I'm not usually very good at.) Jeb was in charge. Trey went to call 911, and the others started to clear a path to the bank. Brian was already in the raft, and was in charge of stabilizing my head, and barked orders at me to look straight ahead. I kept trying to look around and see what was going on, but my friends kept yelling at me to stay still and not move my head. While Becky, Lara, and Amy cleared a path, Jeb and Kevin pushed the raft to the bank of the river.

A couple of the guys had been lifeguards, and some had an idea of what the injury might have been, so they were cautious and knew not to move my head. I'm convinced, in fact I know without a doubt, that their caution is one of the reasons why I am able to utilize as much of my body as I can today. *They rose to the challenge.* If they had not known what to do . . . if they had just tossed me on the raft and not secured my head, my spinal cord could have easily sustained more serious damage.

The strange events continued to unfold. As Trey ran up the bank to call 911, he knocked on the first door he came to. As fortune would have it, the house happened to belong to Dr. John Flannigan, the chief of the emergency room at McKenna Hospital in New Braunfels, Texas. He came down the bank to the river where I was still in the raft with Brian. I received expert medical attention within 5 to 10 minutes after my accident occurred.

Everything is crystal clear in my memory right up until the time they began to place me in the ambulance. I heard my friends assure me that I was going to be all right. As they placed the stretcher in the ambulance, I remember that my thoughts went straight to my mother. "Whatever you do, don't tell my mother," I told the doctor. She had just been diagnosed with breast cancer. She had just started chemotherapy, and I didn't want her to worry about me.

"Whatever you do, just DON'T TELL MY MOTHER."

The next thing I remember is being in the emergency room in New Braunfels. They asked me to raise my arm. I picked up my arm, then it just flopped. They asked me to raise my other arm. Again, I picked it up, and it just flopped. Then emergency room personnel told me that they were going to airlift me to Northeast Baptist Hospital in San Antonio. I spent that first night in the ICU not knowing whether my paralysis was temporary or permanent.

My challenge had arrived. My neurosurgeon walked into my room that next morning, and he would deliver the news I did not want to hear. He informed me that I sustained a spinal cord injury (subluxation of C4–5). He told me I would never walk again, and that I would be lucky if I would be able to touch my nose, let alone do anything that my 23-year-old body had grown accustomed to doing.

That night after I heard the news, a lot of things went through my head. I believed that I would walk, but I had lingering thoughts of how

I would handle the situation if I were unable to walk. Walking would be the big goal, but what about life's other small tasks? I never thought about the daily activities. What if I was unable to pick up my arms? What if I was unable to brush my teeth, wash my hair, or shave? I thought more about the bigger picture then I did the daily living. Simple things that I had always taken for granted. Hugging, two-stepping with a pretty girl, settling down, getting married, having kids, holding a baby, playing catch with my kids. I was petrified at the thought of not being able to experience these feelings. I had always dreamed about having a family. It was a huge part of my upbringing. I wanted kids, and I wanted to be there to help them through their little league days, but I could not even move my arms. How could I throw a ball if I couldn't move my arms?

The most amazing thing happened later. Over the next couple of days, hundreds of people showed up at the hospital to show their support. Thousands of letters poured in. My family and many of my closest friends would stay at the hospital throughout those first few nights. I had so many people (and so many Aggies) who were there for me. They wanted to make sure that I had their support *so that I could rise to this challenge*. It would be one thing if I let myself down, but there was no way... no way that I would let them down.

I dedicated myself to rehab (asked for the meanest physical therapist —that's exactly what I received) and spent six months doing in-patient rehab and an additional year and a half in out-patient therapy. I thought to myself—I must rise to this challenge. But, in the end it was not really me that rose to the challenge. It was a mother, who after driving to work and then to radiation treatment and then another hour to my hospital, who was there every night... *she rose to the challenge*. It was a father who drove me to outpatient rehab every day for a year and half... *he rose to the challenge*. It was my brother and my closest friends (who are here tonight) who would spend every night with me during those first two trying weeks and then after that every weekend they brought laughter to my room... *they rose to the challenge*. It was the Aggie community and my hometown community of Marion, Texas, that supported me... *they rose to the challenge*. I drew strength from them—and they tell me that they drew strength from me.

And, yes, with the aid of a walker, I was able to stand up and put one foot in front of the other. It was walking, and it wasn't pretty. But I did it. We did it. I realize now that the hard work that I did during those four years was not so that I could walk, but it was for something more. I don't ever need to question whether I will be able to live life to the fullest. Most nights now, my wife, Jennifer, and I will take our five-year-old to the front yard, and I will throw the ball to him, and he will clobber it. If I wasn't pushed so hard with love and support (if I had not relied on my faith) I might have never been able to throw a ball, and Kieran would not be able to experience baseball with his dad. And soon I'll be playing ball with Jennifer and our new baby, Sawyer. I am so thankful to be able to experience all of those feelings. . . those feelings that my neurosurgeon said I would never experience again.

Many of those here in the reunion Class of '61 were born in 1939. That same year, baseball great Lou Gehrig was battling the disease that would one day bear his name, and he delivered his now famous speech at Yankee Stadium where he declared himself "the luckiest man on the face of the earth." I, too, know how he feels because I have felt that love and support. I have felt that love and support from this Aggie family. It can help a man or woman face any challenge that is presented. There will no doubt be many more challenges that you and I face, and we will rise to those challenges because we are part of a great family. Friends, I hope you feel that love and support from this Aggie family tonight as we answer "Here" and spend the rest of our lives celebrating what they have given to us. Softly call the Muster.

# John R. Hoyle '57

## *2012—Reed Arena*

John R. Hoyle '57. Photo from editor's collection.

John Richard Hoyle was born February 2, 1935, in Rush Springs, Oklahoma. Professor emeritus of educational administration at Texas A&M University, Hoyle was a forerunner in leadership education and assessment and an authority on the visioning process and future studies.

His peers named him one of America's four "exceptional living scholars" in educational administration/leadership. He received the inaugural 2007 Hoyle Leadership Award of Texas A&M University's Administrative Leadership Institute for making a positive difference in the lives of students as well as the Living Legend award, given by the National Council of Professors of Educational Administration and its Texas affiliate. He also received the Golden Deeds Award for distinguished service to Texas education.

Hoyle authored more than half a dozen books and over 150 scholarly publications during his forty years in higher education. With his son, John Hoyle Jr., he produced a three-volume series of books, *Good Bull*, which recall humorous escapades of Aggies over the past fifty years. While a student at A&M, he was a member of the Corps of Cadets and played on a Southwest Conference championship baseball team. He was a public school teacher, coach, and administrator, as well as a professor and administrator at six universities. He served on the executive committee of Texas A&M's first Faculty Senate. Hoyle spoke at Aggie Musters throughout the world for three decades. He and his wife took groups of education students to A&M's Study Abroad Center in Italy.

Hoyle died March 12, 2013, after a brief illness.

## We Fight to the Finish*

Howdy and good evening! I am deeply honored to share this precious time of remembrance and celebration of lives well lived. First, I want to thank the Student Muster Committee for selecting me to be your speaker, and since we are together as the Aggie family, I would like you to meet my family. My lovely wife, Carolyn, has advised me now for 54 years and is a TCU graduate; our son John Jr. and his wife, Julie; and our daughter Laura—all Aggie graduates. Also our grandson David and his wife, Gloria—also Aggies; grandson Michael, a current student; grandson Winston, a former student, and his sister Jennifer, a senior at A&M Consolidated recently admitted to the Fightin' Texas Aggie Class of 2016. This all began with a baseball scholarship and a great education at Texas A&M University.

How do you ever give back enough to an institution that gave you so much? Sometimes we fail to realize just how much we owe to our former professors and advisors. My first sight of this campus was not very pretty. I remember the humidity, cows grazing near the main administration building, a water tower, and several military-style Corps dorms. Someone said that it looked like "Sing Sing on the Brazos." When my folks left me in this strange land to return to Tulsa, Oklahoma, I had thoughts of hitchhiking back home. I had no idea there were no women on campus, and did not realize that the Corps of Cadets was mandatory. A shaved head, khaki attire, running in heat late for class, and unkind words from upperclassmen were part of the daily routine, but like many of you, whether in the Corps or not, I refused to quit.

Colonel Joe Davis, our Commandant, told 2,000 of us in our first command meeting at the Grove, "Look to your right and look to your left, because neither of them will be here to graduate with you in four years." Our Class of '57 beat those odds very well with over seventy percent graduating.

Tonight, we gather here to softly call the Muster for those loved ones we lost during this past year. Oh! How we loved them and grieve their loss to families, friends, and the entire Aggie nation. We miss their love

*Speech title derived by editor from speech contents

for family and friends, and the fun and laughter they shared. No other university around the world sets aside such a sacred time to honor loved ones lost from their families. This evening, we also honor the Class of 1962, who graduated from this great university 50 years ago. We congratulate you and thank you for the sacrifices you made for us in Viet Nam, your successes in business, the military, medicine and education. Also, we thank you for your community leadership in building a better state and nation, and your fifty years of generous support of our great university. Much has changed in Aggieland since your time on campus, while much remains the same. You sat on the grass for your Muster ceremonies held in front of the MSC [Memorial Student Center]. You also remember Silver Taps, Corps trips, Bonfire, Ol' Army Lou, Pinky Downs, Zarape's, the clay pits, Uncle Ed's, and other hangouts. You have stayed in touch with each other, which is the Aggie way.

Mike Dillingham '35 of Bryan, Texas, recently celebrated his 100th birthday. He recalls an enrollment of 3,000 students; Reveille I was a black and white mutt and led the Aggie band onto the field during halftime. Dillingham was in the Corps and a member of the baseball team that won the Southwest Conference championship. Two years ago at age 98, he threw the first pitch at an Aggie home game. He told the Bryan Eagle newspaper, "We are all Aggies. We like one another. We keep up with one another." That is exactly why we are gathered here tonight.

In 1942, the love and devotion for Texas A&M was never more poignantly displayed than when a news dispatch reported that twenty-six Aggies led by General George F. Moore '08 mustered at the mouth of the Malinta tunnel in the Philippine Islands. "As they sang Texas songs," the report continued, "Japanese artillery on Bataan peninsula banged away and the big guns on Corregidor roared in reply." Those brave, devoted Aggies knew that roll call for the missing might soon include them, but their dedication, friendship and Aggie loyalty inspired what has become our greatest tradition. After fierce combat against overwhelming odds, Corregidor fell to the enemy, and all twenty-seven Aggies either died in combat or were taken prisoner.

Among those captured and thrown into a despicable prison cell was Urban C. Hopmann '37, who was one of the 25 who attended the Muster at the Malinta tunnel. Hopmann endured starvation and brutal treatment, but he refused to give up. According to the August 1992 *Texas Aggie,* Hopmann protected his cherished Aggie Ring from Japanese guards by hiding it in a secret pocket in his ragged short pants during the day and burying it in dirt under his body at night. After Hopmann was liberated by American forces, he told other Aggies that "They took my wristwatch, but they were not going to get my Aggie Ring!" He proudly wore that ring for the rest of his life. Aggies honor and keep sacred traditions.

Heroes? I can give you thousands of Aggies who have served this country with integrity and honor wearing their Aggie Ring. Your Muster speaker two years ago, Colonel Stephen Ruth, '92, called a few days ago from Baghdad wishing me well with this presentation and expressed his great love for Texas A&M University and what it stands for. Yes, he was proudly wearing his Aggie ring!

A few years ago my wife, Carolyn, and I chaperoned a group of Aggies for a spring semester to Texas A&M's study abroad center in Italy. The students and I decided that we would hold the first Muster ceremony at the Center. We invited students from Kansas State and Colorado to join us, and after the candle lighting, roll call, and the reading of "The Last Corps Trip," they were truly impressed and deeply moved that our university would set aside a time to honor loved ones who had died the past year. Yes, Mike Dillingham, "we keep up with one another" and cherish the precious time we had together.

Muster inspires approximately three hundred groups of Aggies and friends worldwide from the Piney Woods of East Texas to the battle zones of Afghanistan to come together for food and fellowship and call the roll for the missing. Tonight we also are together to fondly remember the humorous, perhaps exaggerated "Good Bull" stories told by deceased loved ones about their days on campus. They told about their professors: their eloquent or boring lectures, and perhaps their brilliance, excessive rigor, personal mannerisms, and confusing assignments.

In my time we had nicknames for our professors, i.e., Spittin' Sid, who taught Shakespeare and who often became so excited during a lecture he showered the first three rows with spittle. We solved the problem by wearing ponchos and helmets to his class. Also, we had Screamin' Al, a history professor who became so excited while telling stories about Teddy Roosevelt, Abe Lincoln and others, that he often jumped up on his desk, spread his arms and screamed his lecture that could be heard from the third floor of the Academic Building to the YMCA. He was also a preacher at a local church on Sunday—a fine teacher and preacher was he!

We also remember fondly "Notes" Nance, "Bluebook" Benton, "Get it" Greer who said "get it" after every sentence, and "Dirty Shirt" Nelson. We called him Dirty Shirt because he changed his shirt once a year whether it was needed or not. Dirty Shirt taught biology in the 1950s to 200 freshmen at a time. One morning, Dirty Shirt arrived at 7:45 a.m. for an 8:00 class, placed his old worn hat on the podium and went to the restroom. At 8:00 o'clock, 200 sleepy and exhausted, bald-headed freshmen entered the room, sat down and promptly removed their caps. They next checked their watches. After 10 minutes with no Dirty Shirt, they declared a walk and scrambled for the windows and doors and sprinted to the Memorial Student Center for coffee. At that moment Dirty Shirt entered the room, saw the escape in progress and remarked, "I'll get them the next class period!" The next class, he told his 200 fish that he was really irritated at them for running out of his class and with loud emphasis yelled, "When you see my hat here, that means I am here, and if you leave the room you will get an 'F'; is that clear!" "Yes Sir!" they shouted. Two days later, Dirty Shirt walked into the 8:00 class, looked up and saw 200 hats sitting on the desks. These "Good Bull" stories are part of the fabric of A&M culture and reach back into our early beginnings in 1876. A story is told about how our first six students used their sabers to ward off a pack of wolves circling them on their way to chow! The only wolves today are cars circling to find a parking place!

My thirty-five years on the faculty pushed me to earn the label of Texas Aggie. I knew in my heart that I was representing Texas A&M University, and my challenge was always to be well prepared and know I represented something far greater than myself. Five years ago, I taught a class of eighteen graduate students who earned their bachelor's degrees at other universities ranging from the University of Iowa,

Florida State University, and yes, the University of Texas. During the first class, I told them that since they chose to be in my class, they were now Aggies whether they liked it or not. I enthusiastically proceeded to share our traditions, history, a few Good Bull stories and my high expectations for their performance and my pride in the high national rankings of our department. The next day all eighteen students walked into class proudly wearing Aggie T-shirts. Now that earns a big Whoop! After telling these stories to one of my classes, I walked in to find only hats sitting on the desks. Be careful of the Good Bull stories you tell.

Texas A&M University is highly respected, ranked first in the nation by *Smart Money* magazine in "pay back ratio"—what graduates earn compared to the cost of their education. We rank first in Texas in student retention rates for minority students, both African American and Hispanic. These high rankings and other signs of excellence are in large part due to the 2020 Vision effort driving our great school to reach a top ten ranking based on several benchmarks of excellence. State funding for higher education has been cut severely and other sources have been reduced due to times of budget reductions. Our exemplary success as a leading institution is driven by external research funding secured by creative faculty and the excellent efforts by the Texas A&M Foundation, the Association of Former Students, the 12th Man Foundation, and generous contributions made by Aggies around the world who want to support their beloved university. This generosity is clearly displayed when approximately seventy-nine percent of our students receive some form of financial aid. We also have the most student-friendly president in the nation in Dr. Bowen Loftin.

I believe we will reach our 2020 Vision dream because Aggies do not believe in finishing second to any other university. We have moved up to the Southeastern Conference, and in time, with your support, we will be the SEC leader in both academics and athletics. Aggies believe the glass is half full and do not engage in "Stinkin' Thinkin'," even though we take our losses hard. We tell each other to "wait until next year" or "we just ran out of time" or "we needed one more at bat." We all remember failing a quiz or two, but we hit the books harder to pass the next one. Aggies turn disappointment and failure into successes.

Writer Mitch Albom says it best about us: "We are in love with hope!" As an Aggie graduate teacher told her students, "Remember, students, 'good, better, best—never let it rest until your good is better and your better is your best.'" Our reach for the best is clear in Aggieland. There are three reasons that our school will strive to lead the nation and the world in research, teaching, and service. First, we have a profound vision of service beyond self that is embodied in the Aggie Spirit; second, we communicate and impart that vision to others; and third, we persist to accomplish our vision. We fight to the finish.

Tonight, I am honored to share the story of a great Aggie hero who had a vision of service beyond self, carried out that vision by serving his nation, and persisted as a warrior for peace until the end. This Aggie hero and Medal of Honor winner is Staff Sergeant George Dennis Keathley '37. His story is told in Colonel James R. Woodall's excellent book *Texas Aggie Medals of Honor*, published by the Texas A&M University Press in 2010.

Sergeant Keathley gave his last full measure of devotion in a furious and vitally important battle in the mountains of northern Italy on September 14, 1944. Against overwhelming odds and faced with a fourth German counterattack, Keathley and his men stood their ground during a heavy attack from enemy hand grenades, automatic weapons, and mortar shells. Keathley shouted his orders precisely and with determination to his warriors and the enemy was beaten back, suffering numerous casualties. Then an enemy grenade struck near Keathley, inflicting a mortal wound to his left arm and chest area. Rising to his feet, and holding his wounded side with his left hand, he fired his M-1 rifle with his right hand and killed an attacking German while continuing to shout orders and inspiring his men. For 15 minutes he continued to lead his men and fire his rifle. The German counterattack was defeated, but Keathley fell and died in the arms of his friend Sergeant Charles Dozier. Sergeant Dozier said, "I had witnessed the death of the bravest and most heroic man I have ever known. I heard his final words, 'Please write my wife a letter and tell her I love her and I did everything I could for her and my country.'" Sergeant Keathley was posthumously awarded the Congressional Medal of Honor on April 11, 1945. He is buried in the American Military Cemetery near

Florence, Italy, because he had told his wife, "If I am killed in action, I want to be buried where I fought."

My wife and I visited this cemetery near Florence unaware that Keathley was buried there. I had told his story of heroism to several Musters around the state and nation and wondered about the location of his final resting place. We asked the caretaker if he knew if any Aggies were buried here among those 4,000 graves. He was not sure but handed us a note with a row and grave number. As we approached the grave, I saw it was Keathley and I fell to my knees in reverence and thanks to read the words on his white cross. "George D. Keathley, S. SGT 338 Inf. 85th Div, Texas, Sept. 14, 1944." Adorning the cross at the top was a star and on the lower part are the words Medal of Honor.

There are thousands of other Aggie heroes who are in love with hope and excel in various fields and exemplify the spirit of service and leadership. These heroes persist when times are tough and never take the easy way out. Our core values are embraced by the thousands of Aggies who believe that they will make a positive difference in a sometimes troubled world. Those we honor tonight are part of that great Maroon Line that has made a positive difference. So tonight God has given us more time to live and love our family, friends, school and nation. We have been given more time to tell the Aggie story to all who would listen. Remember we are in love with hope! Our love for Texas A&M University is a lifetime passion, and tonight we are deeply honored at this Muster ceremony to call the roll for our missing loved ones. Thank you and Gig 'em!

# Bill Jones '81

*2013—Reed Arena*

Bill Jones '81. Photo from editor's collection.

Bill Jones earned a degree in business management from Texas A&M University. He was Outstanding Freshman in the Corps of Cadets, was on the Ross Volunteers Honor Guard, and was First Brigade commander. Jones earned his law degree from Baylor University School of Law in 1985. He was named the Baylor Young Lawyer of the Year in 1997.

After graduation, he joined the firm of Liddell, Sapp, Zivley, Hill & LaBoon, LLP, and in 1991 formed Cash Jones & Springhetti, LLP (now known as Cash Allen, LLP), in Houston. He served as general counsel to Governor Rick Perry from 2000 until 2003, when he became a partner at Locke Liddell & Sapp, LLP, in Austin. In 2006 he joined Vinson & Elkins LLP and then in 2010 formed the Jones Firm in Austin.

He was president of the Texas Young Lawyers Association and sat on the State Bar of Texas Executive Committee and the State Bar Board of Directors. He was on the boards of the Baylor Law School Alumni Association, the Capitol Area Boy Scouts of America, the Memorial Hermann Healthcare System Foundation, the Texas Public Policy Foundation, and the Texas A&M Association of Former Students.

Jones was appointed to a six-year term on the Texas A&M Board of Regents by Governor Perry in 2003 and served on the Finance and Academic and Student Affairs Committees.

# Friendship—Family—Freedom*

Howdy! Thank you, Rachel, for that wonderful introduction.

It is truly an honor and a privilege to be here with you this evening and to be asked by the campus Aggie Muster Committee to bring this presentation. It was the first time as a lawyer that I was actually speechless when I got the call.

I am from a family of Aggies. My wife, Johnita, of course is an Aggie. My brother-in-law is an Aggie, both brothers-in-law actually are Aggies, my sister-in-law, nephews, and nieces. When we moved to Austin, Texas, my daughter who at the time was about nine years old asked me, "Well, if we move to Austin, can we still be Aggies?" I said "Absolutely." I'm often asked what it's like living behind the Orange Curtain. I will tell you it's tough sometimes living among a bunch of people who worship the golden cow. I seem to recall some folks got in trouble about that some years ago, but that's another story for another time.

We have enjoyed the wild success of our football program this year, and I'm often asked if I gloat as I'm hanging out with my Austin friends. And I say, "No, I don't gloat. That's really not my style. But I do enjoy the peace and quiet."

I'd like to send out a special welcome to the Class of '63. I would have you know that I was born within a week or two of when you started your freshman year. We both have had an interesting fifty-three, almost fifty-four, year journey since your freshman year. But welcome to Aggie Muster.

My wife and I were having dinner a few months ago with some friends, and she told them about my speech. Neither one of them were Aggies, and they asked me, "Well, what is Aggie Muster?" I found myself struggling trying to explain to them exactly what this ceremony was about. It's somewhat like trying to describe to someone who's never flown an Air Force jet what it's like to do that, or to race a Formula One race car. You can describe it as best you can, but it mostly has to be felt. You see, it's more than just a gathering of people.

*Speech title derived by editor from speech contents

We gather for several events at this Institution. Various campus clubs, organizations, socials to meet people on campus, fraternities, sororities, student-led organizations, the Corps of Cadets, Aggie clubs, mother clubs, reunions, football games, tailgates, domino night, and all sorts of gatherings, all which are very important. But this one is very different.

It is not a funeral, although it is solemn. It is not Taps or Silver Taps, although that is a part of it. It is really not like anything else, anywhere in the world, at any other Institution. It is unique to Texas A&M. It is unique because it is a celebration and a time to remember. It is a solemn celebration when Aggies get together to celebrate that Aggie Spirit and to remember those who are no longer with us and the legacy that they left us. As we celebrate this Aggie Spirit, we celebrate the friendship, and we celebrate Aggie Family, and we celebrate the fight for freedom in this country.

We first celebrate friendship. The first thing that you learn when you hit this campus is the word "Howdy." It is used often. You are taught it, and you are expected to use it. I even hear of students stopping from their texting to say "Howdy!"

We also celebrate the friends that we make here on this campus. Now, I have a friend who I met here, and eventually married. We have three children together, and I won't go into that friendship. That's kind of personal. But I have other friends that I will tell you about. Like my friend Daryl Fitzgerald, who was a member of the Aggie Band. You see, Daryl talked me into staying in the Corps when I was ready to give it up after the first few months, and we celebrate that friendship. Later, Daryl served his country as a member of the Air Force, flying in the AWACS plane. When he retired at the Pentagon, another friend, Curtis Donaldson, and I flew up to the Pentagon to be with him during this celebration. Two friends, one black, one white, and both Aggies.

Friends like Rob Butler, my fish old lady (for those of you who are visiting with us today, that's a roommate). Later that year, Rob told me that I was the first African American that he really got to know, because he grew up in San Antonio and went to mostly Catholic schools. He later asked me to be his best man in his wedding when he asked Cindy to marry him. I was honored to do so. Several years later, Rob was the manager of the Killeen Luby's cafeteria when on October 16, 1991, a gunman ran his truck into the front of that store and took out his gun and shot twenty-three of the patrons dead and wounded another twenty. It was the worst massacre in American history up until the Virginia Tech massacre a few years ago. Fortunately, it was Rob's birthday and he wasn't there with his family. Several months after that incident, Rob came to Caldwell to be with me and my brother working cattle all day. The store hadn't reopened yet. He spent most of that day talking, and I spent most of that day listening. Why? Because we're Aggie friends, and that's what we do.

Several years later, Rob and all of my fish buds from Company A-1 showed up when I was sworn in to the Board of Regents here at Texas A&M. They flew from all over the country. Why? Well, because we're Aggie friends and that's what we do. You see the Aggie friendships survive the geographical location of Aggieland. And the four, five, and in some cases six years it takes to leave this place. It is a friendship that lasts a lifetime. And that is why we celebrate the Aggie friendship as we Muster.

We also celebrate the Aggie family. You see the family crest is recognized everywhere. It is known as the Aggie ring. Former students have ring stories that they will tell you about recognizing that ring in long lines in airports, in foreign countries, in business meetings, on the battle field. They all end the same with a smile, a handshake, and an introduction and a simple question. . ."What class are you?" One day, students, you will have stories of ring recognition and a full appreciation of what the Aggie family really means. Because the Aggie family is not just the members of the sorority, or the fraternity, or the dorm, or the Corps, or the athletic program, or whatever organization you happen to be with while you are here as a student. It is the 300,000-plus former students, all who share a common bond. And like a family, we span generations.

We have a young generation of Aggies that are students, and they are the flowing springs and the headwaters supplying the rivers of Aggies yet to be. I encourage you while you are here, students, to pull alongside your fellow students. Don't let differences of opinions, or looks, or beliefs turn you away from helping fellow students. You see, I received help from the most unlikely of places. His name was Larkin O'Hern, and he was my sophomore. Now, you may find that strange that I would say that Larkin O'Hern helped me when he was here, because the relationship between a sophomore and his freshman is, at best, strained. But he was of a generation of Aggies closest to me. He was the Class of '80, and he didn't run me off. He trained me. Sometimes hard, but always fair. He taught me leadership skills that I use to this day. And for that, in his own way, he made me a proud member of the Aggie Corps family. If you are a student, bring someone alongside to make them a member of the Aggie Family. Even if they look a little different than you, talk a little differently than you do, and believe differently than you do. For the Ol' Ags among us, nurture some young Aggie along.

Fred McClure '76 gave this Muster address when I was a student here. He was the first African American Student Body President at Texas A&M University. I admired him from afar for years. I knew who he was long before we were introduced. After I graduated, I called him, and the only qualification I had for talking to him, this man that I had admired from afar for so long, was that I was an Aggie. He took my call, met me at a restaurant in Houston, Texas, and has been my mentor in my professional career ever since that day.

There's also another man by the name of Vel Hawes. He's an Ol' Ag, Class of 1958. His son, Sam, was a fish bud of mine, fellow member of the Class of '81 and A-1. We had the same major in the same year. Mr. Hawes and Connie would open their home to all of us when we would go up for Corps trips in Dallas, Texas. We would invade their home and eat their food and drink their beverages and try not to leave too much of a mess. But Mr. Hawes graduated in the Class of '58. On the first visit to his home, he pulled me aside away from the other cadets and he grabbed my arm and he gave it a squeeze. He looked me in the eyes and said, "Now you can come back to my home anytime, and you don't need to bring Sam with you when you come. In fact, we'd rather you not bring him!" That simple act of kindness was significant, because when Mr. Hawes graduated in 1958, one year before I was born, blacks were not allowed to attend Texas A&M University. He had no black classmates. There were no black members of the football team, or black coaches, or black leaders in the Corps, or administrators, or professors, or deans. And yet, in this moment he was reaching across a generation and racial lines, and welcoming me to the Aggie Family. . . like his own son.

And we celebrate that today. You see our challenge should always be, "Who else can we include in the family?" We should seek to reach across barriers to include others even though their look, their dress, their belief, and their worship may be different than ours. Like family, we will not always agree. But we will work out our disagreements with honor and forbearance. So we Muster to celebrate the Aggie family. All of us.

We also celebrate freedom. Freedom isn't free, as is inscribed on the Korean War Memorial. Someone has to pay, someone has to sacrifice, someone has to step up and say, "I will fight for it." And since the A&M College of Texas opened, Aggies have stepped up in every major engagement. Aggies have fought for the freedoms we enjoy in this country. Sometimes entire classes have stepped forward in the service of our country, putting themselves in harm's way and willing to pay the ultimate sacrifice for us. Often engaging in missions, some of which we may never know about. We celebrate freedom at this hour as we gather at Muster.

Our nation is at war for freedom to protect our shores from terrorists. Aggies will be called to the front lines and the supply lines and put in harm's way. Whether it was Afghanistan, or Iraq, or here on our home turf, friends, husbands, daughters, sons, wives all act as pilots, tank commanders, infantry, ordnance, engineers, helicopter pilots, Army, Navy, Air Force, Marines, on naval ships, pitched tents, humvees, they fight. And yet, wherever they fight, they too will stop today and they will celebrate the Aggie Spirit of camaraderie that is known to all Aggies. And they will talk about the good ol' days at Sparky's [pizza parlor]; Loupot's [bookstore]; Lakeview [a dance hall]; Texas Hall of Fame [a dance hall]; Rother's bookstore; Reveille [a convenience store]; the [Dixie] Chicken [a bar and restaurant at North Gate]; Chicken Oil Company [a hamburger place]; pond jumping (whatever that is); Yell Practice; band practice; Bonfires of years past; pushups; crapouts; Sbisa

[Mess Hall]; Duncan [Dining Hall]; [the dormitories] Krueger, Mosher, Dunn, [and] Legett; Cain Hall [an athletic dormitory demolished in 2016]; MSC [Memorial Student Center]; Kyle Field; Reed Arena; G. Rollie White [Coliseum]; where when it was hot you opened the windows and when it was cold you closed the windows. And then they will pause, remember the fallen, and reflect on whether at next year's Muster someone might answer "Here" for them. So we celebrate the fight for freedom so that we may Muster in peace.

And finally, we are here to remember those who are no longer with us. You saw from the Reflections Display in the MSC today that it showed their lives, their service to A&M, to their fellow members of their class, to the country. When we announce "Here," what we are saying tonight, families, is that they have not been forgotten. Remember, whatever they may have been to their biological families, to us they were Aggies.

We also reflect on how precious life is and how little time we have to accomplish our mission. In the movie *Lonesome Dove*, Gus McCrae was played by Robert Duvall, and he eulogized one of his cowboys that had died. It was very short. He said, "Life is short, shorter for some than for others." Now unfortunately, ol' Gus may have been right. And we're not given an hourglass to know how much time we actually have. So Muster is a reminder for those of us that are here to step up. To say, "Send me. I will serve."

Whether it is your profession, your community, your fellow Aggies, and your school, Texas A&M University, your church, your synagogue, your place of worship, your little league teams, your Boy Scout, Girl Scout, or whatever 4H club or organizations that you can serve in, it's time to step up and say, "What is my mission?" To speak up for what is right regardless of the cost, to support our military and the sacrifices they make for us, and to do our part to give.

Last week I received a letter from a young lady that I will share with you tonight, if you will indulge me. This letter epitomizes everything that we have spoken about tonight. Her father, whom I knew in the Corps of Cadets when I was here, was Class of '80 and his name was Brien Hickman. He was tragically taken from us last year. He is not on the Muster list here tonight because he is going to be honored in his home county. But if you will indulge me, I will read this letter to you from Katie.

Howdy, Mr. Jones!

Thank you for responding to me. I have actually just become aware that my county did not have a Muster Chair this year or last year. I was saddened and disappointed, so I decided about two hours ago (and this was last Thursday) that I was going to have a small, last minute, Aggie Muster ceremony at my house on Sunday. I have done some public speaking, but never about anything so near and dear to my heart. My life without my father will never be the same, just as my life without Texas A&M would not be the same. If you have any words of advice you can share with me, I would greatly appreciate it.

Thanks and Gig 'em,
Katie '11

Now, first of all, she started off the letter with "Howdy!" And secondly, she took advantage of the friendship that her dad had with me from the Class of '80. She reached out to another generation of Aggie and she asked for help. But most importantly, Katie said that she was stepping up to fill in the gap for her father. You see, when one of us falls, when one of us is taken from here, we mourn because we hurt and we will miss them. But we pick ourselves up, we wipe away the tears, we take up the Aggie flag of tradition and honor and duty and we run to the front line and we answer "Here" for the ones that are no longer with us. And we give of ourselves, our resources, and our time, and yes, sometimes even our money. Why? Well, because we are Aggies and that's what we do. And that is why we Muster.

May God bless each and every one of you, and may God bless this institution that we all love called Texas A&M University. Thank you.

# Bill Youngkin '69

## *2014—Reed Arena*

Bill Youngkin '69. Photo from editor's collection.

Billy Jack Youngkin was born January 19, 1947, in Gilmer, Texas. He served as head yell leader, a Ross Volunteer in the Corps of Cadets, a class officer, and was recognized as a Distinguished Student. After graduation, he served in the US Army in the 18th Airborne Corps and was in Vietnam from 1971 to 1972. He graduated from Baylor Law School in 1975.

A practicing attorney for forty years, Youngkin is the principal at Youngkin & Associates in Bryan, Texas. He has handled cases in the Courts of Civil Appeals, Fifth Circuit Court of Appeals, and the Texas Supreme Court.

Youngkin was the 1991 president of the Association of Former Students and the Former Yell Leaders Association, on the advisory board of the Corps Development Council, and on the Executive Committee of Texas A&M's 12th Man Foundation. He established 12th Man Endowed and Corps of Cadets Scholarships. Youngkin and his wife, Marilyn, were named the Texas A&M Parents of the Year in 2000–2001. He was a member of the President's Blue Ribbon Panel for the Corps of Cadets and was inducted into the Corps of Cadets Hall of Honor in 2014.

## Explaining from the Inside*

Howdy. I am honored to be this year's Muster speaker, but I will admit to you that I am also a little nervous. The last time I faced this many

*Speech title derived by editor from speech contents

good-looking Aggie faces was when I was Head Yell Leader my senior year.

I don't know if you have been asked, "If you could do one thing in your life over again, what would it be?" Without any hesitation, my response would be when I was a Yell Leader at A&M. I think I must have gotten a lot cuter after I was elected Yell Leader, because my social life took off like a rocket.

I also want to issue a special Howdy to the Class of '64 members who are commemorating their 50th year reunion. I have heard stories about you guys from the Classes of '66 and '67 who were your sophomores and "fish" and my seniors and juniors. I don't know how accurate their stories about the Class of '64 are, because I have not seen any of you carrying pitchforks or have horns growing out the side of your head.

I am sure the Class of '64 will agree with me that a ton of change has occurred at A&M since their days on campus. For example, where we are today was a cow pasture then. There were more freshmen admitted this year than there were students on campus when I enrolled in 1965. Despite all these changes at A&M, it has, for the most part, remained the same. How can I say that?

When discussing Texas A&M, most often you hear people say, "If you are on the outside looking in, you can't understand it, and if you are on the inside looking out, you can't explain it." Well, I am going to try to do what is said you can't do, explain A&M from the inside.

I have been an Aggie since 1965 when I arrived as a "fish" in the Corps of Cadets. I returned to Brazos County in 1975 after I graduated from Baylor Law School, and I have lived in this community since. Marilyn and I raised two daughters who attended A&M—Libby, Class of 2000, and Katie, Class of 2003. I have been a witness to most of the changes that have occurred at A&M during the past 49 years. People say A&M is different from other universities, and I agree, but how is it different?

A&M is a large public university, but there are others all over the country.

A&M has over 50,000 students, but there are seven universities in America that have such populations on one campus.

A&M is a superior academic and research university, but it is one of

60 similar institutions who are accredited as such in the United States.

You can say that A&M has outstanding faculty, but many others will be able to make that claim also.

These statistics don't make it different, but we all know it is different. The question is what makes it different? What makes it different are the people, you and me, Texas Aggies. You and I, as Aggies, are part of what is often referred to as "The Aggie Family." Are we really family? Yes. And it is something I can prove.

This is my proof. Around 4:00 a.m. on November 18, 1999, Marilyn and I were awakened by a call from our daughter Libby followed by a call from our daughter Katie letting us know that Bonfire had fallen and that they were okay. I could not go back to sleep. I walked outside my home and I could see the emergency vehicle lights reflecting off the clouds above campus.

Our campus and our community was in a state of shock. That day you could see the grief on the faces of everyone. As the day passed, the news became worse. That afternoon it was announced that a special service would be held at Reed Arena at 6:00 p.m. I drove to Reed Arena, which was almost full when I got here. I sat on the aisle steps just below the top row because there was no other place to sit. All the seats and all the aisles were full of grieving Aggies. I sat there and listened to the service and my heart hurt. The service ended but no one left. Instead we locked arms over the shoulders of those next to us with our heads bowed. In the semi-darkness of Reed, not a sound was made until a young lady sitting on the floor started to sing, "Amazing Grace, how sweet the sound." We all joined in, and when it was over, we filed silently out of Reed, just as you would at a Silver Taps ceremony.

That sense of loss, that kind of grief, only happens when you lose someone close to you from your family. I had never met those young Aggies, I did not know their families, but I felt that kind of grief, as did everyone.

The football team canceled practice, went to the site and hauled the logs away on their shoulders, so the bodies could be recovered. The game was played and the University of Texas could not have been more honoring or more respectful of our loss. What they did is what good friends and neighbors do when their friends and neighbors suffer such a devastating loss. The game was played and, some say by divine intervention, the Aggies won.

All of this confirmed for me that I was part of a very large family called Texas Aggies. We may have different last names like Mahomes, Gutierrez, Wong, and Rayburn but we all wear an identification that tells the world we are part of the same family: our Aggie Rings.

If we are a family, what makes us a family? The answer is our traditions. If your personal family is close-knit, it is probably because they maintain certain family traditions, like gathering every summer at Garner State Park or having Christmas at the family farm. For my family, it is Aggie football games. We sit together, we tailgate together and as a result we stay close as a family. My grandsons know their cousins, and they will know the next generation of cousins.

I want you to know that all of the younger classes are my heroes. By younger classes, I mean from the Class of '70 to the Class of '17. They are my heroes because they have maintained, perpetuated and enhanced the Aggie traditions I experienced as a student at A&M. At any point in time, they could have chosen to not participate in the 12th Man or attend Fish Camp or observe Silver Taps or any number of Aggie Traditions. But you did, and that is why we are holding Muster today, because of the choices all of you who wear this ring, that has a number on it greater than mine, have made.

I will tell you from firsthand experience that the other institutions are jealous of our traditions. How do I know this? I was once held as a prisoner of war at Baylor University while I attended law school. They are jealous of A&M, but they are especially jealous of our traditions.

But it was in 1987 I learned the real importance of our traditions for all of us. I have a story for you, Ags, but it is not a fable. I was on the board of the Association of Former Students then and I was invited by Dr. Malon Southerland, who was with student services here at A&M, and who would later become the Vice President of Student Services, to attend a gathering at his house after one of the football games. He introduced Marilyn and me to a group of students and in his introduction he mentioned that I had been the Head Yell Leader.

Most of the group of five to six kids were "fish," and one asked me what caused me to decide to become a Yell Leader. I responded by saying that near the end of my fish year—when I realized the upperclassmen were not going to kill me and eat me for breakfast, and academically, if I continued to work really hard, I might be able to graduate some-day—I started looking at my upperclassmen to see who I would most like to be like when I was a senior. There was this one guy who was Head Yell Leader, an RV [Ross Volunteer], the CO of his outfit, and a distinguished student. I never quite measured up totally to all he was, but I tried. I told those fish that, probably the saddest thing I had to do at A&M was to go to Temple, Texas, as a member of the RV Firing Squad and fire at his funeral, because he was a casualty of the Vietnam War. It was there that I got to see his wife with his little baby that he never got to hold. That guy was Joe Bush '66; he was my role model and he always will be.

About that time, I felt a tug on my sleeve and I looked down at this young lady who had tears streaming down her cheeks and who said, "Mr. Youngkin, Joe Bush was my Dad, and that baby was me." Well, it was all I could do to keep the tears out of my eyes. I told her how much I appreciated her dad and what a special role model he was to me and to all Aggies because Joe died saving others on a mountain top in Laos.

I was able to visit with Robin, Joe's daughter, over the next few years. Before she graduated she said, "I'm so glad I was able to attend A&M, because I feel like I have gotten to know my dad for the first time in my life because I was able to experience the things he did, and I now understand and appreciate the kind of man he was."

That was when I realized the true importance to all of us in maintaining our Aggie traditions. Those traditions allowed Joe Bush's daughter to get to know her dad, and they will also allow my grandsons, your children or future children to share in our traditions and to make that connection to each of us and understand why we are members of the Aggie family.

Family is what makes A&M different, and our traditions are what make each of us members of that Aggie Family. When we leave this place today, I ask that each of us do all we can to perpetuate, to enhance and to preserve our traditions, our bonds. Our traditions are what make us family, and that is what makes A&M different from all the rest.

I mentioned earlier the changes that have occurred at A&M and in my life, but there are more changes to come in my life and yours. However, there are two things we cannot change. We are and shall always will be Texas Aggies. The only question is, what kind will we be? The other thing we cannot change is someday we all will be eligible to have our names called at this Muster ceremony. If we continue to support, enhance, and perpetuate our traditions, when that day and our time does come, a member of our Aggie Family will answer "Here" and will remember and care. We are the Aggies; the Aggies are we. May God grant that it always be so.

# Will Hurd '99

*2015—Reed Arena*

Will Hurd '99. Photo from editor's collection.

William Ballard "Will" Hurd was born August 19, 1977, in San Antonio, where he attended John Marshall High School. During his time at Texas A&M, he served as student body president at the time of the college's greatest tragedy—the Bonfire collapse of 1999. As president, he worked to keep the students calm and organized. His leadership skills were shaped that night, organizing student volunteers to help rescue crews. Hurd used the lessons learned from that fateful night and his overall Aggie experience to help him succeed. "I learned a lot of stuff during that process, and I would give up all those lessons if those kids were still alive," Hurd said, "But it was an honor to serve the Aggie community in its darkest hours."

After college, Hurd served as an undercover officer in the Central Intelligence Agency in the Middle East and South Asia for nearly a decade. Upon leaving the CIA, he became a senior advisor with a cybersecurity firm, covering a wide range of complex challenges faced by manufacturers, financial institutions, retailers, and critical infrastructure owners. He also partnered with a strategic advisory firm helping businesses expand into international markets. In 2015 he was elected to represent Texas' Twenty-third District in Congress, chaired the Information Technology Subcommittee, and served on the Committee of Oversight and Government Reform, the Homeland Security Committee, and as vice chair of the Border and Maritime Subcommittee.

# Work Hard to Make This World Better*

Howdy!

Folks, I couldn't be happier or more honored to be in College Station today with you at Campus Muster.

But before we get started, I want to get an idea of who is here today. I'm going to make a series of statements, and if the statement is true to you, I want you to whoop. I'm giving everyone senior privileges for this exercise. Here we go. I'm a senior? I'm a junior or a sophomore? I'm a proud member of the fighting Texas Aggie Class of 2018? I'm from El Paso? I grew up in San Antonio? I'm from Mentone? Mentone is the county seat of Loving County, which is the least populated county in America with 95 people. I've met 72 of them, and I've been trying to meet the remaining 23.

Up until a few months ago, I thought I'd be celebrating Muster in either San Antonio or DC. But I can tell you without hesitation, today there is nowhere I could be more honored to be than here with you in Aggieland!

I want to thank the members of the Muster Committee for selecting me as tonight's speaker.

This is actually my second time to speak at Campus Muster. Us Aggies say that once something happens twice at A&M, it's a tradition, so I'm going to be really upset with the Muster Committee if I'm not invited back next year to speak again.

It's been exactly 15 years since I last spoke here at Muster. It was my last official duty as Student Body President. In preparation for Muster, you're always told to tone down your remarks and not outshine the former student speaker. It's clear from the amazing job Kyle Kelly did that your outgoing student body president didn't heed that advice. Kyle, you and I are going to have some words after this.

When I was standing here 15 years ago as a 22-year-old, fifth-year senior, it was just months after the worst tragedy this campus has ever faced. On November 18, 1999, at 2:42 in the morning, the entire Aggie family learned far too much about loss when Aggie Bonfire fell.

*Speech title derived by editor from speech contents

On that morning and over the following days, we lost 11 students and a former student, and another 27 were injured. Those 12 students' names were among the many names called at that year's Muster. It was devastating.

It's strange to think that there are many people here today that never witnessed the frenzy of activity, camaraderie and shenanigans that occurred at Stack while building Bonfire, but for those of us who had, it was jarring to see the Polo Fields, where Bonfire was built, transformed into a very tragic place. In the days following the collapse, countless members of the community dropped everything to spend their days and nights at Stack helping in any way they could. It was inspiring to see the Aggie Spirit manifest itself in the acts of compassion and self-lessness performed by those first responders.

One of the things I'll always remember about those few days after Bonfire fell involves one of the greatest honorary Aggies of all time, football coach R. C. Slocum.

He and the entire football team rushed out to Stack and, piece by piece and log by log, helped move the rubble so that students trapped underneath could be located. I don't know how many they helped save, but these were the same folks that would take the field in a week's time and beat the hell out of that team from Austin. But that night, nothing could stop them from being out there helping the 12th Man who had supported them on the gridiron so many times.

I also remember the efforts of the Traditions Council, led by their chair Schuyler Houser, Class of 2000. Days after the collapse, Traditions Council led thousands of students, former students, faculty, and members of the community in a candlelight vigil surrounding the site of the Bonfire. That inspiring group of people lit candles, locked hands and prayed. They prayed not only for the ones we lost, but also prayed for the strength that we Aggies would need that day and in the days ahead.

The night after the Bonfire tragedy, the University and several student groups organized an amazing memorial service, right here in Reed Arena. Then-Lieutenant Governor Rick Perry was the last speaker, and when he concluded his remarks, there was a moment of silence that seemed to last an eternity. And then one voice in the crowd—to this day I don't know who it was—began beautifully singing "Amazing Grace."

In a few moments, thousands of voices joined with her. It was the most beautiful tribute I've ever been a part of. When it stopped, you could hear a pin drop, and I don't think you could find a dry eye in the crowd. It's only been recently that I can listen to that song without tearing up. Whenever I hear it, the emotions we all felt at the candlelight vigil, the Memorial Service and throughout that tragedy flood my memories.

Seeing the Aggie Community respond to such a devastating loss taught me about the importance of the Aggie Family and the importance of our traditions.

When you're asked to participate in one of A&M's oldest and biggest traditions by speaking at Muster, one of the first things you do is reach out to people you know that have spoken at Muster before. When I did this, everyone said, "You've got to tell the story of what it means to be an Aggie, and you've got to share some old army stories about the class celebrating their 50th reunion."

Dan Harmon, the creator of the TV show "Community," says that a great story starts with a character setting out on a journey seeking something he or she desires. They arrive at an unfamiliar place, adapt, and ultimately find what they are seeking. But only after paying a heavy price. After this experience, they are changed forever.

It's hard to think of a class of students that experienced more change or paid a higher price than those in the Fightin' Texas Aggie Class of 1965. Not only have you lived lives that have made everyone at this University proud, you've given back in ways that every class after you has cherished. We're proud to honor you during your 50th reunion.

Back when I was on campus, I had the opportunity to work alongside a member of the Class of '65, Dr. J. Malon Southerland. Dr. Southerland was the Vice President for Student Affairs while I was here. Day after day, he opened his home to host dinners and lunches for students. He led by example, and he is a man that still constantly and consistently gives back to the University. The University wouldn't be the same without Dr. Southerland and former students like him.

But to understand the Class of '65, you've got to picture how they experienced Aggieland when they were students here. The campus has changed a lot since Dr. Southerland was here as a student. For example, to get around College Station for most of the day today, I pulled out my cell phone and ordered an Uber. But when Dr. Southerland needed to get home from campus at the end of the semester, he went to the MSC [Memorial Student Center] and checked a bulletin board called "The Hitchin' Post," where students with cars would post notes about how many seats they had open and where and when they were headed home.

And think about how campus looked from the eyes of Sallie Sheppard. Ms. Sheppard was one of the first women to graduate from Aggieland. She received both a bachelor's and master's degree in mathematics from A&M. She worked on the Apollo program at NASA, then returned to campus as an assistant professor of computer science and later as an associate provost. It's easy to make comments about how much campus has changed now, but it's much harder to imagine what a previously all-male, all-military campus looked like from the perspective of a smart, talented woman like Ms. Sheppard. She helped open doors for thousands of women, and the change she helped usher in made the Aggie experience even more enriching for all of us.

Our campus wasn't the only part of America experiencing changes during those years. Y'all may have seen or heard about the movie "Selma." The movie memorializes "Bloody Sunday" and the march from Selma to Montgomery led by John Lewis, now Congressman John Lewis. This happened on March 7, 1965, right before the Class of '65 graduated.

This march was inspired by the violent and unnecessary death of Vietnam veteran Jimmie Lee Jackson. He was only 27 years old when he was killed following a nonviolent protest for the right to vote. Before his death, he had tried to register to vote for four years straight but was never able to, because of Jim Crow laws. Many of the folks who marched were students. They marched to protest Jimmie Lee's death and in support of the right to vote. They were beaten by police. They were beaten by citizens helping the police. They were beaten, but they were not beat. Their fearlessness and their tenacity sparked a revolution that led to landmark legislation ensuring every American's right to vote.

Earlier this year, I had the opportunity to travel with Congressman Lewis and several of my colleagues to Selma for the 50th anniversary of

Bloody Sunday. That trip was a remarkable reminder that we all stand on the shoulders of giants, and it gave me a new appreciation of the struggle that ensured my ability to exercise my right to vote.

In my current job, I talk a lot about how it's unfortunate that 50 years ago a group of people were willing to endure beatings and humiliation in their struggle for the right to vote, and now we struggle to get people—especially young folks—to the polls to vote. Too many people take this right for granted. Some folks believe that their vote doesn't matter. My good friend Martha McSally and I were elected to Congress at the same time. She won her election by 167 votes. Ask Congresswoman McSally if every vote matters. Your vote matters. Your voice matters. Make sure you're heard.

One of the things I have to do a lot in order to keep my job as a member of Congress is raise money for a never-ending campaign. Like almost every other skill I've used over the past 15 years, I learned how to do that right here at Texas A&M just a few hundred yards away at our Memorial Student Center. The first lesson I learned about fundraising came from a proud member of the Class of '65, Frank Muller. I can't remember what I was raising money for, but I do remember it was my sophomore year and my first call was to Mr. Muller.

I was probably three or four minutes into my script when Frank tore into me. He gave me some pointers in the way only Frank Muller can, and I still use those valuable lessons today. Frank, I appreciate the lesson and I'll see you later tonight. But I've got to warn you; I've gotten way better at asking for money.

Frank Muller is also someone who comes to mind when I think about a character going on a journey, paying a heavy price, and returning home a changed person.

Frank went directly from being a member of the Fightin' Texas Aggie Corps of Cadets to serving eight years on active duty with multiple tours in Vietnam, earning 17 awards for valor.

Frank, like many of his classmates from the Class of '65, sacrificed a great deal for this country.

Many of those who served in Vietnam like Frank came back home to help build our country into what it is today. To those, I want to say thank you and welcome home.

We're not only here to honor and remember the Class of '65, we're also here to think and laugh about our own times at A&M, and what it means to be part of the Aggie family.

To me, the Aggie family is all about the bonds of friendship you create while making your way through your four. . . or five. . . or, for some of y'all, six years here. I will always remember the night that my friends Mike Whittington and Matt Hobson stayed up with me all night painting my student body president campaign logo, a yellow smiley face, on a bunch of ping-pong balls. We had this great idea to dump thousands of these painted ping pong balls into Rudder fountain to promote my campaign—this was guerrilla marketing before guerrilla marketing existed. We stayed up for hours painting these things until we had dozens of large bags full of them. We snuck out early in the morning to Rudder Fountain and emptied every single one of those bags into the pond. Less than five minutes later, all the balls had collected in one corner of the fountain and you could barely notice there was anything in the fountain at all.

It was a horrible idea, but at least we tried to do something different. The point of coming to A&M is to gain experience trying to do something meaningful and hard. Sometimes, you may fail and sometimes you may look like an idiot, like we did with our ping-pong balls, but you will leave with some great friends, some amazing experiences and a better appreciation of the Spirit that can ne'er be told.

The Aggie Spirit never goes away. One of the reasons it doesn't go away is because of Aggie Muster. There's no more important thing we do as Aggies than assemble together on San Jacinto Day every year. The years since I was here last have given me the time to think about the importance of Muster and I've come to the following conclusion:

The reason why, for more than a hundred years, Aggies have gotten together every April 21st to eat a little, reminisce over their days at A&M, and answer the roll call, is because it causes us to reflect on why we are all here on this Earth.

A few of you may know that before I served in Congress, starting right after I graduated from A&M, I began working at the Central Intelligence Agency as an undercover officer.

For nearly a decade, I lived in places like Afghanistan, Pakistan, and

India and served with some of the most dedicated diplomats, intelligence officers, and military professionals our government has ever produced.

The day I started my drive from San Antonio to Washington, DC, to start my job at the CIA was the day Al-Qa'ida operatives steered a small boat to the USS *Cole* and blew it up in the Gulf of Aden off the coast of Yemen. Less than a year later, Al-Qa'ida terrorists flew airplanes into the twin towers and the Pentagon. The next day, I became the fourth employee to join the unit that helped infiltrate almost 100 CIA officers into Afghanistan to make Al-Qa'ida and the Taliban pay for their acts of terrorism on our soil.

I remember being on duty the night that we got the call that Mike Spann had become the first CIA officer killed in the invasion of Afghanistan. Mike was a dedicated public servant who was fighting in hostile territory so that we could continue to exercise the freedoms enshrined in our Constitution.

I was in the office when his wife and children were informed of his death.

I cherish the memory of Mike Spann and the memories of others like him, because it reminds me of how they lived and what they lived for. To me, there's no better way to think about what we each should be doing with our own life than to reflect on the lives of those who are no longer with us.

Author Brendon Burchard captured precisely how I feel, so I am going to borrow from and paraphrase his words:

> The greatest misery that any of us can endure, is
>
> Knowing that we didn't speak up when we should have,
>
> That we didn't work when we should have, and
>
> Didn't love or live when we should have,
>
> We honor the memory of those who are no longer with us when we "faithfully, actively and lovingly fight for a better life for ourselves and others."

Remember this today when you answer here. And remember it when you go out into the world as a member of the Aggie Family, and as the protector of the memory of someone you may have lost. Work hard to make them proud, and work hard to make this world better for yourself and for others.

Remember that Jimmie Lee Jackson died fighting for the right to vote, so go out and vote.

Remember that my colleague Mike Spann lost his life protecting our freedoms, so exercise your right to life, liberty and the pursuit of happiness.

Remember that those 12 Aggies who died that fateful day in 1999 will never get to meet up with their Aggie buddies every year at a Muster ceremony, so answer "here" every year.

Today when we are calling "here" for those who have left us behind, do not mourn—rejoice. Rejoice because they are in a better place. Rejoice because today, you get to commit to living your life to the fullest... because, my friends, that is what they would want us to do.

Let us call and answer "Here..."

# R. C. Slocum

*2016—Reed Arena*

R. C. Slocum. Photo from editor's collection.

Richard Copeland Slocum was born November 7, 1944, in Oakdale, Louisiana. He was an All-District end at Lutcher Stark High School (now West Orange–Stark High School) in Orange, Texas, and lettered four years at McNeese State University in Lake Charles, Louisiana. He graduated with a BS and a master's degree in educational administration.

He began his football coaching career at Lake Charles High School before becoming freshman coach at Kansas State University. In 1972 he joined Emory Bellard's staff at Texas A&M, coaching receivers before moving to defense and then becoming defensive coordinator. He was defensive coordinator at the University of Southern California in 1981, leading the PAC 10 Conference before returning to A&M the next year as defensive coordinator for Jackie Sherrill. In 1985 he was named assistant head coach. Over the next four years, his style of play was characterized as "The Wrecking Crew." In 1989 he started a fourteen-year run as Texas A&M's head coach, during which the Aggies never had a losing season. Slocum's tenure is the longest in A&M's history, and his 94 wins in the 1990s was the most by any Division I program in the state of Texas. He reached his 100th victory faster than any other active coach, and his 123 wins in fourteen years placed him eighth on the all-time coaching list.

He was named president of the American Football Coaches Foundation in 2001 and was appointed special advisor to the president of Texas A&M University in 2002. Slocum was inducted into the Texas A&M Athletic Hall of Fame, the Texas Sports Hall of Fame, and the National Football Foundation College Football Hall of Fame. His recognition includes the General Robert Neyland Award in 2011, the Lifetime Achievement Award of the American Heart Association Bryant Awards in 2013, and the Amos Alonzo Stagg Award of the American Football Coaches Association in 2014.

## "What Will I Leave Behind?"

Howdy!

I am honored to be here this evening as your Muster speaker. Of all our great traditions, *this is the one that is the most meaningful to me*. It is one that I have participated in for the past 45 years.

I was hired to coach football at Texas A&M in December 1971 and reported for work on Jan. 2, 1972. That first spring that I was here with new head coach, Emory Bellard, we took the entire football team to the campus Muster in G. Rollie White [Coliseum]. Since that time, I have attended Muster somewhere each year. I have spoken at Musters in San Diego, Los Angeles, San Francisco, and at Fort Ord in California. I have also spoken in other large cities like Phoenix, Denver (twice), Chicago, and Washington, DC. I have traveled out of the country to Musters in Mexico City and Panama City, Panama. Here in Texas, I have enjoyed some of the smaller places like Refugio, Laredo, Longview, Marble Falls, and my home town of Orange, Texas. Last year, I spoke in Lubbock. Since we joined the Southeastern Conference, Aggies have been kind of lonesome out there. I wasn't sure I wanted to go because of the tortillas they've thrown at us out there.

Although I have been the speaker at Muster many times, *I have always realized that the ceremony is not about the speaker*. Muster is much bigger, and more meaningful than the speaker. This cherished ceremony has special meaning to each of us, but it is one of the foundations of what it means to be an Aggie. *It symbolizes the bond that Aggies have to Texas A&M, and to each other, forever.* I am sure that each of you has your own special reasons of why Muster is important to you.

For the next few minutes, I would like to share with you some of the thoughts that I have had during the many Musters that I have attended, and what Muster means to me. I have organized the thoughts that I have at Muster into three categories, the past, the present and the future.

First, the past. We gather on this date to remember, honor, and celebrate those who have gone before us, family members and friends who are dear to us. One such person that I always think of at Muster is a man from my childhood, an Aggie named Homer Stark, Class of 1945. I think of him because of his love of A&M, his example of being an Aggie, and the role that he played in my life. In my hometown of Orange, Texas, he was from the most affluent family in town. My high school, Lutcher Stark High, was named after his father.

My family was from the other side of town. I lived in the projects for much of my childhood in a place called Riverside. It was a low-rent housing development with rows of duplexes. There were some wonderful people there, but also there were the problems that are typical of that kind of neighborhood. Most families were there because of a lack of education. During that time in my life, I shined shoes in the local barbershop and threw newspapers for the Orange Leader.

Kids from Riverside all went to elementary schools that were in the projects. However, in junior high, kids from all over Orange went to the same school. I got to know some kids from backgrounds different from mine. It was then that I became friends with one of Homer Stark's daughters. She invited me over to their house and introduced me to her dad. For some reason, he took an immediate interest in me. That was the beginning of a life-changing relationship. He was the first Aggie that I had ever met, and he immediately began to tell me all about Texas A&M. Since then, one thing that I have realized is when you meet someone that is an Aggie, it won't take long for you to know it. Homer was so proud of A&M. He had Aggie items all over his house and Aggie stickers on his cars and his jeep. He talked about the Aggies all the time.

It wasn't too long until he invited me to go with him and his family to Bonfire and the annual A&M-t.u. football game. It was the first time I had ever been on a college campus. At the bonfire, for the first time, I saw the Fightin' Texas Aggie Band and witnessed the "Spirit that can ne'er be told." I was hooked on the Aggies. That was the first of many trips that I took with Mr. Stark and his family. He opened my eyes to another side of life. He was always polishing on me and teaching me about life. He was doing what Aggies have always done, helping others. There was not one thing that I could do for him. He was helping me because he saw it as a chance to affect a life in a positive way. It was a chance for him to give back. That is what Aggies do. They help others, and give back.

Not long ago, I heard a great quote [by Maya Angelou] that is relevant to what Homer was doing. I quote, "One cannot go through life with a catcher's mitt on both hands. At some point, you have to throw some back." I watched Homer's example of being an Aggie, and throwing back, for the rest of his life. He was a great mentor for me, and I always think of him at Muster. Several years ago, while speaking at Muster in Oklahoma City, I got to answer "here" for my friend Homer.

At Muster, I also think of many other Aggie giants that I have known personally who are no longer with us. Men who forged very successful careers after leaving A&M and who gave A&M credit for helping them develop the skills they needed for high achievement. Many of these names would be familiar to you. They are on buildings all over campus, and are symbolic of their devotion to Texas A&M. Names like [H. R. "Bum"] Bright, [John] Blocker, [Bob] Frymire, [J. L.] Huffines, [Tommy] Lohman, Richardson (both Joe and Bernie), [George] Mitchell, [Michel] Halbouty, [H. C.] Heldenfels, [John] Lindsey, [Royce] Wisenbaker, [L. F.] Peterson, [Bill] McKenzie, [Ford] Albritton, and [H. B. "Pat"] Zachry. For many of you, these are just names on buildings, but I knew these men, and witnessed, first hand, their great respect for, and devotion to Texas A&M.

I heard their personal stories of working their way through A&M by waiting on tables at Sbisa [Mess Hall], working at Loupot's [bookstore], roughnecking in the oil field, and countless other similar jobs. There were stories about leaving A&M and heading immediately to serve in the military, often directly into combat. They told me of starting their businesses, many times with the help of other Aggies. I watched them as they *always answered the call* when A&M needed their help. They were anxious and proud to give back to Texas A&M. For you young Aggies in the audience, it is important for you to understand that we did not just happen to become one of the world's great universities. These marvelous buildings on campus did not just pop up out of the ground. The outstanding faculty here did not just show up on campus one day. There has been a long line of Aggies who experienced what this school can do in the lives of young people. They wanted to provide to future generations the opportunity to share their experience. For this reason, they gave tirelessly of their time, effort and financial resources to make things better for you. They left you big shoes to fill as an Aggie. I always think of them at Muster.

There are others that I did not know personally, but that are always in my thoughts at Muster; those who fought for the freedoms that we enjoy here in America. Tonight, we are honoring the survivors from Corregidor. Thanks to you brave men for your service and thank you for adding so much meaning to this year's Muster. On a trip to France several years ago, I visited Normandy with a group of Aggies. We were so proud to see General Rudder's name so prominently displayed all around the area. We visited the American cemetery. Rows and rows of crosses denoting young Americans that died so that you and I could live the great lives that we enjoy today. You talk about giving back— everyone in our group was overcome by emotion. There was not a dry eye in the group.

I will never forget that scene. I always think of it at Muster. It serves as a great reminder that "freedom is not free." Even as we are gathered here for this event, there are men and women in uniform around the world that are risking their lives in our behalf.

For several years now, at Muster, my thoughts go back to the last Bonfire. I vividly recall the early-morning phone call telling me that the stack had fallen, and it was bad. I remember going over with the team and watching as my players, along with members of the Corps and non-regs, all joined together to remove the fallen logs in search of bodies of fellow classmates. Each from different backgrounds, but working together, and practicing one of the great lessons of Bonfire, that Aggies are tied to each other.

There were discussions about canceling the game. I weighed in strongly that the game should go on because then, as today, we gain strength and comfort from being with each other as part of the Aggie family. When I spoke at the memorial service at Kyle Field, November 25, 1999, I paraphrased words from President Lincoln's speech at Gettysburg and adapted his remarks to the fallen young Aggies that we were honoring. I quote:

The brave young men and young women, living and dead, who worked to build Bonfire this year have demonstrated those feelings far above our poor power to add or detract. The world will little note, nor long remember what we say here tonight, but will never forget what they did here. It is for us, the living, to be dedicated to the unfinished work which they have thus far so nobly advanced. It is rather for us here, to be dedicated to the great task before us— that from these honored dead, we take increased devotion to that cause for which they gave the last full measure of devotion. That we here highly resolve that these dead shall not have died in vain, that this university, under God, shall have a new birth of the spirit that can ne'er be told, and that the love and support of Aggies for their school and each other shall never perish from the earth.

I always remember some special Aggies at Muster.

This year, my heart is especially heavy as I remember and will answer "Here" for my good friend John David Crow ['58]. What a man! He is truly an Aggie legend. He is gone but will never be forgotten. When I travel around the country over the years, wherever I went there were so many people who asked me, "What about John David Crow? What's he doing?" I was so proud to tell them, "He's still here, he's my friend. I see him every day or so." But he's not here tonight, and I'll proudly answer "Here" for him and he's here in spirit.

Another special person on my mind tonight is one that played a role in me being your speaker. Several months ago, I went to the video lab at Kyle Field to do an interview for the 12th Man Foundation. About the time I got there, my longtime friend [Russell W.] "Rusty" Thompson ['85] showed up with several students. He said they would like to sit in on the interview. I thought it was a little strange, but told him it would be no problem. When I finished my interview, Rusty, with a smile on his face, said the students had a question they wanted to ask me. The group stood, and one young lady, Madeline Kinnaird, asked me the question, "Will you be our speaker at the on-campus Muster this year?" How ironic, that tonight Rusty's name will be among those called. I will be one of those answering "Here" for him. I know that he is here in spirit.

Now, for a little about the present. This is always the upbeat, fun part of Muster to me, and it has been a little different everywhere I have been. Actually, one time I was on a little, small ranch down in South Texas. It was a very informal deal, but it had a great flavor. It is where old classmates and friends catch up with each other. Tonight, we are celebrating the 50th reunion of the great Class of '66. I had a great time visiting with them today at lunch. I hope you are having a great time. We are pleased to have you back on campus.

Muster is where you see the youngsters dressed up in Aggie attire and learning about A&M. It is when families get together and celebrate their love for A&M. I am very proud to have several members of my family here tonight. Some are A&M graduates, some are currently in school, and the younger ones here are being indoctrinated daily and are future Aggies. Muster is where the Mothers' Clubs have all the cool auction items so that they can raise money for scholarships for local kids. Often, the winners of those scholarships are recognized at Muster, clearly reinforcing the time-honored tradition of Aggies helping future Aggies.

Muster is where you get great food with a local flavor like barbecue in Refugio, fajitas in Laredo at the La Mantia ranch on the banks of the Rio Grande, or gumbo in Orange, as well as the great homemade cakes and pies. It is where you see the passion of Aggies, both young and old, for making sure that the tradition of Muster is ongoing. It is the one event that every Aggie has on their calendar in answer to the charge from long ago that *"If there is an A&M man in one hundred miles of you, you are expected to get together, eat a little, and live over the days you spent at the A&M College of Texas"* [from *Texas Aggie*, March 1923]. This tradition has stood the test of time, and it is getting even stronger today.

Over the past several months, I have witnessed, firsthand, the enthusiasm of the on-campus Muster Committee. These young people have spent hours organizing and planning for this event. I had the pleasure of meeting with them on campus a few weeks ago in a planning session, and I had dinner with them last night. What an amazing group of young Aggies. I assure you, the future of this tradition is in good hands. I want to thank each of them at this time for their special efforts and especially for the nice personal notes. Special thanks go out to my direct contact, Daniel Moore, who has guided me through this whole process and has been a great friend.

The third area of thoughts that I always have at Muster involves the future. We all live very hurried, busy lives and seldom take the time to really think about our own mortality. At the heart of the Muster ceremony, during that somber time when the roll is about to be called, I am always reminded that at some point in time, my name will be called—R. C. Slocum.

I ask myself, when that time comes, what I will have left behind? What will people remember about me when they hear my name called? Hopefully, it is more than winning a few football games. My concern will be more along the line of; is someone's life better because I lived? Was I kind and helpful to others along life's way? Did I apply the Golden Rule of treating others as I liked to be treated?

Did I give of my abilities and resources to make things better for those less fortunate? Did I add to society's problems, or was I part of the solutions? Did I sow discord and hatred, or did I promote harmony and respect? Did I see faults in others, or did I look for the best in them? Did I hold grudges and try to get even for perceived wrongs done to me or did I forgive and move on? Did I treat each person I met with respect regardless of their background? Did I reflect the Aggie core values of Excellence, Integrity, Leadership, Loyalty, Respect and Selfless Service? I invite each of you to ask yourselves these questions tonight, for you too one day will have your name called. For each Aggie here, I would like to add one more question. I know that you are better because of Texas A&M, but is A&M better because of you? In closing, I have some good news: Each of us here tonight still has time to make sure that we have good answers to these questions when our names are called at Muster.

As I said in the beginning of my remarks, Muster is one of our great traditions at Texas A&M. I want to thank each of you for being here to participate in this evening's ceremony. I sincerely thank you for allowing me the honor of sharing my thoughts on Muster with you.

God Bless and Gig 'em Aggies!

# Eddie J. Davis '67

## 2017—Reed Arena

Eddie J. Davis '67. Photo from editor's collection.

Eddie Joe Davis was born January 20, 1945, in Wichita Falls. After growing up in Henrietta, he became the first member of his family to go to college. He enrolled with an Opportunity Award Scholarship at Texas A&M University where he earned a bachelor's degree in agricultural journalism. Davis was commander of A&M's Corps of Cadets, a member of the Student Senate, and active in the Memorial Student Center and the Student Conference on National Affairs. He served four years with the US Army, including a tour in Vietnam with the 173rd Airborne Brigade. He retired from the military as a colonel in the Reserve.

After earning master's and doctoral degrees from Texas A&M, he served the university as chief operating officer and executive deputy chancellor for the Texas A&M University System, interim president of Texas A&M University (2006–2008), a tenured professor in educational administration, and president of the Texas A&M Foundation. He retired from the Foundation in 2016.

## "A Gig Line in Our Minds"

Howdy!

Let me begin by saying for all of our fellow Aggies around the world watching this ceremony via the internet, I bring greetings from the center of the civilized world . . . "Aggieland, USA."

Please bear with me a moment while I acknowledge a few very special people.

First, thanks to my friends and relatives who decided to attend tonight.

That includes my best friend and partner, my dear wife of almost 50 years, Jo Ann. She has had to endure more than a few weeks of me fretting over getting these remarks just right.

I also want to thank the Student Muster Committee and especially the speaker selection committee, composed of Bailey McCracken, Daniel Lang, Blake Jones, and Brandon Williams. I'm not quite sure what process the committee used; I can only guess that they somehow applied good Aggie bioengineering and found some thread of maroon blood pumping through my veins. If anyone has any doubts about these kids or the future of this country, hang out with these kids a little while and you'll be very, very satisfied that we're in good hands.

I also want to add my special welcome to the families who've lost loved ones this year. I hope that this Muster experience will reinforce the sense of family, respect and love that will forever create positive memories of the time your special Aggie spent at Texas A&M.

It is one of my greatest honors to speak at Campus Muster and particularly on the occasion of my class—the Class of 1967's—50th reunion. No question that I am under some additional pressure—my classmates are watching and listening. We were an irreverent group and I wouldn't be surprised to hear a horse laugh or even have a projectile or two sent my way . . . especially if I go too long.

My remarks this evening will, in part, relate to my class and their unique place in the history of Texas A&M, and how the changes we experienced relate to our great Aggie Muster Tradition.

If I were to name my speech, I would call it "A Gig Line in My Mind." I'll try to explain that a bit later.

The Class of '67 began their journey at Texas A&M in September 1963, a scant three weeks after A&M's name was changed from the Agricultural and Mechanical College of Texas to Texas A&M University. Thus, we were the first class to attend this newly named institution through its first four years as a full-fledged university.

The new name was one of three controversial transformational changes that occurred during this time. No doubt, you are familiar with all three: name change, admission of women, and the elimination of compulsory participation in the Corps of Cadets.

Our class was at the centroid of the experience during this time of tumult and inflection.

Most controversial was the admission of women. Perhaps it comes as a surprise to the happily ensconced 30,000 or so Aggie women enrolled today that there was a protracted, emotional battle over the admission of their mothers and grandmothers.

The battle included debates on the campus, with the faculty firmly in favor and the students hotly opposed. There was significant coverage in the state and national press and even several lawsuits. One actually reached the Supreme Court and was denied because of venue.

This continuing skirmish ended in the spring prior to our freshman year. On April 27, 1963, then-Board Chairman Sterling Evans announced that women would be admitted on a limited basis. General Earl Rudder, who was the president at the time and who has been given appropriate credit for the decision to admit women, had a staunch partner in Sterling Evans, Class of '21.

When I first became president of the Texas A&M Foundation in 1993, I learned that Mr. Evans, the namesake of the campus library, had made an estate gift of $10 million dollars to support the holdings and the operations of the library. I may not be a mental giant, but when I noticed that there were no other $10 million gifts outstanding to Texas A&M, I thought it best I go see him in person.

Mr. Evans lived in Brackettville, Texas, the home of Fort Clark Springs, an early US Cavalry post near Del Rio. We had a wonderful evening, including a couple of whiskeys and a chicken fried steak that lapped over his plate—that's only significant because he was 95 years old at the time. During our conversation, I asked him when he became so committed to coeducation at Texas A&M.

He said, "Well young man (since he was 95, everybody was a young man to him) . . . I think it was in 1917 when I got off the train in College Station and found that there were no women there."

Intrigued, knowing about the long controversy in the fight over women, I asked him how he managed to do it. He told me that he went to John Connolly, then-governor of Texas, and said "I want you to appoint three regents in this cycle who will support coeducation. I just need three more votes. If you don't, I'll bust every one of your appointees during the senate confirmation process and you won't have any regents." That was one of my earliest and best lessons in power politics.

So, all of you Aggie women out there should say a silent prayer of "thanks" to Mr. Sterling Evans, bless his soul, for the 46-year campaign he waged to bring women to A&M.

So, why were so many ol' Ags opposed in the first place? I think, it had a lot to do with the fact that people don't like change, they fear it and they worried about the impact on traditions, Muster being a really good example.

They should have known better, if for no other reason than the passion and loyalty that had been shown by the A&M Mothers Clubs for almost a century. There were no more staunch supporters of "everything Aggie" than A&M mothers.

Proof of this is an apocryphal story about General Haydon Boatner. Before being activated during the Korean War, then Col. Boatner was the commandant at Texas A&M. During the Korean War, he was activated and became the assistant commander of the 2nd Infantry Division.

A prisoner of war camp was built on Goje Island just off the Korean coast to house Chinese and North Korean prisoners of war. Because of the number of enemy soldiers captured on the Korean peninsula, the POW camp swelled beyond its original capacity and housed some 170,000 POWs.

There was chaos when gangs formed and communist leaders of the camp promoted insurrection. General Boatner was assigned to put down the uprising. As he came into the job, he was asked by a reporter if he was concerned about these angry and riotous prisoners.

Reportedly, he said, "Why would I worry about a few hundred thousand North Koreans and Chinese? As commandant at Texas A&M, I had to deal with the A&M Mothers Clubs."

His statement, whether true or mythical, demonstrates the deep passion Aggie Mothers had for this place. And, Aggie women students brought the same passion with them and to this day carry the Aggie Spirit with unbelievable energy and passion. Hindsight is a wonderful cleanser. All I can say to those who opposed the admission of women . . . is that they were simply . . . stupid. The traditions they were concerned about, like Muster, are more powerful and stronger today than ever before.

I would also like to point to a few leadership positions on this campus that have been, or are now, occupied by women: student body president, president of the senior class, Corps commander, president of the MSC [Memorial Student Center], Muster chair, RHA [Residential Housing Association] president, and on and on . . . and on. Perhaps, just perhaps, old Ags feared they would never lead again.

The other profound change that our class experienced was the decision to make participation in the Corps of Cadets non-compulsory. That also was hotly debated before and during our admission. It was not until September 1965 that the Corps became totally non-compulsory.

It was a challenging time; Texas A&M was not growing. It was a place for poor kids or those who wanted a degree in engineering, agriculture, or a military career.

Vietnam was heating up.

Parenthetically, I just finished reading Frank Vandiver's book *Shadows of Vietnam*.

Dr. Vandiver, a prominent historian, was the president at Texas A&M when I returned as the chief financial officer in 1983. His book revealed that in July 1965, the summer of our sophomore year, Lyndon Johnson made the pinnacle decision to escalate the war in Vietnam. The future of our class was immediately predestined.

The culture of A&M at that time was male, Spartan, and more than a little Darwinian. Henry Dethloff's *A Centennial History of Texas A&M University, 1876–1976* described students of our era as well disciplined, courteous, friendly, ambitious, courageous, and hardworking—perhaps a little less sophisticated, but loyal to the state and nation with a belief in the American way of life, a supreme being, and a capacity for initiative and leadership.

With all due respect to my classmates, we WERE those things, but I think he may have overshot the runway a bit. Note that he did not speak to our academic prowess. I want all of you current students to think back to the anxiety you felt applying to Texas A&M. The competition was stiff and the pressure was intense.

It was . . . let's just say . . . similar in our day. There were four primary criteria for admission:

1. You had to be a male.

2. You had to have graduated from an accredited Texas high school.

3. You had to agree to be in the Corps of Cadets, and finally

4. You had to have no communicable diseases.

The good news: they would waive two out of four.

We were a scraggly bunch, mostly from the farm or refinery. We knew education was the way out. Thank goodness political correctness had not yet been invented. We were a bit cynical and at times, borderline fatalistic.

A popular campus saying when we decided to disagree with a new rule or change at the University was, "What the hell are they going to do, send us to Vietnam?"

The tradition of out-of-classroom education was equally strong if not as well organized in those days. Our saying about that was "Never let what's happening in the classroom get in the way of our education."

Without women, we had to invent things to occupy our time. President Young, I am not endorsing such activities today, but some are worth a footnote in history. As I recall the football team was 2-7-1, but the Class of '67 during the fall of our freshman year, became the Southwest Conference mascot stealing champions. I think at least five were successfully stolen—including Bevo [mascot of the University of Texas]. That's when the stuff really hit the fan.

We were marched into old Guion Hall and reminded by a Texas Ranger that cattle rustling was still a hanging offense in Texas. Bevo magically showed up the next morning. I expect some who were involved would still be serving time today had they been caught, but through pure Aggie good luck, they are sitting in the audience tonight.

President Rudder knew exactly who we were and how we thought. He was a man of few words, tough as nails and stubborn as a bull. Anyone who has ever seen the cliffs at Pointe du Hoc understands this truth.

In those days, the last interview for commander of the Corps of Cadets was with President Rudder. I came to his office at 9 o'clock in the morning. When I showed up, his secretary, Nelda Green, said, "Have a seat, he's not having a particularly good day." My life immediately flashed before my eyes.

His office door was ajar and to put it mildly, he was having quite a colorful phone conversation. When he finished, I went in, and General Rudder stood up, shook hands, and we chatted for a moment.

Then, he said, "Eddie Joe, you're a fine looking young man. I have one question for you . . . are you tough enough?" After a moment of near stroke-level paralysis, I said, "Mr. Rudder, I'm as tough as I need to be." He smiled and said, "That's all I needed to hear." You can be assured that my answer got tested a number of times in 1966 and 1967.

Proof that "what goes around comes around," when I served as interim president in 2006–2007, the Commandant General John Van Alstyne told me one day that he had selected the Corps commander, Nick Guillmette.

I reminded him of my history with President Rudder and I suggested that Cadet Guillmette should come see me in my office as I had gone to Rudder's office 40 years earlier. Before he was anointed, I told Nick I was going to ask him the same question Rudder asked me. I still believe that Van Alystne clued him in, because he said, "Dr. Davis I am as tough as I need to be."

So, what do these stories of change that occurred during our time at Texas A&M have to do with the Muster Tradition? Well, we all left here and we thought the future was cast in stone: Ol' Army is dead. The place will never be the same.

Well, one out of two ain't bad. This place is infinitely better. Ol' Army is not dead, it is alive and well and not only in the Corps of Cadets, but among the beautiful, multicolored students and former students who have left here carrying on the most revered traditions of any institution in the country: the 12th Man, Silver Taps, and today's penultimate tradition, Aggie Muster.

To emphasize the sacrifice of Texas Aggies through time and the values they hold dear, I want to tell you one final story of the Class of '67 that has special meaning and reflects the importance of these Musters.

It's the story of our classmate 2nd Lt. Donald Matocha, a civil engineer from Smithville, Texas. In those days, kids in the Corps had nicknames. Mine was "EJ", short for Eddie Joe, and Don's was "Yogi," short for Yogi Bear. You can imagine what he looked like. Yogi was a quiet, soft-spoken, bright young man who worked hard and had a great sense of humor. Not content to accept a commission in either the Army or Air Force, Yogi spent his summers in the Marine Platoon Leader's Course—not exactly a vacation.

Like thousands of other Americans, along with most of the Class of '67, he was sent to Vietnam. After six months in country, Yogi was given R&R [rest and recuperation] for a week to return home. Before he returned to Vietnam, he told his mother in measured, unemotional terms, that there was a good chance that he would not be returning and that she should not worry for him or be resentful or bitter for his loss. Like a true Aggie, Yogi knew the danger in his mission. He had already assumed that dedication to duty and love of comrades could lead to sacrifice.

Yogi was killed in a firefight in April 1968 near Danang. The gunfire was so intense that Yogi's body could not be recovered. A second Marine was killed when a reaction force went back the next day to try to recover his body. For more than 35 years, our Aggie buddy Don Matocha was missing in action.

In 2004, Yogi's body was discovered and brought home. In 1968, a former North Vietnamese soldier named Nguyen Van Loc found his body while on patrol and buried him in a bomb crater, marking it with wooden planks. Many years later, Mr. Nguyen was able to identify the location. It's notable that he also lost two brothers in the war, one of whom was still MIA [missing in action]. Clearly, he understood the importance of his actions.

Yogi's family finally gave him a proper burial on August 22, 2004, in Smithville, Texas. Many of his Aggie classmates attended and, in good Muster style, 36 years later, answered "Here" when his name was called.

Many in our class have had long and fruitful careers blessed with good health, life partners, children, and grandchildren. Unfortunately, our buddy Yogi never got the chance to experience such blessings. In a split second his life was cut short. His mother said he only wanted two things in life: to be a Texas Aggie and a US Marine.

I'm proud to say that I knew him and he accomplished both goals.

So, let's return to "A Gig Line in Our Minds." What is a gig line anyway? All the young people in the Corps of Cadets know that a gig line is the line formed by the inseam of your trousers, your belt buckle, and the front seam of your shirt.

You will never find a cadet or even an ex-cadet who will not have their gig line perfectly aligned. It is simply a habitual result of the Corps training process.

But, I do believe that it also can be used as a metaphor for thinking about keeping what we have in our minds and in our souls aligned. It's a perfect metaphor for keeping personal values straight and knowing right from wrong. It's not just what we see on the outside; we should all have a gig line to keep us straight in our minds.

So tonight, as we conduct this hallowed Muster tradition let's do *what's right* and answer with a reverent, but enthusiastic "Here" to the roll call for the absent. Let's do it knowing that all the Aggie Donald Matochas who have gone before us had a gig line in their minds and did the "right thing."

Indeed, this Muster tradition is the "right" thing. For all of you who hold an empty space in your heart tonight for a lost loved one, this ceremony symbolizes that others care—indeed that this University, this Aggie culture cares.

Some of you lost current students, with lives cut short; those are the toughest to endure. We can't replace; but be reassured that you— Moms, Dads, sisters, brothers, grandparents, all—and they who have left us will always be a part of this Aggie Family.

And as we remember those who have gone before us, let's think about why we so fervently hold to this precious Muster tradition—-because in the year after we are gone, Aggie comrades will answer "Here."

I am enormously proud, grateful, and comforted for that special honor as a Texas Aggie.

Thank you and God bless Texas A&M.

# Appendix I

*Campus Muster Speakers,
Locations, and Sources*

| Date | Speaker | Speech Title | Location | Source |
|---|---|---|---|---|
| 1943 | | First Muster Packets Mailed Worldwide | | |
| 1944 | Everett Eugene McQuillen '20 | First Memorial Roll Call | Guion | *The Battalion*, April 22, 1944 |
| 1945 | Lt. Clifton Henry Chamberlain '40 | Speech | Guion | Reported in *The Battalion* |
| 1946 | Gen. Dwight David Eisenhower | "Speech for Texas Agricultural and Mechanical College"* | Kyle | Texas A&M University Archives |
| 1947 | Col. Willard Townshend Chevalier | Build Character and Culture† | System | *The Battalion and Bryan Eagle*, April 22, 1947 |
| 1948 | Sam Bernard Hill | 1948 Campus Muster* | System | *Bryan Eagle*, April 22, 1948 |
| 1949 | James William Aston '33 | Only Aggies Can Understand† | Guion | Texas A&M University Archives |
| 1950 | Marion Somerville Church '05 | Live to Honor San Jacinto† | Guion | Texas A&M University Archives |
| 1951 | James Harold Pipkin '29 | "Son, Remember . . ."* | MSC | Texas A&M University Archives |
| 1952 | Joseph Searcy Bracewell '38 | Destroying the Bridge† | System | Texas A&M University Archives |

| 1953 | Colorado Gov. Dan Thornton | "America's Immeasurable Strength"* | MSC | Texas A&M University Archives |
| 1954 | Texas Gov. Allan Shivers | Understanding the Aggie Spirit† | MSC | Texas A&M University Archives |
| 1955 | Gen. Otto Paul Weyland '28 | Guarding Our Heritage with Honor† | MSC | Texas A&M University Archives |
| 1956 | Maj. Gen. James Earl Rudder '32 | Honesty, Integrity, and Common Sense† | MSC | Texas A&M University Archives |
| 1957 | No Campus Muster | Easter recess | | |
| 1958 | Gen. Bernard Adolph Schriever '31 | The Human Factor† | MSC | *The Battalion*, April 22, 1958 |
| 1959 | Olin Earl Teague '32 | Bold Leadership† | MSC | Texas A&M University Archives |
| 1960 | Lt. Gen. Andrew Davis Bruce '16 | A Pledge and Responsibility† | MSC | Texas A&M University Archives |
| 1961 | James William Aston '33 | Do We Know the Truth?† | MSC | Texas A&M University Archives |
| 1962 | Eli Lamar Whiteley '41 | A&M Can Change† | MSC | *The Battalion*, April 24, 1962 |
| 1963 | Leland Fred Peterson '36 | Program of Excellence† | MSC | Texas A&M University Archives |

| Date | Speaker | Speech Title | Location | Source |
|------|---------|--------------|----------|--------|
| 1964 | Earl King Gill '24 | A&M's 12th Man—The True Story[†] | System | Texas A&M University Archives |
| 1965 | Clarence Darrow Hooper '53 | Dynamics of Change and Innovation[†] | System | Texas A&M University Archives |
| 1966 | Penrose Blakely Metcalfe '16 | Never, Never, Never Die[†] | System | Texas A&M University Archives |
| 1967 | Maj. Gen. Raymond Leroy Murray '35 | Knowledgeable, Dedicated Leadership[†] | System | Texas A&M University Archives |
| 1968 | Maj. Gen. Wood Barbee Kyle '36 | Aggie Marine Corps Generals[†] | System | Texas A&M University Archives |
| 1969 | Mayo Joseph Thompson '41 | "Texas A&M: An Island of Light"[†*] | System | Texas A&M University Archives |
| 1970 | Yale Berger Griffis '30 | A Sacred Trust[†] | System | Texas A&M University Archives |
| 1971 | Jack Kenny Williams | In the Footsteps of Giants[†] | GRW | Texas A&M University Archives |
| 1972 | Larry Byron Kirk '66 | Heritage[†] | GRW | Texas A&M University Archives |

| Year | Speaker | Title | Location | Source |
|---|---|---|---|---|
| 1973 | Capt. James Edwin Ray '63 | Enduring Hardships† | GRW | *The Texas Aggie*, July 1973; *The Battalion*, April 23, 1973 |
| 1974 | Sheldon Joseph Best '63 | Quality of Life† | Kyle | Texas A&M University Archives |
| 1975 | Reagan Veasey Brown '43 | Rendezvous with Life† | GRW | Texas A&M University Archives |
| 1976 | Charles G. Scruggs '45 | "How Will You Answer the Muster Calls of the Future?"* | GRW | Texas A&M University Archives |
| 1977 | Maj. James Edwin Ray '63 | Discipline and Human Relations† | GRW | Texas A&M University Archives |
| 1978 | Col. Tom Dooley '35 | The Corregidor Muster of 1942† | GRW | Texas A&M University Archives |
| 1979 | Lee Herman Smith '57 | Not Just a Memorial Service† | GRW | Texas A&M University Archives |
| 1980 | Henry Gabriel Cisneros '68 | Soldier, Statesman, Knightly Gentleman† | GRW | Texas A&M University Archives |
| 1981 | Frederick Donald McClure '76 | "The Signs of the Times"* | GRW | Texas A&M University Archives |
| 1982 | William Bernard Heye Jr. '60 | Quality = Spirit and Leadership† | GRW | Texas A&M University Archives |

| Date | Speaker | Speech Title | Location | Source |
|------|---------|--------------|----------|--------|
| 1983 | Haskell Moorman Monroe | What Kind of Aggie Are You?[†] | GRW | Texas A&M University Archives |
| 1984 | Jack Morris Rains '60 | A&M's Strong Maroon Line[†] | GRW | Texas A&M University Archives |
| 1985 | Lt. Gen. Ormond Ralph Simpson '36 | "So You Think You Are a Texas Aggie?"[*] | GRW | Texas A&M University Archives |
| 1986 | Alfred Webb "Head" Davis '45 | What Is a Great University?[†] | GRW | Texas A&M University Archives |
| 1987 | Robert Lowell Walker '58 | What Is the Aggie Spirit?[†] | GRW | Texas A&M University Archives |
| 1988 | Gerald Duane Griffin '56 | Meeting the Challenge of the Future[†] | GRW | Texas A&M University Archives |
| 1989 | Thomas Chester "Chet" Edwards '74 | The Meaning of Aggie Muster[†] | GRW | Texas A&M University Archives |
| 1990 | Mason Lee "Red" Cashion '53 | Aggie Spirit—Live It, Share It, Give It[†] | GRW | Texas A&M University Archives |
| 1991 | Adm. Jerome Lamarr Johnson '56 | Leadership Is a Duty[†] | GRW | Texas A&M University Archives |
| 1992 | Frank Wallace Cox III '65 | Where Else but Aggieland[†] | GRW | Texas A&M University Archives |

| 1993 | Jack Garner Fritts '53 | That Certain Feeling[†] | GRW | Texas A&M University Archives |
| 1994 | Andrés Anthony Tijerina '67 | Becoming a Texas Aggie[†] | GRW | Texas A&M University Archives |
| 1995 | Lee James Phillips '53 | The Ties That Bind[†] | GRW | Texas A&M University Archives |
| 1996 | Errol Dean Gage '65 | "The Meaning of M-U-S-T-E-R" | GRW | Texas A&M University Archives |
| 1997 | Henry Bartell Zachry Jr. '54 | What Can I Do for A&M?[†] | GRW | Texas A&M University Archives |
| 1998 | Eugene "Gene" Stallings '57 | Doing the Very Best You Can[†] | Reed | Texas A&M University Archives |
| 1999 | William Mike Baggett '68 | Character, Leadership, Teamwork, Emotion[†] | Reed | Texas A&M University Archives |
| 2000 | James Randel "Randy" Matson '67 | Traditions Set Us Apart[†] | Reed | Texas A&M University Archives |
| 2001 | Joe Earl West '54 | A Spirit Can Ne'er Be Told[†] | Reed | Texas A&M University Archives |
| 2002 | James Richard "Rick" Perry '72 | Freedom Is Not Free[†] | Reed | Texas A&M University Archives |

| Date | Speaker | Speech Title | Location | Source |
|---|---|---|---|---|
| 2003 | Edwin Hanson Cooper '53 | Manifestations of Spirit† | Reed | Texas A&M University Archives |
| 2004 | Jon Lewis Hagler '58 | "The Spirit's the Thing"* | Reed | Texas A&M University Archives |
| 2005 | Clayton Wheat Williams Jr. '54 | Texas A&M Is Unique† | Reed | Texas A&M University Archives |
| 2006 | Bill Edward Carter '69 | Aggie Spirit in Action† | Reed | Texas A&M University Archives |
| 2007 | Brooke Leslie Rollins '94 | "In Fire, Gold Is Tested"* | Reed | Texas A&M University Archives |
| 2008 | John Alfred Adams Jr. '73 | "Spirit and Mind"* | Reed | Texas A&M University Archives |
| 2009 | Robert Michael Gates | Character and Integrity† | Reed | Texas A&M University Archives |
| 2010 | Maj. Stephen Gerard Ruth '92 | We Are Called to Serve† | Reed | Texas A&M University Archives |
| 2011 | Tobin "Toby" R. Boenig '95 | "Rise to the Challenge"* | Reed | Texas A&M University Archives |

| 2012 | John Richard Hoyle '57 | We Fight to the Finish[†] | Reed | Texas A&M University Archives |
| 2013 | Bill Jones '81 | Friendship—Family—Freedom[†] | Reed | Texas A&M University Archives |
| 2014 | Billy Jack Youngkin '69 | Explaining from the Inside[†] | Reed | Texas A&M University Archives |
| 2015 | William "Will" Ballard Hurd '99 | Work Hard to Make This World Better[†] | Reed | Texas A&M University Archives |
| 2016 | Richard Copeland "R. C." Slocum | "What Will I Leave Behind?"[*] | Reed | Texas A&M University Archives |
| 2017 | Eddie Joseph Davis '67 | "A Gig Line in Our Minds"[*] | Reed | Texas A&M University Archives |

[*]Speech title provided by speaker
[†]Muster speech title derived from speech manuscript

*Location notes:*
Guion—Guion Hall (demolished 1971, replaced by Rudder Auditorium)
Kyle—Kyle Field
System—System Administration Building, front lawn (Jack K. Williams Building)
MSC—Memorial Student Center, front lawn
GRW—G. Rollie White Coliseum (demolished 2013 for Kyle Field expansion)
Reed—Reed Arena

*Source note:* All sources listed at "Texas A&M University Archives" come from the editor's collection, donated upon completion of this book.

# Appendix II
*Muster Poems*

## The Heroes' Roll Call
*by Dr. John Ashton '06*

In many lands and climes, this April day
Proud sons of Texas A&M unite.
Our loyalty to country, school, we pay,
And seal a pact with bond of common might.

We live again those happy days of yore,
On campus, field, in classroom, hall, at drill.
Fond memory brings a sigh—but nothing more:
Now we are men, and life is one great thrill!

On fortress isle one year ago today,
A group of gallant Aggies, led by Moore,
Held simple rites which to us all doth say:
The spirit shall prevail o'er cannon roar!

They thought of home and all we hold most dear:
Where are they now—those boys we knew so well?
Ask of the winds, let smile repress a tear,
Think only of their glory when they fell!

Corregidor! forever more a hallowed name
To countless sons of Texans yet unborn;
Symbolic like, it stands for deathless fame:
A shrine sublime till Resurrection morn!

Softly call the muster,
Let comrade answer, "Here!"
Their spirits hover 'round us:
As if to bring us cheer!

Mark them "present" in our hearts,
We'll meet some other day.
There is no Death but Life Eterne
For heroes such as they!

In early 1943, E. E. McQuillen '20, executive secretary of Texas A&M's Association of Former Students, asked English professor Dr. John Ashton '06 to write a poem in honor of the Texas Aggies who had defended Corregidor the previous spring. The poem has been slightly modified during its continuous use in Aggie Muster ceremonies. This is the original version.

## In Memoriam
*by David Harrigan '68*

We stood a little taller, and a little Prouder then
When we heard the call of Muster and the Roll Call just begin.
We stood there all together and wiped away the tears
When our names were called out softly and answered with a HERE!

...and so we've joined together with our brothers of the past
To make our final resting place at Aggieland our last.
We take a toast to our brotherhood wherever they may roam,
For us the trek is over, Aggieland we're coming home.

From *Texas Aggie*, March 1977. This poem was written by David Harrigan in memory of his classmate, Kevin Rinard '68, who died in Vietnam. He writes, "I hope that all Aggies might read this and realize their love for each other and know that a part of themselves has never left Aggieland."

## Muster
*by James C. Greene '70*

The assembly,—
In solemn silence stands,
Listening to the call.
Remembering in our soul
Replying to the roll.
"Here"!—

Here, in spirit and heart.
Here, in present with the past.
While lighted candles recall—

A flagpole
Clanging in the dark,
Bugles sound the final call
Burning spirit binding all.
Muster of A&M.

From *Texas Aggie*, April 1987 and August 1993; originally printed in *The Austin Aggie*.

## A Single Candle
*by Lynnette A. Cardenas '86*

Today we come together here
On this, a special day,
To honor those both far and near—
The friends who've passed away.

We burn for them this single light,
A sign to show we care—
A single candle burning bright
To let them know we're there.

Although they're gone, each memory
Will live within us yet.
And we, their Aggie family,
Will pledge not to forget.

Now let us take a solemn vow
With those who've mustered here:
That if indeed the fates allow,
We'll meet again next year!

From *Texas Aggie*, August 1993. The poem was written for the 1993 Muster ceremony held at A&M's branch campus in Koriyama, Japan.

## Silver Taps
*by Mabel Clare Thomas*

Silently they gather, moving shadows
Under restless trees. Tight-lipped boys,
Full by day of rough, gay comradeship,
Have nothing to say tonight.

Clustered in hundreds 'round the Old Main Building,
They come to bid a last "Farewell"
To a fellow Aggie, whose footsteps
Will never tread familiar campus paths again.

Silently they wait, gazing far up at the dome
Rounded against the midnight sky.
The hour strikes, and four straight figures
Move to the corners of the turret,
Raising silver trumpets to their lips.

And then, tearing at the heart as does no other sound,
The notes come clear and sweet, and sad;
Silver Taps for one more Aggie who has gone
To join the bright Battalion in the sky,
Where brave young men need never die.

Then, as the last, long, unearthly note
Fades into the night, the cold, dark silence bursts,
And guns send forth their final, grim salute!
Stand at attention, Aggies! Once more we honor them,
The Silver Taps Battalion of Texas A&M.

From *Aggieland*, 1956 and 1961; reprinted in *Texas Aggie*, June 1987.

## The Shadow of a Century: 1876–1976

*by Jeanette Hennigan*

In the shadow of a Century
Stands a school surpassed by none
In its love for God and Country,
Opportunity and battles won.
Stands a heritage from its founders—
Texas men who held so dear
The principles of democracy
As they blazed a wild frontier.

The military men of A&M
Have written their own history,
Through leadership in both war and peace
They have kept America free.
And the Fighting Texas Aggies
Have a legacy all their own;
For their pride, and honor, and loyalty
Form the Spirit of Aggiedom.

In the echoes of a Century
Our hearts are quick to recall
The reverence of a Silver Taps—
A comrade's "Here" at Muster call.
Yes, the whisper from the shadow
Stirs emotions—bows the head.
Let us never forget the sacrifice
Of Aggies—now and dead.

Or the leaders who nurtured A&M
To its maturity of today—
Men like Gathright and Williams,
Who stand a century step away.
And a hundred years of tradition
Remains deeply ingrained in this school,
"Standing Ready" is its motto,
—Education is its tool.

As the men and women of A&M
Take their place among the best,
Like their Aggie parents before them,
They stand a cut above the rest.
And they leave a changing A&M—
Even taller than the shadow it cast—
Always reaching for the future,
With a firm hold on the past.

From *Texas Aggie*, November 1975. Thomas S. Gathright was A&M's first president (1876–79); Jack K. Williams was president of A&M (1970–77) a century later.

### Silver Taps at A&M
*by Jeanette Hennigan*

You hear about the Aggie Band
And the Spirit of Aggieland,
But few have heard the Farewell Hymn
Of Silver Taps at A&M.

All day the flag flies at half-mast.
A sign to us of a solemn task,
To bid farewell to one who's gone.
With Silver Taps, he's not alone.

The Night is dark and very still.
Where Sully stands the area fills
With a silent crowd of those who care,
Their hearts all joined in silent prayer.

The Ross Volunteers, the honor guard,
Speak for us all as their guns discharge.
Twenty-one guns now blast the air
And fade away in the darkness there.

Then taps blows loud from the tower near.
And twice again so faint, so clear.
Like rustling wings of a soul in flight,
Silver Taps fades in the night.

You stand spellbound, you scarcely breathe
With heavy heart you turn to leave.
Your Aggie friend no more you'll see,
Till Silver Taps is blown for thee.

Silver Taps at A&M
Will always be our farewell hymn.
To those who've gone to heights unknown,
With Silver Taps, he journeys on.

From *Texas Aggie*, March 1974. Jeanette Hennigan was an editorial assistant at *Texas Aggie* magazine; her husband was James K. Hennigan '54.

### Muster Song
*by Margaret Rudder*

We gather here to mark the day
Aggies proudly stand
To honor those who've gone before
To the promised land.

Each name is called upon the roll
Comrades answer "Here!"
Trumpets sound their sad goodbye
To those we held so dear.

All heads are bowed in silent pledge
Never to forget
While rifles fire their last salute
Echoes answer yet.

To their memory we'll be true
We will take their place
One for all and all for one
Ever in Thy grace.

We'll meet again another day
Reunion while we pray
To ask Thy blessings on each one
On this Muster Day.

Aggie Muster Day.

The poem was sent to James E. Ray '63, with "admiration for a great Aggie!" Margaret Rudder was the wife of James Earl Rudder '32, president of Texas A&M (1959–70) and chancellor of the Texas A&M University System (1965–70).

### Silver Taps in the Rain
*by James C. Greene '70*

Rain against my face
The night's black embrace
The gathering mass appears
And through the drizzling tears,
The silence gathers all.—

Through this blackened wet
The echoing marches yet
The silent guns are raised.
And through the flashing blaze,
The thunder echoes all.—

Reigning through the night
The trio of horns invite
The soaking saddening sound
The melody echoing around,
And the pain encompasses all.—

The fading mass retreats
Back,—through the drizzling streets
And the darkened silence is all
Of the wetting black to recall,
The tribute of A&M.—

From *Texas Aggie*, April 1987.

### The Ghosts of Kyle Field
*by J. J. Risch '79*

I took it in my head one night
To run around the track,
The night was cool, the sky was clear,
A slight breeze at my back.

As I walked into Kyle Field,
Dark and ghostly then,
I thought back through the years
Of the other times I'd been.

I'd seen our mascot buried,
I'd been to midnight yell,
I'd seen the Aggie halftime show
Performed so very well.

And now as I jogged around the track,
I could see thousands, it seemed,
Filling the entire stadium,
Coming out to support their team.

The yelling filled my soul,
There was swaying on the decks,
The sound rose to a crescendo:
"Hullaballo, caneck, caneck!"

I whooped, then all was silent,
The only sound, the air.
I looked at empty bleachers
And the Ags that were not there.

I finished up my running
And turned my steps away
To leave Kyle Field for present
And return another day.

There're one hundred thousand Aggies,
And of these I am one,
I saw them all and was part of them
That night I went to run.

From *Texas Aggie*, March 1977.

# Index